WITHDRAWN

# THE NATIONWIDE COMPETITION FOR VOTES

*Also by Ian McAllister*

The Northern Ireland Social Democratic & Labour Party

*Also by Richard Rose & Ian McAllister*

United Kingdom Facts

*Also by Richard Rose*

Understanding Big Government
Understanding the United Kingdom
Can Government Go Bankrupt? with Guy Peters
What Is Governing? Purpose and Policy in Washington
Managing Presidential Objectives
Northern Ireland: A Time of Choice
The Problem of Party Government
International Almanac of Electoral History, with T.T. Mackie
Governing without Consensus
People in Politics
Influencing Voters
Politics in England
Must Labour Lose? with Mark Abrams
The British General Election of 1959, with D.E. Butler

*Edited by Richard Rose*

The Territorial Dimension in United Kingdom Politics, with Peter Madgwick
Fiscal Stress in Cities, with Edward Page
Presidents and Prime Ministers, with Ezra Suleiman
Electoral Participation
Britain: Progress and Decline, with William B. Gwyn
Challenge to Governance
Elections without Choice, with Guy Hermet and Alain Rouquié
New Trends in British Politics, with Dennis Kavanagh
The Dynamics of Public Policy
Comparing Public Policies, with Jerzy Wiatr
The Management of Urban Change in Britain and Germany
Electoral Behavior: A Comparative Handbook
Lessons from America
European Politics, with Mattei Dogan
Policy-Making in Britain
Studies in British Politics

# THE NATIONWIDE COMPETITION FOR VOTES

## The 1983 British Election

Ian McAllister & Richard Rose

**Frances Pinter (Publishers), London and Dover, N.H.**

in association with the

CENTRE FOR THE STUDY
OF PUBLIC POLICY

University of Strathclyde

Frances Pinter (Publishers) Ltd
5 Dryden Street, London WC2 and
51 Washington St, Dover NH 03820

ISBN 0-86187-383-1

Library of Congress Catalog Card Number 84-42500

This book has been set in 10 on 12 Baskerville type by
computer, through the Oxford University National Facility for
Computing in the Arts.

The designer of the book is *Professor Richard Rose* .

Printed in Great Britain

 British Library Cataloguing in Publication Data

McAllister, Ian
    The nationwide competition for votes.
    1. Great Britain. *Parliament* ──Elections,1983
    2. Voting──Great Britain──History──20th
    century
    I. Title   II. Rose, Richard, *1933-*
    324.941'0858     JN956

    ISBN 0-86187-383-1

Printed by S.R.P. Ltd., Exeter, Devon.

# Contents

84-4427

# Tables and Figure

viii

# THE NATIONWIDE COMPETITION FOR VOTES

# INTRODUCTION
# Understanding Electoral Competition

The nationwide competition for votes involves many things: a contest for parliamentary seats as well as for popular votes; a contest for government as well as for seats; pressures dividing the electorate along class lines as well as territorial lines; and the paradox of dividing a national electorate in order to produce a government enjoying unitary authority.

Nothing is more public than the result of a general election. Newspapers and television cameras follow the campaign trail and seek to foretell the outcome before the last vote is counted. The victors are televised entering office, and the results can be read by the naked eye and in even more copious detail by computers. Yet nothing is more disputed than the meaning of this nationwide registration of popular preferences. Politicians have a vested interest in foisting particular interpretations upon election outcomes and political commentators, speaking or writing against a media deadline, only have time to articulate a few simple generalizations.

While many books are published about how politicians campaign or how individual electors vote, relatively few books systematically relate votes cast to constituency contests and their aggregate implications for national government. This book is a study of psephology proper, that is, a study of the election results that collectively determine which party, if any, wins control of government at a nationwide election. It sets out a framework for analysing the common pressures affecting parties and voters nationwide. It uses straightforward statistical techniques to test the relative electoral importance (or unimportance) of a host of socio-economic and territorial influences: class, housing, immigration, urban-rural differences, centre-periphery differences, and so forth. Cluster analysis groups socially similar constituencies together whether or not they are close to each other geographically, and identifies the hegemonic party in each cluster. To understand the outcome of a nationwide election, constituency results must be added up to see whether or not parties with similar shares of the national vote receive similar numbers of seats in Parliament.

Clarity is a necessary condition of understanding the nationwide competition for votes. Therefore, Chapter I outlines the different dimensions of electoral competition that in sum constitute an election outcome. But public choice does not take place in a vacuum; every decision about voting is made in a specific political, economic and social context. In order to demonstrate the practical significance of ideas, it is necessary to use concepts to analyse actual election results.

The 1983 British general election provides a robust test of psephological analysis, for it had many unusual features. In terms of seats, the Conservatives enjoyed the biggest victory in nearly half a century--but the Conservative share of the popular vote actually went down. In the 650 constituency contests, Labour, the country's second party and the official opposition in Parliament, more often finished third than second. The Alliance won a larger share of the popular vote than that taken by major partners in many European coalition governments, yet the electoral front of the Liberal Party and the Social Democratic Party won only two more seats than Nationalist and Ulster parties.

In order to understand whether or not the Conservative Party will dominate British government into the 1990s, it is necessary to understand how vulnerable it is to a conventional swing to the Labour Party or to the unconventional Alliance. Insofar as the Conservatives appear secure against conventional shifts in votes, it is necessary to consider the prospect of a turbulent electoral environment producing an unconventional shift of votes to both Labour and the Alliance.

## Objects of the Book

The first object is to examine why characteristics common to the whole nation (for example, language) or influences having a common impact nationwide (for example, inflation or threat of war) do not produce the same electoral outcome in each parliamentary constituency, or government by a party of national unity or a grand coalition of parties eschewing competition, as happened in Britain in the Second World War.

Elections involve competition between parties offering differing views of national (or sectional) interests. In a free society, no one party expects to win all the votes. If one social division such as class were equally present and strong in all parts of a country, then the party of the manual workers would win nearly every constituency, because manual workers are a majority of the electorate. Notwithstanding the disproportionality of the first-past-the-post British electoral system, no party expects the electoral system to deliver it all the seats. Even though the Conservatives won the 1983 British election with an extraordinarily large lead over Labour, the Conservatives failed to win 253 of the 650 seats in Parliament. Similarly, even though Ronald Reagan won 91 per cent of Electoral College votes in the race for the American Presidency in 1980, he took only 50.7 per cent of the popular vote. In a first-past-the-post electoral system a party that concentrates support and faces divided opponents can turn a marginal advantage in popular votes into a landslide victory.

The influences that affect voters in common throughout the United Kingdom are identified in Chapters II to IV. Britain is not only unitary in constitutional theory but also in politics and public policy (Rose, 1982). In the years between election day, Westminster is the focus of party competition. This is true not only in parliamentary debate and in media reporting of politics, but also in the policies that collectively constitute the benefits and costs of the contemporary mixed economy welfare state. The management of the British economy under the government of Margaret Thatcher affects all parts of the United Kingdom. A rise in unemployment and a fall in the rate of inflation touch every constituency. The 1982 Falklands War was an event which emphasized the unity of the Kingdom against a foreign enemy. Chapter II shows how the Alliance's challenge to the Conservatives and Labour--unlike the challenge in the 1970s of Scottish and Welsh Nationalists-- was a challenge Britainwide. Given the importance of the territorial dimension in electoral competition, Chapters III and IV present analyses of the territorial policies of the Thatcher government, contributed by Jim Bulpitt, and of Labour's territorial strategy for Britain, by Michael Keating.

Party competition thrives upon differential responses to political events, and differential outcomes from constituency to constituency. Competition can persist only if the party that loses an election nationwide is nonetheless able to win some seats in particular parts of the country. Proportional representation systems of election guarantee this. The formula used to convert popular votes into parliamentary representation is based upon multi-member constituencies, resulting in multi-party representation in Parliament. By contrast, in Britain or in the United States, only one candidate can win a single-member constituency, however small or large the candidate's share of its vote. However, the victorious party will differ from constituency to constituency.

Because a parliamentary constituency or a Congressional district is only a very small part of a large country, we rarely think of units this small when considering the areas where one party is particularly successful or unsuccessful in electoral competition. Often reference is made to regional differences in partisanship: we speak of the North of England being a Labour stronghold, or the South of England being a Conservative stronghold in Parliament. In a federal system of government, the constituent states are often the object of analysis . In America wouldbe Presidential nominees fight to win primary elections on a state-by-state basis in order to fight winner-take-all contests for each state's votes in the Electoral College.

In British politics there is an ambiguity in references to nationwide competition. On the one hand, the phrase can refer to the whole of the United Kingdom or to Great Britain excepting Northern Ireland. Insofar as there is a nationwide competition for votes and seats in Britain, then there would be much the same lines of division from Land's End in Cornwall to John o' Groats in Scotland. Alternatively, in a multi-national United Kingdom elections could be four concurrent contests, one in England, another in Wales, a third in Scotland, and a fourth in Northern Ireland. From this perspective, election outcomes would be expected to differ substantially from nation to nation. The overall United Kingdom result would not be a single nationwide contest but the sum of different outcomes in each of its four parts. Chapters V to IX systematically examine the extent to which divisions of votes and seats differ among the nations of the United Kingdom, and whether these differences reflect distinctive national characteristics or simply variations in social structure influencing votes Britainwide.

The British party system today can no longer be described as a two-party system, or as completely British. In the 1983 general election, three different parties or groupings - Conservatives, Labour, and the Liberal and Social Democratic Alliance - fought and won seats in the House of Commons Britainwide. In addition, seven un-British or anti-British parties won seats. Each nation has a distinctive party system. England is the only one of the four parts of the United Kingdom without a Nationalist party. In Northern Ireland, no party fighting seats in Great Britain competes, leaving two pro-British Unionis and Loyalist parties , and two anti-British parties informally linked with groups in the Republic of Ireland promoting Irish unity.

Thinking about election results in terms of maps with a sea of blue constituencies in England and a sea of red constituencies in Scotland and Wales is not proof that votes are determined by distinctive national influences, or by regional differences between the South and North of England, or between red Clydeside and the non-red Scottish Highlands. The second object of this book is to test systematically the extent to which territorial differences between nations and regions are of major electoral importance, or whether election outcomes are determined principally by differences in social structure. Another possibility is that social differences are territorially skewed, for example, between the North of England (more working-class and industrial) and the South of England (more middle-class and non-industrial).

The relative importance of Britainwide social structure as against distinctive national characteristics is tested separately for each of the major parties contesting the seats within each nation of the United Kingdom and among regions within each nation. Chapter IX draws together the results, demonstrating the greater importance of Britainwide divisions of social structure as against territorial divisions between regions and nations.

Insofar as an election outcome is determined by social structure and territorial influences, then results should be relatively predictable from election to election. A nation's social and economic structure changes slowly, and territorially distinctive characteristics are even more resistant to sudden change. The small shift in votes that can make control of government change hands obscures the fact that the base vote of major parties has tended to persist from election to election and decade to decade.

Part III examines the political implications of the distribution of the base support for political parties in Britain today. Insofar as voters with similar socio-economic characteristics tend to be clustered together, then even if parties divide the national vote evenly, most constituencies will remain relatively safe for one party. For example, a working-class constituency will consistently return a Labour MP, and a middle-class constituency a Conservative MP. In Britain, the tendency of socially similar people to cluster together results in the great majority of parliamentary constituencies being safe seats.

The political geography of a country is determined by a combination of social and territorial characteristics. Chapter X identifies clusters of constituencies with the greatest degree of similarity in social structure. It also shows the extent to which there is a more or less accidental clustering of people with similar social characteristics in a given nation or region. Cluster analysis identifies similar constituencies that are widely dispersed throughout Britain, for example, inner-city slum constituencies with high unemployment and much council housing.

In a turbulent political environment, understanding the implications of an election requires a sensitivity to novel elements that could destabilize a seemingly established party system. Chapter XI is a study in the psephology of discontinuities. It commences by considering the stable pattern of party competition from 1945 to 1970, involving a swing back and forth between two and only two parties, Labour and Conservative. The 1974 general elections appeared to threaten this pattern in two different ways: Liberal support more than doubled in England, accounting for one fifth of the vote. In Scotland and Wales, protests against the status quo favoured the Nationalist parties, but their strength tended to be exaggerated (Van Mechelen, 1982). The rise of Nationalist parties in Scotland and Wales created differences in two parts of the United Kingdom, but by definition Nationalists could not break the pattern Britainwide. British parties collectively took 89 per cent of the vote in Wales in October 1974, and 70 per cent in Scotland, when Scottish Nationalists were at their peak. By 1979, and even more by 1983, the Nationalist tide had receded.

The 1983 British general election succeeded in breaking the mould of British psephology . While the Alliance did not break the Conservative monopoly control of government, it did break Labour's monopoly claim as the opposition party, for the Alliance finished second to the government in twice as many constituencies as did Labour. By contrast with the Nationalist parties, the

Alliance is a Britainwide protest party, addressing the same broad appeal from Caithness to Cornwall and winning seats at both extremes of Britain. It has also won seats in places in between, such as Bermondsey and Rochdale. The chief Alliance weakness is not its vote, which was only two per cent less than that of Labour, but the evenness with which its vote has been spread. Had the Alliance vote been concentrated like Labour's in a limited number of constituencies, in 1983 it would have won enough seats to deprive the Conservatives of their House of Commons majority.

Discontinuities occur when changes of degree are transformed into changes of kind. A first-past-the-post electoral system is particularly sensitive to small changes in votes across the critical threshold that separates the winning party from the also-ran parties. In the 1983 British general election the Alliance did not cross the threshold at which it would start winning seats in proportion to (or in excess of) its share of the vote. But by finishing second to the Conservatives in most seats won by the governing party, it makes it that much more difficult for Labour to return to office. Labour needs a conventional swing of more than 12 per cent to gain control of government, and Alliance a swing of almost 20 per cent.

The concluding chapter explains why it is misleading today to think in terms of a conventional swing. A shift in votes sufficient to turn the Conservatives out of office at the next general election would require a discontinuity in electoral competition. The 1983 election made some kind of a discontinuity more likely by pushing all three parties nearer to the threshold at which the traditional relationship between winning votes, winning seats, and winning control of government is destabilized.

Because the counting of votes determines how elections are won and lost, any psephological study will inevitably be a book full of tables. In the past two decades the British census has slowly been making more data available about parliamentary constituencies. Concurrently, the development of high-speed computers has made practical the systematic statistical analysis of the importance of a multiplicity of influences upon constituency results. To assist the reader, each table in this book has been designed to concentrate attention upon significant patterns. Details of the individual constituencies that collectively constitute nationwide patterns are placed in Appendix A, so that technically minded readers can examine results more fully. Using a limited number of standard statistical techniques also makes it easier for the reader to comprehend the logic of analysis. Statistics are indispensable in the analysis of elections, but they are no more and no less than a means to the end of understanding electoral competition.

# Alternative Approaches to Election Studies

The functions of elections are multiple; voters, politicians and social scientists approach the subject in many different ways (cf. Rose and Mossawir, 1967). This book differs from the series of Nuffield College studies of British general elections produced by David Butler and others (e.g., Butler and Kavanagh, 1984). The Nuffield studies are centralist concentrating upon a few square miles around Parliament. There is no doubting the importance of the politics of Westminster, an importance now magnified by television. In an election, parties plan their campaigns in Westminster, and press conferences there are daily televised to audiences nationwide. Even when party leaders go to Manchester, Newcastle or Cardiff for the day, much of what they do or say is intended to catch the eye of media editors in London. The small world of a few hundred election strategists and those they meet daily is the focus of the Nuffield election studies.

An election is not decided in Westminster; victory goes to the party that can successfully win a majority of 650 seats nationwide. Less than one-sixth of parliamentary constituencies are in the Greater London area; a party that only carried London would suffer a defeat. A party that won every seat south of the Thames from Dover to Land's End but none elsewhere would suffer a landslide defeat greater than Labour's loss in 1983. To win a British general election, a party must mobilize support across a broad territory. This book is about the other half of a British election, the half that consists of the constituencies where voters collectively hold the fate of government in their hands.

The literature of voting studies concentrates upon who votes how and why. It does not ask what effect votes have in determining the composition and control of Parliament. Understanding the motivations of individual voters reveals much about the social psychology of the people of Britain, especially about how they do (or do not) think about politics. But a study of the lifelong process by which attitudes are formed, reinforced and altered does not tell us anything specific about a particular general election. This book thus differs from the series of surveys of British voters produced from 1964 to 1970 under the auspices of David Butler and Donald Stokes (1974) and from 1974 to 1979 by Bo Sarlvik and Ivor Crewe (1983), as well as a variety of studies of British voting by the authors of this volume (see e.g. Rose, 1968; Rose, 1974; Rose, 1980; Kelley, McAllister and Mughan 1983; Kelley and McAllister, 1983).

In order to understand an election outcome, we must study votes cast and seats won as well as the attitudes of voters. In the craft union world of the social sciences, psephology (that is, the study of votes) is sharply differentiated from the study of voters (that is, the people casting ballots). The difference is substantive, and not simply a play on words. In political terms, the question of first importance is not why 25.4 per cent of the electorate voted Alliance and

27.6 per cent voted Labour, but why Alliance won 3.5 per cent of the seats in the House of Commons whereas Labour won 32.0 per cent. Examining the characteristics of individual electors will help us understand how individual votes are cast, but votes are only a means to the end of winning seats in the House of Commons. To understand how an election is won or lost, we must concentrate upon how and why parties win (or fail to win) the seats necessary to control British government.

Rather than directing attention upon what might be--a proportional representation system for electing MPs (Bogdanor, 1981) or a hung Parliament with a minority or coalition government (Butler, 1983)--this book concentrates attention upon what is, an electoral system that normally manufactures a parliamentary majority supporting single-party government. Ironically, the rise of the Alliance has made it easier for a single party to win a majority by lowering the threshold of votes needed to win a seat. The Conservatives' landslide victory in 1983 was achieved with a smaller share of the total vote than that gained by the losing party at every British general election from 1950 to 1964, and in 1970 as well. Advocacy of change in the electoral system or speculation about hypothetical results is useful as a reminder that electoral competition is variable in place and time. The final chapter considers under what psephological circumstances the 1983 British general election would become a major step in electoral discontinuity.

While this book gives full attention to national differences within the United Kingdom, it is profoundly not a book about nationalism in the way in which this term is conventionally used. In effect, it is a book about the British nation. Use of the term Britain emphasizes things that people in England, Scotland, Wales and Northern Ireland share in common, particularly participation in a United Kingdom general election. The rise of Nationalist parties in Scotland and Wales in the 1970s stimulated a considerable amount of writing that often threw a distorting light upon the politics of the United Kingdom. To write a book about Scottish Nationalism (Brand, 1978) or Welsh Nationalism (Butt Philip, 1975) is to focus upon only one part of the United Kingdom, and upon a minority party within that nation. Similarly, to write a book about the Scottish political system (Kellas, 1973) is to assume what remains to be proven, namely, that the things differentiating Scotland from England are politically more important than what Scotland and England have in common, such as government by Westminster. It is more accurate to speak about British government in Scotland or British government in Wales, leaving open to empirical investigation whether, and in what ways, politics in one part of the United Kingdom differs from another (cf. Rose, 1982). Only in Northern Ireland can one properly start from the assumption that government and politics are in fundamental respects un-British.

To write about national differences in British politics and leave out England is like writing about Shakespeare and leaving out Hamlet, all the other tragedies, and the comedies as well. To view a British general election principally through the prism of the Welsh or Scottish Nationalists or Provisional Sinn Fein is to let the tail wag the dog. Territorial differences in British politics do not start at the Irish Sea, the Welsh Marches, or the Scottish Border. Examining differences within England leads to questions about cross-national similarities in the way that nations divide. The rediscovery of the North of England by London-based journalists shows that a "two-nations" hypothesis may differentiate English regions. The systematic examination of the territorial dimension in England concentrates attention where attention should focus in an election, where 523 of the 650 seats in Parliament are to be won.

In writing about the United Kingdom, we have had the advantage of eight years of collaboration with colleagues in the Work Group on United Kingdom Politics, an affiliate of the Political Studies Association that brings together academics from its diverse parts to discuss the territorial dimension in government and politics. Given the diversity between England, Scotland, Wales and Northern Ireland, it is valuable to have such meetings to avoid insularity (to which English analysts are peculiarly prone), as well as to curb the hubris of national exceptionalism (Wha's like us, in braid Scots). The chapters on Mrs. Thatcher's territorial politics written by Jim Bulpitt, on British Labour's territorial policy by Michael Keating, and on Wales by Denis Balsom and J. Barry Jones, are contributed by members of the United Kingdom Politics Work Group.

The preparation of this book was made possible by a grant from the Nuffield Foundation to the Work Group. This grant allowed the first-named author to return from Australia to Britain for a period of months to undertake the great bulk of the statistical work presented here. The Australian National University also provided assistance in preparing this book for the press.

In writing and revising the manuscript, useful comments were received from D.K. Britto, Hugh Bochel, Paul McKee, T.T. Mackie, Edward Page, and Denis Van Mechelen. Within Strathclyde the production of this book was greatly advanced by the assistance of June M. Roberts and Graeme Leonard of the Centre for the Study of Public Policy; The University of Strathclyde Computing Centre and Social Statistics Laboratory especially Mrs. Sarinder Hunjan; and Malcolm McLaren and Pat Fenton of the Printing Unit. The Australian National University gave assistance, and the National Facility for Computing in the Arts of Oxford University made possible the prompt translation of this book from typescript to typeset book.

Ian McAllister                                    Richard Rose

# Part One
# The British Dimension

# I
# Electoral Competition
# In Many Dimensions

Elections are singular events, yet an election outcome must be examined in many dimensions if it is to be fully understood. We are not only interested in how people vote, but also in the nature of the parties that compete for popular support. Within a single constituency the most important fact is which party wins the right to represent it in Parliament, rather than the number of votes or the percentage of the vote won by particular candidates. When the losing parties collectively secure more than half the vote, as usually happens in Britain and sometimes happens in America, the winning party's position is less secure in the electorate than in Parliament.

To understand an election outcome we must examine at least four dimensions of electoral competition. First of all, we must consider a paradox: how the division of votes can give one party a mandate to exercise the unitary authority of government. Secondly, it is important to comprehend how both territorial differences and differences in social structure can significantly influence election outcomes. Thirdly, the translation of votes into seats is contingent not mechanical in the first-past-the-post electoral systems used throughout the English-speaking world. A share of the vote likely to guarantee victory in one constituency may lead to defeat in another. The final step in a multi-dimensional psephological analysis is to understand the pattern of party competition nationwide: the party that finishes first or second in one seat may be a poor third or fourth elsewhere. A nationwide election campaign can involve a multiplicity of constituency contests between different pairs of competitors.

## The Paradox of Division and Unity

Free elections are an expression of political divisions within society, yet they are also meant to unite a country in accepting the legitimacy of the authority of the victor.

Free elections can be held without any division of the electorate. Traditionally, many British MPs were returned unopposed by their constituency, a practice that persisted well into the nineteenth century. This occurred not only where the candidate (or a rich relative or patron) literally owned the votes of the constituency, but also where the candidate was thought to be the appropriate representative for a community. The cost of contesting an election when the expense had to be paid by the candidates not the Crown and electors could be extortionate in their demands was a further inhibition to competition in seats where the result was foregone. When a constituency returned two members, it could differentiate its loyalties by returning two MPs of complementary political outlooks. The number of unopposed returns was consistently high, and the return of MPs unopposed was not ended simply by the passage of the First Reform Act. More than half the members of the House of Commons were returned unopposed in four of the nine elections held after 1832, and the number of unopposed returns never fell below 28 per cent between 1832 and 1885 (Craig, 1981: 158).

The absence of electoral competition in mid-nineteenth century elections is succinctly explained by Hanham (1959: 191): 'general elections were not general'. The electorate was not expected to choose between two parties or leaders competing to control government. Instead, elections were seen as choosing--or, in the case of unopposed returns, legitimating--local representation in a national Parliament. MPs could form cabals or coalitions within Parliament, but these groupings, even if called parties, were not parties organized nationwide as they are today. A House of Commons of 650 members was an assembly of notables; MPs were not the candidates of a nationwide party organization.

The expansion of the franchise and the creation of nationwide party organizations progressed together in late nineteenth century Britain. The creation of nationwide party organizations was a crucial step in the advancement of both electoral divisions and national integration. The creation of party labels meaningful in all parts of Britain turned a collection of local contests into a nationwide competition between parties in which votes in each constituency could be related nationwide to partisan issues and leaders.

The creation of nationwide party organizations also meant a major increase in the number of contested seats. In 1885, the first election after the major 1884 expansion of the franchise, all but six per cent of seats were contested. The exhaustion introduced by that election caused unopposed returns to rise to 33 per cent in 1886. Between 1885 and 1910 the percentage of unopposed returns averaged 21 per cent. Further expansion of the suffrage in 1918 and the rise of the Labour Party made competition at elections general. In 1929, 99 per cent of all seats were contested at the general election, and since 1945 every seat has normally been contested everywhere in the United Kingdom. Two or more parties offer voters, wherever they live, the opportunity for choice.

While parties seek to maximize their votes, no party is foolish enough to believe that it will win all the votes in a competitive election campaign. In the first-past-the-post electoral system, a party does not need to win half the vote to gain a majority of seats in Parliament, if more than two parties nominate candidates. in the last four British general elections, the victorious party has on average won 40.7 per cent of the votes and in the 12 elections since 1945 the winner's share has averaged 45.2 per cent of the popular vote. The Conservative and Labour parties each target their appeal to particular parts of the electorate. The Liberal Party has been electorally weak because of its appeal to voters without regard to their social characteristics. The Alliance substantially increased its votes in 1983, but this scarcely affected seats won. Appealing equally to all voters produces fewer MPs than appealing selectively to blocs of voters.

The unitary authority of government in Britain is not created by the nationwide competition for votes, but by institutions of parliamentary government. Unlike the United States, where control of government is constitutionally divided between the President and Congress, in Britain party government concentrates control. A party with a majority in the House of Commons, however large or small its share of the vote, constitutes the Cabinet that enjoys all the authority of government.

## Social and Territorial Bases of Electoral Competition

Given a nationwide competition for votes, the question then arises: what are the bases of electoral competition? The potential sources of electoral division are great in number. A party can base its appeal for votes on any number of primary group loyalties, such as identification with class, religion, race, region, language, or national identity. Examples of each type of party can be found in Europe (Rose and Urwin, 1969). There have also been unsuccessful attempts to mobilize voters along lines of social divisions not previously important in politics, such as age or sex. Furthermore, new parties can be launched that appeal to voters irrespective of their social characteristics, such as the issue-based Ecology Party. The decline of party allegiances rooted in traditional class or religious visions of society encourages parties to seek votes by invoking "brand loyalty" to party labels. A party can also try to put together ad hoc coalitions of diverse blocs of voters with catchall appeals. Insofar as these appeals are insufficient to maintain electoral support because of lacking a firm anchor in the structure of society, then fluctuations in party support will increase.

Two divisions must occur in every society: the electorate is differentiated along class lines, and territorially as well (Rose and Urwin, 1975: Figure 1). Only a primitive society would be without divisions along lines of occupational class. Only a postage-stamp size city-state such as San Marino would be without territorial divisions, whether these divisions are denominated in terms of nations, regions or parliamentary constituencies. By contrast, many primary social characteristics, such as religion, language and race, can be a source of national unity in societies in which virtually everyone shares the same religion, speaks the same language, and is of the same race. When we say a society is homogeneous, we mean that social divisions are reduced to the ineluctable differences of class and territory. Descriptions of Britain as a homogeneous society do not deny that there are class differences , or claim that Scots, Welsh and Ulstermen (or Yorkshiremen) are just the same as Englishmen. No more is asserted than that Britain is relatively united in terms of language,religion and race.

Concepts and theories of class differences are familiar and pervasive. Society is differentiated in terms of occupations; many other social differences, including education, income, trade union membership, and housing are expected to flow from occupational differences. Collectively, these can be described as the socio-economic divisions of society. In the most deterministic theories of class politics, all other types of social differences are thought to be submerged, explained, or "explained away" by the overwhelming importance of class differences. A review of the social bases of party competition in 15 Western nations shows that class differences are one of the principal influences upon electoral divisions in all but two of the countries (Rose, 1974a: 17).

Britain, like Scandinavian countries, is distinctive because of the pre-eminence of class-related divisions as the principal determinant of party loyalties. In Britain housing and trade union membership appear to be of substantial influences upon voters as well as occupation (cf. Rose, 1982a). Even more than Scandinavian parties, British parties have been competing for the support of an electorate that is "only" divided along socio-economic and territorial lines. By contrast, in many Continental European countries religious differences--between practising Catholics and anti-clericals, between Catholics and Protestants, or both--have been of great historical importance in determining the structure of party competition.

The translation of social divisions into electoral divisions need not lead to political conflict. Notwithstanding the thousands of sociological and ideological treatises written about class conflict, the party systems which have been most inclined to divide voters along class lines--the party systems of Norway, Sweden and Denmark--have been marked by the persistence of "civic" competition, that is, agreement by Socialist and bourgeois parties to differ within limits acceptable to both sides (Berglund and Lindstrom, 1978). In Britain too, competition for votes along class lines has not led to violent conflict in the streets.

The electoral articulation of class differences can actually promote national integration. Because class differences occur in every constituency, an election can be fought on the same terms from one end of the land to the other. Class is not the only means of uniting blocs of voters nationwide. In Belgium, Catholic and anti-clerical Liberals as well as Socialists parties succeeded for a century in appealing to voters along lines that integrated French-speaking Walloons and Flemish-speaking voters across territorial and linguistic boundaries. In India the Congress Party has succeeded in forging a nationwide parliamentary majority, notwithstanding the multiplicity of territorial, linguistic, caste and class divisions in India's electorate.

In Britain the Conservative, Labour and Liberal parties, and now the Alliance, have each sought to be effective agents of national integration by contesting seats throughout the United Kingdom, or, since 1974, everywhere except Northern Ireland. The success of each party is different in England, Scotland and Wales. The important point here is that the very fact of seeking to win seats in all parts of Britain makes each party anxious to stress appeals overriding territorial differences, in order to avoid being labelled as a party of only one of the nations that make up the United Kingdom.

Since the 1960s the importance of class differences in party politics has tended to decline, as have other traditional sources of electoral division such as religion. In the United States, where class voting has never been consistently strong, the Republicans under Ronald Reagan have resurrected an appeal to working-class voters greater than the party had enjoyed for more than half a century. The French Communist Party, traditionally a *parti du combat*, in 1981 joined in government as the weaker coalition partner of French Socialists. In Italy Communist deputies have kept a Christian Democratic government in office as part of a *compromesso storico* (historic compromise). In the Netherlands Catholic and Protestant parties that were traditionally separate pillars of the Dutch party system have now buried their theological differences in a single Christian Democratic appeal.

In Britain the rhetoric of party leaders such as Margaret Thatcher and Michael Foot has tended to emphasize class differences, but the realities of social change have done the opposite. Occupation is no longer so closely linked with other social differences. In the past quarter-century the influence of class-related differences upon party preferences has declined by more than half. The Conservatives today draw about half their vote from working-class electors, the Alliance parties draw working-class votes almost exactly in proportion to their size in the electorate, and the Labour Party has contributed, to the decline of class politics in Britain by becoming a failed ghetto party. It is no longer the party of most working-class voters; in 1983 it failed to win the votes of 64 per cent of the country's manual workers (Rose, 1984).

The decline of class-based voting (or of voting anchored in such contingent social divisions as religion) leaves parties with three different albeit potentially complementary strategies to adopt in competing for votes. One school of electoral studies sees voters casting their ballots principally because of a psychologically grounded party identification. The only social cue necessary to guide a voter is a minimal recollection that this is how he or she (or the voter's parents) have usually voted (see Campbell et al., 1960; Butler and Stokes, 1974). But this view of electoral divisions is difficult to justify. It is static, whereas electoral outcomes increasingly emphasize change. Party identification is not firmly grounded in family loyalties. Only two-fifths of the electorate have clear cues from both parents about how to vote, and even in this group a fraction vote otherwise. Strength of party identification has been declining steadily for two decades. As of 1983, only 26 per cent of the electorate strongly identified with a political party, and only two- thirds identified with either the Conservative or Labour Party (Crewe, 1983: table 3).

Another school of thinking sees parties as issue-based. Social structure and party identification theories do not deny the importance of issues. Rather, they assume (but to a lesser extent demonstrate) that a voter's views about major political issues are formed by their social class (manual workers favouring welfare state spending and the Labour Party; middle-class voters favouring lower taxes and the Conservative Party) or by their party identification (Labour voters disliking the Common Market because the Labour Party has opposed it, and Conservative voters approving it because it is endorsed by the Conservative Party). However, conventional views of class or party determination of issue preferences cannot explain observed contradictions between voters' views on major issues, and their party vote. From 1964 to 1974 much evidence was produced showing that the majority of voters (including Labour voters) tended not to agree with Labour Party positions on many major issues (Rose, 1974b: chapter 11). Yet Labour won four of the five elections in the period. Issue preferences can provide a post hoc basis for predicting how people vote, but it has yet to be shown whether, or to what extent, attitudes about issues are formed independent of party and social loyalties (cf. Sarlvik and Crewe, 1983).

The leadership or personality theory of voting behaviour repudiates the significance of social loyalties, party identification and issue preferences. The personality of the leading contenders for office are assumed to be the primary determinant of how people vote, and leaders are regarded as only loosely linked to parties, as is the case in America. Whereas a party cannot change its image at will and a voter cannot easily change class or religion, a shift in party leadership can be made very quickly. A leader-oriented electorate is therefore a volatile electorate. But such theories leave open the grounds on which voters make assessments of politicians whom they have never met, or only viewed vicariously on television. Surveys consistently show that there is a strong correlation between voters' views about party leaders and their party preferences. Insofar as party preferences persist, this shows that party loyalties do more to shape views of political personalities than the opposite. Nor can the personalities of leaders such as Margaret Thatcher, Michael Foot or Neil Kinnock be divorced from their views about issues.

Another way to fill the vacuum left by the increasingly visible inadequacy of class models of electoral competition today is to see competition occurring along territorial lines. Since the 1960s there has been a resurgence of interest in territorial politics throughout Europe. The phenomenon is variously labelled as a demand for regional devolution, national autonomy, independence, or as a peripheral protest movement. Books have appeared with pessimistic titles such as *The Failure of the State*, (Cornford, 1975) or *Ethnic Conflict in the Western World*, (Esman, 1977); optimistic titles, such as *Resolving Nationality Conflicts*(Davison and Gordenker, 1980); or more ambiguously, *Economy, Territory, Identity*(Rokkan and Urwin, 1983). Instead of being seen as a romantic, nineteenth century phenomenon, territorial and nationalist protests have become viewed as normal, and even growing.

The extent to which regional or national differences affect party competition can easily be exaggerated. Books about ethnic differences risk losing all electoral relevance when they concentrate attention upon groups with 50,000 or less people in countries where millions of votes are cast in a national election (cf. Krejci and Velimsky, 1981). Attempts to reduce national protest movements to expressions of cross-regional or cross-national economic and social inequalities are also unsuccessful (cf. Hechter, 1975, with Page, 1978). Regions have registered some measurable influence upon party competition in nine of 15 Western nations, but in none of these countries is regionalism the principal influence upon party competition (Rose, 1974a: 17). Explicitly regional, autonomist or national independence parties enter electoral competition in a number of European countries, but doing so reveals their weakness, not only in national vote totals,but also within their own heartland region (cf. Rose and Urwin, 1975).

Class differences are normally regarded as most important, but even the author of the epigram--'Class is the basis of British party politics; all else is embellishment and detail' (Pulzer, 1967: 98)-- would admit that this phrase excepted Northern Ireland, and perhaps Scotland and Wales as well. In the nineteenth century, the territorial concerns of nationalist movements were of central importance. Liberals such as William Gladstone and Woodrow Wilson saw popular choice and national self-determination as two sides of the same coin of democracy. Within the United Kingdom, national differences were central in the House of Commons from the entry of Irish Nationalists in the 1880s to agitate a single issue, home rule for Ireland, until 1921, when the old United Kingdom was disrupted by the grant of independence to a 26-county Irish Free State.

By European standards Britain is distinctive because it has a multiplicity of Nationalist parties, and in the period since the late 1960s Nationalist parties have been successful in securing a toehold in Parliament (McAllister, 1982). Institutionally, the United Kingdom has always been multi-national, reflecting its creation by the incomplete amalgamation of different territories under a common Crown and Parliament (Rose, 1982). But the existence of distinctive institutions of government in Scotland, Wales and Northern Ireland--and thus, by a process of subtraction, for England as well--has been offset by the political unity resulting from the domination of elections by parties competing Britainwide. In 1964, all 630 seats in the House of Commons were won by parties seeking to represent the whole of the United Kingdom, rather than a single nation or region within it. In 1983, the House of Commons contained MPs for seven different regional parties; the Scottish National Party (SNP); Plaid Cymru (the Welsh Nationalist Party); two Irish nationalist parties, Provisional Sinn Fein and the Social Democratic & Labour Party (SDLP); and three different Ulster Unionist and Loyalist parties.

The strength of nationalist parties has been variable across time, and also from nation to nation. Table I.1 illustrates both these contrasts. In 1964, when the aggregate Conservative and Labour Party vote was divided almost evenly, there were notable differences between nations in the strength of each party. The Conservative vote was highest in Northern Ireland, where it was then in alliance with the Ulster Unionist Party, and in England; the Labour share of the vote was highest in Scotland and Wales. In the October 1974 general election, the Nationalist vote reached an unprecedented height. But Nationalist strength varied greatly, for the Scottish National Party won almost three times the share of the vote taken by Plaid Cymru in Wales. By 1983, Scottish and Welsh Nationalists showed a greater degree of parity--but it was an equality of weakness. By contrast, in Northern Ireland the whole of Ulster's vote was given to parties not linked with parties in Great Britain.

The rise of nationalist parties commenced in 1966, when Gerry Fitt was elected as a Republican Labour MP from West Belfast. He was joined in the House of Commons by a Plaid Cymru by-election victor later in the year, and by a Scottish Nationalist in 1967. An outbreak of civil rights demonstrations in Northern Ireland in summer, 1968, brought Northern Ireland into the spotlight at Westminster, and the election of Bernadette Devlin at a 1969 by-election intensified this. An outbreak of rioting and killing in August, 1969, followed by British troops being called into action, confirmed the status of Northern Ireland as a very different part of the United Kingdom from so-called

Table I.1   THE TERRITORIAL DIVISION OF VOTES BY NATION          I9

| | 1964 | Oct 1974 | 1983 | Change 1964-83 |
|---|---|---|---|---|
| | | (% vote) | | |
| **England** | | | | |
| Conservative | 44.1 | 38.9 | 46.0 | +1.9 |
| Labour | 43.5 | 40.1 | 26.9 | -16.6 |
| Liberal/Alliance[a] | 12.1 | 20.2 | 26.4 | +14.3 |
| **Wales** | | | | |
| Conservative | 29.4 | 23.9 | 31.0 | +1.6 |
| Labour | 57.9 | 49.5 | 37.5 | -20.4 |
| Liberal/Alliance | 7.3 | 15.5 | 23.2 | +15.9 |
| Plaid Cymru | 4.8 | 10.8 | 7.8 | +3.0 |
| **Scotland** | | | | |
| Conservative | 40.6 | 24.7 | 28.4 | -12.2 |
| Labour | 48.7 | 36.3 | 35.1 | -13.6 |
| Liberal/Alliance | 7.6 | 8.3 | 23.7 | +16.1 |
| SNP | 2.4 | 30.4 | 11.8 | +9.4 |
| **N. Ireland** | | | | |
| Ulster Unionist Party[b] | 63.0 | n.a. | n.a. | -63.0 |
| All Unionist[b]/Loyalist | n.a. | 62.1 | 57.1 | -5.0 |
| NI Labour/APNI[c] | 16.1 | 6.3 | 8.0 | -8.1 |
| All Irish unity | 18.2 | 29.8 | 33.2 | +15.0 |

[a] Liberal in 1964 and Oct 1974; Liberal-SDP Alliance in 1983.

[b] In 1964 the Ulster Unionist Party was allied with the British Conservatives and its votes were included in the Conservatives' total vote.  The parties split in 1972.

[c] In 1964 NI Labour; 1974 and 1983 Alliance Party of N. Ireland.

Sources:  Rose and McAllister (1982:  Table 4.1 to 4.4), updated by the authors.  Votes for other parties excluded.

"mainland" Britain (Rose, 1971). The defeat of the two Nationalist by-election victors at the 1970 general election was widely interpreted as the end of Nationalist pressures.

The February, 1974 general election result once again put nationalism in Great Britain on the agenda of Parliament. The surprise election of seven Scottish Nationalist and two Welsh Nationalist MPs was striking in itself, and politically crucial in a Parliament where the Labour government lacked an overall majority. In October 1974 the SNP won 11 seats and Plaid Cymru, 3; together, the 14 Nationalist seats were greater than the Labour government's majority. This was an important factor in making devolution to Scotland and Wales a major parliamentary concern. But the resulting devolution Acts were unambiguously rejected in the March 1979 referendum in Wales and ambiguously endorsed in a low-turnout referendum in Scotland. The Scottish Nationalists then helped bring down the Labour government.

The 1979 British general election marked a shift in emphasis in territorial concerns. The Scottish National Party lost nine of its 11 seats, and the Welsh Nationalists saw their vote drop. But in England, territorial divisions were brought into sharp focus by the election of a Conservative government with nearly four-fifths of the seats in the South of England and a Labour opposition claiming two-thirds of the seats in the North of England, as well as two-thirds of the seats in Scotland and Wales. Curtice and Steed (1982: 297) forecast that the widening gap between North Britain and South Britain was likely to continue, 'producing parliamentary parties that are less likely to aggregate across geographically differentiated interests'. Curtice and Steed saw territorial conflict between an economically declining North Britain and a relatively prosperous South Britain as increasingly likely.

While many changes were registered in the 1983 election result, there remain some broad similarities in voting patterns across two decades. First of all, Britainwide parties have been dominant throughout. Nationalists win the votes of only a minority of a minority. In Scotland, 88 per cent of the vote went to British parties, and in Wales, 92 per cent. In Northern Ireland, parties seeking to withdraw from the United Kingdom won but one-third of the vote; parties loyal or fervently ultra-loyal to the United Kingdom won two-thirds of the popular vote. In 1983 as in 1964, the Conservatives polled the most votes in England, and Labour polled more votes in Scotland and Wales. The Alliance came third in votes in all three nations. The one great structural shift occurred in Northern Ireland. Because no British party seeks to win votes and seats there, the Irish Sea is now a gulf between party competition in Great Britain and in Northern Ireland.

In no sense was the 1983 election simply a return to the status quo as of 1964. Only one group, the Liberal and Social Democratic Party Alliance, saw its vote change at much the same rate in all parts of Britain. The Labour vote fell in all parts of the United Kingdom, but it did not fall equally. Labour's vote went down most in Wales and least in Scotland. The Conservative vote differed in the direction as well as the scale of change. In England and Wales the Conservative vote went up slightly from 1964, a good showing given added competition from the Alliance. However, the Conservative vote fell by nearly one-third in Scotland, and it disappeared from electoral competition in Northern Ireland. Nationalist parties, starting from different levels of support in 1964, grew at different rates, rising most in Northern Ireland, where Irish unity candidates have always been relatively strong, and least in Wales, where Welsh Nationalist have always been relatively weak.

The 1983 election reflected very different patterns of party competition from nation to nation within the United Kingdom. In England, Labour and the Alliance were only 0.5 per cent apart in their share of the popular vote. In effect, they compete to finish a poor second, since the Conservatives are nearly 20 per cent ahead of each. In Scotland and Wales, Labour finished first, but its lead over the Conservatives is much reduced. In Wales, Labour was 28.5 per cent ahead of the Conservatives in 1964 in popular vote; in 1983 it was 6.5 per cent ahead. The Labour lead over the Conservatives in popular votes dropped only 1.4 per cent in Scotland, because both major parties saw a substantial decline in Scottish support from 1964 to 1983.

The net result is that the British party system today consists of three very different types of parties, varying in the degree to which their popular vote appears skewed along class or territorial lines (cf. Rose, 1980; McAllister 1982).

1.  Class-skewed and territorially skewed vote
    Labour Party

2.  Territorially skewed but cross-class support
    Conservative Party
    Scottish National Party
    Plaid Cymru
    All Northern Ireland parties

3.  Not territorially skewed and having cross-class support
    Alliance (Liberal Party, Social Democratic Party)

Whereas only one-quarter of the electorate cast their votes for a party whose support was very heavily class-skewed, three- quarters cast their votes for parties whose support was territorially skewed. Both class and territorial differences appear to affect the electoral success of parties today, but they do not affect all parties equally, nor are they of the same importance in all parts of the United Kingdom.

One way to explain the apparent puzzle of very different national patterns of partisanship is to redefine territorial boundaries. This can most readily be done by dividing each nation of the United Kingdom into regions. The regional analysis of voting reveals substantial differences within England. Up to the 1983 general election, the Labour vote in the North of England had been higher than the Conservative vote, and in 1983 it was almost equal to the Conservative vote. By contrast, in the South of England, where Labour has usually run the Conservatives second, Labour dropped to third place in electoral competition in 1983. The Conservatives won more than three times as many votes as Labour in the South of England. Regional analyses of party support in Wales, Scotland and Northern Ireland show that there can be bigger differences within a nation than between nations, for example between the Welsh-speaking parts of Wales and industrial South Wales, between the Scottish Highlands and industrial Clydeside and in Northern Ireland between constituencies east and west of the River Bann (see Chapters V-VIII).

Disaggregating nations into a number of regions still masks within-region differences. The most populous regions of Britain tend to be heterogeneous, not homogeneous. This is most true of the South-East of England, which encompasses decayed inner-city areas of London, old and new suburbs of owner-occupiers and council house tenants, and rural areas which may mix commuters, light industry, and farming. Every major metropolitan area within the United Kingdom, from London to South Glamorgan, Strathclyde and Greater Belfast, is a combination of disparate social groups. Inner-city areas in different parts of Britain are likely to have more in common with each other than inner- city and suburban areas belonging to the same metropolitan conurbation.

The more territorial parts of the United Kingdom are disaggregated in order to delimit boundaries containing socially and politically homogeneous areas, the more important appears the socio-economic base of electoral competition. The identification of within- nation or within-region or within-conurbation differences is but another way of describing socio-economic similarities among inner-city areas, suburbs, or rural areas throughout Britain. A major task of psephological analysis is to test the relative importance of socio-economic as against territorial influences upon electoral competition in the United Kingdom today.

## From Votes to Seats

Elections are about winning seats as well as votes; the party with the most seats in Parliament is deemed the winner of a general election, gaining the right to form a government. Twice in post-war Britain, in 1951 and again in

February 1974, the party winning the greatest share of the popular vote did not win the greatest number of seats in the House of Commons, and thereby lost control of government.

While modern election campaigning is highly centralized, both in terms of party leadership and media coverage, the effects of the campaign are registered nationwide. Since the breaking of the power of the House of Lords in 1911 and the abolition of University seats in 1948, power in Parliament is determined solely by winning territorial constituencies. To win a majority in the House of Commons, a party must win 326 of the 650 constituencies.

Table I.2  THE TERRITORIAL DIVISION OF SEATS BY NATION

|  | | Seats | | Change |
| --- | --- | --- | --- | --- |
|  | 1964 | Oct1974 | 1983 | 1964–83 |
| England | | | | |
| Conservative | 262 | 253 | 362 | +100 |
| Labour | 246 | 255 | 148 | −98 |
| Liberal/Alliance | 3 | 8 | 13 | +10 |
| Wales | | | | |
| Conservative | 6 | 8 | 14 | +8 |
| Labour | 28 | 23 | 20 | −8 |
| Liberal/Alliance | 2 | 2 | 2 | 0 |
| Plaid Cymru | 0 | 3 | 2 | +2 |
| Scotland | | | | |
| Conservative | 24 | 16 | 21 | −3 |
| Labour | 43 | 41 | 41 | −2 |
| Liberal/Alliance | 4 | 3 | 8 | +4 |
| SNP | 0 | 11 | 2 | +2 |
| N. Ireland | | | | |
| Ulster Unionist Party | 12 | 0 | 0 | (−12) |
| All Unionist/Loyalist | n.a. | 10 | 15 | (+15) |
| NI Labour/APNI | 0 | 0 | 0 | (0) |
| All Irish Unity | 0 | 2 | 2 | (+2) |

Sources: Rose and McAllister (1982: Table 4.2) updated.
        Party groupings as in Table I.1.

Constituencies are not allocated on a United Kingdom basis; they are allocated by four separate sets of Boundary Commissioners for England, Scotland, Wales and Northern Ireland. Hence, there are small but noticeable differences in the number of seats per nation. Whereas in 1983 there was one MP for every 67,201 electors in England and for every 61,778 electors in Northern Ireland, in Wales there was one MP for every 55,628 electors, and in Scotland, one MP for every 53,985 electors. Even more important are the big differences in the number of seats that each party wins (Table I.2).

In theory, a party's share of the popular vote could be distributed among constituencies in any number of ways. At one extreme, the vote of each party would be virtually the same in every constituency. If that were the case, then at the 1983 election the Conservatives, instead of winning 61 per cent of the seats, would have won 100 per cent of the seats, finishing first in every seat, with Labour trailing well behind in second place, and Alliance third.

At the other extreme, in the first-past-the-post electoral system a party could so concentrate its vote that it would win an absolute majority of seats with only one-quarter of the popular vote. If a party gained one more than half the vote in 326 seats, it would be assured of a parliamentary majority, even if it did not win a single vote in the remaining 324 seats. With 25 per cent of the vote and 50.1 per cent of the seats, it could take 100 per cent of the power of government.

In practice, extreme disproportionality has never occurred in a first-past-the-post election in modern times. A systematic comparative analysis of the degree of disproportionality in electoral systems shows that it is very limited. On average, the median country with a first-past-the-post system departs only 13 per cent from a purely proportional outcome, and a proportional representation system departs only five per cent. Another way of saying this is that first-past-the-post systems tend to be 85 per cent proportional in translating popular votes into seats, and proportional representation systems tend to be 95 per cent proportional (Rose, 1983: Table 8).

The 1983 British general election result was unusual in the degree to which it departed from proportionality (Table I.3). In 1964, the degree of proportionality between votes and seats was high, 89 per cent. In October 1974, when Nationalists and Liberals were polling well, the degree of proportionality was 81 per cent, and it rose to 85 per cent in 1979. By comparison, in 1983 the index of proportionality fell to 77 per cent. The distribution of votes and seats was close to pure proportionality in the case of the Labour Party, and of Nationalist and Northern Ireland parties. It departed substantially from proportionality in the case of the Conservatives (42.4 per cent of the vote and 61.1 per cent of the seats in the House of Commons), and the Alliance, (25.4 per cent of the popular vote, and 3.5 per cent of Commons' seats).

When the distribution of parliamentary seats by nation is compared with the distribution of popular votes, the distorting effects of the first-past-the-post

Table I.3 PROPORTIONALITY IN ELECTION OUTCOMES BY NATION

|  | 1964 | Oct 1974 | 1983 | Change 1964–83 |
|---|---|---|---|---|
|  | (Index of Proportionality) | | | |
| England | 87 | 81 | 76 | −11 |
| Wales | 81 | 86 | 79 | −2 |
| Scotland | 88 | 79 | 79 | −9 |
| N. Ireland | 64 | 80 | 70 | +6 |
| Total, United Kingdom | 89 | 81 | 77 | −12 |

Sources: Tables I.1-2.  The Index of Proportionality is the sum of the differences between each party's share of seats and votes, divided by two and subtracted from 100.

electoral system are most evident. The degree of distortion differs between nations, and can also differ from election to election. In England, the chief beneficiary of the first- past-the-post system in 1983 was the Conservative Party,but this is not always the case. In Wales and in Scotland, the Labour Party is consistently the chief beneficiary. In all three parts of Britain, the Alliance suffered from the electoral system, but its disadvantage was only half as great in Scotland as in England. Northern Ireland is the only nation of the United Kingdom in which one bloc, the Unionists and Loyalists, can consistently win a majority of the votes as well as a majority of the seats in the House of Commons.

The outcome of a British and, for that matter, almost every first-past-the-post election tends toward proportionality because most constituencies are not a social cross-section of the country. A party that comes second in the nationwide competition for votes comes first in a substantial number of constituencies if two conditions are met: (1) Its appeal to the mass electorate is biased toward particular sub- divisions of the electorate; and (2) the section of the electorate to which it appeals is territorially clustered, rather than being evenly spread across the country. Both the Conservative and Labour parties meet these criteria. As Labour's vote has fallen, it has more and more depended for parliamentary representation upon constituencies with disproportionately large numbers of working-class voters. The Conservatives have done well in winning seats in the House of Commons by combining an appeal to middle-class voters, who tend to be concentrated in suburban and rural areas, with a substantial working-class vote. Nationalist parties, including Northern Ireland parties, can do relatively well in matching their share of votes to seats because their vote is concentrated in one part of the United Kingdom.

The upsurge of votes for the Alliance in 1983 demonstrates the parliamentary frustration that faces a group that does not appeal to well defined and territorially clustered blocs of voters. The Alliance failure to win many seats in Parliament is not because it finished third in total vote; the disparity in seats between Alliance and Labour is far greater than the disparity in votes. The Alliance's problem is that its vote is spread relatively evenly throughout Great Britain. In 1983 the standard deviation of the Alliance's constituency vote was only 7.4 per cent, compared to much higher levels of dispersion for the Conservatives, 13.2 per cent, and Labour, 15.7 per cent.

Given the potential difference between votes won and seats won, it is important to distinguish carefully between the analysis of voting behaviour and of election outcomes. Evidence about a party's nationwide share of the vote is not per se evidence about its success in winning seats in the House of Commons. To understand that, we must consider both the social sources of a party's vote and the territorial concentration of its electoral support.

## Patterns of Competition for Government

Many patries can compete for votes, but only one party can represent a given constituency in Parliament. Parliament remains more or less representative of diverse political outlooks because different parties finish first in different constituencies. A losing party in one place will be a winning party in another constituency.

In a pure two-party system, each of the two parties competing at the polls will finish first in some constituencies and second in others. Because many seats will be held by big margins of votes, competition for government is effectively concentrated in a limited number of marginal seats. In Conservative-held marginal constituencies, a small swing of votes to Labour would make the seat change hands, and with it control of government. In a Labour-held marginal, a small swing to the Conservatives would strengthen the position of a Conservative government.

Party competition in Britain today is impure rather than pure. When three parties compete there are six logically possible combinations of parties that can finish first and second in England. If the Liberals and Social Democrats are treated as separate parties rather than as a single Alliance, then the logically possible combinations of parties finishing first and second doubles. the number of different patterns increases much more when the Nationalist parties are also taken into account. While only one of these combinations can be valid at any one time in any one place, all of them can be valid when 650 constituencies are examined collectively.

In the 1983 general election, there were 11 different patterns of party competition within Great Britain, that is, constituencies in which there were different pairs of parties finishing first and second. The complexities of Northern Ireland politics add an additional nine patterns of competition for 17 Ulster seats. Collectively, there is now turbulence, because of the multiplicity of patterns of party competition in 1983. Nor is the turbulence confined to peripheral parts of Britain. Within England constituencies collectively display six different patterns of party competition.

When there are multiple patterns of party competition, the identity of the competing parties is contingent not certain in any one constituency. While the Conservatives are indubitably the first party in Britain today, it is not clear which is now the second party . Collectively, third force parties (that is, the Alliance, Nationalists and Northern Ireland parties) were second in 1983 winning 30 per cent of the total vote, as against 28 per cent won by Labour. In terms of seats in the House of Commons, Labour finished second. But in terms of constituency competition, Labour was more likely to finish third rather than second, trailing the Alliance as well as the Conservatives. Labour lost 119 deposits by failing to win one-eighth of the constituency vote, as against the Alliance loss of 11 deposits. The first priority in evaluating any particular constituency contest is to ask: What is the pattern of party competition here?

Whatever the names of the parties finishing first and second, the conventional idea of a seat changing hands by a swing of votes between the two leading parties is no longer true. Swing is appropriate when there are two (and only two) parties contesting a seat. In such a circumstance, the gain of votes by one party must equal the loss of the other party. But when three parties contest a seat, then one party's gain can be obtained in a variety of of ways from the two other parties, and one party's loss can benefit either or both competitors. If the leading party has more than half the vote, any three-way exchange of votes is unlikely to threaten the incumbent MP with defeat. However, at the 1983 election less than half of all MPs won an absolute majority of votes in their constituency.

When a party is defending a constituency with less than half the vote, competition for the seat is multi-dimensional. There are several ways in which a seat might be retained or lost besides a conventional swing in votes between the first and second party. A conventional swing could be negated if the leading party compensated for votes lost to the second-place party by gaining votes from the third-place party. Alternatively, a second-place party could take a seat without the incumbent losing a single vote by attracting sufficient support from the third-place party to pull ahead of an incumbent without an absolute majority. Where a Conservative now holds a seat with a substantial lead over a second-place Alliance candidate, the Conservative could be helped by a revival of Labour fortunes, even if it involved Labour winning some votes from the Conservative. That would make it less likely for the governing party to lose votes to Alliance, now the challenger in most Conservative-held seats.

The competition for votes is turbulent because the very distinctive 1983 general election results are an unstable base for any projection about the next general election. There is a gross disparity between the seats and votes of the two groups of parties contending for the title of Opposition. If the Alliance could concentrate its vote to win seats in proportion to votes, this would threaten both the Conservative and Labour parties. But the Alliance has the psephological misfortune to spread its support evenly. Its lack of a well defined base within the social structure of Britain causes great fluidity in the Alliance vote, which nearly doubled in 1983 from the Liberal total at the previous election. Because the Alliance's support is volatile,it is vulnerable to its vote being halved at the next general election.

The outcome of any one election is half the story of the next election . It is an important half, because it sets the position from which each party starts. Parties do not enter an election campaign as equals, especially when one party is already in government because of a landslide victory. Yet because most seats are held by a minority vote, the governing party could readily lose if the opposition united. Reciprocally, it could retain office if its opponents continue to be divided relatively evenly.

In an era in which parties as well as voters appear to be becoming dealigned, future patterns of party competition will be determined by actions of party leaders as well as voters. But these actions occur in the context of an extraordinary 1983 election outcome. The British party system can today be described as a two-party system only by giving that term a radically new definition. There is one whole party, the Conservatives, with upwards of half the vote and more than half the seats. Labour and the Alliance, share more than half the vote but less than half the seats, constituting the two half-parties in the system.

# II
# Common Problems
# of British Government

Parties divide but problems unite the electorate. The mass of the electorate tends to agree about the concerns to which British government should give priority. Problems of war and peace, inflation, economic growth and unemployment are important nationwide. Politicians too tend to agree about the principal problems facing the country. In a system of free elections, they could hardly do otherwise. Disagreement is about which party's policies or which party's leaders are best qualified to deal with common concerns of the electorate (cf. Rose, 1984).

Cabinet discussions, debates in Parliament, and the activities of Whitehall departments give collective force to the British dimension in the government of the United Kingdom. The problems that command most political attention are problems Britainwide. When divisions occur between spending ministries and Treasury opponents, between MPs favouring free enterprise as against Socialist planning, or within the governing party, the lines of divisions are likely to be functional, not territorial. They usually reflect economic interests found in all parts of Britain, rather than regional interests confined to one part of Britain.

Common British concerns are more important than distinctive national concerns in a multi-national United Kingdom. At Westminster the British dimension is consistently more important than the Scottish dimension, the Welsh dimension, the Ulster or Irish dimension, and the rarely articulated but potentially powerful English dimension. In an ever-widening circle of territorial identifications, from the neighbourhood to global concerns, Westminster is the political focal point. It is more central than the regional dimension, and far stronger than the institutions representing the European or the United Nations dimension.

The institutions of British government are profoundly centralist and the authority of the Crown in Parliament is unlimited. But the Union that constitutes the United Kingdom is in no sense uniform. It is an eccentric unitary state, for there are separate ministers in Cabinet for Scotland, Wales, and

Northern Ireland, albeit none for England. While the content of health, education and housing policies are much the same in all parts of the United Kingdom, responsibility for these important welfare state programmes is dispersed among four ministries, a functional ministry concerned primarily with England, and three territorial ministries (Rose, 1982: chapter 5). The ministries that have Britainwide responsibilities are relatively few but nonetheless of great importance: the Treasury, the Foreign Office and Defence.

Party politics is the force that makes common functional concerns dominate territorial differences. Parties compete for votes throughout Britain, and the Cabinet is kept in office by a parliamentary majority consisting of MPs more or less united along functional lines. A Cabinet minister cannot show favouritism toward his own constituency; to do this would be to mobilize the rest of the Cabinet against him (Gregory, 1980). Even more, a Scottish, Welsh or Northern Ireland Office minister cannot pursue an independent line when the minister's seat in Cabinet depends upon support from a parliamentary party principally consisting of MPs from English constituencies. MPs divide about the best way to tackle problems of inflation, unemployment, and health everywhere in the United Kingdom.

The problems that dominated the Conservative government of Margaret Thatcher from 1979 to 1983 were pre-eminently Britainwide concerns. Inflation everywhere affected the value of the currency. The nationwide rise in unemployment created anxiety about economic conditions in households throughout Britain. The challenge to the party system thrown up by the creation of the Liberal and Social Democratic Party Alliance involved a nationwide competition for votes; it was not concentrated solely in remote Celtic constituencies, or in trendy and equally atypical parts of London. The Falklands War was uniquely an issue encouraging national unity in opposition to an external enemy. By contrast with the preceding Parliament, devolution, the shibboleth of particularism, was of no consequence in the 1979 Parliament. The greater the extent to which the problems of British government are common to all parts, then the more strongly the partisan divisions of the electorate should reflect socio-economic rather than territorial differences.

## A British Government with Britainwide Problems

The chief problems facing the Conservative government of Margaret Thatcher on entry to office in 1979, like those facing her predecessors, were pervasive, affecting every household in the United Kingdom. This was most evident in foreign policy. While politicians might differ about the definition of Britain's national interest, they agree that this interest can only be articulated on a unitary basis for the whole of the United Kingdom. Immediately, the United

Kingdom's position within the European Community was a cause for concern, because of the size of the British cash contribution to the Community in relation to cash benefits received. Negotiations in the European Community are very much negotiations between sovereign states, in which Westminster speaks for the United Kingdom as a whole.

The management of the economy is also an issue in which policy choices affect the whole of Britain, because of the relatively great importance of the government's role in the economy, and the very high degree of centralization of that responsibility in Westminster. Even within central government, decisions are further concentrated in the Treasury. While differences can be found in the economic structure of different regions and nations of the United Kingdom, they tend to be limited; they are differences in degreee rather than differences in kind (McAllister, Parry and Rose, 1979). Economically, the United Kingdom is a relatively homogeneous late industrial society.

The priorities of the Thatcher government--reducing inflation, reducing public sector borrowing and limiting the growth of the money supply--were necessarily decisions of central government. Inflation rates and interest rates are common throughout the whole of the United Kingdom. Borrowing is controlled by the Bank of England; notwithstanding its name, it is the bank for the whole of the United Kingdom. Ingenious economists can suggest ways in which the effects of central economic policies may be modified on a territorial basis, but Mrs. Thatcher had no wish to modify an economic strategy that she believed to be widely applicable because based on universal principles.

A distinctive feature of the 1979 Parliament was the supersession of concern with inflation, felt evenly throughout the United Kingdom, by concern with unemployment. Unemployment rose from 5 per cent at the time of the 1979 general election to 13 per cent by 1982. Instead of being an isolated or transitory phenomenon, unemployment became a matter of widespread concern. There was in principle no reason for the effects of unemployment to be the same throughout the United Kingdom. In the 1930s, for example, there were very large national differences between levels of unemployment in Wales and England, and within England between the depressed North East and the relatively prosperous South of England.

For a quarter-century after the Second World War, unemployment was extremely low. In 1951 nationwide unemployment was 1.3 per cent of the labour force, and in 1961 it was virtually the same, 1.6 per cent (Table II.1). While low, unemployment was very unevenly distributed among the nations of the United Kingdom. In 1951 unemployment in Northern Ireland was six times higher than in England, and more than double that in Wales and Scotland. These differences remained great in 1961.

Table II.1   UNEMPLOYMENT DIFFERENCES NARROW, 1951-83

|              | 1951 | 1961 | 1971 | 1979 May | 1983 June | Change 1951-83 |
|--------------|------|------|------|------|------|------|
|              | (Unemployment as % of UK) |||||  |
| N. Ireland   | 469  | 469  | 226  | 196  | 162  | -307  |
| Wales        | 208  | 162  | 126  | 141  | 123  | -85   |
| Scotland     | 197  | 194  | 166  | 135  | 116  | -81   |
| England      | 77   | 81   | 86   | 91   | 95   | +18   |
| % Unemployed UK | 1.3 | 1.6 | 3.5 | 5.4 | 12.5 | +11.2 |

Sources: 1951-71 Rose and McAllister (1982:158);   1979
and 1983, Department of Employment Gazette.

The limited and gradual rise in unemployment in the 1960s and 1970s was coincidentally accompanied by a narrowing of between-nation differences in the levels of unemployment. Economic expansion caused unemployment in Northern Ireland, Scotland, and Wales to fall from 1961 to 1966; it then rose relatively slowly by comparison with unemployment in England. The subsequent increase in the total number of unemployed, which passed the million mark in 1975, involved a reduction in differences between parts of the United Kingdom. In May 1979 unemployment in Northern Ireland was substantially down relative to England, and in Scotland and Wales the differential had fallen too.

When unemployment more than doubled during the 1979 Parliament, inequalities between parts of the United Kingdom reduced because the rise in unemployment hit hardest in regions that had previously had full employment. By 1983 unemployment in Northern Ireland was two-thirds above the English average. In Wales unemployment was one-quarter more than the English average. In Scotland, the unemployment differential dropped to one-fifth above England. When levels of unemployment are examined by English regions, the Scottish level is lower than unemployment in the formerly very prosperous West Midlands, or in the North West or the North East of England. In Wales, unemployment is also below that of the North East of England, which is approaching a level of unemployment previously found only in that historic black spot for jobs, Northern Ireland.

Before the increase in unemployment, it was fashionable to interpret changes in living standards or differences in living standards between nations as a major influence upon electoral behaviour (cf. Goodhart and Bhansali, 1970), and even as a cause of territorial conflict (Hechter, 1975). The difference between 1.3 per cent unemployment in England and 2.9 per cent in Scotland in 1966 and the four per cent differential in earnings then was invoked as a cause of political protest benefiting the Scottish National Party. Such an interpretation is, however, contrary to the experience of the 1930s, when higher levels of nationwide unemployment were accompanied by bigger differences between nations. In 1930, when unemployment in the United Kingdom as a whole stood at 15 per cent, it was above 25 per cent in Wales. The result was not a rise in Nationalist votes in Wales and Scotland; Nationalist movements were weak by comparison with the 1970s, even though other social differences, such as language and religion, were far greater then. Instead, unemployment differentials created an upsurge of support for the Labour Party, endorsing Aneurin Bevan's view that the solution of the problems of the economically depressed regions of Britain could only be achieved through centralized action at Westminster. This view is still voiced today; for example, Neil Kinnock argued it in opposition to Welsh devolution in 1979.

The sharp rise in unemployment increased the importance of central government, albeit against the wishes of a Thatcher administration wishing to reverse the growth of government. Rising unemployment made such welfare state services as unemployment and supplementary benefit payments more important. Unlike education, which is delivered by local government, unemployment benefits are paid directly by central government. As the recession increased, employment in the private sector contracted, thus increasing the proportion of the population receiving its weekly income from government as public employees or as pensioners or recipients of unemployment benefits. With nearly one-third of the labour force in some form of public employment--and more in Wales, Northern Ireland and the North East of England (Parry, 1981)--Westminster's importance is everywhere palpable. The Treasury's role in collecting taxes nationwide in accord with ability to pay and distributing funds according to need is to the advantage of poorer regions (cf. Rose, 1982: chapter 6). People who see the British Treasury as the provider or guarantor of their income are more inclined to guide the hand that feeds them rather than bite it by voting for Nationalist parties.

In 1983 as in 1979, the problems that most concerned the electorate affected the whole of Britain (Table II.2). Concern with the economy was foremost. When voters were asked to name the two biggest problems facing the country, in 1979 the responses covered a range of economic topics: inflation, unemployment, industrial relations, and taxation. On average, the economy received at least one mention from each voter. By 1983, attention was very

Table II.2 THE MOST IMPORTANT PROBLEMS FACING THE COUNTRY

| | 1979 GB | 1979 Scot'd | 1983 GB | 1983 Scot'd |
|---|---|---|---|---|
| | % | % | % | % |
| Prices, cost of living, inflation | 42 | 45 | 20 | 18 |
| Unemployment, jobs | 27 | 42 | 72 | 72 |
| Industrial relations, strikes, unions | 20 | 16 | 3 | 3 |
| Taxation, incom tax | 21 | 20 | 4 | 5 |
| Other economic issues | 4 | 2 | 3 | 2 |
| Incomes policy | 3 | 4 | 1 | 1 |
| Nationalisation | 3 | 2 | 1 | 2 |
| Defence, nuclear weapons | 2 | 1 | 38 | 30 |
| International peace | 1 | - | 1 | - |
| Falklands War | na | na | 1 | 1 |
| Common Market | 4 | 3 | 5 | 3 |
| Health | 4 | 3 | 11 | 14 |
| Pensions | 7 | 8 | 8 | 10 |
| Education | 8 | 5 | 6 | 5 |
| Welfare benefits | 3 | 4 | 1 | 1 |
| Law & order, crime | 11 | 12 | 5 | 2 |
| Northern Ireland | 1 | 1 | - | - |
| Immigrants, race relations | 5 | 1 | 1 | - |
| Devolution to Scotland, Wales | - | 3 | - | 1 |
| Scotland's interests, N. Sea oil | - | 4 | - | 3 |
| Other | 12 | 8 | 11 | 10 |

Question: 'Think of all the urgent problems facing the country at the present time. When you decided which way to vote, which two issues did you yourself consider most important?' Answers tabulate % naming issue as one of two most important.

Sources: Gallup Political Index, No. 226 (June 1979), p. 10 and calculated from 1983 Gallup Poll BBC election survey.

much concentrated upon a single issue: 72 per cent named unemployment as a major problem. In 1979, concern with welfare state measures such as education and pensions ranked second in importance, further emphasizing the importance of public policies underwritten from Westminster. In 1983, the rise in international tension made foreign affairs and military defence second in public concern. Defence and nuclear weapons uniquely affect the whole electorate.

The principal issues of concern to the electorate were much the same in Scotland as in Britain overall. In 1979 and 1983, the BBC commissioned the Gallup Poll to conduct election day surveys of Scottish voters parallel with Britainwide interviews. Gallup Poll evidence shows that voters in Scotland have much the same concerns as voters elsewhere in Britain. If anything, Scottish voters are more concerned with central economic issues. Differences in the surveys are normally well within the range of sampling fluctuations. Moreover, where differences would be expected to be greatest, namely, in attitudes toward such Scottish issues as devolution, popular interest is lowest. In May 1979, only eight weeks after a referendum on devolution in Scotland, only three per cent of Scots said that they regarded devolution as one of the most important issues facing the country, and only four per cent referred to Scotland's special interests, such as North Sea oil, as important. In 1983, one per cent referred to devolution, and three per cent referred to special interests of Scotland.

Consistent with the priorities of the electorate, the party manifestos concentrated attention upon economic issues important from Land's End to John o' Groats and South Tyrone, and, for that matter, important in Sicily and Schleswig-Holstein as well. More than one- third of the Conservative manifesto was devoted to economic issues, and another quarter to welfare state concerns. The Conservatives published a separate manifesto for Scotland but except for its title, it differed little from the London edition, simply having nominal amendments concerning parallel Scottish institutions for local government, agriculture and fishing. The Conservative Scottish manifesto gave more space to international affairs than to distinctively Scottish issues.

Labour's manifesto similarly emphasized economic concerns and welfare programmes. Devolution to Scotland was given a quarter-page in the main British manifesto. The section on devolution in Labour's specially printed Scottish manifesto was similarly brief. Labour's Scottish manifesto devoted twelve times more space to Westminster's policies toward the rest of the world than to the devolution issue. Similarly, the Alliance manifesto treated decentralizing government as subordinate to electoral reform as a means of transforming the political system. Devolution to Scotland was a subsidiary part of this secondary theme. The main topics of the Alliance manifesto were Britainwide and international issues.

The 1983 United Kingdom election was, if anything, more emphatic in the weight given to the British dimension than elections in the 1970s. The devolution debacle made Westminster politicians shy of raising an issue that they had patently mishandled in the 1974-1979 Parliament. Economic recession increased similarities between the parts of the United Kingdom, albeit in economic misery. It made evident the dependence of poorer regions--which, subjectively, could today mean virtually all parts of the United Kingdom-- upon revenues centralized at Westminster. Common experience of economic difficulties did not lead to political agreement about how economic difficulties should be handled. But it did emphasize the resolution of policy differences by nationwide competition for control of government at Westminster.

## A Challenge to the Party System Britainwide

In the 1970s the chief challenge to the British party system came from outside, that is, from un-British or anti-British Nationalist parties that were not and did not wish to contest seats throughout Britain. In Northern Ireland, the challenge was extreme, for the break up of the United Kingdom was pursued with bullets as well as ballots (Rose, 1976). In Scotland and Wales, Nationalist parties failed to win a majority of votes, but in the Parliament elected in October 1974, the Scottish and Welsh Nationalist parties together held more seats than the Liberals.

The 1979 general election result was initially interpreted in Parliament as marking a return to the status quo ante, that is, the two-party system familiar since 1945. The combined Conservative and Labour share of the vote rose to 81 per cent; it was below the 89 per cent median of postwar elections, but rising. The Liberal share of the vote fell by one-quarter, the Scottish Nationalist vote fell by nearly a third, and Plaid Cymru's vote was still lower. More importantly, the two major parties together held 96 per cent of the seats in the House of Commons, and one party had a clear working majority.

The third party, the Liberals, was in no sense a Celtic fringe party. In 1979 the Liberals won a majority of their seats in England. Of the total Liberal vote, a disproportionate share, 90 per cent, was in English constituencies. The Liberals contested nearly every seat in England, but failed to contest one-fifth of the seats in Wales, and nearly one-third of Scottish seats. With support rising in London suburbs and the South East of England. In the language of centre-periphery politics, the Liberals appeared to be retreating toward the centre.

Academic commentators were much less certain of a return to the status quo ante. John Curtice and Michael Steed (1982) argued that the previous decades had seen an increase in political divisions within England, reflected in a reduction in the total number of marginal seats, Conservative hegemony in the

South of England, and Labour hegemony in the North. William Miller (1981) provocatively entitled an analysis of Scottish and English 1974 voters *The End of British Politics?*(cf. Van Mechelen, 1982). A major study of voting behaviour described the 1970s as *A Decade of Dealignment* (Sarlvik and Crewe, 1983).

The career of the party system in the 1979 Parliament falls into three well defined phases, each dominated by a different party: Labour, the Alliance, and the Conservatives (Table II.3). The initial period of Labour dominance reflected a conventional swing of votes from the government to the opposition party. The second period, dominated by the Alliance formed in consequence of a Social Democratic break-away from the Labour Party, appeared to mark the start of a new era of multi-party competition. The third period, starting with the sharp rise in Conservative fortunes after the outbreak of the Falklands War, restored the governing party to a dominant position, but it did not restore the two-party system as before.

The ups and downs of the parties in the Parliament reflected a large amount of popular dissatisfaction with established parties, leaders and policies. In the 1974 election the rise in third-force voting reflected a combination of Britainwide protest and, in Scotland and Wales, a measure of Nationalist protest as well. The consequences differed. A vote for the Liberals was a vote to break the mould of two-party politics, whereas a vote for Nationalists supported those who wanted to break the mould of Union. In the 1979 Parliament, protest votes concentrated upon an Alliance that wished to break the established party system but to maintain the Union.

From June 1979 to the end of 1980, the British party system appeared to be returning to a degree of normality unknown for a decade; there was a pendulum swing from the Conservatives to Labour. As the Parliament progressed, the swing against the government increased to the advantage of the Labour opposition. By March 1980 Labour was favoured by 49.5 per cent of the Gallup Poll. Since the Conservatives were supported by 37 per cent, the total support for the two major parties was up five per cent from the 1979 general election. The Liberals were losing ground and the Nationalists too.

The Social Democratic break from the Labour Party in January 1981 opened a dramatic second phase in party competition. As soon as the opinion polls could find a way to measure support for the Social Democrats and the Liberals, the Alliance was claiming one-third or more of the vote and support for the two established parties fell drastically. By December 1981 the Alliance was supported by a majority in the Gallup Poll. By-election victories at Crosby and Croydon North West confirmed that the Alliance strength was a reality at the ballot box as well.

In England, the surge in Alliance support was entirely in keeping with the pattern of previous Parliaments, especially Conservative Parliaments, which had been marked by a series of Liberal revivals, each slightly stronger than the

Table II.3   THREE PERIODS OF PARTY COMPETITION, 1979-83

| | Con | Lab | Lib/SDP Alliance[a] | Party lead | |
|---|---|---|---|---|---|
| | | | (monthly average % support) | | |

**1st)  Labour dominant in normal two-party competition**

| | Con | Lab | Lib/SDP Alliance | Party lead | |
|---|---|---|---|---|---|
| Jan 1979 | 42 | 43.5 | 12 | 1.5 | Labour |
| Jul-Sep 1979 | 41 | 45 | 12 | 4 | Labour |
| Oct-Nov 1979 | 39 | 43.5 | 15 | 4.5 | Labour |
| Jan-Mar 1980 | 37 | 45.5 | 15 | 8.5 | Labour |
| Apr-Jun 1980 | 39 | 44.5 | 14 | 5.5 | Labour |
| Jul-Sep 1980 | 38 | 44 | 15 | 6 | Labour |
| Oct-Dec 1980 | 37 | 46 | 14 | 9 | Labour |
| Jan 1981 | 33 | 46.5 | 18.5 | 13.5 | Labour |

(formation of Social Democratic Party)

**2nd)  Alliance dominant in three-party competition**

| | Con | Lab | Lib/SDP Alliance | Party lead | |
|---|---|---|---|---|---|
| Feb-Mar 1981 | 33 | 35 | 30 | 2 | Labour |
| Apr-Jun 1981 | 30.5 | 36 | 31 | 5.5 | Labour |
| Jul-Sep 1981 | 30 | 38.5 | 29 | 8.5 | Labour |
| Oct-Dec 1981 | 26 | 27 | 44 | 17 | Alliance |
| Jan-Mar 1982 | 29 | 32 | 36 | 4 | Alliance |
| Apr 1982 | 31.5 | 29 | 39 | 7.5 | Alliance |

(Falklands)

**3rd)  Conservatives dominant in three-party competition**

| | Con | Lab | Lib/SDP Alliance | Party lead | |
|---|---|---|---|---|---|
| May-Jun 1982 | 43 | 26.5 | 29 | 14 | Con |
| Jul-Sep 1982 | 45 | 28 | 25 | 17 | Con |
| Oct-Dec 1982 | 41 | 33 | 23.5 | 8 | Con |
| Jan-Mar 1983 | 42 | 31 | 24.5 | 11 | Con |
| Apr 1983 | 40.5 | 35 | 22.5 | 5.5 | Con |

[a] Includes respondents expressing a preference for Liberal, SDP or Alliance candidates.

Sources: Gallup Political Index, monthly.

previous one. In Scotland and Wales, the Alliance had a more striking impact, capturing much of the protest vote that for more than a decade previously had been cast for Nationalist candidates. In 12 by-elections in Scotland between 1966 and 1979, the Liberals contested only seven seats, and in each contest finished behind the Scottish National Party, which polled an average of 29 per cent of the vote. In the three Welsh by-elections in the same period, Plaid Cymru won one and finished second twice, polling an average of 39 per cent of the vote, and leaving the Liberals well behind.

The emergence of the Alliance as a Britainwide protest party effectively stopped the Nationalists from filling the vacuum created by the reaction against the Conservative government. Shortly before the formation of the Alliance, the SNP had finished a reasonable second in a by-election, with 29 per cent of the vote; no Liberal candidate stood. In the by-elections in Scotland and Wales which the Alliance fought, it polled substantially better than its Nationalist opponents, and confirmed its superiority at the 1983 general election.

The third and climactic phase of electoral competition in the 1979 Parliament was dominated by an issue unifying electoral opinion, a short and successful war with Argentina to reclaim the Falkland Islands in spring, 1982. The Falklands War was a uniquely consensual event, making manifest a latent British patriotism that is a a force for national unity (Rose, 1984a). The primacy of British identity was demonstrated by the fact that there was no significant difference in any part of Britain in the reaction to the Falklands War. By contrast, in the Republic of Ireland, the Taisoeach, Charles J. Haughey, refused to support the British cause in sympathy for the "national unity" claims of Argentina. No such reaction was forthcoming in Scotland and Wales. British patriotism and British loyalties were dominant during the Falklands conflict, just as they are evident in other patriotic contexts, such as responses to royalty (Rose and Kavanagh, 1976; Blumler et al, 1976).

The upshot of the Falklands War was the re-assertion of Margaret Thatcher's hold on the government, and even more, the re-assertion of the Conservative hold on the electorate. The revival of Conservative support occurred Britainwide. It was less in Wales and Scotland only because Conservative strength was less there in 1979. Whereas Conservative support in December 1981 had fallen to 23 per cent on the Gallup Poll, by July 1982 Conservative support had doubled, giving the party a 19 per cent lead over Labour. Its double-digit lead was maintained up to and including election day.

In the first Thatcher term of office, party preferences registered far greater and more rapid shifts than in any other postwar Parliament. The election outcome of 9 June 1983 was not the culmination of a long-term trend, but the consequence of the Conservatives being the chief beneficiaries of the last change of direction by the electorate. In the midst of rapid and unexpected shifts, one point was clear: the flow in electoral favour occurred Britainwide.

The one exception to this pattern of national integration underlines the importance of taking national integration for granted. In 1981 two by-elections were held in Fermanagh & South Tyrone, in which national integration or disintegration was the issue. In the first by-election, the victorious candidate was Bobby Sands, an IRA hunger-striker seeking to further a united Ireland by force of arms. After Sands died in his prison hunger-strike, the victor at the second by-election was another uncompromising supporter of Irish unity, Owen Carron, who showed his rejection of the United Kingdom by efusing to participate in the Westminster Parliament.

## Farewell to Devolution

When the House of Commons assembled after the May 1979 general election, economic issues were undoubtedly the first concern of the great majority of MPs. The election had been fought on the economic performance of a Labour government that had disappointed its supporters, and fuelled a free-market Conservative reaction. Margaret Thatcher was pledged to get the economy moving again. The next four years were to see many changes in the economy, and one steady feature, an increasing number of unemployed.

Scottish, Welsh and Ulster MPs were as concerned about the state of the British economy as their counterparts from English constituencies. But these MPs were also confronted with unfinished business concerning devolution from the previous Parliament. The two 1978 devolution acts granting assemblies to Scotland and Wales had not been put into effect, pending a vote in Parliament. Northern Ireland had a form of "temporary" direct rule by British ministers without any local political base in the Province.

Public opinion showed a broad negative consensus against the creation of elected assemblies (Table II.4). Consistently, English voters rejected the idea of elected regional assemblies within England, favoured by only five per cent. According to the 1979 British Election Survey, only 27 per cent supported the anodyne statement: 'Some other way should be found to make sure the needs of each major region in England are better understood by the government in London'.

In Wales and Scotland support for the status quo was substantial. This was shown in Wales by an 80 per cent vote against a devolved Welsh assembly in the 1979 referendum. The ballot confirmed the unrepresentativeness of a Westminster Parliament that had sought to impose an assembly on Wales. In Scotland there was no clear majority for any specific constitutional reform. Among the registered electorate, the largest single group of Scots consisted of those who did not vote in the 1979 devolution referendum. Among those who did vote, there was a narrow majority for the assembly. But about one-fifth of

Table II.4  ATTITUDES TO ELECTED ASSEMBLIES BY NATION

| | National view | |
|---|---|---|
| | Voters | Electorate |
| | % | % |
| England | (1979 survey) | |
| For elected regional assemblies | 5 | 5 |
| Against | 95 | 88 |
| Don't know | n.a. | 7 |
| Wales | (1979 Referendum) | |
| For Devolution Act | 20 | 12 |
| Against | 80 | 47 |
| Not voting | n.a. | 41 |
| Scotland | (1979 Referendum) | |
| For Devolution Act | 52 | 33 |
| Against | 48 | 31 |
| Not voting | n.a. | 36 |
| N. Ireland | (1973 Border Poll) | |
| For United Ireland | 1 | 0.6 |
| Remain in UK | 99 | 57.6 |
| Don't know/not voting | n.a. | 41.8 |

Sources: Referendums, Rose and McAllister (1982: 103–5); England, responses to 1979 British Election Study.

this group favoured independence, with the assembly being but a means to this end (cf. Rose and McAllister, 1982: 116f).

Ironically, Westminster's devolution efforts reinforced the status quo. The Welsh assembly act was repealed without difficulty in the opening session of the 1979 Parliament, and the proposal for a devolved assembly for Scotland was also repealed, albeit against the votes of many Labour MPs. Constitutional change for Scotland and Wales was effectively dead as an issue for the life of the Parliament. The Conservative government was firmly committed to maintaining the status quo, and the Labour Party had neither the desire nor the power to bring forward an issue that had proven so divisive within its own ranks in the previous Parliament. Moreover, public opinion in Scotland and Wales was acquiescent. Surveys of protest potential in Scotland and Wales found few predisposed to engage in extra-parliamentary protest against parliamentary decisions about devolution (Miller et al., 1982).

During the 1979 Parliament the rise of the Alliance had the incidental effect of increasing votes for a party with a general rhetorical commitment to devolution all around. The Liberal Party has been the one party consistently committed to territorial devolution, or to a vaguely described federal Britain. Social Democrats, in need of instant policies on every issue, were attracted to devolution as part of a package of proposals intended to encourage popular participation in politics. A committee of Social Democrats headed by Professor David Marquand, a former Labour MP, set out detailed policy proposals in 1982 under the heading Decentralising Government. The case for decentralization was argued on both political grounds (the need to strengthen local voice and choice, and to reduce loads on central government) and on economic grounds (decentralization was expected to stimulate economic development in less prosperous regions, and secure a better allocation of public expenditure). Decentralization was meant to apply to the whole of Great Britain, including English regions. The Alliance excluded Northern Ireland from these proposals.

The eagerness with which some Social Democrats promoted decentralization was not welcomed by ex-Labour Party members who had been prominent opponents of devolution in the previous Parliament. The 1983 Alliance manifesto considerably toned down the Marquand committee's proposals, while remaining sympathetic to the general approach. The Alliance manifesto promised 'immediate action to set up a Scottish Parliament', and to set out 'the framework for decentralization to assemblies in Wales and the English regions as demand develops'. It did not promise devolution all-round, asserting: 'We do not believe that devolution should be imposed on nations or regions which do not wish it'. For England it proposed economic development agencies and a reform of local government.

Accidents in part accounted for the strength of the Alliance's commitment to devolution for Scotland. David Steel, the Liberal leader, was a convinced devolutionist and represented a Scottish constituency. In 1977 he had made devolution for Scotland a condition (and, it turned out, the only condition) of a pact supporting a Labour government. The SDP leader, Roy Jenkins, like most Welsh politicians of his generation, had held conventional views in favour of the status quo. Through a fluke, he became the Social Democratic candidate in the Glasgow Hillhead by-election of March 1982. This forced Jenkins to take an unequivocal stand on devolution; Jenkins came out for a Scottish assembly too.

Only in Northern Ireland did Westminster take positive action in favour of devolution during the 1979 Parliament. Northern Ireland had the unusual experience of having a devolved Assembly forced upon it. The Westminster government was anxious to create an elected Assembly in the Province, believing, without evidence to support its belief, that this could lead to a power-sharing devolved government involving Protestant Unionists and the Catholic-based Social Democratic & Labour Party. Both Official Unionists and Dr. Ian Paisley's Democratic Unionist Party opposed the assembly, the former because it advocated complete integration at Westminster without any intermediary Ulster Assembly, and the DUP because it opposed power-sharing with adherents of a united Ireland. The SDLP opposed the assembly because it did not explicitly include an Irish dimension. In the Northern Ireland Assembly election of October, 1982, 91 per cent of the vote was cast for parties opposed to the Assembly; an absolute majority of votes and seats went to Unionist and Loyalist candidates implacably opposed to a power-sharing executive (Elliott and Wilford, 1983). The Assembly was stillborn.

The British dimension is very much present in Northern Ireland. The Province would not remain a part of the United Kingdom but for the determination of Ulster Protestants, expressed forcefully and electorally. The security forces as well as the majority party leaders in Northern Ireland work to maintain it as part of the United Kingdom. The problem of Northern Ireland arises from the fact that the British dimension collides with an Irish dimension. The confrontation of two nationalisms has never been resolved, and is the source of unending difficulties. From the point of view of two-thirds of the Northern Ireland electorate, there is no doubt about their commitment to the United Kingdom. But many British voters, as well as Ulster Catholics, wish to weaken the British dimension in favour of an Irish dimension (Rose, McAllister and Mair, 1978; Rose, 1982b).

The opposition of the 1979 Conservative government to devolution, except in the unique and peculiar circumstances of Northern Ireland, was underscored by the thoroughness with which the government emphasized the supremacy of its parliamentary majority over local authorities, in existence since 1974 as the creation of an Act of Parliament that reduced their previous number by more than two-thirds.

More important than generalized Conservative rhetoric in favour of local autonomy has been the Thatcher government's desire to reduce public expenditure and local authority rates. This goal collided with the tendency for local government expenditure and rates to rise. In order to limit local authority expenditure, the Conservative government pushed through Parliament bills giving central government unprecedented powers affecting local authority expenditure. Labour politicians who for generations had promoted centralized policymaking in order to guarantee minimum or common standards throughout the United Kingdom suddenly became defenders of local autonomy against central authority. The Conservatives, formerly self-appointed proponents of localism, insisted upon using the full force of the law to assert Westminster's supremacy Britainwide. The dispute was not about centre-periphery relations but was a battle fought along party lines about an issue applicable to the whole of the United Kingdom.

# III

# Thatcherism and Monetarism: the Development of Territorial Management

## JIM BULPITT

*University of Warwick*

Thus arguments about the state and the market are arguments quite as much about centralization and decentralization as about the intrusion or exclusion of political influences (Cairncross, 1976 : 128).

The great tragedy of the drive to centralization, as of the drive to extend the scope of government in general, is that it is mostly led by men of good will who will be the first to rue its consequences (Friedman, 1963: 3).

The first Thatcher government was associated with a watershed in the development of territorial politics in Britain. It implemented, or was forced to implement, a number of measures, which, in combination, either broke or threatened to break, many of the established, though fraying, conventions of territorial management.

At the outset three problems of analysis need to be noted. The first concerns the use of the term territorial politics, which has been defined as: 'that arena of political activity concerned with relations between the central political institutions in the capital city and those interests, communities, political organisations and governmental bodies, outside that central complex but within the accepted boundaries of the state which possess, or are commonly perceived to possess, a significant geographical or local/regional character' (Bulpitt, 1983: 1). This definition requires some comment. It suggests an analytical range more extensive than the traditional focus on the relations between central departments and elected local authorities. It also carries a double inference: the interests of local governments and those of their citizens are not necessarily synonymous; and there are methods of promoting local interests other than by elected local government. Moreover, it accepts that territorial politics cannot be divorced from the examination of political activity in the wider system. In what follows, for example, it will be argued that monetarism was forced on the Conservatives in the mid-1970s by general political circumstances at the time. To view its adoption solely as a more effective and bloody-minded method of controlling local expenditures is too simple.

Secondly, despite their obvious differences, most general commentaries on the first Thatcher government, from Marxists, social democrats and Thatcherites, have shared one common assumption, that it was a consistently radical administration deliberately breaking the mould of the postwar Keynesian consensus. Similarly, interpretations of its territorial policies have contrasted these unfavourably with a Keynesian golden age of British territorial politics. In this age the centralizing logic of the unitary constitution and structure of politics was miraculously avoided; the British, if not the Irish, squared the circle and managed to run a unitary polity with a sufficient degree of local democracy, ordered decentralization, and a co-operative partnership between central and local governments, such that everyone involved was satisfied and awkward things like power and one-sided victories did not occur. Thus our views of the Thatcher government will be influenced by our reading of the history of territorial politics during the era of the so-called Keynesian consensus. The analysis requires an historical dimension.

Thirdly, plausible objections could be mounted against the use of the words Thatcherism and monetarism in the chapter title (Bosanquet, 1983). But these were the terms which dominated the public debate about Conservatism in Britain between 1975 and 1983 and, despite their imprecision, they have a greater connection with reality than alternatives. To put it another way: monetarist ideas offered a life-line to the Conservatives in the mid-1970s and Mrs. Thatcher increasingly became associated with them. Monetarism, of course, may be 'merely the beginning of a much more far-reaching plan' (Bosanquet, 1983: 89). But by 1983 matters had not advanced much further than the beginning.

## The Way We Were

The *ancien regime* of British territorial politics existed roughly between the mid-1920s and the early 1960s. Examining this period provides us both with a means of assessing the "rosy view" of past territorial arrangements and a baseline from which to identify subsequent important territorial developments (see Bulpitt, 1983: Chapter 5).

The regime emerged out of the era of territorial turbulence which occurred just before and after the Great War, an era marked by struggles over the Irish Question, Home Rule All Round in Britain, Welsh Disestablishment, Poplarism and, the threatened growth for the first time in British history of a powerful central state machine. Its development represented a defeat for all those forces hoping to alter radically the structure of territorial politics throughout the United Kingdom. In essence this regime was a reconstruction of past territorial practices or aspirations. Its principal sponsors were Conservative leaders in government. For a variety of reasons, Labour, the main opposition party, also accepted the management code of this territorial regime.

The most important feature of this code was the principle of the division of labour: national governments and politicians concentrated on what were perceived to be national issues or matters of high politics, and local governments and politicians confined themselves to local, or low politics. Intergovernmental relations were left largely to bureaucratic accommodations dispensed amongst a variety of separate policy communities. Wherever and whenever possible territorial politics was depoliticized, a process which was enormously helped by the dominance of parliamentary party leaders over their grass roots followers and backbench MPs, plus the failure of local parties to colonise most governmental agencies at the local and regional levels. The bias in this system was towards a centre-periphery or court-country territorial dichotomy; the operational result was a dual polity, in which local and national politics were to a considerable extent insulated from one another.

The key was the centre, in this period a small political-administrative community of cabinet ministers, top civil servants, with, ad hoc additions, possessing few administrative resources of its own outside the limited confines of S.W.1. It defined high politics responsibilities narrowly; foreign and Commonwealth affairs and defence were its major interests. Once autonomy from peripheral forces was achieved on these issues it was prepared to grant significant reciprocal autonomy to territorial governments in matters of low politics.

Even when the centre accepted formal responsibility for a domestic policy sector, it often attempted to hive off much of the detail of policy and administration to peripheral agencies of government. The welfare state is a prime example: its management was left to elected and non-elected governments at the local and regional levels. Keynes's ideas posed little threat to this system. Although macro-economic demand management placed responsiblity for policy firmly in the hands of the centre (specifically, the Treasury and the Bank of England) it did not require any great degree of centre intervention in peripheral economic affairs. It was not much concerned with local government economic activity. Above all, Keynesianism sought to depoliticize economic policy-making, to abstract it from the incoherences of the party political world and put its management on an automatic pilot in the Treasury. (See e.g. Skidelsky, 1977; Hirsch, 1977; Schaefer and Schaefer, 1983). This peculiar structure of territorial politics was reflected within territorial communities throughout Britain. Most local governments and politicians enjoyed a similar autonomy and insulation from their own local citizens by the simple expedient of not doing much, abstracting themselves from local party control, appeasing, when necessary, potentially awkward opposition groups, such as ratepayers organizations, and permitting local bureaucrats to play a major role in policy formulation (Birch, 1959; Lee, 1963; Bulpitt, 1967).

Although popular in a negative sense (at the time there were few who could think of or wanted anything better) this regime hardly fits the "rosy view" of the past so popular with the Thatcher government's critics. Not only is it difficult to label this territorial structure as centralized or decentralized, but also it requires considerable powers of imagination to see many signs of a thriving local democracy or a positive and benign central-local partnership in the period between the mid-1920s and early 1960s. It may be, that the golden age of British territorial politics occurred later, in the 1960s and 1970s, but few people have been prepared to perceive those years in that light.

This dual polity was extremely fragile. Indeed, given its inherent weaknesses and contradictions, its longevity is remarkable. The point is best illustrated if we list those factors which sustained this regime: (a) a continuous supply of deferential collaborators among local politicians, particularly Labour politicians; (b) a Parliament and central government composed of people socially distinct and distant from peripheral residents; preoccupied with defence and foreign affairs issues, and willing and able to dole out ever-increasing amounts of grants-in-aid to local governments; (c) the continued ability of Cabinets to run the economy effectively by negative Keynesianism; macro controls by the Treasury and little direct interference with the supply side of the economy; and (d) the acceptance by politicians and officials at the centre that their own autonomy in politics was not adversely affected by the reciprocal autonomy allowed their peripheral counterparts in matters of low politics.

If we are to assess the Thatcher Government as a radical break with past territorial practices, then we need to be clear about what those practices were. Equally important, the operation of the *ancien regime* does not endorse traditional Conservative Party rhetoric about the virtues of local self-government and local democracy. Insofar as these catch phrases had any meaning for the party leadership they were always subordinate to the grand design of central autonomy. Reciprocal autonomy for local governments was allowed only so long as it did not interfere with that grand design (Bulpitt, 1982). And whatever democracy meant for Conservatives in the constituencies it was not regarded as sufficiently attractive to override the inherent dreariness and financially burdensome nature of local government affairs.

## The Mess of 1968-1976 and Labour's Response

Thatcherism was born out of the general problems affecting British politics in the mid-1970s and the specific difficulties facing the Conservative Party in that period. But the Conservative response cannot be understood in a vacuum. Both the general and specifically territorial problems which emerged in British politics between 1968 and 1976, and the Labour government's reactions, must be examined as well.

The mess which developed was not a crisis as many hoped, feared or argued at the time. There were few indications that the system was likely to collapse, or had become ungovernable. What was developing from the late 1960s was a problem of central management, which involved considerable confusion and loss of confidence among the national political elite, not so much about what to do, but about how to create a structure of politics which would allow effective system management whatever the policies. We need to note four of the principal causes of this state of affairs: (a) the advent of a more malign world political economy; (b) the successive failures of major party strategies, to achieve economic growth or resolve problems such as inflation and unemployment; (c) the decline in the willingness of such intermediate elites as union leaders to collaborate with central government designs; and (d) the emergence of a less partisan and more volatile electorate.

The territorial components of this central mess were significant. In their search for remodernization, economic growth or simply the solution to particular problems such as inflation, successive governments abandoned reciprocal autonomy, interfering increasingly in peripheral affairs. Regional planning experiments, industrial relations reforms, and incomes policies were all examples of interventionism affecting local economies. Changes in the structure of local and regional governments, the Education Act, 1976, and various inner-city initiatives were examples affecting the more traditional aspects of central-local relations. By 1976 little of this positive action by the centre appeared successful. The particularly crude form of pseudo-Keynesianism which underlay these policies (Bosanquet, 1983; 87) had promoted a climate in which national and local elites lost confidence in each other, and lost the confidence of the general public as well. Moreover, both the increase in the scope of national party colonization of local authorities following the structural reforms of the early 1970s and the growing neo-corporatist character of many aspects of the local policy-making process brought centre and periphery together more often than hitherto. Finally, the thorny question of controlling local government expenditure became more pressing with increased economic difficulties. By the mid-1970s the nature of British territorial politics had changed considerably.

Labour's reactions to this general mess must be regarded as a necessary element in the story of the Thatcher government. At the national level, the Labour government made three moves affecting high politics: it incorporated monetarist instruments, such as monetary targets and cash limits into its macroeconomic management strategy; it continued to rely on income norms to restrain inflation; and it concluded the Lib/Lab parliamentary pact to provide it with a majority at Westminster. Its 1974 response to the specific territorial problems posed by Scottish and Welsh nationalism, the devolution gambit, received renewed and necessary backing from the Lib/Lab pact.

Local government spending produced a complex reaction from Labour, one of great significance in terms of Conservative policies after 1979. Successive central governments had dropped the old dual polity principle, interfering in more detailed fashion in the affairs of the periphery. Yet this new approach was not actually accompanied by serious attempts to control local authority expenditure patterns. The result was that from the early 1960s to the mid-1970s local government current and capital expenditure rose from less than one-quarter of total public expenditure to nearly one-third, and local government employment as a proportion of total public employment grew from 32 per cent in 1961 to 41 per cent by 1974. This expansion of local government activity was increasingly financed from central government grants, which by 1975 formed 45 per cent of total local authority income, and increases in rate levies and precepts, especially on industrial and commercial premises (Cmnd 6453, 1976: 356; Cmnd 8449, 1981: chapter 10). Inflationary pressures, compounded by the oil price rises of 1973/74, forced the Labour government to act on the issue. As Joel Barnett (1982:75) Chief Secretary to the Treasury, later put it: 'By 1975 when expenditure constraints were clearly becoming necessary, we realised that something had to be done'.

In fact, the process of doing something about local expenditure had started in December 1974. The Department of the Environment sent a circular to all local authorities asking that they 'play their part in the achievement of national objectives by limiting the rise of expenditure ... to what was absolutely inescapable'. At this point the government appeared to be offering local authorities a deal: if they curbed the volume of their spending in line with new national objectives, then the government, by increasing its grants to them, would help them avoid the unpopular rate increases brought about by inflation (Wright, 1982; Greenwood, 1982). To provide the organizational resources for this deal, in 1975 Labour established the Consultative Council on Local Government Finance to act as a forum for joint discussions on financial problems between central departments and local authority associations.

However, the 1976 pound/IMF crisis forced the Cabinet to take more stringent measures: central grants to local government were reduced, annual targets were set for local expenditure, and, in 1977/78, cash limits were imposed on the rate support grant (Barnett, 1982: 78). In addition, the government altered the distribution of their grant between different types of local authorities, such that the pro-Labour metropolitan areas were favoured and the pro-Conservative shire counties disadvantaged. As Dr. Greenwood has coyly put it: 'Whether the switch was motivated by political considerations, or by a commitment to assisting the deprived areas of the metropolitan cities is not entirely clear' (Greenwood, 1982).

One possible interpretation of this particular aspect of Labour's territorial policies is that it was a reasonably effective operation, well within the established parameters of consensus politics. The Labour government asked for and received co-operation from local authorities in facing the country's economic problems. Chaps continued to collaborate with one another, local autonomy remained, and the central-local partnership was maintained. A second interpretation is that even though the partnership survived, it operated within a framework which had changed in important ways; central government now accepted that local expenditure could not be divorced from the general state of the economy and the centre's macro-economic strategy. The third interpretation is that Labour fudged the whole issue. Despite the changes in the Whitehall official mind, the Labour government undertook no radical reform of local government finance, even though many people, including the Layfield Committee, believed this to be necessary. Indeed, when the government did suggest some reforms in the grant structure and capital expenditure controls, they allowed the local authority associations to reject them (Cmnd 6813, 1977; Binder, 1982). By 1979 most people accepted that the central government had the right to demand that local spending fit its macro-economic strategy. 'Hard times' had shifted the parameters of high politics (Hood and Wright, 1981). But central government still did not possess the power to influence the spending of individual local authorities, leaving considerable potential here for future conflict.

## Problems, Monetarism and Thatcherism

In mid-1973 a Conservative MP wrote: 'The state of the Tory Party following upon defeat at the next election does not bear thinking about' (Critchley, 1973). He predicted considerable difficulties for the party in terms of both its internal management and future electoral prospects if Heath failed to be returned to office. In many ways Margaret Thatcher's election to the party leadership in February 1975, the so-called peasants revolt, reflected the arrival of those difficulties. Why else choose a woman as leader? Why else ignore the legitimate claims of her more senior colleagues? And why else select someone who was opposed by the bulk of the Shadow Cabinet and who was not particularly popular with the constituency associations?

Early in 1975 the future of the Conservative Party looked grim in the extreme. The party's problems were threefold. First, it had failed to win four out of the last five elections. In doing so it had lost more than three million voters. Moreover, the geographical basis of the party's support had altered significantly: by the mid-1970s the constituencies which it held were disproportionately south of a line from the Severn to the Wash. Secondly, Labour's election victories, plus the policies pursued by Conservative governments since the late 1950s, especially since Macmillan's counter-coup against his Treasury team in 1958, suggested to many in the party that the country was slowly moving down a path which was always favourable to its opponents. Labour introduced socialism and Conservative governments either accepted it, or, in the case of the Heath government, even advanced it (Joseph, 1975). Thirdly, in Harold Wilson the Conservatives were faced with an opponent who possessed a talent for winning elections and was determined to show that Labour had replaced the Conservatives as the natural party of government. The experience of the Heath government appeared to indicate that there was no way the Conservatives could come to any agreement with the unions, particularly those in the public sector. This implied that the Conservative Party could never develop a viable macro-economic strategy, because union hostility would obstruct the effective implementation of an incomes policy. Since at the time an incomes policy was regarded as necessary to achieve national economic recovery the Conservatives appeared in a hopeless position. Edward Heath's final attempt to crack this problem - his talk about the need for a government of national unity during the October 1974 election campaign - had confused the party faithful, and underlined the enormity of the Conservatives' problems.

In 1975, therefore, the Conservative Party faced an awkward task: how could it persuade people (and itself) that it could actually govern effectively if it won an election? This was a problem of statecraft, or central management. It reflected the management mess general in the United Kingdom. How did the Conservatives tackle these difficulties between 1975 and 1979? The Thatcherite response stresses that the Conservative Party successfully changed 'the hearts and minds' of the people by emphasizing the dangers of inflation and pressing home the threats to economic prosperity and individual liberty arising from the expanded state and trade union power. ('The First Two Years', *The Sunday Times*, 3 May 1981). Others would argue that the party turned away from the postwar Keynesian welfare consensus and adopted the hard line of nineteenth-century liberal political economy in its twentieth-century guise, monetarism.

Reality was, at one and the same time, both more complex and more simple.

It is true that in this period the Conservatives did constantly emphasize the dangers of inflation and an expanded state. It is also true that from the early 1970s monetarist economic theory assumed much greater prominence in Britain, particularly as a result of the support it received from, first the IEA, then Enoch Powell and, finally, Sir Keith Joseph (Congdon, 1978). But at the top (and that is the only place where it matters in the Conservative Party) Mrs. Thatcher was faced with a divided shadow cabinet, full of Heathmen suspicious of these new ideas. Thus, in the beginning the necessary reformulation of party policy was a cautious and moderate affair, full of calls for balance or common sense, emphasizing that the party did not claim 'a monopoly of the truth' (Conservative Central Office, 1976). All this reflected the scepticism of Hayek, rather than the easy certainties of Friedman. (Bosanquet, 1983). On more specific issues, such as economic and union policies, the party's internal divisions often led to considerable incoherence in policy statements (Maude, 1977).

Nevertheless, in time the party did associate itself with many monetarist prescriptions. Given the split in the party at the top, a key question is: What were the attractions of monetarism for the moderates, the wets? Why did they accept the new strategy? The answer is simple: it was (and still is) the only governing life-line available. Monetarism, in so far as it is a coherent doctrine (cf. Laidler, 1981; Tobin, 1981), appeared to offer a method of resolving inflation and more generally of managing the economy, without making a future Conservative government a neo-corporatist pawn to the TUC and CBI, as had occurred during the Heath government. Specifically, it did not require an incomes policy. The guiding precepts of the theory -- control of the money supply, cash limits on public expenditure, and the inherent foolishness of incomes policies as a counter to inflation -- all fitted perfectly the requirements of Conservative statecraft. These were matters over which governments could claim some control; the return of a macro-economic automatic pilot to the centre was once again possible. At the time, it was expected that this would not bring about any sustained and irreversible rise in unemployment.

With the wets support, the use of monetarist techniques to achieve political aims remained unchanged up to the 1979 election. For a number of reasons, however, the rhetoric surrounding it grew increasingly strident. One was Mrs. Thatcher's growing confidence in her job. Another was that public opinion polls showed a number of policies traditionally associated with Labour were becoming unpopular. But perhaps the most important influence was the covert adoption of many of the early Thatcher policies by the Labour government under Callaghan and Healey. As a *Times* commentator put it:

> The political ground chosen by the Conservative party since October 1974 has, no doubt for dubious reasons, been occupied by Mr. Callaghan and the Cabinet as

squatters. The Conservatives now need ground where Mr. Callaghan cannot tread (Wood, 1978).

Viewed this way, Thatcherism was (and is) a gift of the idiosyncratic British Labour movement to the Conservatives. In its initial form at least Thatcherism was not a radical departure in British politics, but an attempted reconstruction of the traditional Conservative statecraft of centre autonomy, as had been possible during the Keynesian political economy, as well as earlier. When Mrs. Thatcher argued after 1979 that there is no alternative, this applied as much to Conservative statecraft as to policies. Changing the hearts and minds meant creating a country governable by the Conservative Party.

Given this general strategy, what was the Conservative attitude to territorial politics between 1975 and 1979? The party had to do two things: formulate a response to two specific problems (Scottish and Welsh devolution and local government finance) and, if possible, ensure that any general territorial code fitted the macro-economic strategy discussed above. There are three possible interpretations of its approach to this task.

The first is to suggest that early Thatcherism was inherently centralist in character, interested only in curbing local government and willing to treat local authorities as agents of the state to achieve that aim. On this view, there was, and is, a close and adverse connection between monetarism and the territorial code (Meadows, 1981; Jackson, 1982). Admittedly there is evidence to suggest that Mrs. Thatcher has a profound dislike for local government (Wapshot and Brock, 1983: 105). Nevertheless, as an interpretation of this particular period this is far too narrow a view to be taken seriously.

A second, and superficially more plausible, interpretation is that between 1975 and 1979 the Conservatives developed no viable territorial code at all. There was only a mish-mash of separate policy recommendations which combined possessed no coherence and no obvious link with its macro-economic strategy. Evidence to support this view is not hard to find. For example, the Conservative attitude to devolution, particularly Scottish devolution, was incoherent throughout the decade. At one time or another the party supported practically every policy option available on the issue (Russel, 1978: 124-133). A similar view could be taken about its stance on local government. The party favoured cuts in local expenditure but it appeared that this was to result mainly from more intelligent pay bargaining and the elimination of unspecified "waste". The previous commitment to rating reform was dropped by 1979. Otherwise it was ad hoccism; e.g., hostility to the "feudal" system of municipal housing and more money to be spent on the police service.

The third interpretation is to argue that there was a very close link between the macro-strategy and the territorial code. The crux was that the Conservatives were interested in territorial politics only in so far as it affected the desire for centre autonomy in macro-economic strategy. Local authority spending was to be curbed, central financial assistance cut, and the distribution of grants altered to avoid the biggest grants going to high-spending authorities. Nevertheless, within this framework councils were to continue to be allowed to determine local spending patterns. Like industrial relations and industrial policy, territorial governments were to be run on the same automatic monetarist pilot (see Bulpitt, 1983: 203f; Crompton, 1982: 35). The new code was supported by the interest shown in the privatization of local government services. Concern was also shown for the influence of trade unions on local authority policies. The Conservatives endorsed the view that 'in pursuing their own self- interest, local authority employees are potentially a distorting force in local democracy' (Thomson, 1982: 107). Finally, the Conservatives emphasized the need to increase the role of individual citizens within the local political process, for example in education. Very often these various themes - greater economy, less central control, privatization, anti corporatism, and more freedom for the individual - were incorporated in one policy sector. Housing is an illustration.

Thus, the principle of centre autonomy dominated both the general Conservative strategy and their territorial code prior to 1979. Where territorial politics was concerned this autonomy was to be sustained by a return to the dual polity structure. But it was not a complete return. For the first time the Conservatives were thinking of interfering, albeit indirectly, in the local political process, to secure what they considered the proper management of low politics. Whether this complex and subtle code was fully understood by all those meant to direct it is open to question. More to the point, whether running central-local relations on a monetarist automatic pilot would succeed, was not very clear.

## The Development of Territorial Management, 1979-1983

The 1979 election result was undoubtedly a great triumph for Mrs. Thatcher, but there was a considerable element of luck in the whole proceedings. The opportunity to exercise statecraft is ultimately dependent on chance. James Callaghan's decision to soldier on in the autumn of 1978, when the opinion polls indicated the possibility of a Labour victory, meant that he then faced the unions with a five per cent wage norm. The result, the 1978-79 winter of discontent, was a significant electoral bonus for the Conservatives.

The most convenient method of examining the first Thatcher government's territorial policies and the changing nature of its management code is to identify the different phases of its operations. Three periods can be singled out.

1. May 1979 - December 1980. In this period the government attempted to implement most of the policies it had formulated in opposition. The Cabinet concentrated on its primary policy goal, the defeat of inflation, through policies designed to reduce public expenditure and the size of the public sector generally. This was expressed in the March, 1980 medium term financial strategy: a progressive reduction of 3 million, cash limits tightened, and a forecast decline in the PSBR as a proportion of GDP. On the territorial front, local authorities were to be allowed discretion to set their own priorities within this broad framework. The government also indicated a desire to reduce the number of petty central controls over local authorities and alter local politics in ways more favourable to individuals and private enterprise.

These plans were enormously facilitated by the unexpected demise of the devolution issue, especially as it applied to Scotland. Following the repeal of the Scotland Act in June 1979 the Scottish Office and the Scottish committees of the Commons (sometimes meeting in Edinburgh) were employed as the prime managers and articulators of the Scottish interest within the Union. These Whitehall and Westminster parameters ensured that Scottish politics took place in arenas dominated by the Conservative Party, a necessary manoeuvre given the electoral weakness of Thatcherism north of the border. Scotland and its problems did not vanish from the scene, but they were tackled within a Britainwide framework. Money and public expenditure are, at root, forces favouring uniformity in territorial management.

Many of the government's initiatives in this early period were designed to facilitate changes in the local political process. The White Paper *Central Government Controls Over Local Authorities* (Cmnd 7634, September 1979), and the Education Act 1979, were each intended to free elected local governments from central supervision, the one in general, and by and large innocuous ways, and the other more specifically by the removal of the statutory enforcement of comprehensive education at the secondary level. The 1980 Housing and Education Acts were primarily attempts to expand the rights of citizens in relation to local authorities. The former gave council house dwellers the right to purchase their houses on favourable terms, and also removed many restrictions on tenants. Local education authorities were forced to provide more information regarding their schools and parents were given more choice, in theory, in the selection of schools for their children. This individual rights/anti-corporatist theme was, so the government argued, behind the abolition of the area health authorities in England by the Health Service Act, 1980, and influenced the 1981 Education Act, which was concerned, in part, with the rights of parents in the special education sector. There were also a number of measures designed to assist and stimulate local private enterprise, especially in inner-city areas. Examples were the abolition of regional economic planning councils, the repeal of the Community Land Act, the powers given to the DoE to direct local authorities to sell land 'demonstrably surplus to their requirements', the establishment of urban development corporations and enterprise zones and more commercially oriented regulations for direct works departments.

The centrepiece of the government's territorial policies in this period, at least for England and Wales, was the Local Government, Planning and Land Act, 1980 (Bulpitt, 1983: 206-209; Gyford and James, 1983: Chapter 8). This was a composite measure which, at the time, the government clearly regarded as its final solution to the problem of local spending. The Act instituted the block grant (an idea which Labour had played with and the Conservatives opposed in the late 1970s): it gave central government, for the first time, the means to influence, via grant penalties, the budgets of individual local authorities spending more than the centre's estimates of their expenditure, the so-called grant related expenditure assessment. Strenuously opposed inside and outside Parliament by supporters of local government, this legislation was an embarrassment to many Conservatives, while Labour, playing the John Stuart Mill card, described it as an assault on local representative government. In the course of the Bill's passage through Parliament the government argued the primacy of the national mandate and central macro-economic strategy over local mandates and strategies. In addition, it argued that central-local relations was not only a matter for ministers, MPs, and councillors, but should give scope to free choice by citizens as well. The Conservatives thus publicly rejected the traditional link between local authorities and local democracy.

The territorial strategy formulated in opposition was implemented very quickly, perhaps too quickly, after May 1979. Cash limits on public expenditure devolved responsiblity for cuts down the line. The centre was thus able to avoid awkward decisions about what to cut, this was a matter for local discretion (Wright, 1982: 42). In addition, local citizens had been given additional rights, private enterprise assisted, and the Cabinet seemingly gained the power to influence the budgets of individual local authorities. Everything, it appeared, had gone as far as it needed to go.

Even at this stage, however, the view needed to be qualified. When some local governors refused point blank to collaborate with the centre's expenditure cuts demands, they were replaced by appointed Commissioners. This happened to the Lambeth Area Health Authority in August 1979. The DHSS's action was later declared illegal on a technicality by the courts. Again, much of the legislation designed to assist local citizens and private enterprise included clauses which increased the powers of central departmental ministers over local authorities. Finally, in late 1980 the Scottish Office introduced the Local Government (Miscellaneous Provisions) (Scotland) Bill. This allowed the Scottish Secretary to reduce the grant to individual local authorities in Scotland immediately after their budget and rating decisions had been made if, in the Secretary's view, their expenditure was 'excessive and unreasonable'. Coupled with the fact that Scottish local authorities, unlike their counterparts in England and Wales, had no power to levy supplementary rates, this was a far more centralizing measure than anything attempted south of the border. It even surprised and initially displeased the DoE. (Midwinter, Keating and Taylor, 1983; Crompton, 1982: 37).

2. January 1981 - June 1982. The Thatcherite territorial programme was launched with considerable confidence. But when that programme encountered problems the Cabinet's reactions became confused and largely ineffective. This produced doubts about the utility of the initial territorial code, a realization that central autonomy could no longer be supported by allowing a reciprocal autonomy for local politicians and governments. In the second phase the most important problems to emerge were three: the control of local government expenditure, race relations in inner city areas, and a decline in the propensity of some regional and local governments to collaborate with the centre.

In January, 1981 the DoE sent a letter to all English local authorities asking them to reduce their expenditure 5.6 per cent below their levels of 1978/79. This move marked the acceptance by the government that the 1980 Local Government Act had proved an ineffecive instrument in curbing local councils' expenditure. It also caused considerable confusion in both central and local government since few of those involved were clear whether local authorities would suffer grant penalties on the basis of their block grant assessed expenditure or on the basis of the new guidelines contained in the letter. In any event, the new initiative had little effect. By the autumn of 1981 the Government was still faced with what Michael Heseltine called 'a 1 billion overspend ... the extravagant consequences of political licence' (Bulpitt, 1983: 213).

In England and Wales the Cabinet's response to this continuing and embarrassing problem was threefold: the Local Government Finance Act, 1982; further general cuts in housing subsidies and rate support grant: and the publication in December 1981 of the Green Paper, *Alternatives to Domestic Rates*. The Local Government Finance Act was the most interesting since, as well as establishing a new Audit Commission for local authorities, it abolished supplementary rates and precepts, one of the principal methods local councils had employed to get around the government's policies. This measure was passed only after an earlier bill, which included provision for local referendums on rate increases, had been withdrawn following considerable opposition from Conservative backbenchers. This was just one example of the considerable confusion within the government concerning the details of this new initiative. In Scotland, these matters were managed more efficiently and drastically. The Secretary of State had already taken powers to intervene directly in the local budgetary process and threaten grant reductions. The Local Government and Planning (Scotland) Act of 1982 extended his control even further. The Secretary of State was now given the power to force those councils whose expenditure he regarded as 'excessive and unreasonable' to lower their rates and reimburse ratepayers.

In July 1981 race riots occurred in London, Liverpool and Manchester. Race and territory together were an explosive mix. Potentially these disturbances marked the beginnings of a new and awkward phase in race politics, in which the issue went out of "court" into "country" politics; black interests were beginning to be articulated by blacks and not, as hitherto, by white liberals. Two of the government's reactions to these events were classic: the appointment of Lord Scarman (the quintessential white liberal) to inquire into the disturbances in Brixton, across the river from Westminster, and an increase in public expenditure devoted to inner city areas.

A more novel response was to appoint Heseltine to preside over Merseyside's problems. A Merseyside Task Force was established, composed of civil servants and persons from the private sector, to promote ways of improving Liverpool. Heseltine took his job more seriously than the Cabinet required. According to press comment, he produced a report which suggested considerable ministerial intervention in all inner-city areas. This was rejected by the Cabinet (*The Economist*, 13 March, 1982), a case of the Thatcherite centre gaining autonomy from one of its own ministers. Nevertheless Heseltine (1983) maintained non-Thatcherite views about intervention in inner-city problems.

Finally, as Heseltine constantly pointed out, the government's programme was suffering from a marked decline in collaboration by some office holders at the local level. There were a number of reasons for this: the failure of the government's macro-economic strategy; the unfair incidence of public expenditure cuts in particular areas and services; intense, if not general, opposition to increased controls over local governments; the scale of Labour victories at the local elections of 1981 and 1982; and public opposition to many of the government's policies from the Conservative wets in Parliament and local government. The government's response to this challenge to its authority varied. Massive grant penalties were applied to some local authorities, especially the Greater London Council, the metropolitan county councils in England, and Lothian Regional Council in Scotland. In December 1981 centrally appointed commissioners were sent to administer the sale of council houses in Norwich. In June 1982, four regional health authority chairmen, known to be hostile to the handling of the health service pay dispute, were replaced. Indirectly, party support was given to individuals and local councils prepared to take high-spending Labour authorities to court, e.g., the private action taken against the GLC's "fares fair" scheme of transport subsidies in December 1981 and the challenge to a similar scheme of the West Midlands

County Council from Solihull in January 1982. For a party traditionally opposed to the politicization of central-local relations, all this was a peculiar development. The government was moving, by a series of ad hoc expedients, towards a territorial code very different from what it espoused when it gained office.

3. July 1982 - June 1983. Mr. Leon Brittan, Chief Secretary to the Treasury, gave an indication of the Cabinet's new thinking in a speech to the Society of Local Authority Chief Executives at York (Treasury Press Release, 136/82; "The Treasury Defied", *The Times* , 17 July 1982; Jones and Stewart, 1983). The gist of his message was that because of the impact of local government spending upon the national economy the Cabinet could not adopt 'an attitude of casual insouciance' to the financial decisions of local councils. Secondly, local politicians had shown themselves 'less and less willing' to accept that the centre's macro-economic strategy had primacy over local preferences. Thirdly, the results were disastrous in terms of the control of local expenditure. In Mr. Brittan's words:

> In Great Britain in 1980-81 the outturn of local authority expenditure was 5.5 per cent (1,047 million in cash) in excess of public expenditure plans. In 1981-82 the outturn was 7.9 per cent (1,538 million) in excess of plans. In 1982-83 local authorities are budgeting to spend 7 per cent (1,499 million) above plans.

Finally, the minister gave an explicit threat. If local councils failed to stop their overspending, this was 'bound to lead to developments which the friends of local government will find extremely unwelcome. It is bound to cause central government to ... seek ever greater powers over local authority finances.'

In retrospect this can be seen as the formal announcement of a new Conservative territorial code: centre autonomy in the future was to be protected by something other than the old dual polity. At first, however, this change was obscured because both Michael Heseltine and Tom King at the Department of the Environment continued to talk in the language of the old code. King rejected any idea that the government would seek direct powers over local authority rate poundages. Heseltine went further; he continued to extol the virtues of local self-government as a means of preventing the concentration of power (*The Times*, 16 September 1982). Moreover, from autumn, 1982, with a general election in the offing, a climate of financial leniency developed. Local authorities were positively urged to spend more on capital account. In addition, decisions about the closure of Welsh and Scottish steel mills were postponed.

Nevertheless, there were other signs that the government was adopting a more interventionist line. The 1983 Water Act restructured Regional Water Authorities, abolishing local authority representation and placing their general management on lines similar to the nationalized industries. The Department of

Education and Science produced plans for the Management Services Commission to run aspects of technical and vocational education. It also floated the idea that the Secretary of State should have direct control over the use of a small percentage of educational finances. Finally, there was increasing talk of transferring the stricter Scottish system of local expenditure control south of the border.

The 1983 Conservative manifesto confirmed this trend. It promised legislation to curb the rate demands of 'high-spending councils' and a general reserve power to do the same for all councils 'if necessary'. Paradoxically, given its earlier opposition to neo-corporatism local authorities would be required 'to consult local representatives of industry and commerce before setting their rates'. Finally, the metropolitan county councils and the Greater London Council were to be abolished. Notably absent was any commitment to a radical general reform of local government finance.

## An Assessment

Perhaps the best way to describe the first Thatcher administration is that it was government by apprentices; they learned their territorial code on the job. For different reasons, both opponents and supporters of the Thatcher government have wished to stress the radical nature of that administration, its consistency of purpose and its coherence in operation. This examination of territorial politics casts doubts on all three points of that thesis. If by radical we mean a deliberate break with past practices, then the initial territorial code of the Thatcher government cannot be desribed in that way. Rather than breaking with the past, it tried to recreate it. Its attempts to combine centre autonomy in high politics with local discretion in low politics was a bid to reconstruct the dual polity operating prior to the early 1960s. Monetarism can also be regarded as an attempt to reconstruct yet another Keynesian-type automatic pilot for the economy. In its four-year lifespan the Thatcher government did adopt a radical territorial stance, breaking with past practices. But in the process it lost its claims to consistency and coherence.

The consistency theme cannot accommodate the series of territorial U-turns which took place in these years and which, in combination, point to interesting (and embarrassing) similarities with the unfortunate Heath government. The result was a significant change in the Thatcherite territorial code. It is true that at the end of its period of office the goal of centre autonomy was still maintained. But the means to that goal had altered. The primacy of the centre's interests was now to be sustained by increasing its control over peripheral politicians and governments.

The reversal of policy direction was first of all inherent in the traditional Conservative desire to achieve as large a degree of autonomy for the centre as possible. This commitment stemmed, in part, from the dislike of or indifference to local government, especially big-city government, among important sections of the national Conservative elite. And this dislike or indifference was paralleled among Conservative activists at the grass roots. For much of this century it was convenient for Conservative leaders to run centre autonomy with reciprocal autonomy for local government and local interests. But it was only a convenience, not a valued principle.

The Conservatives have always looked at local government and local institutions in terms of a management ethic; they never developed a substantive ideal regarding the virtues of local government and local democracy. Paradoxically, Thatcherism did stumble on such a territorial ideal. But it was the twentieth-century equivalent of that old feudal principle, nulle terre sans seigneur, namely, no house without its owner-occupier. It would be unfair to place too much emphasis on Conservative Party attitudes; in many ways these merely reflect a similar hostility or indifference to local government amongst the general public. The Labour Party too can hardly be described as unambiguously committed to decentralization. This widespread lack of political support for local government as an institution undoubtedly influenced Conservative policies in this period.

The second reason why the Thatcher government changed its code of territorial management arises from the excessive optimism with which many Conservatives viewed the adoption of monetarist statecraft at the end of the 1970s. While Conservatives have traditionally preached that any new rules of statecraft should be accepted with due caution and thought, enthusiastic Thatcherites failed to do this. They assumed that monetarism in one country was possible, that the money supply could be easily defined and controlled, that the institutions and conventions of the social democratic welfare state could be easily overrun, and that the high/low politics distinction could easily be regained. In practice, none of these assumptions proved to be correct. As a result, the government's statecraft had to be altered quickly and simply: the Public Sector Borrowing Requirement and interest rates became the prime instruments of economic policy, with inevitable awkward consequences for central-local relations (Sbragia, 1983).

Fortress Thatcher, attacked on all sides, concluded that it could not afford the luxury of the dual polity code. In the process what many regarded as dubious arguments were put forward concerning the adverse impact on the national economy of local expenditure and local taxes to justify the new controls (Newton, 1981). Equally important, the centre was redefined. Instead of being a cohesive, broad-Church political-administrative community, its parameters became much narrower and its composition more diffuse. It included only those willing to stick with the Thatcherite strategy. 'Is he one of us?' became the test question. One result was the partial politicization of the higher civil service; another was the increasing importance of advisors drawn from outside Whitehall.

Thirdly, by the late 1970s the collaborative peripheral culture was beginning to decline, and after 1979 it collapsed in some urban Labour council groups. We must be careful not to magnify this development. Most Labour councillors, especially those in South Wales, Strathclyde and Birmingham, still accepted the broad authority of the Conservative government. But others, in Lothian, London and South Yorkshire for example, did not. The new breed of local Labour politicians was easily recognizable. Young, leather-jacketed, blue-jeaned and minus ties, they sat in council and committee meetings confident of their abilities, articulate, and determined to resist as much as possible the government's policies. No previous government had faced this breed of councillors. Conservative ministers were both frightened and perplexed by their appearance on the scene, and old style Labour councillors were threatened too. It is not surprising that the Conservatives decided to increase controls rather than hope for a new consensus with militant Labour councillors.

The first Thatcher government pursued a number of nervous, incoherent, and as it admitted, ineffective policies to deal with its principal problems of territorial management. A supposedly radical administration failed to implement any general reform of local government finance. Yet after the summer of 1982 the Cabinet became more relaxed, more confident, and began to make public the outlines of a new and more coherent territorial code. With hindsight, this change in the government's psychology can be seen to reflect the advent of a dry majority in the Cabinet, continual divisions in the Labour party, and a rise in opinion poll support early in 1982, indicating the end of the SDP electoral honeymoon and public acceptance of high unemployment figures. The successful conclusion of the Falklands War in June, 1982 was the final bonus. After this the Conservatives suddenly realized what the future held in store: three million unemployed and an election victory. Monetarist policies had failed to solve the country's economic problems. Monetarist statecraft, however, had succeeded. Thatcherism had regained for the Conservative centre that degree of relative autonomy in high politics necessary to ensure electoral success in 1983. Its failure to reconstruct the dual polity in the territorial arena should not be forgotten however. Increasing central control over local affairs was the easy option with perhaps awkward consequences in the future.

# IV
# Labour's Territorial Strategy
by
## MICHAEL KEATING

*University of Strathclyde*

The politics of territory are a recurrent problem for the British Labour Party. Though it might seek to emphasize its class or ideological appeal, it cannot escape the need to accommodate territorial politics nor the fundamental problem that, while its support is concentrated in the periphery, its strategy requires it to take power at the centre. Over the years, the party has had to weave together three strands of policy in increasingly intricate patterns. First, there is support for peripheral autonomy, inherited from its Liberal Party forebears, reinforced by a traditional base in local government and still a widely supported value. Secondly, there is the tradition of centralism and state planning which has dominated party practice since the 1930s. Thirdly, there is the question of how to satisfy the material demands of the party's supporters in the disadvantaged regions. Between the wars, Labour moved away from its old home rule all-round policy towards the second and third elements. In the 1945 era it was clearly pursuing a centralist strategy (Keating and Bleiman, 1979).

For Scotland and Wales, this was not a purely assimilationist strategy. On the contrary, Labour sought in the post-war years to exploit the peculiar - and in some respects privileged - position of the two nations in the United Kingdom political structure in order to secure them material advantages, while at the same time enjoying the benefits of a unified political and economic system. So the territorial dimension of Labour's strategy did not disappear. Rather, within the framework of territorial politics the pursuit of autonomy was displaced by the pursuit of material advantage, with only a weak form of autonomy retained on some aspects of social policy and in the limited scope for independent initiative of the Scottish and, after 1964, Welsh Offices. This weak form of dual polity was strongly supported by party leaders in Scotland and Wales, so that by the 1950s Home Rule was being opposed precisely because it would put at risk the position of the Scottish and Welsh Offices and thus Scotland and Wales's relative material advantage (Jones and Keating, 1982).

In the English regions there were material demands but not the same concern with autonomy; in the 1960s the strategy was extended to cover English regions. Economic planning, growth and a centrally- directed regional policy could, it was hoped, satisfy territorial as well as sectoral demands without the need for constitutional change. Underlying this hope was a belief in regional policy as a non-zero-sum game which could simultaneously boost development in the declining regions, relieve over-heating in the boom regions, add to national output and reduce overall inflationary pressures. The 1964 Labour government's National Plan recognized a regional dimension. The main institutional expression of the strategy was the Regional Economic Planning Councils and Boards, the former comprising central and local government nominees together with distinguished independent members, and the latter made up of civil servants from the regional offices of government departments. Much has been written on the problems of this system and its ultimate demise but, for our purpose, the key issue is the almost deliberate lack of clarity about power relationships. It was never made clear whether the Councils were there simply to implement the centrally designed National Plan (in which case, why have local authority representation?) or to provide a local or regional input into national planning. However, at the time, the non-zero-sum growth strategy presented both policy and institutions in consensual terms, rendering such questions entirely academic. The prompt collapse of the National Plan removed the issue from the concern of practical politics, and the English regional question disappeared for a while.

It was in Scotland and Wales that Labour's strategy received its first serious political setback. The challenge of the Welsh and Scottish Nationalist by-election victories in 1966-67 was not met by constitutional concessions but by increasing pork-barrel benefits. Following the February, 1974 election, however, Harold Wilson's second Labour government decided to endorse devolution. While this shift was eagerly accepted by some sections of the party and could be legitimized by reference to the old home rule tradition, two points must be emphasized. Firstly, the decisive pressure had come from outwith the Labour movement and not, as in the Labour Party's earlier years, from within. Secondly, the adoption of devolution did not represent a move back to the old home rule tradition, which was based upon principles irrelevant in a modern welfare state and to a party committed to economic and social planning. Both policies had in common a dualist base, but the line between central and devolved policy spheres was drawn at different points. Home rule had distinguished between imperial affairs (foreign policy, defence, customs and a few other items) and domestic affairs. Devolution sees economic and industrial policy as high politics, to be reserved to the centre as well as defence and foreign affairs, while social and environmental policy could, to a large extent, be devolved downwards (cf. Bulpitt, 1983). Indeed, most of the items to be devolved were already handled by the Scottish and Welsh Offices. These matters were now moved from the weakly autonomous sphere of territorial ministries to the more autonomous sphere of elected assemblies. At the same time, the privileged access to the Cabinet represented by the Secretaries of State was preserved.

As a device for having one's cake and eating it, devolution presented all manner of problems. Devolution proved divisive in Wales where - although, ironically it had originated within the party - it was seen as a concession to hostile nationalist forces. In Scotland, it did not meet what was a widely seen basis for discontent, the demand for more control over economic decision-making. Dualist schemes of this nature have come under attack from the left in other European countries, where they are criticized as an expedient for the state to retain control of the major economic levers, in collusion with big capital, while having the periphery to cope with the social costs of coping with economic crisis and transformation (Worms, 1980). For the British Labour Party, however, devolution seemed the only viable solution given the conflicting demands facing it. Ironically, the Scottish devolution scheme, opposed by some in Scotland because it could damage Scotland's privileged claim on central resource, was killed by English Labour MPs fearful that it would give the Scots extra material advantages. Further indications of the disarray of Labour's territorial strategy were the Labour government's inability to find a means of placating hostile English MPs and, indeed, the latter's confusion as to whether they merely wanted to stop the Scotland Act or to use it to engage in territorial bargaining for greater autonomy and access for their own region of England.

After its 1979 general election defeat, the Labour Party's territorial strategy was in disarray. It had a commitment to devolution in Scotland; the decisive referendum rejection in Wales relieved it of obligations there. At the same time, it faced a continuing English backlash against any special favours for Scotland. This coincided with a growing concern about regional policy and the English regional question as a whole. By the late 1970s, the lack of economic growth and of mobile investment had effectively put an end to the old regional policy of diverting investment, based on a non-zero-sum strategy assumption of growth everywhere for everyone. Former boom areas like the West Midlands and Inner London were feeling the beginnings of deindustrialization. In the regions, Labour activists and councillors were beginning to look at the prospects for indigenous growth policies and local government intervention. In the party leadership, there was a recognition that the 1979 election had not been lost in Scotland or Wales and that a new strategy was needed.

In the English regions, local government reform was an unfinished item from the 1974-79 government. For a long time, Labour- controlled city councils in Conservative-held shire counties had been pressing for a restoration of major functions, including education and social services. Opposition was also strongly expressed to the non- elected health and water authorities. In 1976, the Labour Party had committed itself in principle to solving the problem by abolishing the counties, and dividing their functions between single-tier local authorities and regional councils. The latter would take over water, but control of health was disputed by the health service unions who were pushing for what they called industrial democracy. By the time of the 1979 election, practical agreement had been reached only on proposals for 'organic change' whereby powers would gradually be transferred from the counties to larger cities. Only with the major functions safely in the hands of city councillors would the party's local government interests be prepared to countenance the creation of regions.

## Towards a New Strategy at the British Level

The dominant policy concern in the Labour Party after 1979 was the economy and, specifically, the production of the left-wing Alternative Economic Strategy (AES). Pinning down exactly what is the Alternative Economic Strategy can be difficult, particularly in the absence of reference in many of the published versions to the indelicacies of incomes policy. However, it clearly intended to strengthen state control of the economy, with national planning, reflation, selective import controls and withdrawal from the EEC (Holland, 1975; CSE, 1980). Such a programme for strengthening the levers of the state could also allow considerable scope for internal redistribution between regions as well as income groups. Vigorous regional policies could be pursued without the need to worry too much about the response of the private sector or the effect on international competitiveness.

However, the whole strategy raised immense problems. Very little attention has been given in the AES documents to the problem of implementation. There are suggestions that a principal means will be planning agreements with the national and multi-national corporations of the 'meso-economic' sector; but as these will be negotiated, the corollary is that the state will have to make concessions in return. So the strategy is both less socialist and less nationalist than might appear at first sight. While a successful AES might give considerable scope for the pursuit of redistributive regional policies, there would seem little scope for peripheral autonomy, given the comprehensive central planning envisaged. There is, it is true, a commitment to workers' control in most versions of the AES, but the connection between this and the centrally planned economy is nowhere clearly thought out. Nor is much thought given in the AES documents to coping with policy failure, complete or partial. The assumption all too often made is that the strategy is going to work, and that this will, like the growth strategies of the 1960s, allow a Labour government to satisfy all the legitimate demands, sectoral and territorial, which are made on it. Clearly, the political cost of policy failure, in the context of such raised expectations, would be high.

By the early 1980s there was increasing concern felt about the centralist implications of the AES and the need to explore the scope for territorial decentralization within it. This was partly an intellectual reaction and partly a product of the experience of the new generation of left-wing council leaders in London, the West Midlands, South Yorkshire and elsewhere, who were experimenting with various forms of local economic intervention, often in reaction to the run-down in regional policy and the lack of central intervention under the Conservatives. The experience was absorbed and became a part of Labour Party thinking. In the years before the 1983 election, some sections of the Labour left began to think seriously about a decentralized AES.

It was to restore some coherence to Labour's devolution and regional policies and reconcile them with the Alternative Economic Strategy that John Prescott, a Hull MP, was appointed by Michael Foot as spokesman on devolution and regional affairs. We must be clear about the status which this gave him in Labour Party policy-making. As a spokesman, he could present party policy and could propose new ideas, but any proposals would have to make their way through the traditional route of the National Executive Committee and resolutions to party conference. There were other influences at work in those forums, pushing policy in different directions.

The National Executive Committee (NEC) of the Labour Party has rarely seen territorial politics as a priority, but has often been prepared to take a pragmatic line on such questions. In the early 1980s, it was beset by the continuing civil war between right and left and subject to strong pressures from conflicting interests. The party in Scotland was by now firmly committed to the devolution policy, and in 1981 lodged a strong protest against the failure to include any mention of the policy in Labour's interim programme. This oversight - which is almost certainly all it was - was soon put right after protests from the Scottish Executive; after further urging, the NEC issued a statement at the beginning of 1983 unequivocally backing a devolved assembly. The only proviso was that the details of tax powers would have to be considered in the context of reforms for the whole of the United Kingdom.

Within the Parliamentary Labour Party, on the other hand, there was still considerable opposition to devolution. In 1981 the Northern group of English Labour MPs expressed their opposition to any new scheme for Scotland. The Yorkshire group also expressed disquiet, but in a more positive form, claiming a measure of equal treatment for themselves.

Local government interests in the party were divided and, while primarily interested in new powers for the cities, some councillors, particularly in the North of England, were by no means hostile to the idea of regional government. The influential local government sub- committee of the NEC, however, was determined to give priority to the cities rather than to any experiments in regionalism.

The trade unions' interest in territorial government was sporadic but, as part of its reconsideration of economic policy, in 1982 the TUC produced a document, Regional Development and Planning. This recognized the need for a regional dimension in planning, but proposed that this should be done through tripartite Regional Development Planning Authorities. Throughout the debate, both the TUC and individual unions continued to insist that the English regional dimension should be accommodated through corporatist institutions on which they would have direct representation, a contrast with their support for an elected assembly in Scotland.

Prescott (1982) assembled a working group of academics and other interested people to produce the document, Alternative Regional Strategy: A Framework for Discussion, before the autumn 1982 Labour Party Conference. This takes the commitment to Scottish devolution as so far beyond debate that Scotland is dealt with only in an appendix, where the Scottish Council's proposals are laid out. The bulk of the paper is about England and Wales. Given the decisive rejection of Welsh devolution at the 1979 referendum, it is recognized that proposals for Wales would have to be brought in via England. The document approaches the regional question from the perspective of economic and industrial policy, and worked from there to institutions. National and regional economic planning are seen as vital parts of Labour's AES although the limited possibilities for diversionary regional policy in contemporary conditions are recognized.

The Alternative Regional Strategy proposes both a reform of the national machinery for regional planning and the establishment of new machinery at the regional level. There would be regional assemblies and regional planning boards for the regions of England and for Wales. Ultimately, the regional councils would be directly elected and could take over some of the work of regional offices of government departments; initially they would probably be nominated by industry, unions and local authorities. The councils and boards would draw up economic, social and physical plans and be able to comment on the financial plans of all agencies, including nationalized industries. At national level, there would be a minister for English local and regional development with responsibility for regional and local economic policy, including inner-city policy. A Regional Planning Council would bring together all ministers with responsibilities for industry, economic development, expenditure planning and the nationalized industries, together with the Prime Minister and the chairmen of the regional assemblies. There would be a regional input into the annual public expenditure review system with the regions making bids on the basis of their assessment of the total impact of proposed spending levels by the public sector as a whole in their areas. These would be fed through the Regional Planning Council to a Minister for Expenditure Co-ordination. Public expenditure would be broken down regionally as well as sectorally, although the major decisions would continue to be taken at national level. Labour's proposed National Planning Council would also have some regional representation.

The powers and resources of the regional assemblies are not discussed in detail, but it is suggested that in due course they could take over health and water authorities and other appointed agencies. The integration of these bodies and the development of regional expenditure statistics would, it is recognized, take some years to achieve. Scotland would be linked into the system through the Regional and National Planning Councils, thus providing some degree of equality of treatment and, it was hoped, defusing the English backlash. Taxation and finance for regional assemblies were the subject of the working group's further discussions, overtaken by the election announcement.

Three points stand out in an assessment of the Prescott proposals. Firstly, they recognize that equity of treatment as between Scotland and the English regions need not mean institutional uniformity. Rather, the respective demands of each should be met insofar as they can be reconciled with Labour's overall strategy. In Scotland, this means going for a legislative assembly; in England it is more important to promise development agencies, redistribution of public expenditure and a revived regional policy. Secondly, there is an attempt to avoid the 'dualist' trap, by establishing centre-periphery linking machinery. As it is considered neither possible nor desirable to devolve major economic powers, these would be retained by the centre, but the regions would be given more influence over them. Nor are the linking mechanisms seen in the consensual terms of the 1960s Regional Planning Councils and Boards. It is recognized that territorial bargaining and regional planning will be an intensely political activity. Thirdly, for this very reason the proposals would be extremely difficult to carry within the Labour Party or to implement in government. If the territorial bargaining and planning were to be truly political and the proposed assemblies were to have any weight, they would need to be directly elected and control substantial resources. Yet this would cut across the power of many established office-holders in the Labour movement.

In the course of 1982 and early 1983, Prescott travelled around the country to sell his proposals to regional conferences of the party and to local government and union interests. Meanwhile, the working group continued to meet, coming round to the view that any regional authorities would have to be directly elected and could replace the county councils as the tier between central government and the districts. This ran into opposition from both union and local government interest.

The unions' preference for corporatist institutions, which had hampered moves in the 1960s and 1970s for directly elected regional government, was carried into the TUC-Labour Party Liaison Committee, which was extremely influential in the elaboration of the 1983 party programme. At a series of special regional conferences to discuss economic and regional strategies, the TUC document on Regional Development and Planning and the joint TUC-Labour Party Statement, Economic Planning and Industrial Democracy, were discussed alongside Prescott's Alternative Regional Strategy. Differing interpretations have emerged of the mood of these conferences. There was clearly a lot of support for reviving regional policy and tying it into economic planning, but there were also differences on the form of the planning machinery and the role of the trade unions and local government.

Local government interests, having moved away from the organic change proposals towards outright abolition of the county councils, now often favoured unitary authorities for England and Wales. By 1982 this was party policy, endorsed by annual conference, but the means of implementing it were extremely vague. While the regionalists in the party saw the chance of combining the abolition of counties with the establishment of regions, many local councillors were deeply opposed. It was argued that this would merely recreate all the problems of two- tier government and hand over large parts of England to virtually permanent Conservative rule. Whatever happened, there was an insistence that local authorities should maintain their direct links with Whitehall. This would clearly reduce the weight of regions. Neither the NEC nor its local government committee, nor the party conference, nor the party's local government conference was able to give more than vague approval in principle to a regional tier of government, with regional development agencies and regional planning machinery, but without any specification of the form it might take.

## Holding the Line in Scotland

In Scotland the Labour Party organization is the concern of the Scottish Council of the Labour Party, formally a regional council of the party with the same status as regions of England. There is an annual conference which debates policy, passes resolutions and elects the Scottish Executive but constitutionally it is an advisory and not a decision-making body. At Keir Hardie House in Glasgow, the headquarters of the Scottish Council, there is a permanent staff, including a Scottish secretary, a Scottish organizer and a research officer. While these work closely with the Scottish Executive, they are employed by and responsible to the National Executive Committee in London. Policy ideas, mainly on Scottish questions, are formulated by working parties whose influence varies according to the issue; policies can proceed through the Scottish Executive to Scottish Conference. Although this does not make them policy of the Labour Party in Britain, on purely Scottish matters, such as reorganizing Scotland's distinctive local government structure, endorsement by the Scottish Conference usually suffices. In 1974 it was felt necessary to get the support of the Scottish Conference for the Labour Government's devolution commitment, and it was only placed before the Labour Party Conference actually in 1976 when the bill was already in Parliament.

In Scotland the assembly commitment, though bounced through rather hastily in 1974, has gradually become accepted and solidified in the Labour Party. In the aftermath of the 1974 election, the party appeared to be strengthening it, with Scottish Conference resolutions calling in a sweeping way for an assembly with real economic powers. Conference rhetoric, from both union and constituency delegates, however, failed to distinguish between the autonomy and access strands of Labour's Scottish strategy. The Scotland Act of 1978 combined autonomy in the devolved social and environmental sphere with privileged access to the centralized economic sphere. When demands for an assembly with economic teeth were put beside the unshakeable commitment to the economic and political unity of the United Kingdom (often by the same speakers), all that could emerge was another dualist scheme.

A dualist scheme was produced in 1980 by a working party set up by Labour's Scottish Executive. Devolution supporters succeeded in getting a commitment in principle to tax-raising powers and control of the Scottish Development Agency, the Highlands and Islands Development Board and some of the functions of the Manpower Services Commission. However, economic and industrial policy generally would remain with a central government assumed to be promoting an interventionist economic strategy and a rigorous regional policy to the benefit of Scotland and other needy areas. These proposals were presented to the Scottish Conference in interim form in 1981 (Labour Party Scottish Council 1981), and in their final version in 1982.

In essence, this was a restatement of the 1974-79 strategy, an attempt to reconcile devolution with the party's continued centralist commitments, especially in economic matters. This refurbished dualist strategy would be crucially dependent on a Labour government at Westminster, and sufficient economic growth to permit a strongly diversionary regional policy.

However, just as the mainstream of the Labour Party in Scotland had come to terms with the commitment into which it had been pushed in 1974, undercurrents were at work which could render the policy redundant as the old home rule policy was made redundant in the 1930s. While the 1979 general election restored the normal two-party majority government system to the

House of Commons, it did not mark a complete return to traditional voting habits. The major parties' share of the vote was higher than in 1974 but by post-war standards, at 81 per cent was still low. Even more striking was the geographical imbalance. Swings to the winning Conservatives ranged from 6.4 per cent in Greater London to minus 0.1 per cent in Scotland where Labour gained a Conservative seat. The result was a complicated mosaic of territorial politics. Wales appeared to be moving towards a more evenly balanced multi-party system. In Scotland, Labour was more dominant than ever. Since then, while Labour's strength in Scotland has proved remarkably resilient, in the South it has fallen further.

In the past, periods of Conservative government at Westminster have not, at least since the 1920s, led Scottish Labour to contemplate going it alone because that might put at risk the bigger, if distant, prize of power at United Kingdom level. In the 1979 Parliament, dominated by Margaret Thatcher's Conservatives, sections of the party, especially on the left, began talking seriously about the possiblity of a Labour defeat in Britain but a Labour majority in Scotland. In that case, some were prepared to contemplate a policy going well beyond devolution, in the direction of separatism. The argument was strengthened by the declining possibilities for diversionary regional policies. Not only has access to the levers of power at the United Kingdom level been made more difficult, but such access is in any case less valued. It no longer weighs so heavily as an argument against autonomy.

The emergence within the Scottish National Party of the 79 group, on the left wing of the SNP, created common ground between neo- nationalists in the Labour Party and 79 groupers. Both saw Scotland as ripe for socialism but held back by England, and with no hope for a national movement without a base in the working class. This differed profoundly from the Labour party line both before and after the 1974 elections. For the Labour Party, nationalism has been something to be fought as inimical to socialism and working class interest; or it is something which can be handled by devolution devices tacked on to and marginal to the main centralists economic strategy. The nationalist-left analysis harks back to Labour's early days when home rule was a major element in the party's philosophy.

There are countless problems with the nationalist-left analysis, at both theoretical and practical levels. Theoretically, there is the problem of reconciling an advanced home rule or separatist strategy with the Alternative Economic Strategy to which the left is committed and which involves strengthened levers of control at the United Kingdom level. It could be resolved by going for a purely Scottish AES, but this would mean import controls for Scotland, customs posts at the border and Scottish withdrawal from a Common Market of which the rest of the United Kingdom continued to be a member; in short, Scottish economic autarky. Few have gone so far as to recommend this.

Nor has the neo-nationalist left faced up to the philosophical contradictions between the AES, and Bennism generally, which Tom Nairn (1982) is undoubtedly right to see as a form of English nationalism and Scottish nationalism. Certainly there are few English left-wingers who would be prepared to view Scottish nationalist demands as having anything whatever in common with their own demands for emancipation from the EEC and the multinationals.

At a practical level, the neo-nationalist strategy faces the problem of how to carry the trade unions, still firmly committed to the United Kingdom, and of how it could actually be implemented faced with a Conservative government. There has been vague talk of civil disobedience, boycotts and Sinn Fein tactics, but little serious thought of how power could be usurped and exercised, at what cost, or who would back it.

There was a constant worry among Scots pro-devolutionists in the 1979-1983 period that the issue would fade away or become a mere relic, like Labour's home rule policy in the 1930s and 1940s. A ginger group, Labour For a Scottish Assembly, was set up in 1981 under the chairmanship of George Foulkes MP. Foulkes also convened a group of MPs and advisors to consider strategy. A proposal to put a strong devolution resolution to the 1981 national conference, however, was dropped because of the possibility of a defeat which could have put the policy back decades; given the trade unions position, such a defeat was in fact highly unlikely. Meanwhile, all sides were at least agreed that the United Kingdom strategy deserved one more try and that the issue could not be forced in advance of a general election.

## Into the 1983 Election

The declaration of the 1983 general election found Labour's plans for Scotland intact, but its English territorial strategy in disarray, and a British territorial strategy, linking all the elements together, almost non-existent. The Labour manifesto was produced in record time because the gap between left and right was so large that verbal quibbling would have been a waste of time, and the right was unwilling to be saddled with the blame for the looming defeat by trying to dilute Conference policy. The recently produced policy document, *The New Hope for Britain*, became, unchanged, the election manifesto. On Scotland, it declared, that Labour would:

> Establish a directly elected Scottish Assembly, with an executive drawn from members of the assembly. Provide the Assembly with legislative and executive powers over a wide range of domestic policy, including matters such as health, education and social welfare. Ensure a major role for the Assembly in assisting the regeneration of Scottish industry - including the preparation of a plan for

Scotland - within the context of our overall national plan. As well as receiving grants from central government, the Scottish Assembly will have tax-raising powers, thus ensuring that the level of services provided can be determined in Scotland (Labour Party 1983).

As usual, a separate but very similar Scottish manifesto was published by the Scottish Council of the Labour Party albeit sloppily giving its name as the Scottish Labour Party- actually the name of a breakaway left-nationalist group led by Jim Sillars in the 1970s. *The New Hope for Scotland* (1983) contains a paragraph on devolution identical to that in the British manifesto, with an extra few words to explain how the assembly proposed in the 1978 Scotland Act would have protected Scotland from 'many of the worst excesses of Tory rule'.

For local government in England and Wales, the Labour manifesto is appropriately vague:

> We are examining how best to reform local government. We believe that services such as health, water and sewerage should become answerable to a much greater extent to elected members and we aim to end, if we can, the present confusing division of services between two tiers of authority. Unitary district authorities, in England and Wales, could be responsible for all of the functions in this area that they could sensibly undertake.

A separate section on the inner cities pledges to: 'Use regional development agencies to prepare sites, encourage municipal and co- operative enterprise and help improve transport and other facilities'. In the Scottish version, an otherwise identical paragraph substitutes the SDA for reference to regional development agencies. On the composition of the English regional development agencies, the manifesto simply states that Labour will:

> Develop regional development plans with plans also being drawn up at local level by local authorities. Regional development agencies will be established, extending our present commitment to a Northern Development Agency to other English regions in need of them. These agencies will have similar powers and resources to those in Scotland and Wales. We will also consider using new regional job subsidies.

Labour's 1983 election defeat saw renewed moves to push the Scottish party towards a more aggressive home rule stance, with party leaders in Scotland trying to hold the line at the devolution within the United Kingdom approach, giving equal weight to access and autonomy. A post-election meeting of MPs, party officials, trade union leaders and local authority representatives in July was postponed to September because of fears that it would be used to promote a more aggressive approach, including parliamentary disruption and a challenge to the British government's legitimacy in Scotland. Keir Hardie House produced a document warning against a 'little Scotland' strategy, emphasizing the priority of achieving a Labour victory at United Kingdom level (*Scotsman*, 6 July 1983). It was the old dilemma for Labour in Scotland but with a vital difference. In the past, Labour had chosen the United Kingdom strategy because it was advancing; now the party leadership holds to it in retreat.

For Labour at the United Kingdom level, the dilemma is no less acute. While the electoral needs of the party now point more strongly than ever to the need to win more seats in the more prosperous parts of Southern England, the internal weight of interest in the party is against this. Labour is likely to emphasize the needs of its regional and urban bases. With power continuing to drift away from the Parliamentary Labour Party, it could develop a philosophy of local power. Such local powers would rest on fragile institutional support, especially with the Conservatives pledged to abolish the Greater London Council and metropolitan counties and setting their faces against a Scottish assembly. What is clear is that the British Labour Party cannot now return to its old strategy of territorial management, which has failed to achieve both local autonomy and central planning.

Part Two

# The Response by Nations

# V
# Divisions within England

Of all the nations of the United Kingdom, England is indubitably the most important, yet the least written about. If one party could sweep the constituencies of England, it would have a permanent majority in the United Kingdom Parliament. Alternatively, if the division of votes and seats within England is very close, then an advantage in Wales, Scotland or even Northern Ireland could be sufficient to keep a party in office for four years. While it is not normal for a government to win enough seats in England to claim a parliamentary majority solely on that basis, no party seeking to form the government will wittingly jeopardize its appeal to English voters, who collectively elect more than 80 per cent of the members of the House of Commons.

Is it meaningful to speak of an English vote? To do this implies that electoral competition in England is substantially different from electoral competition in other parts of the United Kingdom. Yet there is no English National Party, as there are Nationalist parties elsewhere in the United Kingdom. The nearest approximation to a Nationalist party in England is a very inadequate approximation, the National Front. The National Front concentrates its efforts almost exclusively in English constituencies. In 1979, when it fought 303 constituencies, 297 were in England; in 1983, when its number of candidates fell to 60, all of these contested English seats. However, the National Front vote is derisory; in 1983 it gained only 0.1 per cent of the total. Moreover, the racialism of the National Front favours an all-white Britain; it does not claim that the English are a separate race from the Scots, the Welsh and the people of Northern Ireland.

To suggest that there is a distinctly English form of party competition because of differences from other nations in the United Kingdom is to put the cart before the horse. England cannot differ greatly from the overall United Kingdom pattern, for its votes largely determine the distribution of votes and seats United Kingdomwide. One speaks of other parts of the United Kingdom deviating from a general pattern, because it is England that sets the pattern.

To speak of an English vote is to imply that the voters of England are homogeneous in their party preferences. This is palpably untrue. In ten of 12 elections since the war, no party has won as much as half the vote in England. When the Conservatives succeeded in doing this in 1955 and 1959, it was not because the party's vote was exceptionally high in England; it was also high in Scotland and in Northern Ireland. Competition for the vote is more even in England than in Wales or Northern Ireland, where one-party dominance has been the rule (cf. Table I.1).

A quick glance at the map will vitiate any assumption that there is a homogeneous English voting pattern. Calculation of votes and seats for England as a whole masks major differences between Sussex, voting 59 per cent Conservative at the 1983 election and returning 14 Conservative MPs for its 14 constituencies, as against South Yorkshire, 57 per cent Labour and returning 13 Labour MPs as against one Conservative. The outcome of a British general election may be less determined by differences between nations than by divisions within England.

Divisions within England are often interpreted as opposing two nations, a Conservative South of England, and a Labour North of England. Differential shares of the vote have been common for a century. In 1885 the Conservatives won 54 per cent of the vote in South East England, but only 42 per cent in Northern regions. In December 1910 the Conservatives won 57 per cent of the vote in the South East of England, but their vote fell to 42 per cent in parts of the North (Pelling, 1967: 415). Differences evident in 1983 are described by Curtice and Steed (1982: 256ff) as reflecting a gradual process of change commencing in 1955, with persisting regional differences in swings cumulatively widening the difference in the regional strength of the parties. Following the 1983 election *The Economist* (18 June 1983) concluded that there are now two two-party systems in England, one in the South involving competition between the Conservatives and Alliance, and another in the North of England involving competition between Labour and the Conservatives.

The invocation of the phrase "two nations" to describe divisions within England is a reminder that territory is not the only basis of political division. Traditionally, the two nations of England have been the rich and the poor or, in contemporary language, the middle class and the working class. These divisions exist within every part of England, and even within the shadow of Parliament. Walking from Westminster to the East End of London, where investigators have often ventured to find the second and poorer nation of England, a traveller can pass through 22 Labour seats before stepping into the first Conservative seat in the suburbs bordering Essex. The importance of such social divisions is obliquely recognized by Curtice and Steed, who note an urban-rural division as well as a North-South division within England. *The Economist* reflects the confusion of territorial and social divisions by referring to Labour as 'a party of the periphery and the inner cities'.

The object of this chapter is to test systematically the relative importance of territorial as against socio-economic explanations of electoral divisions within England today. The first section reviews carefully the alternative models, and the extent to which socio-economic and territorial explanations may be complementary rather than contradictory. The second section uses multivariate statistics to measure the precise importance of a number of different hypothesized influences upon the level of Conservative, Labour and Alliance votes. The concluding section demonstrates the implications for representation in the House of Commons and patterns of party competition.


## Territory and Social Structure as Alternative Models


General statements about the importance of socio-economic structure and territory leave many things unclear. Before undertaking statistical analysis, it is important to consider carefully the specific social and territorial influences often said to influence electoral divisions within England.

Discussions of electoral divisions in territorial terms usually imply that there are distinctive political cultures or sub-cultures associated with given areas. People who live in a given place, because they live in a given place, are expected to have certain attitudes and behaviour, differentiating them from people living elsewhere. Just as people who are born or raised in Lancashire will be socialized to support Lancashire at cricket, so people raised in County Durham will be socialized to support Labour at general elections. Territorial differences can persist, since most people living in a region will have been born there. Newcomers to the area will usually arrive in sufficiently small numbers at any one time so that they (or their children) will adapt to local outlooks. Regional differences within England (cf. Allen, 1968) are not derived from physical geography, such as height above sea level or the climate, but from the social consequences of people living together, thereby tending to acquire outlooks in common that also differentiate them from people in other regions.

The basic hypothesis is: *cultural differences between regions cause differences in election outcomes* . The nature and source of these cultural differences is not specified here. The first task is to see whether or to what extent differences exist. This avoids the time-wasting exercise of elaborating theories that lead to predictions of very great regional differences, only to have the theories collapse because the differences hypothesized are far greater than those existing in reality. In the 1970s many writings about Scottish and Welsh Nationalism exhibited just this defect, expatiating upon major historical and cultural differences between the nations of Britain, while failing to note that these did not produce electoral cleavages in proportion to the described differences.

Defining the boundaries of a politically distinctive area is difficult within England in the absence of national divisions comparable to the differences between England as against Scotland, Wales and Northern Ireland. Parliamentary constituencies are too large to constitute an immediate network of neighbourhood relations (cf. Fitton, 1973), yet a single constituency is too small to constitute a city, let alone a region. Moreover, the frequent redistribution of parliamentary seats because of population movements means that most voters do not have a long-term, let alone lifelong association with a particular constituency. The wholesale re-organization of English local government in the 1970s means that local government is no longer local, that is, conducted in the particular town or place where an individual lives, but rather directed from a county or metropolitan headquarters.

For administrative purposes England is often divided into eight standard regions defined by the Central Statistical Office: the South East (which groups London and the Home Counties), the South West, the East Midlands, the West Midlands, East Anglia, the North West, Yorkshire & Humberside, and the Northern region. The regions are defined for administrative convenience; they are not political units with their own elected assemblies or councils. Nor are these regions standard. Dozens of different sets of regional boundaries are used by different Whitehall departments. Hogwood and Keating (1982: 2) conclude: 'The most striking feature of the English regions in terms of their role in British government is a complete absence of a coherent definition of their boundaries, their size or even of the concept of a region'.

To divide England into two regions only, the North and the South, leaves no room for differentiating intermediate areas, such as the Midlands. Moreover, it overlooks the great contrast between the extreme urbanity of London and the prototypical English countryside in counties around London.

After considering carefully the alternatives of a two-nation division of England, or a quasi-standard set of eight regions, we have concluded that the most appropriate regional boundaries for electoral analysis divide England into four regions: the North of England (grouping together the Northern standard region, Yorkshire & Humberside, and the North West); the Midlands (grouping the East and the West Midlands); London (that is, the Greater London Council area); and the South of England (the South-East minus the GLC, East Anglia, and the South West). The regional location of each constituency is given in Appendix A.

The fourfold classification of English regions has the practical advantage of differentiating the indubitably Southern but industrial Midlands from both the North and the South. It also differentiates London from its contrasting Home Counties hinterland. The basic principle of combining like with like is respected. Each of the four regions is relatively homogeneous politically; all three of the standard regions joined together in the North are disproportionately Labour, and the South of England standard regions grouped together are disproportionately Conservative. Each region is sufficiently large to permit the use of multivariate statistics with a reasonable degree of confidence.

However regions are defined and whatever the process sustaining distinctive cultural outlooks, we still want to know: What specific influences are likely to make some regions more Conservative and others more Labour? Propositions that assert regional differences do not ipso facto explain observed differences. Moreover, to refer simply to regional cultures is to risk using electoral data as evidence of both cause and effect.

A variety of writers, stimulated by a literature about uneven development as between first world and third world nations, have sought to explain regional differences in terms of centre-periphery relations (Orridge, 1981). The basic concept is that every country is differentiated into a central core, which normally enjoys political, economic and cultural hegemony, and peripheral areas. Inequalities between regions are said to cause a political reaction, in which peripheral areas sharply differentiate their party loyalties from the central area. The general hypothesis is: *Different locations on the centre-periphery axis cause differences in election outcomes.*

Within the United Kingdom most discussions of centre-periphery relations have concentrated upon differences between nations, with England identified as central and other nations as peripheral. The result has been inconclusive. Sometimes an attempt is made to differentiate an ahistorical "Celtic twilight" periphery from a "centre" that includes industrial South Wales, and industrial Scotland. This approach is incorrect, in that parts of the so-called Celtic twilight, such as Orkney & Shetland and Berwick, are historically areas of Danish or Norse penetration. A Liberal-held seat such as Bermondsey, across the river from the Palace of Westminster, can hardly be consigned to the Celtic twilight. Furthermore, there is substantial evidence of political, social and economic divisions within each of the nations of the United Kingdom (see Rose, 1968: Table 7; Rose and McAllister, 1982: chapter 9)

The concept of centre-periphery is spatial in its basic imagery: some parts of a country are said to be distant from the centres of power, money and prestige. But writers on the subject have usually been vague in defining the terms. At its worst, discussions can confuse two very different types of relationships, a superior/subordinate relationship independent of territory, e.g. the East End of London as a peripheral part of Britain, and a territorial relationship, e.g., between cosmopolitan London and the industrial periphery. In this study, we have used distance from London in road miles as our measure of centrality or peripherality. The measure is precise, and clearly differentiates the areas closest to London from remote parts of the United Kingdom such as Caithness or Fermanagh. It also discriminates areas within England, as between Birmingham (110 miles distant), Manchester (184 miles), Truro (256 miles), and Newcastle upon Tyne (273 miles).

Sooner or later, every discussion of territorial divisions within England begins describing differences in social structure; centre-periphery writings are no exception. For example, the North of England is usually contrasted with the South of England on the grounds that the North is working-class, industrial and urban, whereas the South is said to be middle-class, administrative, and rural or suburban. The co-existence of social structure and territorial divisions within England makes it important to test whether nominally territorial divisions are simply another way of referring to geographically skewed socio-economic characteristics. The North of England may not favour Labour because it has a Northern culture or is distant from London, but because it has a higher proportion of manual workers, and the South of England may favour the Conservatives because it has a higher proportion of middle-class electors.

Party competition in England is normally interpreted as competition between different socio-economic groups. The occupational structure of a constituency is considered far more important than its geographical location. Within London a middle-class constituency of well-to-do people, such as The City of London & Westminster South, is expected to vote Conservative, whereas a few stops away on the Underground line, a constituency which is heavily working-class with many council tenants, such as Bethnal Green & Stepney, is expected to be a safe Labour seat. From this perspective, there is hardly such a thing as political geography. In place of a map of constituencies, there is a hierarchy of constituencies ranging from those ranking highest in socio-economic status to those that are lowest. Political divisions within a city, a county, a region or nation follow social structure, not territorial location. The basic hypothesis is: *social structure differences cause differences in election outcome.*

Social structure is a comprehensive term referring to a host of social and economic differences that are often colloquially described as class differences. Class differences are often reduced to a single measure, occupation. But concentrating exclusively upon a manual/non- manual occupational division discards a large amount of information about economic conditions, for example, unemployment, income and the character of an individual's work. It discards information that is relevant to both social status and economic conditions, such as council-house tenancy or owner-occupation, and it also ignores social characteristics that are important in a wide variety of everyday relationships, such as age and sex. Analyses of voting behaviour in Britain in the past quarter-century consistently demonstrate the importance of social and economic influences upon voting; they also show that the influences are multiple, rather than reducible to the single measure of occupation (see e.g. Rose, 1982a).

The question is not whether social structure influences voting, but rather which particular structural characteristics are of primary importance. The 1981 census employs more than 5,000 different statistical measures to characterize each parliamentary constituency, ranging from details about occupation to age structure and the male/female sex ratio. Given the plethora of census information available, it is necessary to select a limited number of characteristics differentiating constituencies from each other.

Factor analysis is an appropriate statistical technique for identifying commonality among a large number of statistical measures (Kelley and McAllister, 1983). A wide range of different constituency characteristics of potential importance was initially analysed in order to identify those collectively accounting for a high proportion of the variation between constituencies. Those of no statistical consequence were discarded. After a comprehensive analysis of various possible combinations, a solution was reached encompassing 16 measures that produced four factors, each independent of the other, which collectively account for 84 per cent of the variance among the 650 constituencies of the United Kingdom (See Appendix B for details). In the order in which they emerged, the four factors are:

1. *Socio-economic status* (29 per cent of variance). There are both theoretical and practical reasons for exercising care in constructing the principal measure of what is commonly called class differences. To reduce a host of social characteristics to a single measure, whether occupation, housing, or something else, is to presuppose that the measure prescribed is necessarily independent of and antecedent to other social characteristics. But studies of multiple deprivation in Britain consistently emphasize that areas ranking low or high in terms of one important social or economic indicator are likely to have a similar position on a multiplicity of measures.

The factor analysis identified six census measures that effectively constitute a *single* measure of socio-economic status. This factor has three components: an occupation measure of unskilled workers, semi-skilled workers, and professionals and managers; measures of council-house tenants and of owner-occupiers; and the proportion of unemployed in a constituency. The six measures are highly correlated, with an average factor loading of .84. They are also independent of the other three factors, with which their average correlation is .10.

The measure of socio-economic status distinguishes between constituencies relatively high in their proportion of middle-class residents and owner-occupiers and low in unemployed and council tenants (Cheadle and Croydon South rank highest) as against constituencies with a high proportion of unskilled and semi-skilled workers, council tenants, and unemployed, and short of owner-occupiers or middle-class residents. Liverpool Riverside is the English constituency lowest in socio-economic status. This does not mean that everyone in Croydon South or Cheadle is middle-class, an owner-occupier and in work, nor that everyone who lives in Liverpool Riverside is an unemployed manual worker in a council-house. What it does mean is that in these constituencies the proportions in these categories are at the extreme ends of the scale.

The socio-economic status scale is revealing in what it omits as well as what it includes. Education is not statistically significant in differentiating constituencies from each other, when their other social characteristics are taken into account. Given a history of minimum education for the majority of Britons, middle-class occupations recruit some people with only minimum education. Equally significant, the ownership of one or more than one car, often treated as if it were an indicator of household income, was not significant in differentiating constituencies, after allowing for other influences.

2. *Immigrants* (23 per cent of variance). Immigrant constituencies can be clearly identified by a combination of four highly correlated measures: the proportion of the population born in the New Commonwealth, the proportion born in the Irish Republic, and the proportion of households living in furnished accommodation and/or sharing a bathroom or toilet. Immigrants cluster in constituencies where rented rooms allow people to obtain accommodation quickly and easily; gaining a council house can involve a wait of years, and there are financial barriers to house purchase.

The factor analysis shows that race is not the only element of importance, for Irish as well as New Commonwealth immigrants tend to cluster in the same types of constituencies. Equally important, it shows that not all immigrants living in transient housing are poor. Upper-status Chelsea ranks high in immigrants and bed-sitter accommodation as well as low-status constituencies in London's East End. The London constituency of Brent East ranks highest on the immigrants scale, while a number of North East of England constituencies rank lowest; they attract few immigrants because of high unemployment and lots of council houses.

3. *Elderly* (19 per cent). Constituencies with a high or low proportion of the population retired or over the age of 65 are distinctive in ways cutting across other social characteristics. These constituencies not only include middle-class areas, such as Worthing and Hove in Sussex, but also industrial towns in the North of England, where the departure of young people by default has left a relatively large proportion of elderly residents. Nor do these constituencies represent a single housing group, for some, such as Blackpool, have a high level of transient residents, whereas the retirement havens of the South and some industrial areas in the North can have a high proportion of owner-occupiers. Two constituencies on the South Coast of England rank highest in their proportion of elderly, Eastbourne and Bexhill & Battle; Harlow ranks lowest.

4. *Agriculture* (12 per cent). Agriculture does not readily fit analyses of class which assume an urban, industrial population. Farmers may be wealthy in terms of the land they own or have borrowed money to purchase, but they work with their hands. The environment of agricultural Britain is very different from that of industrial cities, and these differences affect people whether or not they actually live on a farm. Hence, constituencies with a relatively high proportion of the labour force working in agriculture are distinctive in a factor analysis. A large number of urban constituencies cluster at the bottom of this scale, for they are without any agriculture; the most rural constituency in England is Holland with Boston.

Population movement from inner-city areas to suburbs and the surrounding countryside and movement between regions are potentially significant for electoral behaviour. Voters who leave an area in which they are born and bred may also leave behind earlier party loyalties. Constituencies full of new housing estates, whether owner-occupiers, council tenants or New Towns, might be expected to be electorally volatile, or open to the appeal of new parties, such as the Alliance. Population change is also important. In 1983 Boundary Commissioners created new parliamentary constituencies in areas of expanding population and merged constituencies contracting in population. However, the factor analysis showed that population change in a constituency is not part of a general syndrome; it does not correlate strongly with the measures of socio-economic status, age, immigration, or agriculture. Nor is population change sufficiently distinctive to constitute a factor on its own; it does not differentiate constituencies beyond what is achieved by the four factors described above.

## Testing the Causes of Divisions

The 1983 election revealed a plenitude of electoral divisions within England. The Conservatives were well ahead with 46 per cent of the vote because more than half the vote was divided among their opponents, with Labour taking 27 per cent, and the Alliance 26 per cent. The mechanics of the electoral system produced a very different allocation of seats: the Conservatives won more than two-thirds of the 523 English seats, Labour more than a quarter, and the Alliance only 13. While the two also-ran parties were nearly even in votes, they differed in their competitive placement. The Alliance finished second in more than half the constituencies of England, and was twice as likely as Labour to finish second to a Conservative winner. Three very different kinds of electoral outcomes thus require explanation: how the parties divide the vote; the division of seats in the House of Commons; and contrasting patterns of party competition. Whereas social structure might be the most important determinant of votes, territorial differences may correlate most with outcomes in terms of seats.

When examining constituency voting patterns, the first concern is the base vote that each party receives rather than the swing registered between parties since the last election, the normal tool of analysis in Nuffield election studies (cf. Chapter XI). Inferences drawn from characteristics of a constituency as a whole are subject to the ecological fallacy, if projected to the behaviour of a small proportion of individuals whose changes of votes produce a small net swing.

A party's base vote is its share of the total vote in the constituency. It is reasonable to compare the socio-economic status of the total electorate with each party's share of the total vote. Concentrating attention upon the base vote is even more important than usual in 1983, for there is no historic record of how the constituencies voted in 1979, since nine-tenths had their boundaries changed by redistribution. Moreover with three parties fighting nationwide, a constituency swing could be the byproduct of a variety of switches in votes. A party could achieve a swing in its favour, even though its base vote contracted (see Chapter XI).

In a three-party system, it is important to examine the Conservative, Labour and Alliance share of the vote separately. Knowing that the Conservatives won a seat does not tell us the name of the second party, let alone the share of the vote won by the party finishing second. In Chelmsford, which the Conservatives won with 48 per cent of the vote, the Alliance finished a very close second with 47 per cent, and Labour was third with five per cent. In Chorley, which also gave the Conservatives 48 per cent, Labour finished second with 30 per cent of the vote, and the Alliance third with 20 per cent.

Another reason for separately examining each party's vote is that there are good theoretical reasons to expect differences in the extent to which each is determined by social structure and territorial influences. The conventional class equals party model of voting implies that social structure and, *a fortiori* , socio-economic status, ought to determine both the Conservative and Labour share of a constituency's vote. This is consistent with much Labour rhetoric-- but inconsistent with the Conservative claim to be a national party appealing to all classes. The Alliance rejects class categories; its supporters argue that Alliance support is derived from a cross-section of the nation, and is not dependent upon the social structure of a constituency. Territorial influences could also differ in their impact upon parties. For example, the weakness of the Labour Party in the South of England need not result in disproportionate Conservative strength. It could reflect disproportionate Alliance strength there.

While the social and territorial characteristics of constituencies may be discussed separately for clarity in exposition, in practice their influence is exercised jointly. The Conservative vote in a constituency may be affected by a constituency ranking high in socio-economic status and being a London suburb. The Labour vote in a constituency may be affected by a constituency ranking low in socio- economic status and being in the North of England. Given a multiplicity of potential influences upon constituency voting, it is necessary to use multivariate statistics to test the relative importance of each of the six measures of territory and social structure discussed above.

A familiar multivariate statistic, ordinary least squares regression analysis, is employed here to test influences upon votes. It is particularly appropriate because, when assessing the importance of each of the six influences, it controls for the effects of the other five. Regression analysis can thus test whether the apparent relationship between distance from London and Labour voting is a centre-periphery difference, or simply an artifact of a higher proportion of working-class electors in constituencies far from London.

The first point demonstrated is that there is a very good fit, as shown by a high proportion of variance explained ($r^2$), between a constituency's social structure and territorial characteristics and the share of the vote won by the Conservative and Labour parties. Altogether, the six different influences can explain 78 per cent of the variation in the Conservative vote in a constituency, and 79 per cent of the Labour vote (Table V.1). But the six influences are not of equal importance.

Socio-economic status is by far the most important single influence upon a constituency's vote. It explains 42 per cent of the variation in the Conservative share of the constituency vote, and 39 per cent of the variance in Labour's share of the vote. The impact of socio-economic status upon a party's vote is shown in table V.1 by the b value, the metric partial regression coefficient. This gives the change in the party's share of the vote from the constant, (24.2 per cent in the case of the Conservatives). For each one per cent change in a constituency's position on the socio-economic status scale, the proportion of the Conservative vote changes by 0.37 per cent. In a constituency at the bottom of the socio-economic scale, the Conservative vote is expected to be 24.2 per cent. In a constituency ranking in the 100th percentile on the scale, the expected Conservative vote would be 61.2 per cent (that is, 0.37 x 100 plus the constant of 24.2 per cent) before allowing for the impact of other less influential characteristics of the constituency. The impact of socio-economic status is even stronger upon Labour's vote: -0.46 per cent for every one per cent change in a constituency's ranking on the socio-economic status scale. The minus sign signifies that it should be subtracted from the constant, 55.3 per cent. In a constituency that ranks 10 per cent from the bottom of the socio-economic scale, the Labour vote, all other influences cancelling out, would be 50.7 per cent (that is, -0.46 x 10 plus 55.3 per cent).

Because constituency outcomes aggregate the behaviour of tens of thousands of voters, the ecological association between socio-economic status and party preferences appears different than in sample surveys of the behaviour of

Table V.1  SOCIAL STRUCTURE AND TERRITORIAL INFLUENCES ON THE VOTE
          IN ENGLAND

|  | Conservative vote | | Labour vote | | Alliance vote | |
|---|---|---|---|---|---|---|
|  | b | % variance explained | b | % variance explained | b | % variance explained |
| **Social Structure** | | | | | | |
| Socio-econ status | .37** | 42 | -.46** | 39 | .08** | 9 |
| Agriculture | .11** | 15 | -.16** | 17 | .06** | 8 |
| Immigrants | -.02 | 2 | .04* | 4 | -.01 | 2 |
| Elderly | .01 | 1 | -.04* | 3 | .02 | 2 |
| **Territory** | | | | | | |
| Miles from London | -.03** | 11 | .01 | 4 | .00 | 1 |
| Region[a] | 2.8** | 7 | 6.9** | 12 | 3.4** | 8 |
| (Constant) $r^2$ | (24.2) | 78 | (55.3) | 79 | (18.1) | 30 |

[a] South of England for Conservatives and Alliance; Labour, North
of England.

*Significant at .05 level          **Significant at .01 level

individuals (see e.g. Miller, 1978: Table 6). Surveys of individual voters
emphasize the limited and declining relationship between socio-economic
status, typically measured by a single indicator, occupation, and individual
party preference. The probability of an individual voting Conservative if
middle-class or Labour if working-class was far less than 1.00 in 1983, and has
been declining steadily in the past quarter-century (Rose, 1980). But there
remains a degree of association between occupational class and party
preference, causing a constituency low in socio-economic status to produce a
high Labour vote, and a high-ranking constituency a high Conservative vote.
This aggregate relationship, though less than a one-to-one fit, has remained
high and steady for decades (Miller, 1978: table 9). Of the 100 British
constituencies ranking highest in socio- economic status, the Conservatives won
99 and Alliance one in 1983. In the 100 ranking lowest in socio-economic status,
Labour won 83 seats, the Conservatives 12, and Alliance 5.

When the vote of one individual is analysed, there must either be a one-to-
one fit between class and party, or no fit at all. But when thousands of votes are

analysed, there does not need to be an all-or-nothing fit; the impact (the b value) can fall anywhere between 1.00 and 0.0. After taking the constant into account, a change in socio-economic status produces a change in party vote that is substantially more than nil, but less than a one-to-one fit.

Just as a cricket or a baseball team does not need to score all the runs to win a match, so a party does not need to win all the votes to win a seat. The higher the b value, the greater the likelihood that social structure can determine whether a party will win sufficient votes to win a seat. In the 1983 election the impact of socio-economic status upon votes was strong enough so that the Conservatives could normally expect more than 50 per cent of the vote, thus guaranteeing the party victory, in the top 30 per cent of constituencies according to socio-economic status. Labour was predicted to get more than 50 per cent of the vote in the bottom 10 per cent of constituencies in socio- economic terms.

Because factor analysis is used to classify constituencies according to a multiplicity of socio-economic characteristics-- unemployment and housing as well as occupational class--both the variety and the inter-relationship of socio-economic conditions are reflected here. It is prima facie reasonable to say that constituencies that have more middle-class residents, more owner-occupiers and less unemployment are likely to have a higher Conservative vote, and that constituencies with more manual workers, more council tenants, and more unemployment are likely to have a higher Labour vote. That is precisely what Table V.1 demonstrates. The use of a multiplicity of indicators to determine socio-economic status maintains the integrity of class as a single concept. It is here treated as a second-order abstraction referring to a multiplicity of attributes. (For the same approach applied to survey data see the description of ideal-types in Rose, 1980: Table 14).

Alternative strategies of attempting to deal with the multiplicity of characteristics associated with the concept of class have considerable problems. For example, when Franklin and Mughan (1978) apply regression analysis to British voting, they treat socio- economic characteristics as if they were separate and independent of each other. But the factor analysis undertaken here, re-inforced by analysis of survey data (see e.g. Rose, 1968 *et seq*) demonstrates that this is emphatically not the case. As Weatherford notes (1980: 461): 'The inclusion of several related components of social class in the same regression equation can lead to mistaken inferences about larger theoretical questions'.

By using a single indicator of class Miller avoids this problem. But the indicator chosen, the proportion of employers and managers in a constituency, is unsuited to explain the total constituency vote, because it averages only 13.3 per cent of a constituency (Miller, 1979: Table 6). A series of inferences about the behaviour of the remaining 87 per cent of the voters is required; Miller does not provide this. Moreover, a realistic model must take into account non-occupational factors in the milieu, since from one-third to one-half of the electorate lacks a current occupation, being retired, a housewife, a student or unemployed (Miller, 1978: 258). Social relationships also reflect such politically important influences as public or private housing and unemployment. It is best to include these by factor analysis, as is done here.

Although the socio-economic status of a constituency has the strongest impact upon its vote, it is not the only characteristic that is important. The agricultural character of a constituency is significant, even after taking socio-economic status into account. A traveller would never confuse an industrial town or a prosperous suburb with a farming area. The agricultural character of a constituency can explain 15 per cent of the Conservative share of the vote, and 17 per cent of the Labour share of the vote. The b values in Table V.1 show that the difference in the Conservative vote between the least and the most agricultural constituency is an 11 per cent advantage to the Conservatives, and a 16 per cent loss to Labour.

An alternative measure of urban-rural difference was also tested, namely, the density of population in a constituency. This distinguishes areas of suburban houses with gardens from city centres as well as from rural areas. However, the distribution of population between compact urban constituencies, suburbs and scattered rural areas has no discernible impact upon the vote (cf. Campbell et al., 1960: chapter 15)

By contrast with socio-economic status and agriculture, the immigrant character of a constituency and the proportion of the elderly in its electorate have virtually no influence on votes *after* the impact of other influences is taken into account (Table V.1). In England the difference in votes between the constituency with the most immigrants and the constituency with the least, controlling for other factors, is a two per cent drop in the Conservative vote, and a four per cent gain in the Labour vote; it is proportionately less in constituencies between these extremes. Where the $m_1$ elderly are most numerous, the Conservative vote is up one per cent and the Labour vote down four per cent, and the constituency with the fewest elderly people registers the reverse.

Whereas socio-economic status accounts for 42 per cent of the variance in the Conservative vote, the immigrant factor accounts for only two per cent, and the elderly for one per cent of the variation. In the case of the Labour vote, a similar pattern emerges: immigrants account for four per cent of the variation in the Labour vote, and the elderly account for three per cent.

The Alliance vote is very different from the Conservative and Labour vote in England, for 70 per cent of the variation in the Alliance vote *cannot* be explained by the social and territorial characteristics of a constituency (Table V.1). Even more striking, the variation in the Alliance vote from constituency to constituency is much less than the variation in the Conservative or Labour vote.

Of the 30 per cent of the variation in the Alliance vote explainable by constituency characteristics, nine per cent is accounted for by socio-economic status. But the impact of status upon the Alliance vote is weak. For every one per cent change in the socio- economic status of a constituency, the Alliance vote alters by less than one-tenth of one per cent; this is one-quarter less than the impact registered by such a change upon the Conservative vote, and less than one-fifth its impact upon the Labour vote. The agricultural character of a constituency is almost as important as socio-economic status in explaining variation in the Alliance vote. But it explains only half as much variance as it does in the Conservative or in the Labour vote. Moreover, the impact of agriculture is also much less; a one per cent rise on the agriculture scale results in only a 0.06 per cent increase in the Alliance vote.

Territorial differences do affect party shares of the vote, but the impact is less than social structure influences. Territorial factors account for 18 per cent of variance explained in the Conservative share of the vote; for 16 per cent of the variance explained in the Labour vote; and for nine per cent in the Alliance vote.

A constituency's location on a centre-periphery axis and its regional location each have some impact upon votes, but their relative significance differs between the Conservative and Labour parties. The Conservative vote in constituencies in the South of England is 2.8 per cent higher than in constituencies in other regions of England, even after allowance is made for the socio-economic status and agricultural character of the constituency. (Because only one region is examined in Table V.1 and it is treated as a nominal variable, the b value of 2.8 per cent is therefore not comparable to other b values in the column). Distance from London has a negative effect upon Conservative voting; for every 100 miles a constituency is distant from London the Conservative vote is likely to be three per cent less than would be expected because of its other characteristics. Thus, in Devon and Cornwall, the advantage of being in the South is offset by the disadvantage of distance from London, and in the North, where most constituencies are more than 200 miles from London, a Conservative candidate will have a distance handicap of six per cent or more of the vote.

The Alliance vote, like the Conservative vote, is boosted in the South of England by 3.4 per cent on average, after controlling for its other characteristics. But within England distance from London does not help or hinder Alliance support. It draws support around Greater London, in Devon and Cornwall, and in Northumberland as well.

The regional effect upon the Labour vote is greater than that upon the vote for other parties. Labour's support in North of England constituencies is increased on average by 6.9 per cent above that predicted by its social structure (Table V.2). This is best interpreted as evidence of a North of England rather

Table V.2  REGIONAL INFLUENCES ON THE VOTE IN ENGLAND

| Region[a] | % Conservative vote | | | % Labour vote | | | % Alliance vote | | |
|---|---|---|---|---|---|---|---|---|---|
| | Act. | Pre-dict[b] | Diff. | Act. | Pre-dict | Diff. | Act. | Pre-dict | Diff. |
| South | 53 | 48 | +5 | 16 | 23 | −7 | 30 | 25 | +5 |
| London | 43 | 46 | −3 | 30 | 26 | +4 | 25 | 25 | 0 |
| Midlands | 45 | 47 | −2 | 31 | 29 | +2 | 23 | 20 | +3 |
| North | 38 | 41 | −3 | 37 | 34 | +3 | 24 | 22 | +2 |

[a] See Appendix A for the definition of regions.

[b] The mean predicted constituency vote for the party, calculated by a regression analysis of the constituency's socio-economic status, agriculture, immigrants and elderly. The predicted votes need not sum to 100.

than a peripheral culture, for distance from London has virtually no impact upon Labour's share of the vote. In East Anglian and South-West of England constituencies distant from London, Labour polls an average or below-average vote.

The best way to measure the extent to which there is a regional effect in all four of the English regions is to compare the vote that a party actually wins in the region with the vote that it would be expected to have on the basis of a regression analysis of its social structure. If regional cultures have no effect, the difference between the actual and estimated share of the vote would be small, caused by more or less random statistical fluctuations. The more a region's actual vote differs from its predicted vote, then the greater the degree of regional effect. Given that regression statistics are much better at determining the Conservative and Labour shares of the vote than the Alliance vote, the method used for testing regional effects ought, if anything, to produce greater differences for Alliance.

In most regions of England there are limited but noteworthy differences between the predicted and the actual share of the vote for each of the three parties. The regional differences do not exceed seven per cent, Labour's shortfall in the unfavourable regional culture of the South of England. The average difference between the predicted and actual regional vote of the parties is 3.25 per cent. Within this range, the regional culture is most favourable to the Conservatives in the South of England, where the party does five per cent better than would be predicted solely on the basis of social structure. The sub- culture is unfavourable in other regions of England, where the Conservatives get about three per cent less than their expected share of the vote. The Labour Party suffers more loss of votes in the South of England than it gains in the North. Because Alliance's vote is not primarily a reflection of social structure differences, its results in Table V.2, which highlights a South of England advantage, should be treated cautiously.

## Constituency Outcomes

When electoral outcomes are defined in terms of winning seats in the House of Commons rather than winning votes in constituencies, regional effects become important. In three of the four regions of England, no party won as much as half the vote and in the North of England the Conservatives came first with as little as 38 per cent of the popular vote. But one party won a majority of the seats in every English region (Table V.3). One-party hegemony was nearly total in the South of England, where the Conservatives won 95 per cent of the 178 seats contested. In London and the Midlands, the Conservatives won more than two-thirds of the seats. In the North of England, Labour won 55 per cent of the region's 162 seats.

The most important feature of regional competition for parliamentary seats is that there is very little competition. Only in the North of England was there

Table. V.3  THE REGIONAL DISTRIBUTION OF SEATS IN ENGLAND

| | Conservative | Labour | Alliance | Total |
|---|---|---|---|---|
| | (% seats) | | | N |
| South of England | 95 | 2 | 3 | 178 |
| London | 67 | 31 | 2 | 84 |
| Midlands | 71 | 29 | 0 | 99 |
| North of England | 41 | 55 | 4 | 162 |
| Total England | 69 | 28 | 2 | 523 |

competition in 1983; the Conservatives were able to win four seats for every five won by Labour. In elections in the 1970s, the Midlands was the highly competitive region, with the Conservatives and Labour each winning a substantial number of seats. The North of England was a Labour stronghold, with Labour taking two-thirds or more of the seats there. The nationwide collapse of the Labour vote in 1983 shifted the locus of competition to the North of England. In the three regions south of a line drawn from Humberside to Merseyside one-party hegemony is currently the rule.

Conventional conceptions of centre-periphery cannot explain the Conservative hegemony. In London, indubitably central in any conception of England or the United Kingdom, the Conservative share of seats and votes was less than in the Midlands. Conservative hegemony is great only in the South of England. If a line is drawn from the mouth of the Thames to just south of Bristol, there is not a single Labour MP south of that line. In geographical terms, Conservative strength in Parliament increases as one moves toward the English Channel, in some places closer to France than to London. From this perspective, an historian could argue that Conservative strength is concentrated in the periphery of the Kingdom of Burgundy.

Regional influence upon parliamentary representation is not a function of regional culture or of social and economic characteristics of the regions; it is primarily a function of the first-past-the-post electoral system. The regional effect upon the Conservative vote averaged three per cent in 1983, but the electoral system manufactured an average difference of 24 per cent between the seats and the votes won by the Conservatives in a region (cf. Tables V.2-3). The average regional effect upon the Labour vote was four per cent in 1983; the mechanics of the electoral system turned this into an average disparity of nine per cent of parliamentary representation. The Alliance vote showed an average regional effect of less than three per cent. The regional effect of the electoral system on Alliance representation averaged 22 per cent.

If Britain were to adopt proportional representation, using regions as the constituencies for allocating seats, then virtually the whole of the discrepancy between seats and votes reported in Table V.3 would disappear. Instead of each region having hegemonic representation by one party, each region would be represented by a substantial fraction of Labour, Alliance and Conservative MPs. No party could dominate parliamentary representation in any English region.

In the first-past-the-post electoral system, the party that finishes second immediately gains nothing in parliamentary representation. But the party finishing second in a constituency can claim to be the opposition, expecting to benefit when the swing of the pendulum deprives the front-running party of votes. Conventionally, the party finishing third is dismissed. A vote cast for a third-place party is regarded as a wasted vote, in a way that a vote cast for a second-place party is not, for a favourable swing could make it the winning party in a constituency.

The three-way division of the vote in England in 1983 did not produce the same ordering of parties in every constituency. Had that been the case then the Conservatives would have won all 523 English seats, and Labour would have finished second 523 times. Of the six logically possible patterns of competition, three account for nearly all the constituency outcomes (Table V.4). In 48 per cent of English constituencies, the Conservative candidate finished first and an Alliance candidate second; in 25 per cent of constituencies the pattern of competition was Labour first and Conservative second; and in 22 per cent the pattern was Conservative first and Labour second (Table V.4).

The regional effect upon patterns of party competition is much less marked than the effect upon the distribution of seats. While every constituency by definition has a two-party system, that is, one party finishing first and another finishing second, only in the South of England is there a consistent pattern of competition between two parties. In the South of England, 82 per cent of constituency contests show the same pattern of party competition, Conservatives first and Alliance second. By contrast, in London and the Midlands there is no single pattern. In London 37 per cent of seats show a Conservative-Alliance pattern, 30 per cent a Conservative-Labour pattern,

Table V.4   PATTERNS OF PARTY COMPETITION IN ENGLAND

|  | South | London | Midlands | North | Total |
|---|---|---|---|---|---|
|  | (N constituencies) | | | | |
| **Conservatives first** | | | | | |
| Alliance second | 146 | 31 | 36 | 36 | 249 |
| Labour second | 23 | 25 | 34 | 31 | 113 |
| Total | 169 | 56 | 70 | 67 | 362 |
| **Labour first** | | | | | |
| Conservatives second | 4 | 22 | 29 | 76 | 131 |
| Alliance second | 0 | 4 | 0 | 13 | 17 |
| Total | 4 | 26 | 29 | 89 | 148 |
| **Alliance first** | | | | | |
| Conservatives second | 5 | 0 | 0 | 4 | 9 |
| Labour second | 0 | 2 | 0 | 2 | 4 |
| Total | 5 | 2 | 0 | 6 | 13 |

and 26 per cent a Labour-Conservative pattern. Similarly, the Midlands has a three-way division in patterns of party competition: 36 per cent have a Conservative-Alliance pattern, 34 per cent a Conservative-Labour pattern, and 29 per cent a Labour-Conservative pattern. In the North of England, there are also diverse patterns of competition; in 47 per cent of the constituencies the order is Labour-Conservative, in 22 per cent Conservative-Alliance, and in 19 per cent Conservative-Labour.

The systematic analysis of the division of votes, seats and patterns of party competition in England emphasizes that the influence of social structure and territory is contingent. It depends upon whether one is seeking to explain the distribution of votes in the mass electrate or seats in the House of Commons. If votes are the focus of attention, then social structure is by far the most important determinant. The social structure of England assures both the Conservatives and Labour a substantial vote. Territory exercises most influence upon electoral outcomes when attention is focussed upon the distribution of parliamentary seats. If attention is directed to party representation in the House of Commons, then regions that are multi-party in terms of votes or patterns of party competition tend to have their parliamentary representation dominated by a single party.

# VI
# The Faces of Wales

by

DENIS BALSOM

*University of Wales*

*Aberystwyth*

J. BARRY JONES

*University of Wales*

*Cardiff*

Welsh politics following the 1979 general election was strongly influenced by two factors; the devolution referendum of 1 March 1979 and the secular decline of Wales's traditional basic industries. In the referendum an overwhelming 79 per cent of the voters rejected the Labour Government's proposals. It was not merely a defeat for the nationalists; it also seriously weakened the Welsh political and cultural establishment. With the exception of the Conservatives, all political parties in Wales had supported devolution, together with the vast majority of Welsh religious denominations and most of the notables in the Welsh cultural community. However, on the evidence of the referendum, only the Conservatives had correctly judged the mood of the Welsh electorate; a factor reflected in the resurgence of the Conservative vote from 23.9 per cent in October 1974 to 32.2 per cent in May 1979. This suggested an erosion of the distinctive character of Welsh politics and its progressive acquisition of politico-cultural values of a wider British system (Foulkes *et al*, 1983:226).

The decline of Wales's industrial base was accelerated by the central tenet of the new Conservative government's economic policy: the attempt to cut back public expenditure. The policy had a disproportionate impact on Wales which in 1979 had approximately 43 per cent of its working population employed in the public sector. The most catastrophic change took place in the Welsh steel industry. On the eve of the 1979 election in Wales, the British Steel Corporation employed 63,000 steel workers; by May 1983 that number had plummeted to 19,000. Manufacturing industries declined from 312,000 to less than 226,000 and the numbers employed in the construction industries fell from 67,000 to 53,000 in the same period. The service sector, one of the few growth points in the Welsh economy during the 1970s, shed 41,000 workers drifting down from 563,000 to 522,000 (Welsh Regional Digest of Statistics 1982). The Welsh electorate in June 1983 voted in a political and economic environment markedly different from that in 1979.

## Political and Economic Developments, 1979-83

The most obvious consequence of the 1979 referendum was the abrupt removal from the political scene of the devolution issue, which had occupied a central position in Welsh politics since Gwynfor Evans' spectacular by-election victory in July 1966. The Conservative Party's argument, that Wales did not require fundamentally different treatment from the rest of the United Kingdom, appeared to be vindicated. The Labour and Liberal parties, impressed by the scale of the referendum defeat and threatened by the electoral advance of the Conservatives, adopted lower profiles on specifically Welsh issues and prudently dissociated themselves from the devolution policy. Furthermore, the problematic concept of a Welsh dimension in the formulation and presentation of central government policies was rendered more obscure and less certain.

However, the political and administrative *status quo* was not preserved by the referendum vote. During the referendum campaign the Conservatives had consistently argued that the problems of public accountability in Welsh administration could be resolved within the framework of the Westminster Parliament. On 26 June 1979, the day the House of Commons repealed the Wales Act by 191 votes to 8, the Welsh Secretary of State, Nicholas Edwards, announced the government's intention to establish a Select Committee on Welsh Affairs to examine the expenditure, administration and policy of the Welsh Office and associated public bodies (SO86A, 25 June 1979). After a series of disputes concerning the chairmanship, eventually resolved in favour of the Labour Party, the Committee came into operation in January 1980.

From the outset the Welsh media and public opinion tended to regard the Committee on Welsh Affairs as a substitute for a Welsh assembly. This was partly because of the tone of the debate during the later stages of the referendum campaign but it was also a point of view shared by a majority of the committee including the first chairman Leo Abse, a leading member of the Gang of Six, Labour MPs who had been largely responsible for defeating the devolution proposals in the referendum. A majority of the committee was enthusiastic to disprove the necessity for an elected assembly by exploiting the committee as a lobbyist for the Welsh interest; an option open to the committee only because of its impeccable anti-devolution credentials. In order to maximize its role the committee successfully sought a consensual approach. It addressed itself to issues with a distinctly nationalist tone: unemployment persistently and substantially above the United Kingdom average, Welsh-language broadcasting, and water in Wales. The committee's intention was not merely to focus the attention of the Welsh public on the Westminster parliamentary process, but also to prevent Plaid Cymru from pre-empting these issues and presenting itself as the sole custodian of the national interest.

The committee's first report published in August 1980 was highly critical of the government's economic policy and warned that there would be 'risks of serious social disorder if there were to be very high and chronic levels of unemployment, particularly among the young' (HC 731, 1980). The report, while not deflecting the government from its policy, proved acutely embarrassing. The committee's recommendations had the unanimous support of all six Conservative members of the committee; an indication of territorial interest taking precedence over partisan loyalties. However, the government rejected all but two of the recommendations (Cmnd 8085, 1980). Subsequently the Welsh Committee avoided direct confrontations on substantive policy issues and attempted instead to influence the policy implementation process, suggesting how the programming schedule for Channel 4 Wales might be planned, how the consumer interest in the Welsh Water Authority might be best protected and advocating an equalization of water rates across the whole of Britain. All were elements in the administration of public policy but none attracted the media publicity and the public interest generated by the Welsh Committee's first report.

The Committee on Welsh Affairs did not become a surrogate for an elected assembly. It failed to maintain the initial high level of public interest nor did it satisfy the, perhaps unrealistic, expectations which some people placed on it. In this situation the committee's intrinsic weaknesses become more apparent: a wide ranging remit which frustrated specialization and membership unrepresentative of the balance of political forces in Wales.

The distinctly Welsh political issues arose from the 1979 election. The Conservative Party, in common with all other parties in Wales, had campaigned with the commitment to establish a separate Welsh-language TV channel in Wales. In September 1979 the Home Secretary, William Whitelaw, announced the government's intention not to do so. The decision provoked widespread indignation in Wales. Attacks were made on TV transmitters in England and Wales by militant members of Cymdeithas yr Iaith Cymraeg (Welsh Language Society). A more circumspect Plaid Cymru organized a campaign of non-payment of TV licence fees. In the early summer of 1980 Plaid Cymru's President, Gwynfor Evans, announced his intention to fast to death from October unless the government backed down. There followed a series of intense negotiations between the government and various Welsh political figures resulting in the government's first U-turn. The Welsh Secretary admitted that the government had lost the middle ground of opinion in Wales and that a Welsh language TV channel would, after all, be established (*Arcade*, 14 May 1981). It was an uncompromising defeat for the government and an enormous boost for the morale of nationalist forces in Wales. It also emphazised the potency of extra-parliamentary action for those activists in the nationalist movement who had always regarded the devolution exercise as irrelevant to the real problems of Wales.

The process of incremental institutional reforms, characteristic of the development of the Welsh Office during the 1970s, was continued. In anticipation of devolution, plans were advanced for transferring responsibility for negotiating and distributing the Rate Support Grant (RSG) in Wales from the Department of the Environment to the Welsh Office, a responsiblity in Scotland already exercised by the Scottish Office. The momentum created was sufficient for this process to be completed despite the referendum. The new procedure, which came into operation in 1980 had two important consequences. It increased Welsh Office control of local authorities, and it separated the Welsh RSG from that of England, permitting territorial comparisons to be drawn. In December 1980 English local authorities complained to the Department of the Environment at the preferential treatment implicit in the Welsh RSG. The evidence appears to support the complaint. In the four years prior to 1981-82 Wales's share of the combined England and Wales RSG was 7.25 per cent. By 1982-83 it had increased to 7.6 per cent, a possible measure of the skill and tenacity with which the Welsh Office has been promoting Wales's case (*Arcade*, 12 December 1980).

The Welsh Office has not yet attained the position in Welsh political life enjoyed by the Scottish Office in Scotland. It emerged from the Welsh Affairs Committee's hearings that the British Steel Corporation in December 1979 had neglected to inform the Welsh Secretary of State of the impending run down of the two major steel plants in Wales. There are also doubts as to the level of consultation with the Welsh Office prior to the Home Secretary's decision to renege on the Welsh TV channel commitment. However the Welsh Office has continued to grow both in numbers and importance. Since August 1980 its 2,500 civil servants have occupied a palatial new building in Cathays Park, Cardiff costing £23 million. The convention whereby the two junior ministers are appointed, one from the north and one from the south, one Welsh-speaking and one not, was preserved and reaffirmed after the tragic death of Michael Roberts while speaking in a Welsh debate on the floor of the House of Commons in February 1983. His successor was John Stradling Thomas, also from the south.

The 1979-83 period also witnessed a fundamental shift in the Welsh economy. In four years the Welsh unemployment rate rose from 8.5 per cent in April 1979, to 16.7 per cent in May 1983. The trigger for this change was the decline of steel-making capacity in Wales. The cutback had serious implications for the coal industry in South Wales, and seriously eroded the rate income of three of the eight Welsh county councils.

The Wales TUC assumed the leadership in fighting BSC's proposals. George Wright, the Wales TUC Secretary called for a Welsh general strike but the hesitancy of the British TUC General Council, the opposition of some Welsh Labour MPs and the reluctance of the South Wales miners to endorse a general strike in a pit-head ballot effectively rejected the idea. In April 1980 James Callaghan, the previous Labour Prime Minister and MP for a Cardiff constituency, suggested setting up a Joint Standing Conference to include representatives of Welsh county and district councils, the Wales TUC and the CBI Wales. Initially, because of its heavy Labour bias, the CBI participated only as observers, but early in 1982 the body was formally established as the Welsh Committee for Economic and Industrial Affairs under the Chairmanship of Lord Cledwyn Hughes, a former Labour Welsh Secretary of State. The committee was intended to identify priority problems and to lobby the government to take account of Welsh needs. Thus, within three years of the government's elimination of the Welsh Council in August 1979, as part of its war on quangos, another body seeking to speak for Wales had arisen.

For a time, it appeared that the most effective reaction to the government's economic policies, would be that of the South Wales miners. In February 1981 the publication of the National Coal Board's plans to close seven Welsh pits, threatening 2,800 jobs provoked an all-out strike in the South Wales coalfield, which rapidly spread to other British coalfields. The government conceded, promising to curb imported coal, to sustain investment and agreed additional subsidies to the South Wales coalfield in excess of £30 million. It was however a short lived respite. Two years later in March 1983 when the Ty-Mawr- Lewis Merthyr pit was earmarked for closure a South Wales coalfield strike won little support elsewhere. The plans to reduce the South Wales coalfield by as much as a third had merely been deferred.

The belief that the economic problems in Wales were qualitatively different from the rest of the United Kingdom encouraged the Wales TUC to investigate the possibility of dealing with the job crisis by establishing co-operatives. In January 1981 representatives of the Wales TUC visited Mondragon Co-operative in the Basque area of Northern Spain as part of a £45,000 feasibility study financed by the Welsh Office. As a result the Wales TUC was instrumental in setting up the Wales Worker Co-operative Development and Training Centre in April 1983, funded equally by the Welsh Office and the EEC social fund, with substantial contributions from the Welsh Development

Agency, Mid Wales Development and all the Welsh county councils. It is too soon to measure its impact.

The economic picture was not entirely black. New jobs were attracted to Wales despite the recession. INMOS, a microchip company, established production facilities in Wales with the promise of 2000 jobs. The Welsh Development Agency continued its extensive factory-building programme, including the Ford Motor Company engine plant in Bridgend, where by the end of 1980 the workforce had grown to 1,800. From 1979 to 1983 the WDA built in excess of 700 factories, for an estimated 10,000 jobs.

Confronted by structural contraction of the Welsh economy, the political parties were curiously quiet. The Conservative Party in Wales could argue the government's policies were vindicated by the party's electoral advances in Wales. Furthermore, consistent with the party's earlier position Welsh Conservatives were reluctant to regard Wales as separate from the rest of the UK or as facing problems distinctly different. However, some Conservatives, members of the Welsh Affairs Committee and the CBI Wales, were apprehensive of the impact of government policies in Wales, and criticized the party's prevailing monetarist philosophy (HC 731, 1980).

The devolution experience had left the Labour Party in some disarray. Following the 1979 general election it set about distancing itself from the devolution policy, a task made easier by the resignation of some pro-devolutionists within the party and the retirement of Emrys Jones, the Welsh Regional Organiser and Secretary, who had been a major architect of the devolution proposals. Devolution ceased to exist as a policy option; it was not even debated in Welsh Labour Conferences. For most party activists it was a painful memory best forgotten. However, the appointment of John Prescott as Labour Party Spokesman on Regional Affairs and devolution was evidence of the PLP's continuing concern - if not commitment. Prescott (1981) noted of Wales:

> There is a strong feeling that devolution as previously put forward is less relevant than ever. However it was made clear to us that reform of local government, the advent of unitary authorities and possibility of regional government, would be acceptable in Wales provided that it was undertaken within the context of the UK framework and not one that treated Wales separately.

The Welsh Labour Party acquired an attitude of circumspection, tending to follow initiatives taken by the Wales TUC and subsequently endorsing the stand taken by Labour groups in Welsh local authorities in declaring the whole of Wales a Nuclear Free Zone in March 1982. The Labour Party in Wales was not riven by the activities of the militant tendency as were many parties in England and Scotland. The vast majority of Welsh Labour MPs were on the right of the party and members of the Solidarity Campaign; the Labour Coordinating Committee was able to recruit only one Welsh MP. The activities of the new hard left made relatively little impact on a traditionally working-class and socially conservative party.

The Welsh Liberals had been discomfited by the 1979 general election and Emlyn Hooson, its leader, lost out to the Conservative challenge in Montgomery. However the party's fortunes were revitalized by the defection of three Labour MPs to the SDP. The first, Tom Ellis, Wrexham's Labour MP, announced his intention to break with Labour in January, 1981. Referring to the traditions of Welsh radicalism, he percipiently advocated an alliance with the Liberals, several months before the idea was broached in the rest of Britain. The Alliance in Wales was forged with little rancour and operated with genuine commitment and enthusiasm.

The party most chastened by the referendum and the general election was Plaid Cymru whose vote was reduced to 8 per cent in 1979. In the post mortem that followed the election, a left-right split emerged between the traditionalists, committed to a decentralized community socialism, and the left-wing, grouped around Dafydd Elis Thomas, who emphasized the need to establish a Welsh Socialist State by means of a popular front movement encompassing nationalists and the Welsh labour movement. The picture was further complicated by the emergence of a splinter group, the Welsh Socialist Republicans, which was highly critical of Plaid Cymru's attachment to constitutionalism. A drift to unconstitutional activities in the years following the 1979 election revealed that Plaid Cymru was in danger of losing the initiative within the nationalist movement. By December, 1980 there had been 42 arson attacks on second home holiday cottages owned by English people. Operation Fire - a joint police action, made a sweep throughout Wales on 31 March 1980, detaining or arresting over 50 people. Eventually four were brought to trial and convicted. During 1981 a series of thirteen bomb attacks led to the arrest of seven men on conspiracy charges. Some were held in custody awaiting a trial which was still pending at the time of the general election.

Gwynfor Evans' decision to retire from the position of party president obliged Plaid to choose between a continuation of the traditional nationalism, represented by Dafydd Wigley, and the strident left-wing socialism advocated by Dafydd Elis Thomas. Many in Plaid Cymru were unhappy with Thomas's sympathetic attitude towards the Northern Ireland hunger strikers and deplored his initiative in moving the writ for the Fermanagh and South Tyrone by-election. While Dafydd Wigley's election as President in October 1981 confirmed that Plaid Cymru would remain a broad left nationalist party the debate was not closed.

Confronted by distinctly different problems, all political parties in Wales were equally confused as to their future role and influence in Welsh life. What was clear, however, was that the tragic death of Welsh Guardsmen in Bluff

Cove did not lead to increased questioning of the British connection, as many nationalists had hoped and expected. In fact the very reverse happened and the Conservatives benefited from the Falkland's factor as much in Wales as in England.

Whereas a constant succession of monthly polls subject public opinion in Britain to intense scrutiny, in Wales such polls are infrequent and irregular. Between May, 1979 and May, 1983, the commencement of the election campaign, four national polls were conducted in Wales. The Welsh pattern mirrors the British pattern but in a slightly different fashion (Table VI.1 and Table II.3). In the face of the growth of support for the SDP-Liberal Alliance, and the later post-Falklands Conservative revival, Labour support appeared to wither. Labour entered the 1983 campaign in Wales endorsed by 44 per cent of popular opinion, their lowest share of the vote at a general election in Wales since 1931. The Conservatives at 38 per cent appeared set for a major triumph. Doubt about the solidity of Conservative support, however, had been raised by the impact upon it during the honeymoon era of the newly formed SDP-Liberal Alliance. The HTV poll taken in September, 1981, showed the substantial support for the Alliance was gained almost wholly at the expense of the Conservative Party. The Alliance, then declined in favour during 1982, in line with British trends. The position of Plaid Cymru in the polls remained relatively static confirming a low base level of support.

Table VI.1   PUBLIC OPINION IN WALES, 1979–83

|  | 1979 | HTV poll 9/81 | Marplan 9/82 | HTV poll 3/83 | HTV poll 5/83 | 1983 |
|---|---|---|---|---|---|---|
|  |  | (% party preference) | | | | |
| Labour | 48 | 44 | 41 | 42 | 44 | 38 |
| Conservative | 33 | 16 | 36 | 36 | 38 | 31 |
| Alliance/Liberal | 11 | 34[b] | 19 | 16 | 14 | 23 |
| Plaid Cymru | 8 | 7 | 4 | 5 | 5 | 8 |

[a]   All results adjusted to exclude minor parties, don't knows.

[b]   Question specifically emphasized SDP/Liberal Alliance.

Aside from local elections, which in Wales are unreliable guides to the potential division of opinion at parliamentary elections, there was only one major electoral indicator of opinion during the 1979-83 period: the Gower by-election. This by-election, held on 16 September 1982, was the first to be called in Wales since that at Merthyr Tydfil in March, 1972. The late 1960s and early 1970s had seen a succession of by-elections at which Plaid Cymru had done much to disrupt the traditional pattern of party allegiances in Wales. The Gower by-election was in an area with a relatively high proportion of Welsh-speakers, and presented the Alliance with its first opportunity to launch a challenge in Wales, with an effervescent candidate, Gwynoro Jones. A number of opinion polls were conducted during the campaign. The Alliance gained considerable ground in the last few days; support was drawn from Labour rather than the Conservatives in the proportion of 2 to 1. But Gower never threatened to emulate Hillhead, Crosby or Croydon North West. Labour retained the seat with 44 per cent of the poll, the SDP returned 25 per cent, ahead of the Conservatives with 22 per cent and Plaid Cymru 9 per cent.

The HTV poll of March 1983, the last taken before the date of the election was known, showed Labour at 42 per cent, less popular than before, while the Conservatives were at a high point at 36 per cent. Questions about issues showed that unemployment, predominantly the most important issue for the electorate, was becoming increasingly depoliticized as the electorate despaired of any party's ability to provide a remedy; almost 30 per cent felt that no party was able to deal with the problem. Wales appeared anti-unilateralist, divided on the deployment of Cruise missiles and continuation of membership of the Common Market. The leadership of Margaret Thatcher was widely acclaimed, while that of Michael Foot roundly deprecated, even by half of those intending to vote Labour. This profile of political discontent was broadly in line with that being reported for the remainder of Britain. Wales showed a more British face than had been seen in modern times.

## Preparations for the Campaign

The electoral map for much of Wales has remained virtually unchanged for many years. The House of Commons (Redistribution of Seats) Act 1949 recommended an increase to 36 in the number of MPs returned from Wales; since then further change had been relatively slight. Thirteen Welsh constituencies had remained unaltered for 60 odd-years, notwithstanding a relatively high degree of social and economic change in Wales.

Since the previous electoral review, a major restructuring of Welsh local government had occurred; this had the effect of both exacerbating the boundary problems yet providing the opportunity for their resolution. On the basis of the old 13-county Wales, grave inequalities in the number of electors had grown up between constituencies; by 1981 the electorate of Merioneth was 27,619 compared with 85,272 in Monmouth. Rule 4 of the Boundary Commission's guidelines (Cmnd 8798) placed a high premium upon respecting county boundaries. After the local government reorganization of 1974, however, this rule was applied only to the eight new counties, leaving the new district authorities available to be divided. The Boundary Commissioners concluded:

> It was apparent, however, that our proposals would have to disrupt long-established ties in safe areas and whilst we recognised that they would cause disturbance, we considered that we would be failing in our duty if our recommendations perpetuated the current inequalities of representation (Cmnd 8798, para 12).

Using the wards of the district councils as their building blocks, and working within the framework of the existing number of seats, 36, a quota of seats per county could be established and provisional recommendations were accordingly published on 25 June 1981. Only two seats remained undisturbed, Rhondda and Cardiff West. Initial reaction to these provisional proposals centred upon the Commission's emphasis upon achieving equality in electorates between constituencies.

> In our electoral system a reasonable parity of electorate has to be a major consideration ... we had begun by applying that criteria fairly strictly. We emphasised, however, that we were prepared to be flexible and that we would welcome constructive suggestions ... (Cmnd 8798, para. 20).

A meeting with representatives of the parties in Westminster led the Commissioners to note with masterly understatement: 'we were left in no doubt as to their general reactions to our recommendations ...' (Cmnd 8798, para. 20). Although debate arose throughout Wales the focus of discontent fell upon the proposals for Gwynedd, Mid Glamorgan and for Gwent and Powys.

In Gwynedd, population size dictated the allocation of only three seats, causing the Commission to combine Anglesey with Bangor and to create a corridor constituency, Aberconwy and Meirionnydd, stretching from Llandudno to Aberdovey. Apart from geographical considerations of size and communications, these recommendations appeared likely to cost Plaid Cymru one of their parliamentary seats. Its opposition was intense. After the public inquiry the Assistant Commissioner advocated allocating four seats to Gwynedd by maintaining Anglesey as one seat (Ynys Mon) leaving Caernarfon unchanged, and dividing the Aberconwy District to form two seats one combined with the tiny Meirionnydd. This scheme:

> ... had the advantage of taking into account not only the special geographical
> considerations applicable to the country, but also community, linguistic and
> cultural factors ... these advantages justified the low constituency electorates and
> recommended ... adoption (Cmnd 8798, para. 88).

Further to some petty quibbles over names this revised scheme was adopted and
Wales had a thirty-seventh constituency.

Mid Glamorgan required perhaps the greatest redrawing of constituency
boundaries, due to the way the old Glamorgan county had been divided
between the new counties of Mid, West and South Glamorgan. Bridgend was to
be created out of the old Ogmore and Aberavon constituencies, as altered by
the new Mid Glamorgan and West Glamorgan boundary. The argument
centred upon whether the division of Ogmore should be made on an East-West
axis, as recommended by the Commission, or on a North-South axis. The
location of the highly lucrative Ogmore Labour Club, now potentially isolated
from the newly proposed Ogmore seat, probably did much to fire the
controversy. In the end the provisional proposals were largely confirmed.
Around Merthyr the Commissioners were accused of being particularly
insensitive to the traditional valley pattern of constituencies. Several
communities were allocated to constituencies whose centre was 'over the
mountain'. In the main these objections were upheld and the proposals revised
accordingly.

The principal objection to the proposals for Gwent and Powys was that the
Commissioners had been sufficiently influenced by considerations of
population size to override their own guide lines of integral counties. In terms of
electorates, Powys had a theoretical entitlement to 1.4 seats and Gwent to 5.6
seats. Together they could be allocated seven seats. Furthermore, within Gwent
the Commissioners' plans had paid scant heed to existing units:

> We had anticipated that the abandonment of the traditional valley pattern in
> Gwent would provoke comment from the public but the strength of the reaction
> convinced us that a different approach for Gwent would be necessary. (Cmnd
> 8798, para 188).

Following the Assistant Commissioner's recommendations, two seats were
allocated to Powys and six to Gwent, enabling the traditional valley pattern to
be largely retained in Gwent. Wales had gained a thirty-eighth constituency.

The net result of the Boundary Commission's recommendations was to align
the new seats with the new counties, leaving only three seats totally unchanged
from the previous review. Seven of the new constituencies were coterminus with
district boundaries and eighteen districts were not divided between
constituencies. Prior to the 1983 election an academic study team attempted to
analyze the political effects of the boundary changes and in Wales estimated

that both Labour and Conservatives would have gained a seat (BBC-ITN, 1983).

Notwithstanding the constitutional changes wrought within the Labour party, no Labour candidate was deselected in Wales. The defection of three Labour members to the SDP, Tom Ellis (Wrexham), Jeffrey Thomas (Abertillery) and Ednyfed Hudson-Davies (Caerphilly) may have forestalled deselection battles.

The division of seats between the Alliance partners in Wales was aided by the fact that none of the three Labour defectors to the SDP had intended to fight their seats again, all affected by the boundary changes. Ednyfed Hudson-Davies elected to contest an English home counties seat. Jeffrey Thomas, formerly MP for Abertillery intended to fight a Cardiff seat and Tom Ellis from Wrexham indicated his intention to stand elsewhere in Clwyd. The Alliance division of seats gave 19 to each party. Using the BBC-ITN notional 1979 results for the new constituencies, the average base figure from which the Alliance had to build was 14.0 per cent for the seats allocated to the Liberals and 8.7 per cent for those assigned to the SDP. However, the Liberal Party had usually polled badly in industrial South Wales, and the SDP hoped to cut into the Labour vote there, as it showed was possible at the Gower by-election.

The biggest intra-party row over nomination came from the unexpected quarter of the Conservative Party. The Boundary Commission recommendations created an additional seat in Clwyd: the existing seats of Denbigh and West Flint were, effectively, re-aligned into three seats, Clwyd North West, Clwyd South West and Delyn, with the former being potentially the safest Conservative prospect. The two sitting Conservative MPs, Sir Anthony Meyer and Geraint Morgan, initially competed against each other for nomination to Clwyd North West; both were outflanked by supporters of Beata Brookes, the MEP for North Wales. As both MPs were somewhat out of step with Thatcherite Conservatism, the hand of Central Office was alleged to have been at work in orchestrating the Brookes nomination campaign. Sir Anthony Meyer resorted to a High Court injunction to have Miss Brookes' nomination overturned and his own assured by a general meeting of the Constituency Association. Legal action was also resorted to by the opponents of Peter Hubbard-Miles, the Conservative candidate, and subsequent new MP for Bridgend. Hubbard-Miles had earlier beaten-off a carpet-bagging intrusion for the nomination from a close associate of Norman Tebbitt, an event which precipitated the resignations of all the officers of the local association. Subsequently, allegations of a packed selection conference led to an injunction being taken out against Hubbard-Miles, but the approach of polling day calmed the furore and local Conservatives closed ranks and set about winning the seat.

When nominations closed for the general election four major-party candidates had been drafted for each of the 38 new constituencies. Plaid Cymru continued to fight all the Welsh seats, even though their prospects in many were known to be minimal.

## The Election Campaign

The 1983 campaign, by comparison with those in the 1970s, was deficient in specifically Welsh issues. The demise of devolution and the dominant role of the media and public opinion polls, both of which tended to adopt a metropolitan orientation, contributed to the essential 'Britishness' of the campaign in Wales. The same issues were raised, standardized arguments deployed and, in most cases, similar conclusions reached.

Despite the referendum, a reaffirmation by the Welsh electorate of their intention to remain unambiguously British, the British parties still found it expedient to defer in some way to the elusive concept of the Welsh identity. All three British major party groupings produced separate Welsh Manifestos, although none was quite as extensive as the 28-page document, *The Only Alternative*, produced by Plaid Cymru. Labour's manifesto, *New Hope for Wales*, claimed 'that Wales, with its unique identity and aspirations, has its own special needs and interests'. In surprisingly similar phrasing the *Conservative Manifesto for Wales* asserted 'Wales has its special characteristics and problems;' while the Alliance document, *The Priorities for Wales*, assumed for themselves 'the strongest possible sense of Welsh identity' and proceded to 'reject the jingoism of Mrs. Thatcher, the isolationism of Michael Foot and the inward-looking nationalism of Plaid Cymru'. The Labour and Conservative manifestos specifically and the Alliance document implicitly emphasized the essential political and economic unity of the United Kingdom. All three manifestos faithfully covered those major policy issues central to the electoral campaign Britainwide.

There were predictable differences between the parties on the vexed question of the Welsh economy. Where Labour argued for increased public investment in the traditional coal and steel industries, a demand echoed in a more muted tone, by the Alliance, the Conservatives emphasized the need to modernize and diversify the Welsh economy, conceding that pits would have to close.

Another specifically Welsh issue to re-emerge was leasehold reform. Both Labour and the Alliance promised to outlaw leaseholds on all new properties but whereas the Alliance argued that a fair price should be established to enable an owner-occupier to purchase the leasehold, Labour emphasized the need for local authorities to be given the right to acquire freeholds. Plaid advocated the complete abolition of the leasehold system. The issue was ignored by the Conservative manifesto. Also ignored by the Conservatives and the Alliance were the tendentious issues of Welsh water charges and second homes. Both were taken up by Plaid Cymru and the Labour Party. Although there were clear differences in tone and presentation, the positions of the two parties was broadly similar. They deplored the repeal of the 1977 Water Charges Equilisation Act and both wanted an equalization policy to close the gap between water rate charges in England and Wales. Similarly on second homes (that is holiday homes owned by English people) both parties wanted local authorities in areas with high concentrations of second homes, estimated by the Welsh Office at 30,000, to be given first refusal to purchase when such properties appeared on the market.

Devolution was conspicuous by its absence from the manifestos. The only named reference to it appeared in the Conservative manifesto which, recalling that devolution had been overwhelmingly rejected in the referendum by the Welsh people, went on to claim that government had been brought closer to the Welsh people as a result of the enlarged responsibilities of the Welsh Office and improved parliamentary scrutiny of its work. Labour in a section entitled *Democratic Change in Wales* studiously avoided the actual word 'devolution' and reiterated its rejection of 'any policies which could separate Wales in any way from the rest of Britain'. However, Labour did call for an Economic Planning Council for Wales consisting of representatives from the Welsh Office, the TUC, CBI and Welsh local authorities, but carefully refrained from detailing its exact functions.

The Alliance manifesto also avoided mentioning the term. Instead it talked about the maximum decentralization of power and the restoration of real responsibility of local government, sentiments remarkably similar to those expressed by Plaid Cymru. Rather enigmatically the Alliance document proceded to declare that its ultimate objective was for democratically elected bodies in Wales to take over functions of undemocratic nominated bodies. This was significantly different from the wording employed by the Alliance in their British Manifesto which talked of providing a 'framework for decentralisation to assemblies (our emphasis) in Wales and the English regions'. When questioned about the discrepancy between the two documents, Lord Hooson, the Alliance's Welsh campaign leader, acknowledged: 'We have not yet done sufficient work on this and it is not part of our priorities' (*Western Mail*, 18 May 1983). This was the closest that any political party came to advocating devolution.

Significantly, Plaid Cymru completely ignored devolution and restored national independence to its pre-eminent position. In the introduction to its manifesto sub-titled, *England's Rule of Wales Must End*, Plaid presented the rationale for its electoral campaign:

> Wales has never elected a majority of Tory MPs. Yet we suffer Tory government most of the time. Wales has different social values and aspirations to England. Yet

we are forced to suffer English right-wing Tory policies because we are tied to England's apron strings.

The central message of Plaid Cymru's manifesto was thus qualitively different from the programmes presented by the three British parties.

The predominance of British issues was even more prevalent in the election campaign in Wales. The broad lines of inter-party dispute laid down by the London morning press conferences were faithfully reflected in the interests, concerns and pronouncements of the Welsh media and politicians. Only at the margins did issues arise which, if not unique to Wales, had a particular significance for the Welsh economy or politics.

The question of EEC membership, which made virtually no impact on Britain as a whole, intruded intermittently throughout the Welsh campaign. On 16 May the *Daily Mail* reported that Nissan, a Japanese car firm, intended to scrap plans to establish a car assembly plant in Britain if Labour won because of the party's commitment to leave the EEC. The story touched a raw nerve in Wales, for three Welsh locations were among the eight British sites shortlisted for Nissan development. Later in the same week at the launch of the Alliance Welsh manifesto, Tom Ellis warned that 100,000 jobs were at risk in Wales if Britain left the European Community.

The European issue was sustained during the Welsh campaign because it so obviously discomfited the Labour Party. It also embarrassed Plaid Cymru whose policy shift to accept EEC membership encouraged other parties to condemn the nationalists for placing electoral considerations (the votes of Welsh farmers) before principle. Labour itself, raised the issue later in the campaign. On 1 June Alan Williams, the Labour candidate for Swansea West, announced after a meeting with Ian MacGregor that the British Steel Corporation feared that their plans to modernize the hot strip mill in Port Talbot might be vetoed by the EEC Commission, which was concerned that this would increase Britain's steel-making capacity. The Conservatives hotly denied Labour's interpretation.

Wales figured early in the round-Britain circus of the party leaders. Michael Foot spoke at Cardiff City Hall on 18 May. Amid scenes of great enthusiasm recalling campaigns of the 1950s Michael Foot attacked the Tories on unemployment. He condemned the Tory Welsh Manifesto as a 'wickedly complacent document and pointed to the fact that the number of people working in Wales is the smallest recorded' (*Western Mail*, 19 May 1983). Five days later Mrs. Thatcher spoke in the same building to similar rapturous applause. In her speech she noted that Michael Foot had been unable to stop the closure of Ebbw Vale Steel Works in his own constituency. She went on to condemn Welsh Labour Party leaders for selling Wales short, 'presenting her to the world with an image of dereliction and hopelessness. Some encourage strikes and disputes, regardles of the jobs they destroyed. The people of Wales have rejected all that' (*South Wales Echo*, 24 May 1983).

Labour's standing in Wales was further compromised by James Callaghan's attack on the Labour Party's unilateralist defence policies, in a speech to constituents in Penarth near Cardiff. Callaghan's multilateralist views were well known, but his decision to repeat his views during the campaign had national consequences, not least the extraordinary 'I'm the leader' declaration made by Michael Foot at Labour's press conference the following day. The reaction in South Wales was immediate and bitter. Ray Davies, Labour's candidate in an adjoining Cardiff constituency, described the Callaghan speech as a 'stab in the back' while Ray Powell from neighbouring Ogmore denounced Callaghan's remarks and declined to share the same platform in a Labour meeting arranged for 3 June in the new - and marginal - Bridgend constituency.

At one time it seemed possible that Plaid Cymru might generate some publicity out of what they described as the 'blatantly unfair carve up' of party political broadcasts; the Alliance was allocated 40 minutes TV time compared to Plaid Cymru's 10 minutes. Plaid Cymru's criticisms reflected the difficulties faced by British broadcasting organizations making decisions where territorial differentiations complicate the Britainwide pattern. Plaid Cymru voiced a similar criticism over the Robin Day *It's Your Call* programme, in which Welsh and Scottish Nationalist leaders were obliged to share a programme, in contrast to the Ecology Party, which had a complete programme. However, after a few days Plaid Cymru quietly let the matter drop.

Not only had many of the geographical names on the political map of Wales altered, after the election their political colour and many of the faces of those who represent them had altered too. With a greater degree of competition existing between the two major parties in Wales the previous certainty of result diminished. Consequently, Wales returned a body of MPs probably more diverse than ever before. The combined effects of SDP defection, new boundaries and electoral change restructured the Welsh parliamentary group. Furthermore, an analysis of the Welsh MPs published shortly after the election (*Western Mail*, 12 July 1983) showed 11 of the 38 to be non-Welsh born. These trends may suggest that Wales is becoming more like England where the local link of MP and community appears weaker, a surprising development when considered alongside increasingly independent Welsh institutional structures, many of which place a high premium upon local origins, and sometimes facility in the Welsh language.

The crucial question arising from the election results is to what extent Wales remains a distinct political entity or has been subsumed within Britainwide influences.

The BBC-ITN notional 1979 results for the new constituencies estimated that the 38 seats in Wales would have divided Conservatives 12, Labour 23 (including the Speaker), Liberals 1 and Plaid Cymru 2. The outcome of the 1983 election, with Wales electing 14 Conservatives, 20 Labour MPs and 2 each from Plaid Cymru and the Liberal-SDP Alliance, showed a change of four seats. The Conservatives lost Montgomery but gained the new constituencies of Bridgend, Cardiff West and Newport West, all of which might have been deemed to have been notional Labour constituencies. Although the Conservatives secured their highest number of seats in Wales this century, their proportion of the poll was lower than that secured in 1979 or 1959. Labour's share of the poll sank to a 60-year low while Plaid Cymru's support remained relatively static at eight per cent. The major change was caused by the newly formed Liberal-SDP Alliance which, in gaining 23.2 per cent of the vote, surpassed the peaks of previous Liberal revivals. The Liberals alone had not secured such a proportion of the poll since 1929, when they won nine seats.

The SDP-Liberal upsurge reduced the majorities of other parties rather than winning seats for the Alliance. Wales has long been an area of relatively low electoral turnover and very large majorities, especially for the Labour Party. The changes introduced by the Boundary Commission altered this, and together with the 1983 shift in votes, transformed the relative marginality of the Welsh constituencies. Ten of the new Welsh constituencies are now highly marginal with majorities of under five per cent, compared with just two after the 1979 election. While Labour still dominates the seats in the super-safe category with majorities over 25 per cent, Dafydd Wigley has made Caernarfon a super-safe seat for Plaid Cymru. The Alliance vote had the effect of reducing Labour majorities; Labour's average majority has declined by ten points from the 1979 results. The net effect has been to increase the number of Labour marginals and of safe Conservative seats, factors of importance at future elections.

A brief examination of the county breakdown of results shows how the face of Welsh politics has been altered. Only in traditional South Wales does Labour retain its dominance; the area of the historic coalfield, now enclosed within Mid and West Glamorgan and Gwent. The new county of South Glamorgan is firmly Conservative, with the Alliance pressing Labour very hard for second place. Rural Wales exhibits genuine multi-party politics with the Conservatives ahead in all four counties. Labour remains relatively strong in Dyfed, due to the West Wales coalfield. Plaid Cymru is virtually equal to the Conservatives in Gwynedd, while the Alliance has a firm foothold in Powys and Clwyd.

The aggregate evidence suggests that the Alliance secured its support almost wholly at the expense of the Labour Party, whereas earlier poll evidence in Wales had suggested that Conservative support might be most vulnerable to the Alliance. A further series of polls conducted by HTV during the campaign allows some analysis of the patterns of partisan movement, the so-called flow of the vote. These campaign polls showed the steady erosion of Labour support and the gradual advance of the Alliance. In line with national polls, there appeared to have been a small swing away from the Conservatives in the last few days of the campaign.

The data also revealed the relatively high degree of volatility among supporters of all political parties. Within the campaign period of four weeks, considerable shifts occurred. This is not a novel finding, but evidence of a neglected phenomena generally hidden by the mutual balancing of shifts between parties. The polls also showed that the greatest fluctuations were between those formerly having a party preference and those reporting they were Don't Know's. An analysis of the preferences of undecided voters provides evidence suggesting a cycle of indecision and decision. Rather than switch directly between parties, most respondents assume an intermediate Don't Know position, and then finally adopt a new party preference. The evidence suggests that 2.5 former Don't Knows were shifting to the Alliance for each one opting Labour or Conservative. Furthermore, the Labour Party exhibited the greatest degree of doubt, losing the highest proportion of its support to Don't Knows.

The party most susceptible to voter volatility in Wales is the Labour Party. During the life of the panel survey Labour voters had four possible courses of action. Consistent Labour supporters maintained their Labour affiliation throughout; of the original Labour sample, 65 per cent proved to be consistent. Waverers recorded a different preference by the first panel recall but then reverted to the Labour Party, a pattern adopted by a further 15 per cent of the original Labour group. The remaining 20 per cent are made up of early changers who had deserted Labour in the first week of the campaign (19 per cent), and late changers who moved away from Labour immediately prior to the election (one per cent).

By adapting the HTV poll of early May 1983, it is possible to construct a socio-economic profile for each of the main parties (Table 6.2). For the Labour and Conservative parties the most distinctive feature is the class bias of their supporters. Labour attracts the support of nearly half the semi-skilled and unskilled workers, the DE social category, yet only 13 per cent of the AB professional and managerial group. The Conservatives attract the support of some 45 per cent of this latter group, while gaining one-fifth of the DE group. This clear pattern of differentiation is not repeated for sex, age or language. By contrast, support for the Alliance appears remarkably uniform. In Wales as a whole, the Alliance polled 23 per cent of the vote; in each subsection of the electorate, defined by age, sex, class, language and employment, the Alliance maintains a similar proportion of support. Support for Plaid Cymru shows two distinct characteristics, a white-collar bias in social groups AB and C1, and a

Table VI.2 PROFILES OF PARTY SUPPORTERS IN WALES 1983

|  | Total | Sex | | Age | | | Class | | | | Language | | Employment | |
|---|---|---|---|---|---|---|---|---|---|---|---|---|---|---|
|  |  | M | F | 18/34 | 35/64 | 65+ | AB | C1 | C2 | DE | Welsh spkr | Non W/spkr | In work | Unemployed |
|  |  |  |  |  |  |  | (% party preference) |  |  |  |  |  |  |  |
| Labour | 38 | 38 | 37 | 40 | 36 | 39 | 13 | 26 | 41 | 49 | 28 | 41 | 31 | 48 |
| Conservative | 31 | 28 | 34 | 32 | 30 | 33 | 45 | 42 | 32 | 20 | 25 | 33 | 36 | 17 |
| Alliance | 23 | 25 | 21 | 20 | 26 | 23 | 27 | 22 | 21 | 25 | 23 | 23 | 22 | 27 |
| Plaid Cymru | 8 | 9 | 7 | 8 | 9 | 6 | 15 | 10 | 6 | 7 | 24 | 2 | 11 | 9 |
| Totals | 100 | 49 | 51 | 31 | 49 | 20 | 10 | 21 | 34 | 35 | 26 | 74 | 36 | 10 |

Source: HTV Poll May 1983, N: 1235, Voting intention weighted to replicate the general election result.

disproportionate strength among the Welsh-speaking population. Overall, it is the division of partisan opinion among the minority who are Welsh-speakers that is the most striking aspect of this analysis. Genuine multi-party politics exists within this section of the Welsh electorate with each party having the support of about one-quarter of the Welsh-speaking population.

Although the Conservatives secured a landslide victory, in Wales Labour retained its overall lead in the vote, winning ten per cent more than Labour's Britainwide total. Labour led in all age groups and among Welsh-speakers and non-Welsh-speakers. Nonetheless, the Conservatives had a clear lead over Labour among middle-class voters. Increasingly, Wales is not a homogenous political community. Just as the impact of social and economic change has been uneven, so the political behaviour of particular localities has varied.

More than before, distinct political regions are discernible within Wales. Such variation that exists between the pattern of political behaviour of Wales and the rest of Britain is most accurately described by concentration upon the politically distinct parts of Wales. For the purposes of this analysis, Wales comprises three distinct political regions: Y Fro Gymraeg, the Welsh-speaking heartland; Welsh Wales, the classic South Wales former coalfield area; and British Wales, the indistinct remainder of the Principality.

To assess the relative importance of regional divisions, a model of voting behaviour in Wales was developed utilizing the known relationships between party support and aggregate socio-economic measures derived from the census. When the estimates of the party vote produced by this model are compared with the actual pattern of votes in each of the three regions of Wales, the relative significance of regions can be discerned (Table 6.3). In most cases the differences between observed and predicted party votes are small. However, a pattern does emerge: in Y Fro Gymraeg, the Labour vote is depressed, and that

Table VI.3   REGIONAL INFLUENCES ON THE VOTE IN WALES

| Region[a] | Con. | | | Labour | | | Alliance | | | Plaid Cymru | | |
|---|---|---|---|---|---|---|---|---|---|---|---|---|
| | Act | Prd | Df | Act | Prd | Df | Act | Prd | Df | Act | Prd | Df |
| | | | | | (% vote) | | | | | | | |
| Y Fro Gymraeg | 31 | 31 | 0 | 19 | 31 | −12 | 20 | 15 | +5 | 29 | 17 | +12 |
| Welsh Wales | 19 | 23 | −4 | 54 | 46 | +8 | 20 | 18 | +2 | 6 | 7 | −1 |
| British Wales | 41 | 38 | +3 | 29 | 31 | −2 | 27 | 19 | +8 | 3 | 6 | −3 |

[a]  See Appendix A for the definition of regions.

for Plaid Cymru is higher; in British Wales the Alliance vote is larger than its social composition would have suggested; and in traditional Welsh Wales the Labour vote remains inflated.

When political regions are included in the model alongside elements of social structure in Wales, the relative importance of each characteristic for each party can be calculated (Table 6.4). The results demonstrate that within Wales region can be at least as important as class as an influence on voting. In British Wales the Conservatives added 11.1 per cent to their base vote; in traditional Welsh Wales Labour added 12.5 per cent; and Plaid Cymru benefited by 10.3 per cent in Y Fro Gymraeg. Only the Alliance vote appears unresponsive to regional or any other influences, confirming Alliance's support independent of any particular cleavage or division within society. However, the most important factor in explaining voting behaviour in Wales is the impact size of the Welsh-speaking population upon support for Plaid Cymru. Any geographic dimension in the pattern of Welsh voting will also be highly inter-related with the concept of subjective national identity (Balsom *et al* , 1982). Although the

Table VI.4   SOCIAL STRUCTURE, TERRITORIAL AND LINGUISTIC INFLUENCES ON THE VOTE IN WALES[a]

|  | Con. | % var. | Labour | % var. | Alliance | % var. | Plaid Cymru | % var. |
|---|---|---|---|---|---|---|---|---|
|  | b | expl'd | b | expl'd | b | expl'd | b | expl'd |
| **Social Structure** | | | | | | | | |
| Socio-ec status | .31** | 14 | −.34** | 17 | .07 | 1 | −.03 | 2 |
| Agriculture | .08 | 10 | −.13* | 18 | .09 | 4 | −.04 | 6 |
| Immigrants | .21* | 10 | −.24* | 12 | .13 | 2 | −.09 | 5 |
| Elderly | .03 | 2 | .01 | 1 | .06 | 1 | −.10 | 8 |
| **Territory** | | | | | | | | |
| Miles Cardiff | .04 | 9 | −.05 | 10 | .02 | 2 | −.01 | 2 |
| Region[a] | 11.1** | 19 | 12.5** | 23 | 1.0 | 2 | 10.3* | 16 |
| **Language** | | | | | | | | |
| Welsh-speakers | −.15 | 11 | −.01 | 1 | .23* | 7 | .41** | 37 |
| (Constant) $r^2$ | (3.0) | 75 | (59.8) | 82 | (14.7) | 19 | (9.2) | 76 |

[a]   British Wales for Conservatives and Alliance,   Welsh Wales for Labour, and Y Fro Gymraeg for Plaid Cymru.

data here does not permit further analysis, it strongly indicates that identity and locale now represent crucial elements in determining voting in Wales.

Further evidence of this territorial dimension within Welsh politics can be gleaned from examining the pattern of party competition in contemporary Wales (Table 6.5). Plaid Cymru's effective challenge is restricted to Y Fro Gymraeg; Labour dominates Welsh Wales, where the Alliance is as credible an opposition as the Conservatives, while in British Wales the Conservatives are dominant with equal opposition from the Alliance and the Labour Party, a situation not dissimilar from that pertaining in Britain as a whole.

The 1983 general election in Wales confirmed the changing pattern suggested by the election of 1979. Welsh identity has always been an elusive concept, complicated by geography, for the central Welsh plateau separates North Wales communities from those in the South. However, the traditional and simplistic categories of a Welsh-speaking agricultural north and an English-speaking industrial south are no longer appropriate for an understandably Welsh politics. Three distinct political areas are emerging in Wales.

Table VI.5   PATTERNS OF PARTY COMPETITION IN WALES

|  | British Wales | Welsh Wales | Y Fro Gymraeg | Total |
|---|---|---|---|---|
|  | (N constituencies) | | | |
| **Conservatives first** | | | | |
| Labour second | 7 | 0 | 0 | 7 |
| Alliance second | 5 | 0 | 1 | 6 |
| Plaid Cymru second | 0 | 0 | 1 | 1 |
| Total | 12 | 0 | 2 | 14 |
| **Labour first** | | | | |
| Alliance second | 0 | 12 | 0 | 12 |
| Conservative second | 4 | 3 | 1 | 8 |
| Total | 4 | 15 | 1 | 20 |
| **Alliance first** | | | | |
| Conservatives second | 1 | 0 | 1 | 2 |
| **Plaid Cymru Seats** | | | | |
| Conservatives second | 0 | 0 | 2 | 2 |

The first area, Y Fro Gymraeg (the Welsh-speaking heartland), encompasses North West and West Central Wales. Here Plaid Cymru is firmly established and to a considerable degree determines the political agenda, the nature and tone of the political agenda and the outcome of elections. Partisanship here is heavily influenced by ethnicity and linguistic considerations which overshadow but never completely eliminate the established British socio-economic determinants. The political debate is largely but not exclusively based on national Welsh criteria. Like all other parts of Wales, Y Fro Gymraeg decisively rejected devolution, under the apprehension that its particular regional concerns and interests would be overwhelmed in a Welsh Assembly dominated by the industrial and anglicised south. Thus, Plaid Cymru's position in this area is as much dependent upon responding to the needs and demands of local interests as in promoting causes relevant throughout Wales. In 1979, for example, the three Plaid Cymru MPs broke ranks with Scottish Nationalists and supported the Labour government in the vote of no confidence after extracting a promise of full compensation for incapacitated slate quarry workers in their constituencies. Similarly, Plaid's decision to change its position on membership of the European Community was eased by the realization that it would not weaken their support among the Welsh farming population

The second area, Welsh Wales, is comprised largely of the industrial valleys of South Wales. This was Labour's Welsh electoral beachhead, from which it spread out to dominate Welsh politics but into which it has now been forced back. Even in this area Labour's dominant position is weakening. Labour partisanship, based on both class and ethnicity, is peculiarly vulnerable on two flanks; to Plaid Cymru, which seeks to compete with Labour for the ethnic vote and to the Conservatives, whose appeal is directed to an emerging Welsh middle class and an anglo-immigrant community. Neither party alone can seriously threaten Labour's dominance but in a four party system, elections become a form of Russian roulette in which any one of three parties could emerge as the significant challenger to Labour's position. In this area Labour's position is also threatened by demographic changes which have already resulted in the elimination of two seats in successive Boundary Commission reports.

The emergence of the third area, British Wales, hinted at in the devolution referendum and confirmed by the 1983 general election, includes those parts of Wales adjacent to England. Here the political conflict in 1983 was Conservatives vs Labour vs Alliance, as in the British pattern. Specifically Welsh issues make little impact and ethnic identity is a factor of negligible significance, save in certain affluent middle class Cardiff suburbs, where a Welsh-speaking professional elite is concentrated. Partisanship unambiguously follows from the established British pattern of socio-economic status. The penetration of British political values into this area has proceeded sufficiently for what was previously an alien phenomenon, the Welsh working class Tory, to become evident.

The prospects for the future of Welsh politics are that the first area will be preserved; that ethnicity with a strong linguistic cultural root will prevail; and that politics will continue to be polarized on the linguistic divide probably to the continuing benefit of Plaid Cymru. The second area seems destined to experience continuing social change. The decline of the coal industry and its mining communities, the progressive depopulation of some valleys and the development of others as dormitory areas for Cardiff, Newport and Swansea would further endanger Labour's position. This, together with an erosion of the non-linguistic Welsh ethnic community will probably see the fatal weakening of the once powerful Welsh political stereotype which provided the political environment and the electoral base for Nye Bevan and more recently for Neil Kinnock.

The expectations are that the third area will continue to prosper and to acquire English immigrants and values. The 1981 census revealed that 20.5 per cent of the Welsh population was born outside Wales. In parts of Powys and Clwyd the penetration of English immigrants is more than 30 per cent. This area displays a social character and a cultural accent more akin to the English home counties than either the Welsh industrial valleys or rural uplands. In the course of the 1970s following the building of the Severn Bridge and western extensions of the M4, South East Wales and particularly the southern half of Gwent and South Glamorgan became increasingly integrated, both economically and culturally with the metropolitan area. On British Rail's 125 Intercity express, Cardiff is only one hour 45 minutes down the line from London. The establishment of electronic high technology industries such as INMOS and MITEL in Newport and Cardiff confirmed that South Wales while on the western extremity is nevertheless part of the M4 sunrise corridor. Thus areas of British Wales have not only acquired the English language and values but are ceasing to be part of the political periphery in either industrial or political terms.

However, there is a paradox. As the socio-economic character of Wales changes, a galaxy of Welsh national institutions created during the ferment of the devolution debate in the 1960s and 1970s have established themselves as part of Welsh political life. The Welsh Office, the Welsh Development Agency, the Select Committee on Welsh Affairs, Channel 4 Wales, the Wales TUC, CBI Wales, and the Welsh organizations, conferences and manifestos of the British political parties are but a few examples. The dynamic for continuing institutional reform is already within the system. The extent to which this institutional development counteracts changes in the Welsh socio-economic environment will determine the future pattern of Welsh politics.

# VII
# Scotland:
# British with a Difference

The 1970s stimulated much confusion about where or how Scotland fit into the United Kingdom: As an integral and undifferentiated part of an indivisible Britain? As a culturally distinctive but politically integrated nation in a multi-national state (Rose, 1970) or, in the words of a knowledgeable Frenchman, Jacques Leruez (1983), *as une nation sans état* ? As a separate policy network integrated in a larger British political system? (Keating and Midwinter, 1983) As a distinctively Scottish political system? (Kellas, 1973) Or whether, in Miller's (1981: 10) words: 'A Scottish governmental machine has been constructed complete with Prime Minister, subordinate ministers, its own civil service and unlimited responsibilities if not unlimited powers'?

In 1979 Scottish voters collectively rendered a pair of ambiguous verdicts. The referendum vote was so narrowly in favour of devolution that its proponents faced the charge that their case was, to use a Scots' law term, Not proven. But unlike Wales, the opponents of devolution in Scotland could not claim that the vote was a rejection of devolution. The May, 1979, general election saw a decline in the vote of the Scottish National Party, but at 17.3 per cent it was higher than the Liberal vote in Britain. The Conservatives gained seats and votes, but Labour comfortably retained its majority of Scottish MPs, albeit a majority manufactured by the electoral system from 41.6 per cent of the vote.

The 1979 Conservative government offered a good test of theories propounded to account for Scotland's distinctiveness in the 1970s. According to those who saw Westminster's legitimacy dependent upon its largesse, the intensification of economic difficulties implied greater political conflict and a boost to nationalism in Scotland. A Conservative majority in Parliament but a Labour majority among Scottish MPs could be used as a rationale for de-legitimating Westminster's authority and encouraging extra-parliamentary protest by Nationalists or socialists wont to make the break with England with Thatcher-style government, or both.

In the event, the break did not come. The 1983 edition of *The Scottish Government Yearbook* was a litany of complaints about the decay of things Scottish--and of the inability (or unwillingness) of Scots to force the British government to alter its course of action. Dr. Henry Drucker (1982: 31) considered this a curious case of a dog that didn't bark; he explained the failure of forecast conflict to occur as evidence that 'Scottish party politics since 1979 has been nationalised...opponents aim their fire as part of British armies, ignoring the Scottish front'. An alternative explanation is that Scotland is no exception to the proposition that the predominant influences upon party competition are Britainwide, and that differences of degree should not be treated as differences in kind. In short, the hypothesized sleeping dog of nationalist and socialist Scottish opinion is "the dog that never was".

## British Government in Scotland

If a nation is defined as the terminal community with which people identify (Emerson, 1960: 25), then Scots have at least three identities: to their locality, e.g. Glasgow; to Scotland; and to Britain as a whole. There is neither logical nor psychological inconsistency in having a multiplicity of identities; a Scot may be British and also a Glaswegian as well as a Scot. Nominal labels mislead if they are treated as establishing exclusive loyalties.

Constitutionally, all government in Scotland is British, that is, acting under authority conferred by the Crown in Parliament, which since the 1707 Act of Union has been solely at Westminster. But Britain is a Union without uniformity (Rose, 1982: chapter 2). There is a network of separately denominated institutions for conducting some of the Crown's business in Scotland. But nominal distinctions do not create autonomous institutions. The Scottish Office remains a ministry in Cabinet, subject to the collective discipline of British party government. Scottish local authorities differ in the apportionment of functions from England, but they too depend upon the Cabinet for the bulk of their funds, and for all of their statutory powers (cf. Page, 1982).

Most institutions of government in Scotland are not Scottish; they are either local or Britainwide. Major welfare state services such as education, housing and social services are provided by local authorities; pensions, unemployment benefits and a host of economic policies are the responsibility of ministries implementing policies Britainwide. The conjunction in 1979 of Conservative control of British government and concurrent Labour control of the two largest local authorities in Scotland, Strathclyde and Lothian regions, induced conflict, but it was central-local conflict analogous to that between a Labour-led Greater London Council and Westminster, rather than England vs. Scotland.

Without intending, the electorate of Glasgow's marginal constituency of Cathcart greatly affected Mrs. Thatcher's choice of a Secretary of State for Scotland in May, 1979, by refusing to return to Parliament Teddy Taylor, the shadow Scottish Secretary of State. In consequence, George Younger was appointed Secretary of State in his stead, a politician with substantial experience of the Scottish Office as a junior minister in the 1970-74 Conservative government, and an individual as emollient as Taylor was a bonny fechter. Younger is a team player, never complaining about rebuffs or boasting of Scottish Office victories, yet free from association with abrasive monetarism.

The motto of Scottish Office ministers through the years has been stated by Malcolm Rifkind (1981: 66), a junior minister from 1979 to 1982.

> Insist upon United Kingdom uniformity when we like what our English colleagues are doing and assert the need for distinctive Scottish solutions when we don't like what they are doing. In plain English (if I can be excused that word in this context), we enjoy eating our cake and having it.

But in British government in the 1980s, as Malcolm Rifkind himself was to preach to unwilling Labour councillors in Scotland, the Treasury was less willing to supply the cake, and there was far more careful scrutiny of the distribution of such benefits as the Treasury was willing to provide (Heald, 1983: chapter 10).

The economic issues that dominated the minds of the Cabinet and the electorate during the 1979 Parliament were Britainwide, even worldwide in their origins and significance. Inflation, unemployment, the decline of old industries and slow rates of economic growth were not distinctly Scottish issues. The policies that Mrs. Thatcher pronounced as the most appropriate cure for these remedies were enunciated as general truths universally applicable. Whereas the interventionist government of Edward Heath had encouraged regional policies intended to discriminate to Scotland's benefit, and electoral politics induced Labour governments to attend specially to Scottish concerns, Mrs. Thatcher was egalitarian with a difference: all parts of the United Kingdom (including Scotland) were in principle to be treated equally in the sharing out of the medicine of monetarism. High interest rates prevailed throughout the United Kingdom, and the subsequent fall in inflation was also common throughout the United Kingdom.

The impact of the Conservative measures intended to roll back the state were of greater immediate importance in Scotland than in many other parts of Britain for four reasons. First of all, Scottish levels of unemployment had been consistently higher than in England. The growth of depressed areas in England meant the gradual erosion of selectivity in economic policy, as difficulties became more and more widespread.

Secondly, the conflict between the Conservative government and local authorities was Britainwide, because it was a central part of the government's economic strategy and political philosophy (cf. Chapter III). The controversy reached its height in Scotland, not England, in a confrontation in 1981 between the Labour-controlled Lothian region and the Scottish Office. Under the provisions of the newly adopted Local Government (Miscellaneous Provisions) (Scotland) Act, the Secretary of State in 1981 notified Lothian Regional Council that a reduction of £53 million in Rate Support Grant was due because of excessive and unreasonable expenditure by the local authority. Lothian was not only the largest of seven Labour-controlled councils affected, but also the most leftwing; its dominant faction was determined not to act unless compelled to do so. Compulsion was introduced after Lothian's cut was reduced to £30 million (Midwinter, Keating and Taylor, 1983). Divisions within the Labour Party were quietly and effectively underlined by the behaviour of the largest local authority in Scotland and the one most securely Labour, Strathclyde Region. It was not threatened with cuts in its central government grant, nor did it join in the outcry raised by other Labour councils. In 1982, its vote went up three per cent in the local elections.

Throughout Britain the battle between local authorities and their related Cabinet ministries was hotly contested in terms of local democracy vs. Westminster democracy. These divisions were Britainwide, and thus incidentally integrative. Lothian Region did not fight for independence from London; instead, it joined with the Greater London Council in seeking to assert local freedom to determine its rates and local spending itself. Nor could conflict have been created readily on a Scotland vs. England basis, for many Scots were very critical of levels of local authority spending. In Lothian Region the dominant Labour group lost its majority at the 1982 regional election; its vote dropped by nearly 10 per cent.

Thirdly, cuts in public expenditure threatened employment in the public sector, which in Scotland had been running at 30 per cent of the labour force, higher than any English region except the depressed North, albeit lower than Wales or Northern Ireland (Parry, 1981: 230). While Scottish wage rates remained equal to or greater than British rates, the total number in employment fell as the private sector contracted. Such visible and important public sector employers as the British Steel Corporation were subject to great cuts in employment Britainwide by a Scots-born director, Ian MacGregor, seeking to reduce losses of hundreds of millions of pounds in the face of a surplus of capacity relative to world demand. BSC kept its Lanarkshire works running, albeit at a lower level of employment.

Finally, housing policy is disproportionately important in Scotland, because 54 per cent of Scottish houses are council tenancies, 22 per cent more than the British average. The government's policy of reducing subsidies for the construction of new council housing, combined with the increased cost of servicing debt on existing council housing due to high interest rates, intensified housing cutbacks commenced under the previous Labour government. The Conservative government's 1980 Act giving council tenants the right to buy their house was meant to end quarrelling between the government and Labour local authorities about a policy subject to great ideological dispute. Labour authorities in Scotland complained that the compulsion to sell council houses was another unwarranted attack upon their autonomy.

With a comfortable overall majority, the government's lack of a majority of Scottish MPs was of no consequence in the division lobbies. Eight of the 22 Scottish Conservative MPs held government office, a higher ratio than in the Conservative parliamentary party as a whole. Backbench Scottish Conservative MPs were occupied in attending committee meetings; and their small numbers made their presence important.

The new system of parliamentary committees established a backbench Select Committee on Scotland under a Labour chairman. The Committee was an alternative to devolution, not a stepping-stone to devolution, emphasized its first chairman, Donald Dewar, himself a devolutionist. He saw the committee's role as useful but limited, aiming 'to throw a little light into dark places' (Dewar, 1980: 22). The Committee also generated considerable heat, as Conservatives disagreed about how partisan its role should be, with Iain Sproat pushing to make it a vehicle for attacking the public sector, and others seeking to improve (and sometimes expand) the public sector. The Select Committee did not prosper. Its initial chairman resigned for a position of shadow spokesman on the Labour opposition team. By the end of the Parliament, the *Scotsman's* James Naughtie (1982: 10) could lament that it was 'ineffective and many of the members uninterested'.

The Scottish Grand Committee not only continued its role of scrutinising government measures introduced for technical reasons as separate bills for Scotland, but also gave symbolic evidence of the Conservative government's response to demands for devolution. The Scottish Grand Committee held some meetings in the Crown Office Buildings, Edinburgh, the old Royal High School building remodelled by the previous Labour government to serve as the home of the proposed Scottish Assembly. The gesture was as weak as it was symbolic. The former President of the European Commission, Roy Jenkins, found the Scottish Grand Committee the place where he could address fellow MPs about the problems of Glasgow taxis.

# Parties less Ambiguous;
# Public Opinion more Ambiguous

Harold Wilson's decision to endorse devolution in principle in summer, 1974 had caught all parties, including his own, off balance. Within each party there was disagreement about whether devolution was too much, too little, or not enough of a response to the challenge of the Scottish National Party. In the years that followed some outspoken MPs enunciated a position of principle and stuck to it. Most MPs were pragmatists, shifting ground as judgements changed about how much, if any, devolution was necessary.

The Parliament elected in June, 1979 was doubly free of Nationalist pressures. The fall in the SNP share of the popular vote reduced the party from 11 to two MPs. The substantial Conservative majority meant that the government had no need to sidle along the opposition benches looking for measures it could sponsor to curry favour with MPs whose votes would be needed to win a vote of confidence. Scottish voters were no longer presented with the anomalous picture of all parties advocating changes in forms of government, as happened for a brief period in the mid-1970s. They are now offered a choice.

As the party of government, the Conservatives had little difficulty in unambiguously endorsing the British system of government as it is. The gestures in favour of devolution, made in opposition by Edward Heath in a 1968 declaration at Perth and in the mid-1970s by nervous Scottish Conservative MPs, were abandoned. No follow up was proposed to Sir Alec Douglas-Home's statement during the 1979 referendum campaign that a vote against the 1978 devolution act did not preclude all changes. The inter-party talks held in the first session of the Parliament identified no common ground for change, and there was no need or will for change in the governing party. The Conservatives had for generations campaigned in Scotland as the Unionist Party, instead of or in addition to using the label Conservative.

The Secretary of State, George Younger, justified Conservative policy in forthright terms:

> I do not believe that most people in Scotland are any longer interested in this subject as a practical proposition--and this for very sound reasons.
>
> First, the present system gives Scotland a very strong and effective role in United Kingdom affairs. Second, the debates of recent years have highlighted the long-standing fact that Scotland gets a larger expenditure of public money per head of population than either England or Wales. Third, the financing of any Scottish Assembly with executive powers would create more problems for Scotland than it would solve.
>
> Nobody has come up yet with a system of such financing which will not either create an area of perpetual friction between Edinburgh and Westminster or an unacceptable and additional burden on the taxpayers of Scotland. (*Scotsman*, 12 January 1983).

In opposition the Labour Party in Scotland became clearly committed to a Scottish Assembly. There had not been time for this to be done in 1974, and many of the divisions within the party evident in the 1979 referendum campaign dated from Harold Wilson's abrupt endorsement of devolution then. The form of devolution endorsed by the Scottish Council of the Labour Party at Keir Hardie House, Glasgow, and by the Scottish conference was more internally consistent than the 1978 Scotland Act, for it favoured an Assembly with its own fund-raising powers. By going further than the previous government's Act, Keir Hardie House appeared to be endorsing a form of quasi-federalism, or asymmetrical federalism affecting Scotland only. This was because it could only speak for the Labour Party in Scotland. It could not commit the British Labour Party to a scheme for devolution including England and Wales (see chapter IV).

Within the Labour Party in Scotland, the conflict between Labour councils and a Conservative-controlled Scottish Office using central powers to take away rather than hand out money reduced opposition to devolution by councillors, an important bloc in the party. A Scottish Assembly would have made a difference, though it is arguable whether it would have had more money to dispense, have dispensed money differently, or have led a fight about the amount of money available for dispensing on Scotland vs. England lines. Within the Parliamentary Labour Party, a ginger Gang of Four, consisting of George Foulkes, David Marshall, John Maxton and John Home Robertson, began to campaign for 'home rule' for Scotland. George Galloway, a former leftwing chairman of the Scottish Council, spoke of the need for 'a full blown effort at parliamentary disruption by Scottish MPs to render Parliament inoperable, as the struggle for Irish Home Rule almost 80 years ago showed' (*Scotsman*, 8 April 1983). The campaigners for home rule soon (by implication, as soon as Labour lost the 1983 election in Britain) argued that a Parliament in the hands of a party without a majority in Scotland lacked the legitimacy to govern Scotland.

The creation of the Social Democratic Party and the Alliance with the Liberals brought about a spate of policy-making proposals for Scotland, with both David Steel and Roy Jenkins representing Scottish constituencies. The Social Democrats, as a British party--and a party whose initial Scottish supporters included some prominent opponents of devolution such as Lord Wilson of Langside--did not talk lightly of a federal Britain. But the SDP was prepared to accept that Scotland was different, and that Scottish devolution should have a priority not dependent upon the completion of negotiations to carry out the decentralization of government Britainwide.

The Scottish National Party, after being defeated in the 1979 election, entered the 1983 election campaign demoralized. The intervening period had been devoted to Nationalists fighting each other. Two issues divided the party. The first, in view of the referendum debacle, was the appropriate position to take on further proposals for devolution. Traditionalists who believed in the doctrine of independence or nothing argued that their position had been justified by events. The 1979 SNP conference endorsed the principle of campaigning for independence as the next step forward. Devolution was not on offer in the 1979 Parliament.

The SNP was also divided about the merits of adopting a consciously leftwing programme. The case for moving left was put by the 79 group, which was formed in the wake of the election defeat by a group of prominent SNP members, including Margo MacDonald, ex-MP for Govan, and Stephen Maxwell, formerly the party's publicity officer. The 79 group urged the adoption of policies that would more or less align the SNP with the Labour Party left. Tactically, the 79 group argued that only by adopting these policies could the SNP hope to defeat the Labour Party and thereby win a majority of Scottish seats, deemed the key to securing independence. When Jim Sillars, an ex- Labour MP and founder of the breakaway Scottish Labour Party, joined the SNP, he added his voice to the 79 group. Sillars and Maxwell were elected to national offices of the party.

The traditional leadership of the SNP reacted against a move left, arguing that the SNP could only win a Scottish majority by uniting Scotland in demanding independence, rather than dividing it on class issues. Traditionalists pressed for the explusion of the 79 group, and steps were put in train at the June, 1982, party conference. But weeks before the 1983 election the party's national council voted to re-admit members of the 79 group in hopes of securing unity in the face of a general election. The 79 group had failed to move the party left, or for that matter to demonstrate that the particular policies it advocated were approved by a majority of Scottish voters.

At the popular level the movement of opinion among the Scottish electorate can be charted on a monthly basis throughout the Parliament, thanks to the polls conducted for the *Glasgow Herald* by System Three, an Edinburgh-based firm. The first 18 months of the Parliament showed a pattern similar to that of Britain generally: a Labour advance at the expense of the Conservatives. Since Labour had finished well ahead of the Conservative in the May, 1979, ballot, further advance brought Labour as high as 59 per cent in September, 1980, a 40 per cent lead over the Conservatives. SNP and Liberal support was steady, and very close to the 1979 result, leaving the parties third and fourth (Table VII.1).

The launch of the Social Democratic Party and its subsequent Alliance with the Liberals brought about greater divergences between Scotland and England. During 1981 SNP support rose to a high for the Parliament of 22 per

Table VII.1 POPULAR SUPPORT FOR PARTIES IN SCOTLAND, 1979-83

| | Con | Lab | Lib-SDP Alliance | SNP | Party Lead | 1st/2nd |
|---|---|---|---|---|---|---|
| | | | (monthly average % support) | | | |
| **1979** | | | | | | |
| June-Sept | 24 | 55 | 8 | 14 | 31 | Lab/Con |
| Oct-Dec | 26 | 49 | 8 | 16 | 23 | Lab/Con |
| **1980** | | | | | | |
| Jan-Mar | 27 | 49 | 9 | 13 | 22 | Lab/Con |
| Apr-June | 23 | 53 | 8 | 15 | 30 | Lab/Con |
| Jul-Sept | 20 | 56 | 8 | 15 | 36 | Lab/Con |
| Oct-Nov | 19 | 55 | 9 | 15 | 36 | Lab/Con |
| **1981[a]** | | | | | | |
| Jan-Mar | 17 (14) | 49 (38) | 11 (28) | 19 (19) | 30 | Lab/SNP |
| Apr-Jun | 17 (13) | 52 (45) | 10 (24) | 18 (17) | 34 | Lab/SNP |
| Jul-Sept | 17 (15) | 51 (43) | 11 (25) | 18 (18) | 33 | Lab/SNP |
| Oct-Dec | 15 | 45 | 21 | 18 | 27 | Lab/SNP |
| **1982** | | | | | | |
| Jan-Mar | 19 | 42 | 22 | 17 | 20 | Lab/All |
| Apr-Jun | 25 | 44 | 17 | 15 | 19 | Lab/Con |
| Jul-Sept | 22 | 45 | 17 | 16 | 23 | Lab/Con |
| Oct-Dec | 28 | 45 | 14 | 12 | 17 | Lab/Con |
| **1983** | | | | | | |
| Jan-Mar | 26 | 48 | 14 | 13 | 22 | Lab/Con |
| April | 24 | 49 | 15 | 11 | 25 | Lab/Con |

[a] From March to August 1981 System Three asked two voting intention questions, the first without a prompt concerning the SDP and the second with. Figures in brackets give the answers to the latter question, combining Liberal and SDP responses. The party lead is calculated from the unbracketed responses.

Source: System Three Polls, conducted for the Glasgow Herald. Figures for combined months are averages.

cent, the Conservative support fell to 14 or 12 per cent, depending upon the measure, and Labour support consistently remained well ahead of the Alliance (Table VII.1). The closest that Alliance came to catching up with Labour was the end of 1981, when Labour's lead over Alliance fell to 13 per cent. A second striking feature of Scottish opinion was that the rise in Alliance support did not detract from SNP support. While Labour remained in front with 40 per cent, third force support for the Alliance and SNP combined was 44 per cent.

Given that the Conservatives finished second in Scotland in 1979, the Conservative revival carried the party much less far than in Britain overall. Conservative support was 19 per cent in Scotland at the time of the Hillhead by-election, immediately before the outbreak of the Falklands War. It rose above 20 per cent in April 1982, and stayed above, but did not go higher than 30 per cent prior to the general election campaign. Because of the four-way division in vote the revival in Conservative support did not reduce Labour's lead. The Conservatives were always at least 15 per cent behind Labour in the System Three polls, a position worse than that at the May 1979 election.

The three by-elections held in Scotland during the Parliament were each so distinctive in time and place that collectively they do not form a pattern. In June, 1980 Labour held Glasgow Central, a very safe seat, on a 43 per cent turnout; the SNP candidate finished second. At Glasgow Hillhead in March, 1982, after one of the longest and most intensive by-election campaigns in the postwar era, the Alliance took the only Conservative seat in Glasgow, but Roy Jenkins returned to Parliament with only 33.4 per cent of the vote, and the SNP candidate drew 11 per cent. Labour won a safe seat at Coatbridge and Airdrie in June, 1982, with the Conservatives finishing a distant second, and the Alliance and SNP candidates losing their deposits.

The volatility of the voters during the 1979 Parliament cannot be explained by attitudes toward the structure of government in Scotland, for the fluctuations were much greater in party preferences than in constitutional preferences (cf. Tables VII.1-2). Opinion polls have asked questions about attitudes toward the preferred form of government in Scotland since 1974, albeit with differences in the phrasing of alternatives between polling organizations. Since the referendum campaign, they have found a high degree of stability in popular opinion. Opinion Research Centre never found a Scottish majority in favour of any of the five alternatives that its interviewers preferred in surveys for the Scotsman. The figures could be interpreted as showing as of April, 1979 that 43 per cent of Scots favoured no change or minimal adaptation without an elected Assembly (options 1 and 2), or that 40 per cent favoured more than devolution, a fully federal Parliament or independence (options 4 and 5).

The MORI poll is politically significant, for the questions used in the 1980s were also used by MORI in conducting unpublished surveys for Harold

Table VII.2  PUBLIC OPINION OF ALTERNATIVES FOR GOVERNING SCOTLAND

Opinion Research Centre

|            | No change | Adapt | Assembly | Fed. | Indep'ce |
|------------|-----------|-------|----------|------|----------|
|            | %         | %     | %        | %    | %        |
| Mar 1974   | 21        | 19    | 24       | 16   | 17       |
| Sept 1974  | 21        | 14    | 17       | 16   | 17       |
| Feb 1979   | 32        | 13    | 16       | 20   | 14       |
| Apr 1979   | 35        | 8     | 13       | 28   | 12       |
| Sept 1979  | 33        | 11    | 13       | 27   | 13       |

MORI (Market & Opinion Research International)

|            | No change | Change | Indep'ce |
|------------|-----------|--------|----------|
|            | %         | %      | %        |
| Feb  1974  | 19        | 59     | 19       |
| Mar  1979  | 35        | 42     | 14       |
| Nov  1980  | 29        | 44     | 19       |
| Feb  1981  | 30        | 46     | 25       |
| May  1981  | 25        | 50     | 25       |
| Sept 1981  | 31        | 46     | 23       |
| Nov  1981  | 26        | 47     | 22       |
| Feb  1982  | 23        | 53     | 19       |
| Apr  1982  | 22        | 45     | 27       |
| Nov  1982  | 26        | 47     | 22       |
| Feb  1983  | 35        | 42     | 14       |
| June 1983  | 22        | 51     | 23       |

(The ORC surveys offered respondents five alternatives;  the MORI
surveys offered three.   For the full text of the questions,  see
Rose and McAllister, 1982: 116-117).

Source:  The Scotsman, Edinburgh; and MORI reports.

Wilson, when the Prime Minister was contemplating devolution as a Labour policy in 1974. The offer of fewer alternatives produced a simpler distribution, with one-quarter or more preferring the status quo, about half 'a Scottish Assembly as part of Britain but with substantial powers', and about one-fifth independence. Interpretation of the results is contentious. Labour supporters could, if they wished, argue that the Labour government's proposals offered substantial powers, but critics could attack the proposals for not offering enough. The impact of Labour's own shift toward promising substantially greater powers for a Scottish Assembly after the 1979 election cannot be measured with the MORI poll, for it does not distinguish between Labour's two proposals.

At a minimum, both the ORC and the MORI polls can be interpreted to show that for nearly a decade a preponderant majority of Scots endorsed statements favouring change in government in Scotland, but there is no agreement about what specifically is being endorsed. Moreover, the 1979 referendum showed that there is no security that polling figures could be used to predict a referendum vote. Recognizing this, John Smith (1981: 46), a major architect of devolution legislation in the 1974-79 Labour government, argued that a new Labour government committed to devolution would have to "front end" the referendum, that is, hold an advisory referendum on a white paper containing devolution proposals and regard the result as 'solid grounds for pressing ahead. It would be ridiculous to stage another referendum after the legislation.'

## The Campaign and the Result

The 1983 election campaign in Scotland opened with little expectation or fear in any party. Scottish politicians did not expect to be much affected electorally by the decline of the Labour vote in England. The Conservatives did not expect to win a majority of Scottish votes nor was Labour afraid of a Nationalist or Alliance breakthrough. Survival, and perhaps a few gains, were the aims of these two parties. The apparent certainty of a Conservative victory Britainwide meant that Scottish MPs could not hope to be a decisive bloc in the next Parliament as they had been from 1974 to 1979.

Redistribution changed the boundaries of the great bulk of Scottish constituencies but it did not alter the total vote of the parties. The 1979 election outcome had produced four principal patterns of party competition, albeit in unequal numbers. In two-thirds of the seats Labour and Conservative candidates were the front- running pair; in another 17 seats the SNP finished second to a Conservative or Labour MP, and in seven seats the Liberals were first or second. Marginal seats were relatively few. Continuing population decline in Glasgow as in other major British cities, meant that its parliamentary representation fell from 15 seats between 1918 and 1970 to 13 in 1974 and 11 in 1983. The initial proposal of the Scottish Boundary Commissioners was to reduce Glasgow representation to 10, but appeals succeeded in increasing the number to 11, thus raising the total number of Scotland's seats in Parliament to 72, one more than at any time before in the modern history of Parliament.

The BBC-ITN (1983:236) analysis of the new constituency boundaries reckoned that the net effect of redistribution was an increase of one in Conservative representation in the Commons. But changes in individual constituencies were forced by the reduction in seats in older centres of population, and the creation of new seats in response to population growth. Ian Sproat, who had won Aberdeen South on its old boundaries by 1.5 per cent, renounced the opportunity to stand for re-election, though the BBC-ITN calculation showed the Conservative lead was virtually unaltered at 1.3 per cent. Sproat was finally adopted for the new constituency of Roxburgh and Berwickshire, which the BBC-ITN reckoned was virtually a dead heat between Conservatives and Liberals as of 1979. Sproat's move was of no avail; he lost his new seat by 10.7 per cent to a Liberal, while his successor held Aberdeen South for the Conservatives by 9.1 per cent.

Three of the four party manifestos issued in Scotland could differ little in the substance of their proposals from party headquarters version issued in London (cf. Chapters II-IV). The Conservative manifesto made no mention of the word devolution. Its reference 'to consider further changes to improve the government of Scotland within the United Kingdom' was contained in a brief section headed *The Supremacy of Parliament* . Labour's manifesto pledged a Scottish Assembly intended 'to give more power to Scotland. At the same time, we shall retain the benefits that come from our links with the rest of the United Kingdom'.

Only the Scottish National Party could be distinctive; this was made evident in the title of its manifesto, *Choose Scotland--the Challenge of Independence*. The commitment to independence was spelled out clearly at the beginning of the manifesto, and the document concluded with a quotation from the preamble of the American Declaration of Independence of 1776. The bulk of the SNP manifesto concentrated upon pragmatic justifications for independence, starting with the argument that successive London governments ruined the Scottish economy, with unemployment rising under both Labour and Conservative governments.

In downplaying devolution the British parties were simply following the declared preferences of the Scottish electorate. Economic concerns, not political institutions, came first with the electorate in Scotland as elsewhere in Britain (cf. Table II.2). When MORI asked Scottish voters during the campaign to say which party had the best policy on devolution, the largest single group, 37 per cent, said they didn't know. Of the rest, 23 per cent rated the SNP best, albeit it favoured independence; 16 per cent Labour; 13 per cent the Conservatives, and 9 per cent the Alliance (MORI, 1983: 93). The broad scatter of answers illustrated the low level of knowledge and interest in the issue in Scotland.

During the election campaign no distinctively Scottish issues were brought forward to distract attention from issues common Britainwide. The Scottish National Party took cognizance of the Britainwide campaign, but only to urge Scots, in the words of the party leader, Gordon Wilson, to use 'blackmail' to wring economic concessions from a Thatcher government at Westminster by voting for the SNP ( *Scotsman* 18 May 1983). A gaffe by Peter Shore came too late in the day for it to be publicised. At Labour's Transport House press conference the day before the election he pointed to a diagram of North Sea oil revenues and declared: 'Here is the wasted wealth of England'.

Two sets of opinion polls were published during the campaign, MORI in the *Scotsman* and *Scottish Daily Express*, and System Three in the *Glasgow Herald* (cf. Table VII.3). Given that the 1979 election result had produced an overall seven per cent Conservative lead in Britain as against a 10 per cent Labour lead in Scotland, the Scotland-only polls were bound to appear different, if only recording no change from 1979. The campaign polls tended to indicate Labour maintaining or even increasing its lead over the Conservatives in Scotland, exactly the opposite of the position reported by polls Britainwide.

Table VII.3  CAMPAIGN POLLS IN SCOTLAND

| | Con | Lab | All | SNP | Labour lead |
|---|---|---|---|---|---|
| | % | % | % | % | % |
| Firm, fieldwork dates | | | | | |
| System Three, 13-17 May, Herald | 32 | 44 | 12 | 12 | 12 |
| MORI, 24-25 May, Scotsman | 34 | 39 | 19 | 7 | 5 |
| MORI, 4 June, Express | 28 | 38 | 22 | 12 | 10 |
| System Three, 4-5 June, Herald | 26 | 40 | 23 | 12 | 14 |
| MORI, 7-8 June Scotsman | 27 | 41 | 20 | 11 | 14 |
| Actual result | 28.4 | 35.1 | 24.5 | 11.8 | 6.7 |

Two interpretations of the campaign polls are possible. The first is that the tendency to overestimate the Labour vote as against the final result reflected the fact that the sampling points in Scottish surveys tend to over-represent the more accessible Central- belt constituencies, where Labour does well, as against the Highland constituencies, extremely difficult of access, where Labour's support is very weak. This would also account for the underestimation of the vote for the other parties. The other possibility is that there was a late swing away from Labour in Scotland. A Gallup Poll taken for the BBC in Scotland on election day found 37 per cent of its respondents Labour, as against 29 per cent Conservative, 25 per cent Alliance, and nine per cent SNP. This suggests that Scottish polls tend to over- represent the Labour vote by about two per cent because of the structure of their sample, and that there was a late swing in Scotland away from Labour to other parties.

The election result in Scotland occasioned little surprise. The distribution of seats--41 Labour, 21 Conservative, 8 Alliance, and 2 SNP--left Labour the dominant party in parliamentary representation, as it had been for two decades. Labour was down three seats by comparison with 1979, but the same as in the October 1974 election. The Conservatives were also down one seat from 1979. The Alliance gain of five seats was a better showing than the Liberals had achieved at any general election in Scotland since 1929, and better than the February, 1974 showing which launched the SNP as a major force in politics in Scotland.

The distribution of the popular vote in Scotland showed a very different picture from the distribution of seats. Labour's share of the vote, 35.1 per cent, was its lowest in Scotland since 1931. If the Alliance and the SNP vote is added together to measure the strength of third force protest against the Conservative-Labour duopoly, then the third force takes the biggest portion of the vote in Scotland, 36.3 per cent. A Labour dismissal of the Conservative claim to represent Scotland because it was not supported by 72 per cent of the voters could be countered by rejecting Labour's claim to speak for Scotland on the ground that it was not supported by 65 per cent of the voters. The 24.5 per cent poll by the Alliance, combined with the SNP vote, meant that the two established parties together took only 63.5 per cent of the vote in Scotland, compared to 68.5 per cent in Wales, and 72.9 per cent in England.

The election outcome showed that Scotland was British--but British with a difference. It was British because 88 per cent of the total vote went to parties contesting the election Britainwide. But it was different because Labour finished first rather than the Conservatives. It was also different because the Alliance was stronger in Scotland. In 1983 the proportion of the third force vote going to an explicitly British party was twice as great as that going to an explicitly Scottish party. The 1983 result supports Denis Van Mechelen's (1982: 4) conclusion from analysing third-party voting in the 1970s: 'Scottish voters turned to the SNP in 1974 as much to express their British concerns as their peculiarly Scottish ones'.

In Scottish constituencies as in English constituencies, socio-economic status was an important influence determining the vote for the Conservatives, Labour and, at a much lower level, the Alliance (cf. Table VII.4 and V.1). Agriculture is a much stronger influence too, for Scotland is not only a land of heavy industry and vast council housing estates, but also of rolling hills, Highlands and open countryside. All other conditions remaining equal, as the socio-economic status of the constituency rises by 10 points on the scale, Labour's vote is likely to fall by 4.1 per cent; as a constituency's agricultural status rises by 10 per cent, Labour's vote falls by 2.7 per cent. Since rural constituencies tend to be higher on both scales, Labour's vote is doubly depressed outside the Central

Table VII.4 SOCIAL STRUCTURE AND TERRITORIAL INFLUENCES ON THE VOTE IN SCOTLAND

| | Conservative vote | | Labour vote | | Alliance vote | | SNP vote | |
|---|---|---|---|---|---|---|---|---|
| | b | % var expl | b | % var expl | b | % var expl | b | % var expl |
| **Social Structure** | | | | | | | | |
| Socio-ec status | .31** | 26 | -.41** | 38 | .11 | 5 | -.05 | 2 |
| Agriculture | .15** | 20 | -.27** | 39 | .06 | 5 | .01 | 1 |
| Immigrants | -.11 | 4 | .06 | 3 | .10 | 2 | -.11 | 3 |
| Elderly | .01 | 1 | .01 | 0 | -.06 | 2 | .05 | 2 |
| **Territory** | | | | | | | | |
| Miles Edinb'h | -.08** | 20 | .01 | 2 | .02 | 3 | .02 | 2 |
| Region[a] | 5.0* | 8 | 2.1 | 4 | 4.7 | 4 | 9.7* | 9 |
| (Constant) r² | (19.7) | 79 | (51.4) | 86 | (19.1) | 21 | (9.0) | 19 |

[a] North of Scotland for Conservatives and SNP; Central Industrial belt for Labour; Lothian and Borders for Alliance.

Industrial belt of Scotland. Another distinctive feature of Scottish social structure is shown by the positive effect of immigration upon the Alliance vote. Given the low proportion of Commonwealth immigrants in Scotland, this may be interpreted as the effect of universities, for university constituencies tend to be high on transient accommodation and to attract as students a disproportionate number of Scotland's immigrants from the New Commonwealth.

The divisions within Scotland are territorial as well as functional. Even after controlling for the effect of socio-economic status and agriculture, there remains a significant portion of the variance in the vote that can be explained by regional differences. Region makes the biggest impact on the SNP. While its vote most nearly approximates a cross-section of Scotland (that is, the lowest proportion of variance is explained by social structure), it adds 9.7 per cent to its vote in North of Scotland constituencies. The regional boost for the Alliance is in the Lothians and Borders, where its vote is 4.7 per cent higher than would be predicted by other constituency characteristics. By contrast, 80 per cent of the Labour vote is determined by social structure, as against six per cent determined by territorial influences.

The Conservative vote is affected by cross-cutting territorinfluences. Ceteris paribus, the Conservative vote goes up by 5.0 per cent in North of Scotland constituencies. But the greater the distance from Edinburgh, the less the Conservative vote; the b value of .08 in Table VII.4 appears small until one calculates that this represents the loss of 4.0 of the vote by a 50-mile move from Edinburgh. This reflects the poor showing of the Conservatives in Clydeside constituencies, to the west of Edinburgh, even after allowance is made for differences in socio-economic status between Glasgow and Edinburgh. It also means that in North of Scotland constituencies the Conservative vote is boosted by a regional effect and the agricultural character of the constituencies, but substantially reduced insofar as the constituencies are distant from Edinburgh.

Whereas Nationalists argue that Scotland is united against England, regional divisions in the 1983 vote show that Scotland is internally far more divided than England (cf. Table VII.5 and V.2). There are substantial differences in the vote for each party from region to region within Scotland, and these differences cannot be explained simply in terms of social structure. In the North of Scotland, the Labour Party polls 16 per cent less than would be expected because of the social structure, and the Conservatives 10 per cent better. In the Central Industrial belt, Labour enjoys an eight per cent advantage beyond that accounted for by social structure. In the Lothians and Borders, both the Alliance and the Conservative Party benefit from a regional effect. The strength of the regional effect in Scotland is particularly striking because of the absence of the language divisions, which in Wales can produce prima facie differences in culture (cf. Tables VII.4-5 and VI.3-4).

Table VII.5   REGIONAL INFLUENCES ON THE VOTE IN SCOTLAND

|  | Con. vote | | | Labour vote | | | Alliance vote | | | SNP vote | | |
|  | Act | Prd | Df | Act | Prd | Df | Act | Prd | Df | Act | Prd | Df |
|---|---|---|---|---|---|---|---|---|---|---|---|---|
|  | | | | | (% vote) | | | | | | | | |
| North | 35 | 25 | +10 | 16 | 32 | −16 | 29 | 21 | +8 | 21 | 26 | −5 |
| Central Industrial | 24 | 29 | −5 | 44 | 36 | +8 | 22 | 23 | −1 | 10 | 14 | −4 |
| Lothian & Borders | 33 | 28 | +5 | 29 | 35 | −6 | 29 | 25 | +4 | 9 | 14 | −5 |

Notes:   [a]   See Appendix A for the definition of regions.

# Union without Uniformity

Comparing the election outcome in Scotland and England shows there is no uniformity. In 1983, Labour secured a vote 8.2 per cent higher in Scotland than in England, the Conservatives 17.6 per cent worse than in England, and the Alliance, 1.9 per cent below its English level. The differences were greater than in any postwar British general election, but they were differences within the Union of England and Scotland. The vote for parties upholding the Union has been rising since October 1974, when it was 70 per cent, to 83 per cent in 1979 and 88 per cent in 1983.

The scale of the Scottish National Party setback is shown by the fact that it lost its deposits in 53 of the 72 seats it fought. This was a higher proportion of SNP lost deposits than at any previous election. In 1970, when the party's share of the vote in Scotland was slightly lower than in 1983, the SNP lost 43 deposits. In addition to winning two seats, the SNP came second in only seven constituencies. At least for the 1983 Parliament, it is an also-ran party in Scotland.

The absence of uniformity in patterns of party competition is far greater in Scotland than in England (cf. Table VII.4 and V.4). Nine different patterns of party competition occur; the most common, a Labour victor facing a challenge from a Conservative, is found in less than one-third of all Scottish constituencies. The second most common, a Labour MP with an Alliance challenger, occurs in more than one-quarter of all seats. Competition between the Labour Party and the Alliance is also significant. Whereas 96 per cent of the constituencies in England have competition between Conservative and

Alliance or Conservative and Labour, in Scotland these two categories of constituencies account for only 60 per cent of seats (Table VII.6).

The contrast between a sweeping Conservative victory at Westminster and Labour maintaining a hegemony of seats but not of votes in Scotland is often interpreted as a 'failure' of the Conservatives to maintain a competitive position in Scotland. In fact, it would more accurately be described as a failure of Labour to maintain a competitive position in the South of England. Whereas the Conservatives managed to win 29 per cent of the 72 seats in Scotland in 1983, Labour won only two per cent of the 169 seats in the South of England. When the Greater London area is included, Labour's strength rises but a little. Labour won only 11 per cent of the 262 seats in London and the South of England. The Conservatives won a larger share of seats and votes in Scotland than Labour won in England.

Table VII.6  PATTERNS OF PARTY COMPETITION IN SCOTLAND

|  | Lothian Borders | Central Indus. | North | Total |
|---|---|---|---|---|
|  | (N constituencies) | | | |
| **Conservatives first** | | | | |
| Alliance second | 4 | 4 | 2 | 10 |
| Labour second | 1 | 3 | 1 | 5 |
| SNP second | 1 | 0 | 5 | 6 |
| Total | 6 | 7 | 8 | 21 |
| **Labour first** | | | | |
| Conservatives second | 3 | 18 | 0 | 21 |
| Alliance second | 3 | 15 | 1 | 19 |
| SNP second | 0 | 1 | 0 | 1 |
| Total | 6 | 34 | 1 | 41 |
| **Alliance first** | | | | |
| Conservatives second | 2 | 0 | 5 | 7 |
| Labour second | 0 | 1 | 0 | 1 |
| Total | 2 | 1 | 5 | 8 |
| **SNP first** | | | | |
| Labour second | 0 | 1 | 1 | 2 |
| Total | 14 | 43 | 15 | 72 |

The effect of Labour's weakness in England is to give Scottish Labour MPs a disproportionately large voice in the Parliamentary Labour Party. After Labour's worst election defeat in nearly half a century, Scotland contributes almost one-fifth of the Labour MPs. But the presence of so many Scottish representatives at the highest levels of Labour policymaking today is a sign of Labour's weakness in Britain. If Labour MPs representing Scottish constituencies are to take office in a British Labour government, then they will necessarily find their weight diluted by the election of an additional 120 Labour MPs representing English constituencies, with only a handful of additional Labour MPs from Scotland.

The Alliance too has its parliamentary representation tilted toward Scotland, for more than one-third of Alliance MPs represent Scottish constituencies. In Scotland the Alliance benefited by an uneven distribution of its vote. The Alliance vote was higher in the North of Scotland and lower in the Central Industrial belt. In this way, the Alliance could take advantage of the fact that in four-party competition a lower share of the popular vote is required to win a seat. While the Alliance can claim to speak for all parts of Britain, it cannot claim to speak equally in Parliament for all parts of Scotland. Seven of its eight Scottish seats are rural constituencies, and the other, Glasgow Hillhead, is even more deviant, having previously been the sole Conservative seat in Glasgow.

Within Scotland, the politicians showed no uniformity in interpreting the election outcome, and a few showed little commitment to the Union. The Secretary of State for Scotland, George Younger, totally rejected suggestions from Labour MPs that the government should take steps to introduce changes in government in Scotland. In response to questions from Labour MPs favouring home rule or devolution he said:

> There is no sign that the people of Scotland have any desire for a further layer of government, with extra taxes on the Scots to pay for it ...
> We consider that the present arrangements for government in Scotland are working well, and we do not envisage any changes at the moment (House of Commons Debates Vol. 45, Col. 879, 13 July 1983).

The Scottish National Party's annual conference in late September 1983 faced both ways on the next steps for the party. The Parliamentary leader, Donald Stewart, MP for the Western Isles, argued: 'I don't accept that we must lower our sights to make the party more acceptable to the people ... We should say that we have a fixed aim of independence without any qualification whatsoever' (*Scotsman* , 1 October 1983). But the party chairman and fellow MP, Gordon Wilson, secured acceptance of devolution as a half-way house to independence, when the conference overwhelmingly voted 'not to obstruct' any steps to devolve legislative and economic powers to Scotland.

Predictably, Labour MPs disagree about the implications of the party's contrasting strength in seats in England and Scotland. The disparity in outcome in the two ends of Britain was sufficient for a former Scottish opponent of devolution, Robin Cook, to announce that he no longer upheld 'the concept of a centralised state on the basis that it gave us alternate bouts of Labour and Conservative rule'. Instead, Cook came out for federal government in the United Kingdom, implicitly writing off England to permanent dominance by the Conservatives in exchange for Labour's long-term hegemony in Scotland (*Scotsman*, 4 July 1983). Collectively, Labour MPs from Scotland are not so ready to abandon their half-way endorsement of devolution. The response of the Scottish Council of the Labour Party has been negative to calls for extra-parliamentary protest and joint action with non-Labour groups interested in promoting devolution. Power at Westminster, not opting out to Edinburgh, remains the principal concern of Labour MPs in Scotland, as it is of nearly all MPs Britainwide.

# VIII
# Northern Ireland: The Importance of Being (or not Being) British

In Northern Ireland, the basic political cleavage concerns the Province's constitutional status, not class as in the rest of the United Kingdom. The organization of the political parties around the union has led to two distinct party systems. On the Protestant side, there are parties which compete solely for the vote of their own community, on a platform of continued union with Britain. Similarly, on the Catholic side the political parties compete for their own community's vote by espousing Irish unity. Despite the existence of the bi-confessional Alliance Party, which has a small but consistent following, these two party systems are distinct from one another, insofar as parties originating in one community neither expect nor attempt to win electoral support from voters of the other community. Party competition within each community thus takes place on the basis of which party provides the best means of securing the community's particular constitutional goal, union with Britain or Irish unity (For introductions, see Arthur, 1980; McAllister, 1983 and Rose, 1976).

Northern Ireland is also unique in that its political system demonstrates what a full commitment to the union produces. The two major Unionist parties, the Official Unionist Party and the Democratic Unionist Party, both support the retention of the British link to the exclusion of all other non-related issues, notably those in the socio-economic field. While the Official Unionists embody this aim in a demand for the full integration of Northern Ireland with Britain (although a significant minority favour the return of a majority rule Stormont Parliament) the Democratic Unionists demand the gradual return of devolution through the medium of the Northern Ireland Assembly elected in October 1982.

Until 1982 the Social Democratic and Labour Party (SDLP) was the unchallenged party representing of the Catholic community. It was formed in 1970 to articulate Catholic political demands within the context of Northern Ireland , the legitimacy of which the old Nationalist Party refused to recognize (McAllister, 1977). By contrast , the SDLP relegated Irish unity by consent to fourth in its list of priorities. However, three factors - the collapse of the power sharing Executive after a Protestant general strike in May 1974, the failure of the 1975-76 Constitutional Convention, and the political vacuum in the late 1970s - forced it to adopt more traditional nationalist aims. In 1977 a policy document declared that 'attempts to solve the problem in a purely British context have failed and will continue to fail' (SDLP, 1977:3). In 1978 the party conference voted for British withdrawal. A similar motion had been narrowly defeated at the 1977 annual conference, with 12 of the party's 17 elected representatives to the Constitutional Convention voting in favour of withdrawal.

The gradual shift in SDLP thinking, plus the radicalization of Catholic opinion caused by the IRA hunger strikes in 1981, provided the background for the electoral challenge of Sinn Fein, the political counterpart of the Provisional IRA. Sinn Fein represents the extreme manifestation of nationalism, insofar as it is the political expression of a movement committed to using physical force to achieve Irish unity. Similarly, the Alliance Party represents the extreme manifestation of political moderation in Northern Ireland, insofar as it is the furthest point voters of either commmunity can go without crossing the sectarian divide.

Within each confessional system,the 1983 general election in Northern Ireland was seen as a major test of political support. Protestants regarded it as indicative of the two Unionist parties' ability to find agreed candidates in the six constituencies where a divided Protestant vote could allow an Irish unity candidate to win the seat. The competition between the SDLP and Sinn Fein made the election a test of the extent to which the SDLP had ceased to be the sole political voice of the Catholic community. From the perspective of the British government's Northern Ireland policy, the Sinn Fein challenge to the SDLP was the most serious threat. Since the early 1970s attempt to institutionalize power-sharing, British government policy had assumed two things. Firstly, it assumed the existence of the SDLP as the sole political group empowered to negotiate on behalf of the Catholic community and to deliver Catholic consent for any settlement. Secondly, it assumed that any governmental structures that were created in Northern Ireland would involve some form of power-sharing between Protestants and Catholics, and that the SDLP would be prepared to participate in such an arrangement. With the intervention of Sinn Fein, these twin tenets of British policy were cast in doubt.

# The Assembly and the Hunger Strikes

The years spanning the general elections of 1979 and 1983 underline the consequences of political organization around the union. The period was significant for two factors. Firstly, the British government renewed attempts to seek agreement between the Northern Ireland political parties, following the failure of the 1973-74 Assembly and the 1975-76 Constitutional Convention. Secondly, a series of hunger strikes by IRA prisoners in the Maze prison, in which ten strikers starved themselves to death, radicalized Catholic political opinion. The two events proved to be a watershed in Catholic politics. The attempt to achieve political agreement through an elected Assembly produced an abstentionist SDLP, a style of politics the SDLP had previously rejected. Although the hunger strikers were effectively defeated by the British government, the sympathy that was generated within the Catholic community provided the mass base from which Sinn Fein was able to mobilize a sizeable vote, culminating in the election of Gerry Adams, Sinn Fein vice president, in West Belfast in the 1983 general election.

The British government's attempts to return devolution to Northern Ireland began shortly after the Conservative government took up office in 1979. The 1979 Conservative manifesto had aimed to restore political accountability to the Province, and 'to establish one or more elected regional councils with a wide range of powers over local services' (Conservative Party, 1979). By contrast, the 1979 Labour manifesto had committed the party to continuing direct rule. However, this appeared to be contradicted by a National Executive Committee statement to the 1981 annual conference, which suggested that Labour should campaign for 'unity between the two parts of Ireland, based on agreement and consent' (Labour Party, 1981:11).

In November 1979 the Conservative government's attempts to restore devolution began with the publication of a White Paper, *The Government of Northern Ireland: A White Paper for a Conference*, which set out the scope of a proposed conference to find areas of agreement between the parties, and the conditions under which powers would be transferred to an Assembly. Of the four parties invited to the conference, the Official Unionists and the SDLP refused to attend. The SDLP refused on the ground that it wished to have bilateral talks with the Northern Ireland secretary, Humphrey Atkins. The party's non-participation in the talks led the leader of the party and one of its six founder members, Gerry Fitt, to resign. Between January and March 1980 the conference held 34 half-day sessions. In July 1980 a further White Paper, *The Government of Northern Ireland: Proposals for Further Discussion*, appeared, setting out a series of ideas for a locally elected administration, and two alternatives for the composition of an executive.

Concomitantly, the British government sought closer links with the Irish

Republic. In December 1980 Mrs Thatcher, Humphrey Atkins and other senior ministers met their Irish counterparts in Dublin . The result was an agreement that civil servants from both countries would draw up plans for closer Anglo-Irish co-operation, including new institutional structures. Nearly a year later in November 1981 the two governments agreed to establish 'an Anglo-Irish Intergovernmental Council' to give expression to 'their two countries unique relationship, particularly in the field of economic co-operation and co-operation on legal measures'.

By this time it was clear that the British government was committed to an Assembly election in Northern Ireland. Atkin's strategy was to let the new Assembly decide on a cross-party basis what powers it would ask Westminster to return to the Province; that policy became known as 'rolling devolution.' A White Paper, *A Framework for Devolution*, outlined this and other alternatives in April 1982. These moves created a variety of problems for the SDLP, which had been consistently distancing itself since the late 1970s from any form of political accommodation within the context of Northern Ireland . Although the Anglo-Irish Council held out the potential to satisfy the SDLP's need for an Irish dimension, from the SDLP perspective it had too few powers and no provision for creating an institutional forum for elected members of the British and Irish parliaments and from Northern Ireland.

The SDLP's long-term approach to seeking political change in the Province was significantly altered by the IRA hunger strikes. IRA prisoners had been spasmodically protesting against the abolition of political status in 1976. These protests had taken the form of a refusal to wear prison clothes (the 'blanket' protest) and smearing excrement on the walls of their cells (the 'dirty' protest). These methods had won few concessions from the British government, and in 1980 a further channel of protest was blocked when four IRA prisoners had their claims of 'inhuman and degrading treatment' rejected by the European Court of Human Rights. It was at this point that the IRA took the extreme step of sanctioning a hunger strike. Although hunger strikes are highly emotive in Ireland and have the potential for radicalizing mass opinion, they also harbour the risk that a prisoner will die and his death will be blamed on the IRA, not the British government. A successful hunger strike is one in which concessions are won on the very brink of death. As part of their continuing claim for political status, seven IRA prisoners went on hunger strike in October 1980, but the protest was called off without concessions after 53 days, when one of the seven was close to death.

A second series of hunger strikes began in early 1981. Bobby Sands was the first to refuse food, and he was followed by others at varying intervals. On 5 March Frank Maguire, the Independent Republican MP for Fermanagh & South Tyrone at Westminster, died. The seat had a relatively small Catholic majority. Initially three Catholic candidates were nominated in the by-election to fill the vacancy: Bobby Sands; Noel Maguire, the dead MP's brother, standing as an Independent Republican; and Austin Currie of the SDLP. Twelve days before the election, the SDLP party executive withdrew Currie's nomination, followed the next day by Noel Maguire, and thus leaving the field clear for Sands, who narrowly won the seat. One SDLP district councillor in Fermanagh, Tom Murray, signed Sands' nomination papers. Sands died on 5 May, and by September nine others had also died on hunger strike without winning significant concessions from the British government. The hunger strikes were called off on 3 October 1981.

Politically, the hunger strikes marked a watershed in Catholic politics in Northern Ireland. Firstly, they brought Catholic political divisions into sharp relief. During the previous decade, the Catholic community was prepared to vote for the SDLP on the grounds that Catholic political unity was of paramount importance, and that the party represented the appropriate vehicle for presenting Catholic political demands to the British government. Thus, the SDLP gained support from moderate nationalists as well as from Catholics with republican inclinations. The hunger strikes split a coalition of Catholic opinion prepared to give the SDLP their support at the political level, and the IRA support at the military level. As the survey findings in Table VIII.1 show, about two-thirds of Catholic opinion had little or no sympathy for the hunger strikers, while the remainder supported the strike. There is no division in Protestant opinion: 97 per cent of the Protestants interviewed had no sympathy at all with the hunger strike.

Secondly, the sizeable section of Catholic opinion favouring the strike led the IRA to feel it had a sufficiently large numerical base from which to mount an electoral challenge to the SDLP. Moreover, the actions of the SDLP horrified many moderate Catholics. In the early 1970s one of the party's major criticisms of the old Nationalist Party had been the latter's collusion with physical force republicanism during elections. An informal agreement existed in the 1950s and 1960s that Nationalists had the exclusive right to contest elections to the Stormont Parliament, while Westminster elections were the preserve of republicans. The SDLP now appeared to be doing the same by standing aside to allow the election of Sands in Fermanagh & South Tyrone, and also doing the same thing when Owen Carron, Sands' election agent, contested and won the second by-election to fill the seat.

The political emergence of a Catholic republican minority after the hunger strike formed the background to the SDLP's decision about contesting the October 1982 Assembly election. The SDLP had already stated its opposition to the principle of the Assembly when the White Paper had been published in April 1982. John Hume, who had succeeded Gerry Fitt as leader, stated that 'any party which accepts without question proposals which can clearly be shown to be unworkable, in order to present an image of reasonableness to the

Table VIII.1  <u>ULSTER ATTITUDES TOWARDS THE HUNGER STRIKE</u>

Q:  How much sympathy do you have with the IRA hunger
    strikers in the Maze Prison?

|  | Protestant % | Catholic % | Total % |
|---|---|---|---|
| A great deal | – | 7 | 20 |
| A fair amount | – | 6 | 15 |
| A little | 2 | 12 | 31 |
| None at all | 97 | 74 | 33 |

Source:  MORI survey for <u>Sunday Times</u>,  18–22 June 1981,
         N = 1,008.

community, is an irresponsible political party' (*Irish Times*, 27 April 1982). The decision about whether or not to contest the election symbolized the party's future approach to the whole Northern Ireland problem. To contest the election and participate in the Assembly would have followed the constitutional, participatory path the party had committed itself to in 1970, and implied that the party felt an internal solution to the problem was possible. To abstain from contesting the election, or to abstain from taking up seats if elected, would imply that the party considered an internal political solution impossible, and that a feasible solution would have to embrace a broader framework, encompassing relations with the Irish Republic.

The SDLP's decision to contest the election but not to take their seats provided a compromise between the two groups within the party, one of which wanted to participate fully in the Assembly, and the other to have no part in it. The compromise that was reached enabled the party to maintain its unity, but also to defend its electoral position against Sinn Fein, which had by then decided to nominate candidates on an abstentionist platform. It was a compromise that once again reflected the divisions within Catholic opinion. A survey carried out just before the Assembly election showed that while 38 per cent of Catholics favoured the idea of the Assembly, 37 per cent had no opinion, and 1 in 4 opposed it (Table VIII.2). By contrast, two-thirds of Protestants favoured the Assembly.

Table VIII.2    ULSTER ATTITUDES TO N. IRELAND ASSEMBLY

Q:  There will be an election for a Northern Ireland
    Assembly on October 10th.    Are you in favour, or
    opposed to the idea of this Assembly?

|            | Protestant % | Catholic % | Total % |
|------------|:---:|:---:|:---:|
| In favour  | 66 | 38 | 55 |
| Opposed    | 8  | 25 | 15 |
| Don't know | 26 | 37 | 30 |

Source: Ulster Marketing Surveys for BBC,    5-6 October
        1982, N = 1,009.

Both the SDLP and Sinn Fein contested the Assembly election, the latter polling creditably with 10.1 per cent of the first preference vote and 5 of the 78 seats, compared to the SDLP's 18.8 per cent and 14 seats. The Democratic Unionists, traditionally the weaker of the two Unionist parties, also polled well against the Official Unionists, winning 23.0 per cent of the vote and 21 seats against the latter's 29.8 per cent and 26 seats. Overall, the combined vote for Loyalist and Unionist parties fell slightly in 1982 when compared to the 1975 Convention election -- from 62.5 per cent of the first preference vote to 58.6 per cent. Through the intervention of Sinn Fein, the total Irish unity vote increased, from 25.9 per cent in 1975 to 31.7 per cent in 1982 (Elliott and Wilford, 1983).

Although no Catholic group attended the Assembly, it met during the remainder of 1982 and throughout 1983, debating and passing motions on such topics as security, Anglo-Irish relations, and the form devolution should take in the Province. The strategy of the Official Unionists was to use the Assembly as a forum to demand from the British government a return to majority rule in Northern Ireland, while the Democratic Unionists argued that the Assembly itself provided an institutional framework for the return of devolution, and that powers could be gradually given to it. These differences in approach surfaced on a variety of occasions, most notably with regard to the role of the committees which were set up to scrutinize the British government's administration in Northern Ireland. While the Democratic Unionists were prepared to accept these committees as a first step towards legislative devolution, the Official

Unionists regarded them as a distraction from the real issue of obtaining full devolution. As a result, the Official Unionists boycotted the committees until February 1983.

Outside the Assembly, the SDLP continued to attack the Protestant community's resistance to political change, along with what they saw as the British government's tolerance of that resistance. In a speech to the 1983 party conference, John Hume attacked the British government for their acceptance of the Protestant position, and argued that they should 'accept that there are other ways and means in which the Protestant identity can be protected' (*Belfast Telegraph*,28 January 1983). The SDLP's position was to move away from any solution involving the United Kingdom alone, and to look towards an all-Ireland solution actively encompassing the Irish and British governments. It was this policy which provided the SDLP with a major plank in their 1983 Westminister election platform.

## The 1983 General Election

In keeping with the rest of the United Kingdom, there was a major revision of constituency boundaries in Northern Ireland. But unlike mainland Britain, the changes had not been initiated by the Boundary Commission's regular revisions to take account of population shifts. Rather, they stemmed from an agreement reached between the Labour government in 1977 and 1978 and the Ulster Unionists MPs, that the latter would support the government in motions of confidence if Northern Ireland's Westminster representation - since 1921 having far more electors per constituency than Britain - was brought into line with the rest of the United Kingdom. The agreement to increase the number of Ulster seats from 12 to 17 was honoured by the incoming Conservative government in 1979.

The subsequent boundary changes resulted in major revisions in all but two constituencies -- North Belfast and Fermanagh & South Tyrone -- and made the task of estimating the religious (and hence the political) complexion of each constituency more difficult. Some approximation of religious affiliation in the 17 constituencies can be made by using the 1981 census, and adjusting for the 19 per cent of the population who failed to answer the religion question.    The proportion of the population refusing to state their religon in the 1981 census varies considerably between constituencies: the largest (23.7 per cent) is found in West Belfast, which has a large Catholic majority, while the lowest is found in constituencies which have a large Protestant majority, such as Strangford (15.4 per cent). There would appear to be prima facie evidence that Catholics are disproportionately represented among the non-stated category. The simplest method of allocating these persons to one or the other religious community is to distribute them according to the religious balance in the constituency: for example, if stated Catholics comprise 30 per cent of the population, then assume that 30 per cent of the not stated are Catholics. This is not a practical solution since it under-estimates the Catholic electorate.

The best practical alternative is to assume some weighting to the Catholic proportion in the not stated category. The weighting used here is one third: that is, it is assumed that the Catholic not stated category is made up of one third more than they appear to be on the basis of the stated proportion in the population. For example, if the stated percentage of Catholics in a constituency is 30 per cent, then it is assumed that the not stated category is 40 per cent Catholic (30 + (30/3)).

Calculations show that 6 of the 17 constituencies have Catholic majorities: West Belfast (71 per cent Catholic); Foyle (68 per cent); Newry & Armagh (60 per cent); Mid Ulster (54 per cent); South Down (53 per cent); and Fermanagh & South Tyrone (50 per cent). The remaining 11 constituencies have secure Protestant majorities ranging from 95 per cent of the population in East Belfast, to 63 per cent in Upper Bann.

Within the Protestant community, the Official Unionist and Democratic Unionists negotiated to reach agreed candidates in the 11 constituencies with loyalist majorities, and in the remaining seats where it was possible that the Catholic majority's vote would be split between the SDLP and Sinn Fein. The Official Unionists were disinclined to negotiate, except for the fact that Enoch Powell would be in jeopardy in South Down if the Protestant vote was split with the Democratic Unionists. A draft agreement was made between the two parties, in which the Official Unionists would nominate candidates in Fermanagh & South Tyrone, South Down and Newry & Armagh, while the Democratic Unionists would contest Foyle, West Belfast and Mid Ulster. The agreement collapsed when the local Official Unionist party in Mid Ulster refused to stand aside for the Democratic Unionist's candidate, the Rev William McCrea. In the event, the agreement partially held, and the Official Unionists were the sole Protestant party in Fermanagh & South Tyrone and Newry & Armagh, while the Democratic Unionists were given a clear field in Foyle. The Democratic Unionists also stood aside in North Down, so as to increase the chances of re-election for James Kilfedder, who had left the Official Unionist Party in 1979 and was contesting the election as a 'Popular Unionist' against an Official Unionist candidate, Robert McCartney.

There were no comparable attempts to agree candidates among the two groups competing for the Catholic vote, the SDLP and Sinn Fein. The Irish Independence Party, which had unsuccessfully contested a few seats in the 1982 Assembly election decided not to contest the election.

The SDLP, recalling the problems they precipitated by failing to contest the two Fermanagh & South Tyrone by- elections in 1981, contested all 17 seats, while Sinn Fein contested 14. The SDLP strategy was to point out the links between Sinn Fein and the IRA, and to highlight their own attempts to broaden the discussion of Northern Ireland to include the Irish Republic. In this latter aspect of their campaign, the SDLP emphasized the New Ireland Forum, an all-Ireland body designed to bring the political parties together to discuss possible constitutional solutions. However, within Northern Ireland only the SDLP agreed to attend the Forum; the other three invited parties, the Official Unionists, Democratic Unionists and Alliance, all refused; Sinn Fein was not invited because of its links with the IRA. The SDLP placed great emphasis on the Forum; Hume claimed during the election that it would 'make a dramatic impact not only on Irish opinion, but on British opinion and international opinion. It will open up the whole debate on the Irish question' (*Guardian*, 21 May 1983).

While the SDLP focused on Sinn Fein's link with the IRA, Sinn Fein itself made no attempt to obscure its support for physical force. At least six of its 14 candidates had either been interned or served prison sentences for terrorist offences, and this was mentioned in their election literature, presumably to enhance their popular appeal. Sinn Fein emphasised the complementary nature of the ballot and the bullet . As Danny Morrison, the Mid Ulster candidate, put it, they approached the election 'with an Armalite in one hand and a ballot box in the other.' In a BBC interview, Gerry Adams, the West Belfast candidate, stated 'The use of force is a question for the IRA and we support their use of force.' (quoted in *Irish Times*, 30 May 1983).

One significant dimension to the SDLP-Sinn Fein competition involved political organisation. Although the SDLP had developed an extensive cross-local political organization in the early 1970s, apathy and a lack of political progress had gradually undermined its effectiveness, particularly in Belfast. By contrast, Sinn Fein had been developing an organization based on local communities, and the October 1982 Assembly election had provided an opportunity to test it. Moreover, they were energetically setting up advice centres to cope with individual grievances, and by June 1983 it was estimated they had eight centres functioning and another five planned. By focusing on local issues such as housing, and raising these grievances with government, Sinn Fein was tapping a tradition of Irish political localism by which public representatives act as mediators between the individual and government, and in return gain the individual's vote(See Bax, 1977 and Sacks, 1976). The SDLP and Sinn Fein also came into conflict at the local level, and after the election the SDLP published a list of incidents in which candidates, canvassers and supporters were attacked or intimidated by IRA supporters (*Irish Times*, 7 July 1983).

The bi-confessional Alliance Party of Northern Ireland vied for the support of both communities. Unlike the SDLP, which had moved away from a power sharing solution within the context of the Northern Ireland state, Alliance adhered to the basic 1973 Sunningdale framework. Its manifesto warned, 'The price of devolution is really an accommodation with constitutional nationalists who totally reject violence and are prepared to give their support to the institutions of the state' (Alliance Party, 1983). It nominated 12 candidates in the election, significantly not contesting West Belfast in the hope that the Alliance vote would go to the sitting MP, Gerry Fitt, who was being challenged by both the SDLP and Sinn Fein. Fitt had previously lost his Belfast City Council seat in the 1981 District Council elections. Rather than mounting a door-to-door canvass, Fitt placed full page advertisements in the Protestant *Belfast Newsletter* and the Catholic *Irish News* (costing £ 2,270 and £ 1,900 respectively) listing details of his parlimentary interjections and speeches from *Hansard* .

The general election result gave the Official Unionists a plurality of the vote , 34 per cent, and 10 of the 17 seats(Table VIII.3). The Democratic Unionists emerged as the second largest party, with 20 per cent of the vote and 4 seats. Within the Catholic community, the SDLP led Sinn Fein in total votes. But each party had one candidate elected. John Hume, the SDLP leader, was returned for Foyle, easily beating his Sinn Fein rival, Martin McGuinness. In

Table VIII.3   THE 1983 ELECTION RESULT IN N. IRELAND

|  | Candidates | Votes | % | Seats |
|---|---|---|---|---|
| Ulster Unionist | 16 | 259,952 | 34.0 | 11 |
| Democratic Unionist | 14 | 152,749 | 20.0 | 3 |
| Other Loyalists[a] | 2 | 23,995 | 3.1 | 1 |
| All Unionist–Loyalist | 32 | 436,696 | 57.1 | 15 |
| APNI | 12 | 61,275 | 8.0 | 0 |
| SDLP | 17 | 137,012 | 17.9 | 1 |
| Sinn Fein | 14 | 102,701 | 13.4 | 1 |
| Workers' Party | 14 | 14,650 | 1.9 | 0 |
| All Irish unity | 45 | 254,363 | 33.2 | 2 |
| Other | 5 | 12,591 | 1.7 | 0 |
| Total | 95 | 764,925 | 100.0 | 17 |

[a]   James Kilfedder in North Down and Billy Gault in North Belfast.

Table VIII.4   PATTERNS OF PARTY COMPETITION IN N. IRELAND

|  | East of Bann | Belfast | West of Bann | Total |
|---|---|---|---|---|
| **Official Unionist first** | | | | |
| DUP second | 4 | 1 | 1 | 6 |
| Alliance second | 0 | 1 | 0 | 1 |
| SDLP second | 2 | 0 | 1 | 3 |
| Sinn Fein second | 0 | 0 | 1 | 1 |
| Total | 6 | 2 | 3 | 11 |
| **Democratic Unionist first** | | | | |
| Official Unionist second | 1 | 1 | 0 | 2 |
| Sinn Fein second | 0 | 0 | 1 | 1 |
| Total | 1 | 1 | 1 | 3 |
| **Other first[a]** | | | | |
| Alliance second | 1 | 0 | 0 | 1 |
| **SDLP first** | | | | |
| Democratic Unionist second | 0 | 0 | 1 | 1 |
| **Sinn Fein first** | | | | |
| SDLP second | 0 | 1 | 0 | 1 |

[a]  James Kilfedder in North Down

West Belfast, Gerry Adams, Sinn Fein vice president, beat both Gerry Fitt and the SDLP candidate, Joe Hendron. The remaining seat went to James Kilfedder in North Down. Despite the apparent SDLP lead over Sinn Fein, if we examine the percentage vote each party received in the constituencies it contested, the lead is much narrower. By this measure Sinn Fein actually received nearly 16 per cent of the vote, only 2 per cent behind the SDLP. The pattern of party competition in eight of the 17 contests involved competition between the Official Unionists and DUP (Table VIII.4). A further three had the Official Unionists first and the SDLP second. There were six different patterns of competition in the six remaining seats.

The distribution of seats was influenced by two complementary factors: the nature of the electoral system and the territorial clustering of party support.

The first past the post system used in Westminster elections favours parties which can maximize their vote in specific areas, and is to the disadvantage of parties whose support is dissipated across a range of constituencies. By contrast,the single transferable vote proportional representation system (STV PR) methods used in Northern Ireland local government and provincial elections, greatly reduces the advantage of larger, territorially grouped parties. This is illustrated by comparing the votes and seats gained by the parties in the 1982 Assembly election, conducted under proportional representation, and the 1983 general election. In the PR election, the discrepancy between the proportion of votes and seats was small, averaging just 3 per cent and as in the general election, the discrepancy consistently favoured the Unionist parties. In the general election, however, the average discrepancy between votes and seats was nearly 10 per cent, ranging from a 24.8 per cent advantage for the Official Unionists to a 12 per cent disadvantage for the SDLP. On the basis of a proportional allocation of seats, the Official Unionists would have returned 6 MPs not 10; the SDLP 3, not 1; Sinn Fein 2 not 1; and Alliance would have elected its first Westminster MP.

Another way to illustrate the territorial clustering of the vote is to examine the party votes in the three major regions of Northern Ireland which have shown to be electorally important over the last half century (McAllister, 1983): Belfast; the region surrounding Belfast to the East of the River Bann; and the region West of the River Bann. Each of the five parties has a distinct regional base(Table VIII.5). The two Unionist parties are weakest West of the Bann and strongest in Belfast. Alliance finds the bulk of its support in Belfast and East

Table VIII.5   REGIONAL INFLUENCES ON THE VOTE IN N. IRELAND

| Party | Total | Deviation from N. Ireland total | | |
| | | E. of Bann | Belfast | W. of Bann |
| | % | % | % | % |
| Official Unionist | 34.0 | +5.2 | −5.7 | −1.9 |
| Democratic Unionist | 20.0 | +6.2 | +2.1 | −2.2 |
| APNI | 8.0 | +3.5 | +5.6 | −6.3 |
| SDLP | 17.9 | −5.7 | −5.3 | +8.2 |
| Sinn Fein | 13.4 | −9.9 | +1.1 | +8.9 |

a.   (For a definition of regions, see Appendix A).

of the Bann, and does worst in constituencies to the West of the Bann, where sectarian tensions are highest. Both the SDLP and Sinn Fein are strongest in the West.It is noteworthy that Sinn Fein does considerably better in Belfast than the SDLP.

The most significant aspect of the 1983 general election in Northern Ireland was the success of Sinn Fein, which increased its vote from 10.1 per cent in the 1982 Assembly election to 13.4 per cent. Two hypotheses can be put forward to account for this increase, each of which have implications for British government policy in Northern Ireland, and for the party system as a whole. The first hypothesis sees the Sinn Fein increase as a protest vote, consisting mainly of ex-SDLP voters who have become disillusioned with attempts to find an internal Northern Ireland settlement and are disaffected with the SDLP's political leadership. Secondly, it has been suggested that it represents the mobilization of a republican vote, which is largely unrelated to the SDLP, representing the turnout of Catholics sympathetic to republicanism, but who had not bothered to vote previously because they did not regard parties rejecting physical force as worth voting for. The protest vote hypothesis implies that there has been a shift in Catholic political opinion, and casts doubt on the practicality of any British-sponsored internal solution. On the other hand, the mobilization of the vote hypothesis means there has been no shift in opinion: republicans have always existed in Northern Ireland, and now are prepared to turn out to vote for a republican party, whereas previously they abstained from voting on principle.

Comparing the SDLP and Sinn Fein vote totals between the 1982 Assembly and the 1983 general election casts doubt on the protest vote hypothesis. Disaffection from the SDLP suggests that it should have lost votes, when in fact its vote increased from 118,891 in 1982 to 137,012 in 1983. Moreover, the turnout between the two elections increased by just over 10 per cent, from 62.3 per cent to 72.8 per cent, bringing an extra 100,000 voters to the polls. Of these extra voters, it would appear that some 43,000 were additional Official and Democratic Unionist voters, around 17,000 were extra SDLP voters, and the remaining 40,000 favoured Sinn Fein, accounting for the party's rise in total votes from 64,191 to 102,701. Clearly, there is strong evidence pointing to the mobilization of a republican vote hypothesis. Rather than there being any decay in the SDLP's electoral position within the Catholic community, Sinn Fein have managed to gain support from individuals who previously preferred to abstain from voting.In other words, Catholic attitudes have changed less than Catholic electoral behaviour. Previously,the division was between SDLP voters and republican abstentionists. Now it is between SDLP and republican voters.

# The Implications of the Result

From a United Kingdom perspective, the 1983 general election once again displayed Northern Ireland's uniqueness. While social class differentiated the major parties in Britain, Northern Ireland's political parties were divided on the more fundamental question of the constitution, with two parties seeing themselves as British, another Irish. Moreover, one in every seven Ulster voters (or one in three Catholics) cast their ballot for a party advocating the violent removal of the British presence from the Province (Table VIII.6).

Examining the religious and class break-down of support for the parties shows that four parties are exclusively confessional, two Protestant, and two Catholic; only the Alliance Party draws its support from both religions. In terms of the social class of supporters, all five gain cross-class support; with all except the Alliance and Official Unionist parties drawing proportionately more from the middle class.

For the British government, the election result has three major implications. Firstly and most obviously, the divisions within communities, expressed by elected MPs, means that a political accommodation is very difficult to achieve. The two Unionist parties are divided about how they should be governed - as a part of Britain, like any other part of the mainland, or with distinctive institutions and administration. The two Catholic parties are divided less on the ultimate aim of a united Ireland than on the methods to be used to achieve this,

Table VIII.6  PARTY PREFERENCE BY RELIGION AND CLASS IN ULSTER

|  | Official Unionist | Democratic Unionist | APNI | SDLP | Sinn Fein |
|---|---|---|---|---|---|
|  | % | % | % | % | % |
| **Religion** | | | | | |
| Protestant | 98 | 95 | 54 | 4 | – |
| Catholic | 2 | 2 | 45 | 96 | 98 |
| Other | – | 3 | 1 | – | 2 |
| | | | | | |
| **Class** | | | | | |
| Middle class | 43 | 30 | 54 | 37 | 20 |
| Working class | 57 | 70 | 46 | 63 | 80 |

Source: Market Research Bureau of Ireland survey for Irish News 30 May–1 June 1983, N = 1,020.

constitutional action or extra-constitutional physical force. The SDLP believes that constitutional change can come with pressure by the Dublin government; Sinn Fein relies on its own forces. The result of these intra-communal political divisions is that no single group can be said to be fully representative of either community and in any negotiations several groups would have to be considered for each. Sinn Fein's electoral success added a further complication in that successive British governments since 1976 had committed themselves not to negotiate with the IRA. Although the Irish Republic had reaffirmed that they would not negotiate with these groups, this commitment is now more difficult for the British when an IRA supporter in Sinn Fein is a member of the Westminster Parliament.

Secondly, the republican movement has traditionally had two wings: one, a physical force organization dedicated to removing the British presence by arms, and the other, a political group supporting the military campaign by non-violent action that could be taken "overground" rather than "underground". From the late 1960s until the early 1980s, the IRA's military wing was predominant. The election result shows that the political wing is now also important. The IRA can try to reap direct political benefits from the military campaign, whereas before the lack of a creditable, competent, political voice meant that the gains to be made from the military side were limited. Indeed, Gerry Adams admitted that Sinn Fein's role was to complement the military campaign, arguing that their strategy was 'to broaden and popularise the armed struggle' (*Sunday Times*, 8 May 1983).

Finally, the election result reaffirmed that devolution remains an impractical option in Northern Ireland, at least in the immediate future. The Unionists are dissatisfied with anything less than majority rule in a provincial Parliament or full integration with Britain. Similarly, the SDLP are committed to abstaining from participation in the Assembly, and to seeking a political solution outside the framework of the United Kingdom, with the aid of the Irish government in Dublin. Temporary direct rule thus remains. . Opinion polls have shown that direct rule is endorsed by a majority in both communities in Northern Ireland as an acceptable short-term solution (Rose, McAllister and Mair, 1978). While they continue to display fundamental divisions about ultimate constitutional goals, temporary direct rule remains by default.

# IX
# The Integration
# of the British Electorate

Explanations of the outcome of elections in the United Kingdom are often asymmetrical. Elections in England are not explained in terms of distinctive English factors. Instead, voting behaviour is explained in terms of social structure characteristics common to every Western nation. The leading studies of voting behaviour in Britain (Butler and Stokes, 1974; Sarlvik and Crewe, 1983) assume generic rather than nation-specific influences. Both sets of authors analyse voting with a conceptual framework developed at the University of Michigan and exported to more than a dozen countries from Australia and Japan to Finland and Italy. Insofar as the framework identifies distinctive national factors, they are common to the whole of Britain, such as party identification or party leaders; they are not factors unique to England.

By contrast, studies of election outcomes in Scotland, Wales and Northern Ireland seek or claim to find unique influences differentiating elections between the nations of the United Kingdom. Focusing a study upon Scotland, Wales or Northern Ireland is more or less assumed to justify emphasizing nation-specific rather than generic influences upon votes. Whereas the generic approach risks ignoring what is distinctive about election outcomes in Britain, focusing on a single nation within Britain is vulnerable to the nominalist fallacy. It assumes that because a study is defined by the boundaries of a nation, then non-Scottish or non-Welsh influences are irrelevant, and that the distinctive feature of Scottish social structure is that it is Scottish.

Northern Ireland *is* unique in being dominated by nation-specific influences. The parties contesting elections in Ulster have no links with parties in what is referred to as mainland Britain. The uniqueness of Northern Ireland is further emphasized by the fact that parties to political conflict there include illegal and active armed groups, such as the Provisional IRA and the Ulster Volunteer Force, acting as alternatives or supplements to electoral organisations (Rose,

1976: chapter 3). Nowhere in Great Britain does political competition take the form it does in Ulster.

Whereas preceding chapters have examined the four nations of the United Kingdom separately, the purpose here is to use data about social structure, territorial differences and election outcomes to test the extent to which the British electorate is integrated. Integration occurs insofar as there are common influences upon voting; insofar as territorial and particularistic national influences are of principal importance, then electoral competition involves different or, in Northern Ireland, dis-integrative influences. In the second section, the extent of national differences in competition for seats is examined. Given that any universe of more than 600 constituencies is bound to have some exceptions, the third section examines the constituencies that deviate from the Britainwide pattern.

## The Dominance of Social Structure

When separate regression analyses for England, Wales and Scotland are compared, the results are broadly similar. Two social structure influences stand out as consistently important: the socio-economic status of a constituency and agriculture. The significance of national differences is further mitigated by the evidence of regional effects dividing each nation. In Wales, Plaid Cymru is a partial exception to these generalizations (Table VI.3). The percentage of Welsh-speakers in a constituency has a greater impact upon the Plaid vote than the socio-economic status of a constituency has upon the vote. However, the proportion of the Welsh vote thus influenced is small, only eight per cent. Moreover, language use divides the regions of Wales from each other.

Analysing all the constituencies of Great Britain together gives full and proper weight to England; the 523 English constituencies will dominate statistical analysis as they do the creation of a House of Commons majority. Excluding Northern Ireland, because Ulster votes are not cast for parties competing in Britain, also follows the political ground rules for constructing a House of Commons majority. By combining the three nations of Britain together, it is possible to test whether or to what extent there is a distinctly national effect in Scotland and Wales, just as separate analyses of Scotland and Wales could test the significance of regional divisions within Scotland and Wales. An all-Britain analysis also tests the importance of social structure common in constituencies from Sussex to Strathclyde, and from Aldershot to Aberdeen.

Analytically, the British electorate can be described as integrated insofar as common social structure influences are the principal determinants of votes rather than territorial factors. The results are clear: social influences do result in the integration of electoral competition (Table IX.1). Four social structure influences can explain 60 per cent of the variation in Labour's vote, and 54 per cent of the variation in Conservative vote. Social structure is less important in determining the Alliance vote, but nonetheless explains more than half of the Alliance vote that can be accounted for by regression analysis.

Where a constituency ranks in socio-economic status is more important than where it is placed on a map. The socio-economic status of a constituency is the single most important influence upon the level of a party's vote. Occupation, housing and levels of unemployment are far more important than regional culture, or centre-periphery measures of distance. The difference in the Conservative vote in constituencies at the top and bottom of the status scale is 36 per cent, and the difference in the Labour vote is 43 per cent. Variations of this magnitude assure the Conservatives of hundreds of safe seats, and Labour of many safe seats too. The relatively weak impact of socio- economic status upon the Alliance vote, nine per cent at the extremes, explains why the Alliance has so very few safe seats. Apparent national differences can also be explained in socio-economic terms. One reason why the Conservative vote is lower in Scotland is not Scottish culture, but because Scottish constituencies on average rank substantially lower in socio-economic status, for the proportion of council

Table IX.1   SOCIAL STRUCTURE AND TERRITORIAL INFLUENCES ON THE VOTE IN BRITAIN

| | Conservative vote | | Labour vote | | Alliance vote | |
|---|---|---|---|---|---|---|
| | b | % var. expl'd | b | % var. expl'd | b | % var. expl'd |
| **Social Structure** | | | | | | |
| Socio-econ. status | .36** | 40 | −.43** | 34 | .09** | 9 |
| Agriculture | .10** | 13 | −.20** | 19 | .06** | 7 |
| Immigrants | −.01 | 0 | −.06* | 5 | −.01 | 1 |
| Elderly | −.01 | 1 | −.02* | 2 | .00 | 0 |
| **Territory** | | | | | | |
| Miles from London | −.02** | 13 | −.01* | 4 | .01* | 3 |
| Region[a] | 4.3** | 9 | −8.0** | 12 | 3.9** | 7 |
| (Constant) $r^2$ | (24.0) | 76 | (60.1) | 76 | (17.2) | 26 |

[a]   South of England for all parties.

tenants in Scotland is about double the English average (cf. Appendix Table B.3).

Agriculture is a second social structure influence important throughout Britain. The Conservative vote rises by 10 per cent in the most agricultural constituency as against urban constituencies, and the Alliance vote rises six per cent, all other things being equal. The Labour vote is even more strongly affected, falling from its urban peak by 20 per cent in the most rural constituencies. A higher level of agriculture in some parts of Scotland and Wales (Appendix Table B.3), results in very industrial areas favouring Labour, and very agricultural areas having a low Labour vote. Thus, social structure can simultaneously create divisions within nations and integrate social groups Britainwide.

The presence of a substantial number of immigrants in a constituency appears to produce a complex reaction. Once the socio-economic status of high immigrant constituencies is taken into account, the Labour vote is likely to be *less* than would be expected. In the most immigrant constituency, Labour loses six per cent of the vote it would be expected to get because of its other characteristics (Table IX.1). Constituencies high in immigrants tend to have a substantially lower turnout; people living in transient accommodation, and especially recent immigrants, are much less likely to vote. The turnout factor, which is not included in the regression, appears to depress the likelihood of pro-Labour immigrants actually casting their ballots.

Examining the proportion of the elderly in a constituency is a reminder that social structure influences are very unequal in importance. By comparison with levels of socio-economic status and agriculture, the elderly have virtually no impact upon the vote in British constituencies. Elderly people tend to be set in voting patterns decades previously by influences already taken into account, such as socio-economic status.

Territorial influences are of secondary importance; they are more important than the age composition of a constituency, but far less significant than its socio-economic status or agriculture. Distance from London has a limited but noticeable impact upon the vote of each of the parties; it accounts for 13 per cent of the variance in the Conservative vote, for four per cent of that in the Labour vote, and three per cent in the Alliance vote, once all other influences are controlled for. The further a constituency is from London, the more likely the Conservative and Labour vote is to fall. This is true within England, as well as being true as between English and Scottish constituencies. The Conservative vote in a Scottish constituency 400 miles from London is likely to be eight per cent lower than in the same type of seat in London, but the party's vote would also be down by five per cent in a North of England constituency 250 miles from London.

The political distinctiveness of the South of England, even after allowance for its socio-economic status and agriculture, is noteworthy too. A total of 12 per cent of the variance in the Labour vote can be explained by its poor showing in constituencies in the South of England, and nine per cent of the variation in the Conservative vote and seven per cent in the Alliance vote can be explained by the strength of these parties in the South of England.

Regional analysis of the whole of Britain combines the four English regions and Wales and Scotland, previously examined separately. The distinctive national element in the politics of Wales and Scotland is preserved by not disaggregating Wales and Scotland into regions. Moreover, doing this increases statistical reliability, given that Scotland and Wales have fewer constituencies than the smallest of the four English regions. The extent to which regional effects are important in each of these six regions of Britain and for each party is assessed here, as in previous chapters, by comparing the vote that the party would be expected to gain because of its social structure with the vote actually obtained (Table IX.2).

In analysing regional patterns in voting, it is crucial to distinguish between the extent and the causes of differences. For example, we can note that there are great differences between the Conservative vote in Chelsea as against Bow & Poplar, but this would not be explained in terms of differences in regional culture within inner London, but by differences in social structure. The extent of regional differences in the vote are substantial in Britain. The mean constituency vote for the Conservatives ranges 25 per cent, from 53 per cent in the South of England to 28 per cent in Scotland. The Labour vote ranges by 21 per cent, from a 37 per cent share in the North of England and in Wales to 15

Table IX.2  REGIONAL INFLUENCES ON THE VOTE IN BRITAIN

| | % Conservative vote | | | % Labour vote | | | % Alliance vote | | |
|---|---|---|---|---|---|---|---|---|---|
| | Act | Pre-dict | Diff | Act | Pre-dict | Diff | Act | Pre-dict | Diff |
| **England** | | | | | | | | | |
| South | 53 | 47 | +6 | 16 | 24 | −8 | 30 | 28 | +2 |
| London | 43 | 44 | −1 | 30 | 27 | +3 | 25 | 27 | −2 |
| Midlands | 45 | 45 | 0 | 31 | 30 | +1 | 23 | 23 | 0 |
| North | 38 | 40 | −2 | 37 | 34 | +3 | 24 | 25 | −1 |
| Wales | 31 | 30 | +1 | 37 | 39 | −2 | 23 | 22 | +1 |
| Scotland | 28 | 30 | −2 | 35 | 40 | −5 | 25 | 22 | +3 |

per cent in the South of England. By contrast, the Alliance vote varies only seven per cent from 30 per cent in the South of England to 23 per cent in the Midlands and in Wales.

Comparing the regional share of the vote that each party would be predicted to have solely on the basis of its social structure with what it actually achieved shows that nearly the whole of inter-regional differences can be explained by social structure. The average difference between the actual and predicted vote for the Alliance in six regions is 1.5 per cent; for the Conservatives, 2.0 per cent; and for Labour, 3.7 per cent. In two-thirds of the cases the differences are two per cent or less, well within what could be caused by rounding and measurement errors. The party most subject to regional effects is Labour and the effects tend to be negative. Labour does eight per cent worse in its vote in the South of England than would be expected from social structure, and five per cent below what would be expected in Scotland.

The two regions which evidence some effect, however secondary, are at the extremes of Britain, the South of England and Scotland. In the South of England the Conservatives would be expected to do well because of its relatively high socio-economic status and agricultural areas. In fact, the Conservatives do six per cent better than expected. The Alliance would be expected to come second because of the social structure; it does, and adds two per cent to its expected vote. Labour suffers from its weakness, polling below the poor vote it would be expected to have in the South of England by eight per cent. In Scotland, the presence of the Nationalists, taking 12 per cent of the vote, increases the likelihood of British parties polling worse than would otherwise be predicted. Labour also polls below its expected vote in Scotland, because the very high proportion of council house tenants in Scotland causes the prediction of a relatively high Labour vote, but council-house tenancy is less a sign of low socio- economic status in Scotland than in England.

Regional differences are nominal, for the sub-cultures of Scotland and Wales are meant to be different in kind from that of London; differences in social structure are differences of degree. The regression analyses emphasize that it is differences in degree-- particularly, the degree to which a constituency is high or low in socio-economic status or in agriculture--that have the greatest impact upon a party's share of the vote. The one influence that can double or halve the Conservative or Labour vote in a constituency is the Britainwide influence of socio-economic status.

## Constituency Competition for Seats

A map of a country's social structure will reveal a degree of variation from one area to another, and so too will a map of election results. What is distinctive about Anglo-American countries is that the first-past-the-post electoral system makes the party first in votes the exclusive representative of a constituency. The winning party enjoys hegemony in the constituency. The concept of hegemony not only means the dominance of one group, but also the presence of a minority to be dominated. If the winning MP secures less than half the total vote, then the hegemony of representation affects a majority of the voters. By being the sole voice of a constituency in Parliament, its MP can claim to represent the whole area, though winning the votes of only a part.

While there is competition for votes in each single-member constituency, in a three-party race the result is always the same: two parties will lose. The presence of any opposition MPs in the House of Commons depends upon the empirical relationship between social structure, party loyalties and constituency boundaries. In a sense, the House of Commons represents the voters in spite of rather than because of the mechanics of the electoral system.

There are two ways in which parties can compete successfully for seats in the House of Commons. On the one hand, a party may claim the loyalty of social groups that tend to be preponderant in particular places, whether parts of a conurbation, a region or nation. Labour's appeal to manual workers, council-house tenants and the unemployed makes low-status constituencies safe Labour seats. Of the 100 constituencies in Britain ranking lowest in socio-economic status, Labour won 91 at the 1983 general election; the Conservatives five (Nottingham North, Basildon, Harlow, the Wrekin, and Corby); the Alliance three (Southwark & Bermondsey, Roxburgh & Berwickshire, and Woolwich); and the SNP one (Dundee East). Reciprocally, the Conservatives tend to have the loyalty of middle class home-owners unconcerned about unemployment. Of the 100 constituencies ranking highest in socio-economic status in Britain, the Conservatives won all 100.

If the social structure of a constituency more or less assures the party half the vote, then it has a safe seat. Even when Labour's vote dropped to 27.6 per cent of the nationwide total in 1983, it could still win 32.2 per cent of all seats in Parliament. In a similar fashion, when the Conservative share of the vote dropped to 35.8 per cent in October, 1974, the Conservatives could enjoy the luxury of over-representation, winning 43.6 per cent of all the seats in the Commons.

The Alliance suffers in the competition for parliamentary representation because its vote is distributed very evenly Britainwide. Whereas the Conservative share of the vote varied from 46.0 per cent in England to 28.4 per cent in Scotland, and Labour's share from 37.5 per cent in Wales to 26.9 per cent in England, the difference in the Alliance vote was much narrower being 26.4 per cent in England, 24.5 per cent in Scotland, and 23.2 per cent in Wales. The Alliance vote was also spread far more evenly among the regions of England than the Labour or Conservative vote.

In an electoral system in which it pays to concentrate political appeal, the Alliance is distinctive in that its vote is not greatly influenced by any salient feature of social structure. In a country where each constituency is not a microcosm of society as a whole, but is usually biased in favour of a party with a definite appeal to particular socio-economic groups, the Alliance is likely to end up second. One of its opponents benefits from the social structure, finishing first, and the other avoids wasting votes by finishing third. As long as Alliance support is so evenly spread, the only way in which it can hope to win a parliamentary majority is by increasing its popular vote to a level much above that required to give the Conservative or Labour Party a majority of seats in Parliament.

The Nationalists concentrate their efforts far more narrowly than the Alliance, only contesting seats in Scotland and Wales. Their derisory shares of the total United Kingdom vote must be multiplied many times to take into account the restricted electorate to which they appeal. Within Scotland, the SNP makes an appeal to all Scots, whatever their socio-economic status. It succeeds in attracting votes across class lines, but it fails to win many seats in Scotland (see Brand, McLean, and Miller, 1983). In February, 1974 the SNP won 22 per cent of the Scottish vote and 10 per cent of the seats; it rose to a high of 30 per cent of the vote and 15 per cent of the seats in October, 1974, before falling to 12 per cent of the vote and three per cent of the seats in 1983.

Plaid Cymru's electoral appeal is concentrated upon a doubly limited section of the electorate. Plaid Cymru not only advocates an independent Wales, but also the promotion of the historic language of the Principality, a language spoken by only one-fifth of the Welsh population. The Welsh-speakers to whom Plaid appeals are concentrated in a limited number of constituencies in North and West Wales. Within these constituencies, the language appeal of Plaid Cymru benefits it even more than Labour benefits from its socio-economic status. For this reason, Plaid Cymru is able to win a relatively larger number of seats than the SNP--5.2 per cent of Wales in the 1983 election, as against 2.8 per cent of Scotland for the SNP--even though Plaid Cymru consistently wins a much lower share of the vote.

Northern Ireland further emphasizes the importance of basing an electoral appeal upon a major social characteristic, in this case religion. Religion tends to determine the share of the vote going to Unionist and Loyalist as against Irish unity candidates. In the constituencies where Protestants and Catholics are fairly evenly balanced in number, one community can lose the election by splitting its vote between two candidates if the other is united behind a single candidate. Where one religion is heavily preponderant, then competition can take place between Protestant parties. Given the constituency concentration of Catholics, if united behind a single candidate Catholic voters can win up to five seats in Northern Ireland.

In the 1983 United Kingdom election, the competition for seats involved two types of parties, those that had an appeal skewed in territorial or social terms or both--the Conservative, Labour, Nationalist and Ulster parties--as against the Alliance. Given the nature of the first-past-the-post electoral system, the former were relatively more successful in competition for seats in the House of Commons.

There is a very skew distribution of parliamentary representation among the regions and nations of the United Kingdom (Table IX.3). In 1983 the Conservatives won 61 per cent of the seats in the House of Commons, but their regional representation varied from 95 per cent of the seats in the South of England to 29 per cent in Scotland. This variation of more than three to one was of far greater magnitude than the difference in the party's vote. The Labour Party's parliamentary representation was skewed more from weakness than strength. Its share of MPs ranged from two per cent in the South of England to 57 per cent of Scottish MPs. The representation of Nationalist parties is by intent concentrated in Wales and Scotland. Northern Ireland representation is 100 per cent different from constituencies in Britain. The Alliance's parliamentary representation is much the same in all parts of Britain only because it is everywhere weak in parliamentary representation.

Every region in Britain is competitive in terms of votes, for no party can claim

Table IX.3   THE DISTRIBUTION OF PARLIAMENTARY REPRESENTATION IN THE UNITED KINGDOM

|  | Conservatives | Labour | Alliance | National't |
|---|---|---|---|---|
|  | (% seats won) | | | |
| **England** | | | | |
| South of England | 95 | 2 | 3 | 0 |
| London | 67 | 31 | 2 | 0 |
| Midlands | 71 | 29 | 0 | 0 |
| North | 41 | 55 | 4 | 0 |
| Total England | 69 | 27 | 2 | 0 |
| Wales | 37 | 53 | 5 | 5 |
| Scotland | 29 | 57 | 11 | 3 |
| N. Ireland | 0 | 0 | 0 | 100 |
| United Kingdom | 61 | 32 | 3.5 | 3.5 |

two-thirds of a region's votes, and usually the leading party takes less than half the vote. But few regions of the United Kingdom are competitive in terms of parliamentary representation. Parliamentary representation reflects balanced competition when at least two parties elect a substantial proportion of MPs for a region. It is hegemonic, subject to one-party domination, if one party elects the great bulk of MPs from a region.

In 1983 only three of the seven regions and nations of the United Kingdom could claim balanced representation: Wales, the North of England and Scotland. In each of these areas, the Labour Party was first in the share of popular votes and first in the share of seats, but only by a limited margin. Labour won 53 per cent of the seats in Wales, 55 per cent in the North of England and 57 per cent in Scotland. Nearly half the seats in the House of Commons from these three areas were taken by also-ran parties. The Conservatives won a substantial fraction of seats in each region, and the Alliance did relatively well.

The fact that the more distant parts of Britain are most balanced in parliamentary representation is a major force for political integration. When an issue arises in the House of Commons, the voices of Scottish, Welsh and North of England MPs are sure to be heard, but they will not be voicing distinctive territorial concerns (see also McDonald, 1982). Their voices will be divided along party lines common to the whole of Britain. Scots MPs will disagree as Conservative, Labour and Alliance partisans, not as Scots versus English.

The importance of balanced representation from Scotland and Wales is underscored by the absence of such representation from Northern Ireland since the Ulster Unionists withdrew from association with the Conservative Party in 1972, and the Labour Party decided to placate the forces of Irish unity rather than contest Ulster seats. Ulster MPs tend to be treated as outcasts at Westminster; they are excluded by party lines that integrate MPs from England, Scotland and Wales.

The 1983 election result was unusual in the weakness of the Labour vote and the size of the Conservative majority in the House of Commons. But the tendency of the electoral system to make parliamentary representation hegemonic rather than competitive is consistent through the years. This can be illustrated by examining the territorial distribution of seats in the 1964 and in the February, 1974 Parliaments, when the two major parties were very nearly equal in the number of seats each won United Kingdomwide.

Even when the Conservative and Labour parties are matched almost evenly overall in the House of Commons, they are not matched evenly in most parts of the United Kingdom. In 1964 only the West Midlands and Scotland could be described as having competitive or balanced representation in Parliament. Labour won 56 per cent of seats in the West Midlands, and the Conservatives 44 per cent; in Scotland, Labour won 61 per cent of seats, against 39 per cent for

Conservative and Liberal opponents. Elsewhere, hegemony was the rule: Labour won 78 per cent of the seats in Wales (rising to 89 per cent in 1966), and Ulster Unionists took all 12 seats in Northern Ireland. In 1974, the pattern was much the same, with Labour winning 55 per cent of seats in the West Midlands, and 56 per cent of seats in Scotland. Elsewhere, one party enjoyed a hegemonic dominance of parliamentary representation. The 1983 election demonstrated a greater degree of within-region and within-nation balance in parliamentary representation.

When attention is turned to patterns of party competition, neither a one nor a two-party system can be said to exist. By definition, there will always be a second party to challenge the winner, however distant the runner up is. Strictly speaking, a two- party system exists only if two parties finish first and second in virtually every constituency. In 1983, however, the Conservative and Labour parties failed to maintain a monopoly of the positions of winner and challenger. Either the Labour or Conservative parties were third or worse in 365 seats, 56 per cent of the total in the House of Commons (Table IX.4).

The 1983 general election produced 20 different patterns of party competition. Of these, only two represent the traditional patterns of the Conservatives ahead of Labour, or Labour leading the Conservatives. Another four represent the increasing importance of constituency competition between the Alliance and the Conservatives, or less often Alliance and Labour. The presence of Nationalist parties in Scotland and Wales creates an additional five patterns of party competition. In Northern Ireland, even though there are only 17 seats, nine different patterns of party competition occur, according to whether competition is between Protestant and Catholic parties across communal lines; among Unionist and Loyalist parties; between parties advocating alternative routes to Irish unity; or between Unionists and cross-confessional candidates of the Alliance Party of Northern Ireland.

In effect, Great Britain has three principal two-party systems today. In 265 seats, competition is between a Conservative front-runner and a second-place Alliance candidate. In 160 seats, the competition is between a Labour front-runner and a second-place Conservative candidate. In only 125 seats does the pattern of competition in the constituency, Labour challenging a Conservative incumbent, match the pattern in the House of Commons as a whole. Altogether, these three patterns of competition, each very different from the other, embrace 85 per cent of the seats in Parliament. The remaining 17 patterns of party competition account for 15 per cent of the seats in the House of Commons. Single-party hegemony is not invincible as parliamentary representation may make it appear, for in every constituency there is always an alternative to challenge the sitting MP.

Although patterns of party competition are varied, the overall effect is to maintain political integration within Britain, for in more than 95 per cent of all

Table IX.4   MULTI-DIMENSIONAL PATTERNS OF PARTY
             COMPETITION IN THE UNITED KINGDOM

|                          | Seats 1983 | |
| Pattern                  | N   | %    |
|--------------------------|-----|------|
| Conservative-Alliance[a] | 283 | 43.5 |
| Conservative-Labour      | 125 | 19.2 |
| Labour-Conservative      | 160 | 24.6 |
| Labour-Alliance[b]       | 53  | 8.2  |
| N. Ireland parties       | 17  | 2.6  |
| Nationalist 1st or 2nd   | 12  | 1.8  |

[a] Includes 18 seats in which Alliance finished first and Conservatives second.

[b] Includes five seats in which Alliance finished first and Labour second.

---

constituencies the parties finishing first and second--the Conservatives, Labour and Alliance--are contesting seats Britainwide. Parties finishing second are well suited to put pressure on front-running parties.

A striking feature of the 1983 election result is that no pattern of party competition is dominant in any one nation. The most frequently occurring pattern in England is a Conservative MP challenged by an Alliance candidate, but this is found in less than half of English seats. In Scotland, the most frequent occurrence is a Labour MP with a Conservative in second place, but this is hardly more frequent than a Labour MP with an Alliance candidate in second place. In Wales the most common pattern is a Labour MP challenged by an Alliance candidate, but this occurs in less than one-third of all Welsh constituencies. Differences in patterns of party competition within nations are much greater than differences between nations, thus strengthening integration Britainwide.

Party competition need not be along lines common to the whole of Britain. In the October, 1974 election, the Scottish National Party demonstrated the parliamentary influence that could be obtained by finishing second. Whilst winning only 11 of Scotland's 71 seats in the Commons, the SNP finished second in 42 more, becoming a major party in three-quarters of Scotland's constituencies, a position that it used to lever a devolution act from the Labour government of the day.

Notwithstanding the very skew distribution of seats among parties, the overall effect is to maintain the integration of Great Britain. In nine of the twelve general elections since 1945, the governing party has needed to win seats in two or three nations of Britain in order to enjoy a majority in Parliament. The three exceptions are Labour's landslide victory in 1945, the 1959 Conservative victory, and the Conservative landslide victory in 1983. In five postwar elections, the governing party has enjoyed a substantial lead in seats in England, but has needed representation elsewhere to be strong enough to form a government. This was the case in the Conservative governments of 1951, 1955, 1970 and 1979, as well as being true of the 1966 Labour government. The 1950 and October, 1974 election outcomes left the two major parties virtually even in parliamentary representation in England. Labour formed the government because of its relatively greater strength in Wales in 1950, and in Scotland too in 1974. In the two elections in which the government's majority was so slim that it could not be long sustained, 1964 and February, 1974, Labour took office with a majority of English MPs supporting its Conservative opponents. Conceding the majority of English seats to the opposition party meant that the governing party was soon forced to call another general election. *In order to win control of government, a party must compete effectively Britainwide.*

## Deviations from the Britainwide Pattern

In a set of 650 constituencies there will inevitably be some seats that deviate from the overall pattern, whether because of a unique idiosyncratic factor (e.g. a spectacular by-election, as at Bermondsey), because of more general factors, such as having a popular incumbent MP, or local or regional traditions influencing party loyalties. Even if only five per cent of constituencies deviate from the general pattern, this still constitutes 32 abnormal constituencies, and the figure rises to 65 constituencies if a tenth of constituencies deviate. In a three-party system, a constituency deviating from the Conservative pattern need not be deviant in Labour terms or vice versa. Thus, the proportion of constituencies deviant in the vote of one or more parties could rise to 200, less than one-third of all constituencies but numerous enough to merit attention.

Conventionally, electoral deviations from the Britainwide pattern are not measured by the discrepancy between a partry's expected and actual share of the vote. Instead, deviant constituencies are described as those in which the swing differs from the national mean (see e.g. Butler, 1965; Curtice and Steed, 1982). David Butler developed the measure of swing to demonstrate the absence of any deviation from nationwide influences upon changes in vote from one election to the next. However, the problems of calculating swing have greatly increased with the rise of the Liberals and then of the Alliance (see chapter XI). Moreover, to measure deviations solely in terms of the change in vote from one election to the next is to assume that the initial constituency vote is totally normal. No evidence for this assumption has been presented in analyses of swing.

Before deviant constituencies can be identified, it is necessary to identify normal constituencies. Regression analysis provides the means to identify both normal and deviant constituencies. The statistical analysis reported in the foregoing pages identifies the social structure and territorial influences that explain 76 per cent of the variation in the Conservative and in the Labour vote in Britain. The ability to explain only 26 per cent of the Alliance vote suggests either that the Alliance vote is independent of nationwide influences, the view of the community politics wing of the Liberal Party, or that factors influencing the Alliance vote, such as political attitudes, are not reflected in the census data examined here.

Fitting the specific social structure and territorial characteristics of each constituency to a regression equation for British voting, using the social structure influences reported in Table IX.1, predicts the Conservative and Labour share of the vote in each of the 633 constituencies of Great Britain. Given the very high proportion of variance explained by these equations, there should be a very good fit between the predicted and the actual vote for the party in the great majority of constituencies. Just as the overall goodness of fit can be measured by the $r^2$ value, so the fit for an individual constituency can be measured by subtracting the actual vote from the predicted vote to obtain a residual measure of error. If the constituency result is normal, then the difference between the predicted and the actual share of the vote will approach 0.0. If the predicted vote is higher than the actual vote, then the constituency deviation is negative, because it is over-predicted. If the predicted vote is lower, then the deviation is positive and under-predicted.

By definition, normality and deviations are matters of degree. The most deviant constituencies are often unique. The Western Isles is the most deviant constituency in the regression analysis, for the Conservative vote of 9.6 per cent was 32.7 per cent below that predicted simply by the constituency's social structure and territorial characteristics. By returning a Scottish Nationalist MP, the constituency deviated from mainland Scotland as well as from nearly every constituency elsewhere in Britain. The constituencies where the Labour vote is most over-predicted are also unique cases. In Southwark & Bermondsey, where the Labour vote was 23.2 per cent below the predicted norm, Labour had fought a disastrous by-election a few months before the general election. In Plymouth Devonport, 22.3 per cent below the predicted Labour norm, the Alliance opponent was the former Labour MP for the constituency, Dr. David Owen.

Once the unique constituencies are allowed for, the residual difference between the actual and predicted vote of a party in a constituency begins to resemble a normal distribution. In the case of the Conservative vote, 95 per cent of all constituency results fall within the range of a 12.3 per cent under-prediction to an 18.2 per cent over-prediction, with the remaining 5 per cent of constituencies divided evenly on each side of this range. In the case of Labour, 95 per cent of all results can be predicted to within a range of an 18.2 per cent under-prediction to a 15.6 per cent over-prediction. Table IX.5 lists the 32 constituencies where the vote is most over or under- predicted for the Conservative and Labour parties. The residual differences for every British constituency are given in Appendix A.

A casual glance at the constituencies deviating most from the British norm indicates a regional effect. Of the 16 constituencies where Labour's vote is well above what would be expected from the social structure, eight are in South Wales. Reciprocally, of the 16 seats where the Conservative vote is well below that which would be predicted by their basic characteristics, 12 are Welsh and another three Scottish; only one is English. Of the 16 seats where the Conservative vote is much higher than predicted, all are English and only two are in the North of England. In the 16 seats where the Labour vote is well below what would be predicted, none is in Wales or the North of England; 12 are concentrated in England south of the Mersey, and three are in rural Scotland (Table IX.5).

Most constituencies are relatively normal, that is, their predicted and actual votes are close to each other. This is just as true for the Alliance as it is for the Conservative and Labour parties. Notwithstanding the lower proportion of the Alliance vote explained by social structure and territorial characteristics, 95 per cent of all Alliance results are within the range of an 8.2 per cent over-prediction to a 12.0 per cent under-prediction. The Alliance vote is not only very evenly spread throughout Britain, but also very close to its norm everywhere. This contrasts markedly with earlier Liberal revivals, which depended upon a constituency becoming deviant in order for the Liberals to win a substantial share of the vote.

Because normality and deviance are questions of degree, they are very amenable to statistical analysis. Just as it is possible to explain a party's share of the vote in a constituency by using regression analysis, so it is possible to subject the residual deviation of the party's vote to multivariate statistical analysis, in order to test to what extent deviant results reflect a pattern different from that affecting most constituencies, or tend to reflect constituency-specific influences.

Table IX.5 <u>CONSERVATIVE AND LABOUR DEVIANT CONSTITUENCIES</u>

| Conservative Underprediction | | Labour Overprediction | |
|---|---|---|---|
| 1. Nottingham North | 20.1 | Southwark & Bermondsey | −23.2 |
| 2. City of London & West. S | 17.8 | Plymouth Devonport | −22.3 |
| 3. Wolverhampton NE | 14.8 | Dundee East | −21.4 |
| 4. Gosport | 13.8 | Havant | −19.7 |
| 5. Chelsea | 13.8 | Gosport | −17.7 |
| 6. Havant | 13.6 | Cheltenham | −17.0 |
| 7. Walsall North | 13.5 | Islington S & Finsbury | −16.8 |
| 8. Peterborough | 13.4 | Nottingham North | −16.7 |
| 9. Nottingham South | 13.3 | City London & West. S | −16.6 |
| 10. Birmingham Northfield | 13.2 | Roxburgh&Berwickshire | −16.5 |
| 11. Manchester Wythenshawe | 13.1 | Angus East | −15.4 |
| 12. Meriden | 13.0 | Chelmsford | −16.3 |
| 13. Liverpool Garston | 12.6 | Eastbourne | −16.1 |
| 14. Corby | 12.5 | Inver's,Nairn &Lochaber | −15.8 |
| 15. Harlow | 12.4 | Yeovil | −15.7 |
| 16. West Bromwich West | 12.3 | Isle of Wight | −15.6 |

| Conservative Overprediction | | Labour Underprediction | |
|---|---|---|---|
| 1. Western Isles | −32.7 | Rhondda | 28.5 |
| 2. Rhondda | −32.1 | Ealing Southall | 26.2 |
| 3. Caernarfon | −28.1 | Blaenau Gwent | 25.3 |
| 4. Ceredigion & Pembroke N | −26.7 | Carmarthen | 24.6 |
| 5. Cynon Valley | −25.3 | Merthyr Tydfil & Rhyney | 23.4 |
| 6. Carmarthen | −24.4 | Barnsley East | 22.9 |
| 7. Orkney & Shetland | −23.4 | Ogmore | 22.5 |
| 8. Merionnydd Nant Conwy | −21.8 | Cynon Valley | 22.1 |
| 9. Ogmore | −21.8 | Workington | 21.5 |
| 10. Glasgow Hillhead | 21.5 | Bolsover | 21.0 |
| 11. Neath | −21.2 | Islwyn | 20.0 |
| 12. Islwyn | −20.2 | Hemsworth | 19.3 |
| 13. Pontypridd | −19.9 | Brent South | 19.1 |
| 14. Ealing Southall | −18.4 | Neath | 18.9 |
| 15. Blaenau Gwent | −18.3 | Newham NE | 18.3 |
| 16. Caerphilly | −18.2 | Crewe & Nantwich | 18.2 |

a  For the residual values for every constituency see Appendix A.
b  For the regression model from which the outliers were calculated, see Table IX.2.

Contrasting causes of deviation are tested here. Two factors are political: the turnout in a constituency and the presence of an incumbent MP as a candidate. Nuffield studies of deviations from Britainwide swings examine both (cf. Butler and Kavanagh, 1980: 421ff). Party organizers are apt to argue that their party did particularly well or badly in a constituency because the party's organization did or did not succeed in getting out the vote. Party organizers imply that a high turnout should produce a higher than average vote for their candidate, and a low turnout a below average vote. But in seats where both parties try to encourage turnout, then the net effect should be nil when competing efforts cancel out.

The presence of an incumbent MP is credited by some MPs with influencing the party's vote. A sitting Member of Parliament has many chances to get his or her name known locally, and to appear in a variety of non-political contexts as well as on party platforms. Insofar as an incumbent MP has more resources and opportunities to campaign, then the vote for a party should tend to be higher than normal where a seat is fought by an incumbent, and below normal when a non-incumbent is fighting the seat (cf. Cain, Ferejohn and Fiorina, 1979). Against this can be set the argument that party identification rather than candidate identification determines votes. This was tested by MPs who switched from the Labour Party to the Social Democratic Party during the 1979 Parliament. Of the MPs who switched parties, 24 were defeated and only four re-elected.

The prominence of Welsh constituencies and, to a lesser extent Scottish constituencies, in the list of deviants is suggestive but not conclusive evidence that territorial differences cause deviant results. The fact that some Welsh or Scottish seats appear on a list of deviant constituencies does not mean that all the constituencies are deviant there.

The regression analysis of constituency deviation demonstrates that national differences account for a significant portion of constituency departures from Britainwide norms (Table IX.6). A constituency in Wales can deviate by having a higher Labour vote than would be predicted from social structure characteristics alone, and a Conservative constituency in Wales will deviate by having a lower vote. In Scotland a Conservative constituency vote is again likely to deviate negatively, and a Labour constituency vote will also be lower than expected.

By comparison with territorial factors, political influences do little to explain constituency deviations in the vote. The presence of an incumbent MP adds on average 0.43 per cent to the Conservative vote; a similar amount, 0.39 per cent, is subtracted from the predicted Labour vote, a reminder that the exposure of a politician to the electorate is not always to a politician's advantage. Turnout also has a limited effect upon a party's vote; a rise in turnout works to the disadvantage of both major parties, and helps the Alliance. A 10 per cent

Table IX.6   <u>CAUSES OF DEVIANT CONSTITUENCY RESULTS</u>

| | Conservatives | | Labour | |
|---|---|---|---|---|
| | b | % variance explained | b | % variance explained |
| % Turnout | -.04 | 1 | -.03 | 0 |
| Incumbent MP[a] | .43 | 0 | -.39 | 0 |
| Scottish constituency[a] | -4.4** | 6 | -4.9** | 5 |
| Welsh constituency[a] | <u>-12.9**</u> | <u>13</u> | <u>9.6**</u> | <u>6</u> |
| (Constant) r² | (4.4) | 20 | (1.8) | 11 |

[a] Scored zero or one.

---

increase in turnout can lower the Conservative share of the vote by 0.4 per cent, and the Labour share by 0.3 per cent.

Taken together, the regression analyses states a theme, the predominance of social structure as the chief determinant of the vote in British constituencies, and a variation, national differences are the chief cause of the limited amount of constituency deviance from Britainwide norms.

Part Three
# Competition for Government

# X
# The Political Geography
# of Britain

In extreme form, the political geography of territorial differences could lead to national disintegration. The twentieth century offers many examples of differences within a country leading to its break up and the creation of several succession states. If the United Kingdom were divided into a Conservative and a Labour half, then the breaking up of Britain into two independent parts--one Labour and one Conservative--would provide a government more representative of each half.

But we have already found that social structure is far more important than region, nation, or distance from London in determining party preferences. The decaying urban areas of inner London are as much Labour strongholds as the same sorts of places in Glasgow and Cardiff. Only in Belfast do voters march to the rhythm of a different drum. The social structure of a constituency, not its geographical location, is the primary determinant of electoral behaviour. Therefore, a proper understanding of the political geography of the United Kingdom cannot be based simply upon maps, for location on a map does not determine votes. To classify constituencies solely by where they are is wrongly to impute a significance to such nominal labels as Yorkshire or Scotland that is not justified by the evidence.

Because social structure is important, political divisions along social lines could cut across territorial divisions, thus promoting national integration. But for this to happen a second condition must be met, namely, the social differences of primary political importance must be evenly distributed throughout Britain. But we would not expect every one of 650 British constituencies to be divided exactly as the average for the United Kingdom. Most seats in the House of Commons can be regarded as safe seats because their social composition is *atypical*, being sufficiently middle-class or working-class to remain consistently Conservative or Labour whatever the swings at a particular election. Spatial skewing of social characteristics occurs between leafy suburbs and inner-city areas; it occurs to a lesser extent between regions and nations of the United Kingdom.

The purpose of this chapter is to construct a political geography of the United Kingdom that recognizes both social structure and territorial factors related to partisanship. To do this we first of all need to group the 650 constituencies of the United Kingdom into a relatively limited number of clusters, each distinctive in terms of one or more social characteristics. Secondly, we need to see whether or not distinctive clusters of constituencies tend to be integrative, that is, Britainwide in scope, or disintegrative, with social differences creating clusters of English-only, Scots-only, Welsh-only and Ulster-only groups. Thirdly, we need to test whether each of these clusters is politically homogeneous, in order to validate the political significance of the classification produced on social structure grounds.

## The Social Structure of Parliamentary Constituencies

The problem faced is simple and practical. Given hundreds of constituencies, each of which can be characterized in terms of a great variety of social conditions--occupation, industrial structure, agriculture, housing, unemployment, age of population, immigration, and so forth--we need a method of reducing the raw information, tens of thousands of observations, to a manageable and meaningful form, grouping constituencies that are socially similar to each other and different from other groups. In this way, we can identify several dozen clusters of constituencies, each of which is socially distinctive and would be expected to be politically distinctive as well.

EM> The raw materials for classifying parliamentary constituencies are provided in great detail by the 1981 census, which has issued in machine-readable form suitable for computer analysis as well as in book form (OPCS, 1983), social characteristics for each constituency. Given that this file contains 3.25 million observations, the census materials were first subjected to a factor analysis in order to reduce the mass of social data to a more meaningful form. Four principal factors differentiating constituencies were identified: socio-economic status, agriculture, immigrants, and the proportion of the elderly in a constituency (See Chapter V and Appendix B). Unlike regression analysis, cluster analysis accepts that social conditions are correlated with each other. Hence, the three different elements in the socio-economic status factor--occupation, housing, and unemployment--can here be entered separately in the analysis in order to identify and refine differences between constituencies.

The procedure used to create groups of constituencies sharing certain social characteristics is known as cluster analysis. This technique calculates measures of similarity between all the units of analysis, and on that basis groups the most similar units into a number of clusters. As the number of clusters is progressively reduced, the most similar clusters are merged. The particular type of cluster analysis used here is based on an iterative relocation algorithm (see Everitt, 1974). The analysis reported here builds upon two earlier studies, the pioneering analysis of the 1951 census, *British Towns*, by Moser and Scott (1961); and statistical analyses of the 1971 census data of parliamentary constituencies (Webber, 1978) and of local authority areas (Webber and Craig, 1978). There is substsantial continuity between the studies, reflecting the persisting importance of a small number of social structure characteristics, as well as obvious differences, for example, the concentration here upon parliamentary constituencies as against local government areas.

In grouping together 650 parliamentary constituencies it is obvious that two clusters would be too few, indiscriminantly lumping together nearly all Conservative constituencies, or all South of England constituencies. Equally, 120 clusters would be too many, averaging little more than five constituencies per cluster. There is no statistically agreed method for determining how many clusters a given body of data should have; the number is empirically determined by the specific analytic purpose and characteristics of the units of analysis. Following Webber (1978), the decision was made to create 30 constituency clusters, a number large enough to register all the logically possible pairs of differentiating characteristics among the six social determinants, to make it likely for Wales to be divided into at least two clusters, and Scottish constituencies to be assigned to at least three clusters. Once the 30 different clusters were identified, the consequences of reducing the number of clusters to 24 was tested. While this removed a number of relatively small clusters by merging them with similar groups, it also created several large and heterogeneous clusters, thus demonstrating the advantage of the more homogeneous 30-cluster classification of parliamentary constituencies.

In effect, cluster analysis groups constituencies as if they were parts of a tree. For example, there are main branches discriminating occupationally middle-class from working-class constituencies, and agricultural from non-agricultural constituencies, and there are additional stems from each principal branch. For example, working-class constituencies can be differentiated from each other by their level of owner-occupation, and middle-class constituencies can be differentiated by whether or not they are disproportionately rural. Each cluster is normally differentiated in at least two respects from other clusters, as well as having things in common with other clusters forming separate stems from the same principal branch.

The description of each cluster in Table X.1 is derived from the characteristics making it different from the United Kingdom means, and from adjacent clusters. The descriptions have a statistical justification, and are not simply an interpretation derived impressionistically from a few constituency

Table X.1 SOCIAL CLUSTERS OF UNITED KINGDOM CONSTITUENCIES

| Cluster Type, Nation[a] | Non man | Own occ | Unemp | Born New Cm | Agr | Elderly |
|---|---|---|---|---|---|---|
| | % | % | % | % | % | % |
| 1. Rural, council ten, Scot | 41 | 39 | 12 | 1 | 3 | 8 |
| 2. Rural, Britain | 47 | 62 | 9 | 1 | 5 | 11 |
| 3. Council ten, elderly, Scot | 48 | 24 | 18 | 0 | 0 | 7 |
| 4. Council ten, manual, unemp, immig, London | 43 | 17 | 22 | 8 | 0 | 9 |
| 5. Own occ, full employ, S Eng | 57 | 64 | 8 | 4 | 0 | 11 |
| 6. Young,cross-class,Eng & Wales | 50 | 61 | 12 | 1 | 1 | 7 |
| 7. Cross-class, Eng & Wales | 50 | 61 | 11 | 1 | 0 | 9 |
| 8. Non-man, immig, London | 67 | 65 | 9 | 7 | 0 | 10 |
| 9. Full employ, non-man, own occ, young, S Eng | 60 | 69 | 7 | 1 | 1 | 7 |
| 10. Own occ, rural, old, S Eng | 53 | 66 | 10 | 1 | 3 | 12 |
| 11. Cross-sections of towns UK | 59 | 58 | 10 | 2 | 0 | 10 |
| 12. Full emp,non-man,ownocc,SEng | 59 | 67 | 7 | 1 | 2 | 8 |
| 13. Young, S Eng | 56 | 48 | 9 | 2 | 1 | 7 |
| 14. Manual, Britain | 44 | 51 | 15 | 1 | 0 | 9 |
| 15. North of England | 48 | 48 | 14 | 0 | 1 | 9 |
| 16. Manual,unem,coun ten,Eng &Scot | 45 | 25 | 19 | 1 | 0 | 10 |
| 17. Rural, full employ, S Eng | 52 | 60 | 8 | 1 | 3 | 9 |
| 18. Immig, old, S Eng | 56 | 62 | 12 | 2 | 0 | 12 |
| 19. Own occ, old, S Eng | 60 | 73 | 10 | 1 | 1 | 14 |
| 20. Immig, manual, Eng & Wales | 50 | 53 | 14 | 6 | 1 | 9 |
| 21. Non-man, immig, London | 70 | 41 | 12 | 9 | 0 | 10 |
| 22. Manual, own occ, old, N Eng | 43 | 63 | 15 | 1 | 0 | 10 |
| 23. Non-man,fullemp,ownocc,Eng&Sc | 72 | 76 | 6 | 2 | 0 | 8 |
| 24. Rural, Scot | 35 | 46 | 13 | 0 | 6 | 9 |
| 25. Full employ, non-man, S Eng | 70 | 69 | 6 | 2 | 0 | 10 |
| 26. Manual,coun ten,unem,old,N Eng | 46 | 39 | 18 | 1 | 0 | 11 |
| 27. Manual, coun ten, unem, N Eng | 44 | 41 | 18 | 1 | 0 | 8 |
| 28. Own occ, Britain | 58 | 72 | 9 | 1 | 0 | 9 |
| 29. Own occ, old, S Eng | 50 | 65 | 12 | 1 | 1 | 11 |
| 30. Manual, unemp, immig, London | 52 | 39 | 17 | 16 | 0 | 9 |
| United Kingdom average | 52 | 55 | 12 | 2 | 1 | 9 |
| Standard Deviation | 11 | 16 | 5 | 4 | 2 | 3 |

[a] If more than half the constituencies in a cluster are from one region or nation, the cluster is labelled by it.

names. The values given for each of the six social structure characteristics used to form the clusters represent the mean value for all constituencies in the cluster and are the same as those used in Appendix A. In each case, the indicator reflects the percentage of each group in the average constituency in a cluster. A constituency in cluster 1, for example, on average would be 41 per cent middle-class, have 39 per cent owner-occupiers, and 12 per cent unemployment, 1 per cent born in the New Commonwealth, 3 per cent in agriculture, and 8 per cent age 65 to 74. Thus, the first cluster is above average on the agriculture scale, and below average in owner-occupiers. The mean value for each social indicator of each cluster enables one to identify how typical or atypical a cluster is by comparison with the United Kingdom average. The cluster to which each United Kingdom constituency is assigned is given in Appendix A, and further details are available in McAllister and Rose (1984).

The logic of cluster analysis can be illustrated by considering as examples the initial clusters. Cluster 1 is distinctive because it is three times more agricultural than the United Kingdom average, and one-quarter less owner-occupiers than average; Angus East is typical. Cluster 2 is similar to Cluster 1 in being very agricultural, being more than four times the national average. But it differs in being above average in owner-occupation, and its population also tends to be more elderly than cluster 1; Ludlow in Shropshire is typical of this group. Cluster 3, like the first two, is working-class and has few immigrants. But it differs from the first clusters in being urban, and has an above-average level of unemployment. The two Motherwell constituencies in Scotland and Jarrow are representative of this cluster. Clusters 3 and 4 are both urban, council-house and working- class groups with high levels of unemployment. But they differ in that cluster 3, which is disproportionately Scottish, is very low in immigrants, whereas cluster 4 has four times the national mean for immigrants, and its residents are disproportionately elderly. Bethnal Green & Stepney and Manchester Central are typical of this cluster.

The number of constituencies in a cluster and their geographical distribution is not fixed, being determined empirically by the distribution of distinctive social characteristics, and co-incidentally by any territorial bias in differentiating characteristics. Cluster 1 is relatively small, having only 12 constituencies. These constituencies--agricultural in character but low in their proportion of owner-occupiers because of council housing and tenancy of farms--are geographically very skewed; nine are in Scotland and three in Northern Ireland. By contrast, cluster 2, which is even more agricultural than the first cluster, is predominantly owner-occupier. It embraces 33 constituencies throughout Britain, reaching from North Cornwall to Fife North East.

Identifying 30 different groups of parliamentary constituencies provides a rigorous additional test of the importance of social structure as a determinant of electoral outcomes. Even more, it can test whether or to what extent social characteristics are so unevenly distributed territorially that constituencies similar in terms of major social characteristics will also be contiguous geographically, clustering in the same region of England or nation of the United Kingdom.

## Territorial and Functional Homogeneity?

Clusters of constituencies defined by their social characteristics must necessarily be homogeneous in terms of functional attributes. Clusters can be territorially homogeneous as well, if all the constituencies with a given combination of attributes are found in one nation or region. It is empirically possible that constituencies grouped in terms of a given set of characteristics are not drawn from throughout Britain, but come almost exclusively from a single region. Insofar as cluster analysis shows that each region or nation of the United Kingdom tends to consist of a few socially and territorially homogeneous clusters, then social differences will reinforce territorial differences and, in a first-past-the-post electoral system, create political homogeneity in representation as well. If this is the case, then the co-incidence of territorial and functional differences will reduce the integrative force of political divisions along the lines of social structure.

How socially homogeneous are the nations and regions of the United Kingdom? Theories of national differences imply that the parts of the United Kingdom should each form discrete and different clusters: one cluster could incorporate all of Northern Ireland, and two clusters could accommodate Wales, differentiating industrial Wales from industrial England, and rural Wales from rural England. In Scotland, three clusters might be expected, dividing industrial Clydeside from the douce area around Edinburgh and from the rural Highlands, as well as differentiating each from English clusters.

In a 30-cluster classification of constituencies, England could monopolize 24 clusters. These might be divided along regional lines as between the North, the Midlands, London and the South of England. There is ample literary justification for three of the regional distinctions; only Midland constituencies might be distributed functionally. But the logic of nationalism suggests that there ought to be integration within England, clustering English constituencies on functional grounds, York and Canterbury being combined, and inner-city areas from Newcastle to London being grouped together. The common thread in theories of national differences is that even if a nation is divided, each of the resulting clusters should be nationally homogeneous, and thus different from other parts of the United Kingdom.

In fact, the United Kingdom is a union in social as well as constitutional terms. The regions and nations of the United Kingdom are integrated in dozens of clusters, because of social characteristics that are widely dispersed throughout the United Kingdom. Table X.2 demonstrates that the 17 constituencies of Northern Ireland are dispersed among 10 different clusters, rather than forming a single homogeneous set. The 38 constituencies of Wales are dispersed among 18 clusters, the same number as the 72 constituencies of Scotland, England's 523 constituencies are dispersed among 29 of the 30 clusters.

An index of dispersion can measure the degree to which constituencies cluster in nationally distinctive groups. If they were dispersed completely randomly, then the index would have a value of 1.0. If the constituencies were exclusively clustered by nation in groups of 20, then the maximum value would be 10 for Northern Ireland, (actual value, 1.7); 9 for Wales (actual value 1.7); 4.5 for Scotland (actual value 1.7) and 1.4 for England (actual value 1.03). In each case, the index values approach complete dispersion.

Notwithstanding its political distinctiveness, Northern Ireland displays a striking degree of social integration with other parts of the United Kingdom. In terms of conventional measures of social structure, Northern Ireland constituencies are heterogeneous. The urban area of Belfast is differentiated

Table X.2   THE SOCIAL HETEROGENEITY OF NATIONS

| Nation/Region (N constituencies) | Clusters | Constituencies per Cluster | Index of Dispersion[a] |
|---|---|---|---|
| England (523) | 29 | 18.0 | 1.03 |
| North of England (162) | 27 | 6.0 | 1.1 |
| Midlands (99) | 23 | 4.3 | 1.3 |
| London (84) | 13 | 6.5 | 2.3 |
| South of England (178) | 24 | 7.4 | 1.3 |
| Scotland (72) | 18 | 4.0 | 1.7 |
| Wales (38) | 18 | 2.1 | 1.7 |
| N Ireland (17) | 10 | 1.7 | 1.7 |
| Total (650) | 30 | 21.7 | n.a. |

[a] Calculated by dividing the mean number of constituencies per cluster by the number each nation or region would have had if constituencies were distributed evenly through all 30 clusters.

from rural constituencies in East Ulster and West of the River Bann, and within Belfast sharp socio-economic distinctions can be drawn between different parts of the city. Even if religion had been included in this analysis, differences would have been emphasized, for the proportion identified as Catholic ranges from 55 per cent in Foyle to five per cent in North Down and in East Belfast.

As well as being different from each other, Northern Ireland constituencies share many characteristics in common with constituencies elsewhere in Britain. North Down is in cluster 12, a group of full employment, middle-class constituencies principally in the South of England, such as Henley and Sevenoaks. South Belfast is in cluster 18, predominantly South of England urban constituencies with high levels of elderly and immigrants, such as the two Brighton seats and Portsmouth South. East and North Belfast, by contrast, are found in cluster 22, which is working-class but high on owner-occupiers and the elderly, like North of England constituencies such as Burnley and Blackburn and such Welsh seats as Rhondda. West Belfast is in cluster 27, with high levels of unemployment and lots of council housing. This not only distinguishes West Belfast from East Belfast, but also makes it similar to such places in England as Sunderland and Hartlepool. The most rural constituencies, such as Mid Ulster, are concentrated in cluster 24, along with very rural Scottish constituencies, such as Argyll & Bute, and a few in England and Wales, such as Holland with Boston.

The integration of Wales with other parts of Britain is reflected by the fact that its 38 constituencies are dispersed widely among 18 different clusters. For example, cluster 6 is a predominantly English cluster which approximates the Britainwide average for socio- economic status, but is relatively young and without immigrants. Four Welsh constituencies--Alyn & Deeside, Caerphilly, Pontypridd and Newport East--are in this category. Cluster 7, similar except for an older population, has one Welsh constituency, Cardiff South & Penarth. The 23 constituencies of cluster 9 are high in middle-class home-owners and low in unemployment; the cluster has one Welsh seat, the Vale of Glamorgan, along with many South of England constituencies such as Chelmsford and Mid-Kent. Cluster 10, similar except for a much higher proportion of elderly people, has one Welsh constituency, Caernarfon. The 17 urban constituencies of cluster 11 include Swansea West. There are a few clusters with a number of Welsh constituencies; for example, the very urban, working class cluster 14 includes six Welsh constituencies. But they are a small minority of the 35 seats in the cluster, as well as being a small minority of the 38 Welsh seats.

The heterogeneity of Scotland is also demonstrated by the cluster analysis. The 72 Scottish constituencies are dispersed among 18 different clusters as diverse as cluster 4, which embraces Glasgow Maryhill in a grouping of 12 principally South of England constituencies high in council housing, unemployment, manual workers and immigrants; and cluster 29, a predominantly South of England group of elderly home-owners, which includes the Western Isles as well as Dover and Great Yarmouth. While Scottish constituencies are scattered in as many different clusters as Wales, because of a larger population, Scottish constituencies can dominate three clusters. In cluster 1, which is rural and low in owner-occupiers, nine of the 12 constituencies are Scottish; in cluster 3, which is heavily urban, working-class and council house, 23 of 28 constituencies are Scottish; and in extremely rural cluster 24, 10 of the 19 constituencies are Scottish. But these distinctively Scottish clusters constitute little more than half of all Scottish constituencies. The existence of some distinctive clusters concentrated in Scotland should not lead one to ignore the other 15 clusters among which Scottish seats are dispersed.

In any classification of the United Kingdom, English constituencies are bound to predominate. In fact, 29 of the 30 clusters have at least one English constituency; the exception is cluster 1, which consists exclusively of rural council-tenant constituencies in Scotland and Northern Ireland.

When England is divided into regions, it is possible to identify territorial biases in social clusters. The region of England least integrated into the United Kingdom is London. The 84 constituencies of London are divided among 13 clusters, five less than the 72 constituencies of Scotland or the 38 constituencies of Wales. The index of dispersion for London constituencies is 2.3, showing more concentration than any other region of England or nation in the United Kingdom. Within London, very working-class cluster 4, high on unemployment, on immigrants and council housing (e.g. Hackney South & Shoreditch) can be differentiated from working-class cluster 30, extremely high on immigrants but not so high on council houses (e.g. Leyton and Tottenham). Within middle-class constituencies, cluster 8, high on immigrants (e.g. Harrow East, and Ilford South) can be discriminated from cluster 21, which is extremely high on immigrants (e.g. Hampstead & Highgate, and Chelsea). The existence of large numbers of predominantly London clusters means that nearly two-thirds of the constituencies in the metropolitan centre of Britain are in four distinct groups dissimilar from the rest of the United Kingdom.

Within England there is a clear tendency for regions to become better integrated in Britain as they are distant from Charing Cross. The South of England and the Midlands are each represented in nearly two dozen different clusters. The North of England comes closest to combining characteristics of all parts of the United Kingdom. Northern constituencies are found in 27 of the 30 constituencies examined here, thus having the greatest degree of dispersion. The only clusters in which the North of England is not represented are cluster 1, a rural cluster without any English constituency; cluster 9, a middle-class grouping very low in unemployment, and cluster 13, an area low in numbers of the elderly, and low in unemployment.

The predominance of England within the United Kingdom means that most social clusters must be predominantly English. Hence, the important question here is: to what extent are clusters exclusively English? If an average cluster were composed of a cross-section of the United Kingdom, it would have 18 English constituencies, two from Scotland, one Welsh and one or none from Northern Ireland. At the other extreme, even with a high degree of integration of Scottish, Welsh and Northern Ireland constituencies, it would still be possible for at least a dozen clusters to be exclusively English. In fact, nine-tenths of the social clusters and 91 per cent of all constituencies are integrated in groups that cut across national boundaries of the United Kingdom (Table X.3). Four clusters are a complete microcosm of the United Kingdom, containing 89 constituencies from all four nations: an urban cluster of medium social status 11; a stable working-class urban cluster, 15; an extremely rural cluster, 24; and a very working-class urban cluster of areas with high unemployment, 27. Another six clusters with 151 constituencies combine constituencies in England, Scotland and Wales, and an additional 91 constituencies in four clusters combine seats from three of the four nations of the United Kingdom.

The degree of integration of constituency clusters varies in strength. An absolute majority of constituencies, 331, are completely British, including seats from at least three of the four nations of the United Kingdom. In addition, another 13 clusters with 246 seats are integrated, for they are not exclusively confined to one nation. There are two clusters that reflect unusual forms of integration, cluster 12, an Anglo-Ulster group, and cluster 1, an Ulster-Scottish group.

National exclusiveness occurs in only three all-England clusters, cluster 5, high on owner-occupiers and low on unemployment (e.g. Windsor &

Table X.3 THE CROSS-NATIONAL INTEGRATION OF SOCIAL CLUSTERS

| | Clusters | Constituencies | |
|---|---|---|---|
| | N | N | % |
| **United Kingdom/Great Britain** | | | |
| All four nations | 4 | 89 | 14 |
| Great Britain | 6 | 151 | 23 |
| Three nations of four | 4 | 91 | 14 |
| | 14 | 331 | 51 |
| **Two Nations** | | | |
| England & Wales | 6 | 146 | 22 |
| England & Scotland | 5 | 85 | 13 |
| England & N. Ireland | 1 | 21 | 3 |
| Scotland & N. Ireland | 1 | 12 | 3 |
| | 13 | 264 | 41 |
| **One Nation** | | | |
| England only | 3 | 55 | 8 |

Maidenhead); cluster 20, a very working-class immigrant urban cluster (e.g. three Coventry constituencies); and cluster 30, consisting of inner-city constituencies very high on immigration (e.g. London Vauxhall and Birmingham Sparkbrook). These three homogeneous clusters, however, constitute only eight per cent of all United Kingdom constituencies.

A third way of examining socially similar clusters is to consider whether any one region is predominant in a given cluster. With four regions of England and three other nations in the United Kingdom, it is possible for a cluster to be integrated, combining constituencies from diverse regions and nations of the United Kingdom, yet still have more than half of its constituencies from one area. Insofar as this is the case, then the territorial bias in the social structure of the United Kingdom would represent a departure from a model of perfect integration, albeit not threatening the disintegration of Britain.

There is a degree of territorial bias in the distribution of social structure within the United Kingdom (Table X.4). Of the 30 clusters, the South of England is predominant in ten, London in four, the North of England in four,

Table X.4  LIMITS OF TERRITORIAL PREDOMINANCE IN SOCIAL CLUSTERS

| Region or nation | Constituencies | | |
|---|---|---|---|
| | In predominant clusters | Total in region/nation[a] | Predominant as % total |
| | N | N | |
| South of England | 128 | 178 | 72 |
| London | 51 | 84 | 61 |
| Scotland | 42 | 72 | 58 |
| North of England | 55 | 162 | 34 |
| Midlands | 0 | 99 | 0 |
| Wales | 0 | 38 | 0 |
| N. Ireland | 0 | 17 | 0 |
| Total United Kingdom | 276 | 650 | 42 |

[a] A region or nation predominates in a cluster if it comprises more than half of the constituencies there.

and Scotland in three. The Midlands of England, Wales and Northern Ireland are completely integrated; they do not predominate in any social cluster. But the bias is limited, a departure from perfect proportionality, not proof of the United Kingdom having mutually reinforcing social and territorial cleavages. London and South of England constituencies usually are in clusters in which they predominate. But overall 58 per cent of all constituencies are not in a constituency in which their own region is predominant.

Most MPs do *not* represent a cluster of social interests that also constitutes a well defined territorial bloc. They either represent a constituency that is integrated with constituencies dispersed throughout Britain, or are in a cluster reflecting their social and economic concerns but not their particular region or nation.

## Social Homogeneity Leads to Political Hegemony

Constituencies can be very homogeneous in terms of some social characteristics; hundreds of parliamentary constituencies are more than 90 per cent urban, 100 per cent without agriculture, and have very few immigrant electors. It is also possible for a constituency to be virtually 100 per cent working class in inner-city areas and almost entirely council house.

Parliamentary constituencies are far more homogeneous socially than electorally. No British constituency returns 90 per cent of its vote for a single party. In the best Conservative constituency in 1983, Bexhill & Battle, the Conservatives won 67.3 per cent of the total vote, and in Blaenau Gwent, Labour won 70.1 per cent of the vote. By definition electoral competiton is about political divisions within a constituency. Even though socio-economic status greatly influences a party's vote, it alters the vote by less than one per cent for each percentage point change in a constituency's socio-economic status.

The first-past-the-post electoral system compensates for the imperfect conversion of social characteristics into votes by awarding a constituency to the party with the largest number of votes. Inasmuch as most constituencies are distinctive in terms of the social structure characteristics influencing voting, then in terms of political representation most clusters should be politically homogeneous. Constituencies clustered together because of high socio-economic status should be represented by Conservative MPs, and constituencies clustered together because of low socio-economic status, overwhelmingly Labour.

A cluster of constituencies can be said to be politically homogeneous if one party dominates its parliamentary representation, as measured by the proportion of seats that the most successful party wins. Given that seats in the 1983 general election were very unevenly distributed, with Conservatives winning 61 per cent United Kingdomwide, and Labour only 32 per cent, we would expect more clusters to have a majority of Conservative MPs. We would also expect Labour to find it much more difficult to establish hegemony within a given social cluster.

Social homogeneity leads to political hegemony. In 25 of 30 clusters, three-quarters or more of the MPs elected are of the same political party (Table X.5). Of the 18 predominantly Conservative clusters, at least three-quarters of MPs are Conservatives in 17 clusters. In ten clusters not a single Labour MP is elected, and in another six, only one Labour MP is returned. Altogether, the 18 clusters returned 348 Conservative MPs at the 1983 election, 22 Labour MPs, and 18 Alliance, Nationalist and Ulster MPs. Conservative MPs thus represent 90 per cent of all the seats with 50 per cent of the vote there.

Of the 10 clusters which are predominantly Labour, eight are clearly under the hegemony of the Labour Party, for even in a disastrous year such as 1983 it elected three-quarters or more of their MPs. In one of the clusters not a single Conservative MP was elected, and only one Conservative was returned in two other clusters. Altogether, these 10 clusters returned 184 Labour MPs, 38 Conservative MPs, and nine Alliance and Nationalist MPs. Labour MPs maintain a hegemony in ten clusters, representing 80 per cent of seats with 45 per cent of the vote.

There are two clusters, 1 and 24, where third-force parties do disproportionately well in winning seats as well as votes. Of their 31 seats, 19 are in Scotland and eight in Northern Ireland. The principal beneficiaries of the atypical nature of these very rural seats are the Liberal-SDP Alliance, and Northern Ireland parties. Neither Scottish nor Welsh Nationalists win a single seat in "Celtic twilight" clusters. The Alliance also does relatively well in predominantly Conservative seats, where it is almost as likely to win a seat in the House of Commons as Labour.

The pervasiveness of one-party clusters of constituencies is emphasized by the fact that only three of the 30 clusters can be described as competitive between the government party and the official opposition. In cluster 20, Labour won 15 seats, the Conservatives 14, and Alliance one. Cluster 20 draws together constituencies that tend to be disproportionately working-class and high on immigrants, but about normal in terms of owner-occupiers. The constituencies are widely dispersed geographically, but the stronger Labour areas, such as the North of England and Scotland, are much under-represented. Its votes are very evenly divided, 39 per cent Labour and 38 per cent Conservative. Twenty-three of the 30 seats were won by margins of ten per cent or less.

Cluster 22 is also very evenly balanced between the parties, with Labour winning 11 seats against nine for the Conservatives, and the Ulster Unionist parties the other two seats. This cluster is disproportionately working class, as is cluster 20, but also above average in home-owners. This Conservative advantage is offset by the cluster being disproportionately North of England; 13 of the 22 seats are there, and another four in pro-Labour Wales. Of the seats in

Table X.5  <u>POLITICAL HEGEMONY IN SOCIAL CLUSTERS:  SEATS AND VOTES</u>

| | Seats | | | Votes | | |
|---|---|---|---|---|---|---|
| | Con | Lab | Other | Con | Lab | All. |
| | N | N | N | % | % | % |
| **Predominantly Conservative clusters (18)** | | | | | | |
| 5. Own occ, full employ, S Eng | 17 | – | – | 51 | 22 | 26 |
| 9. Full employ, non-man, own occ, young, S Eng | 23 | – | – | 55 | 16 | 29 |
| 23. Non-man,fullemp, ownocc,Eng&Sc | 15 | – | – | 58 | 11 | 30 |
| 25. Non-man, full employ, S Eng | 21 | – | – | 56 | 14 | 29 |
| 8. Non-man, immig, London | 19 | 1 | 1 | 48 | 22 | 28 |
| 10. Own occ, rural, old, S Eng | 18 | – | 2 | 55 | 12 | 30 |
| 12. Non-man, full employ, S Eng | 20 | – | 1 | 53 | 14 | 28 |
| 13. Young, S Eng | 11 | – | 1 | 43 | 21 | 26 |
| 17. Rural, full employ, S Eng | 39 | 1 | 1 | 52 | 16 | 28 |
| 18. Immig, old, S Eng | 15 | – | 1 | 49 | 18 | 25 |
| 19. Own occ, old, S Eng | 18 | – | 1 | 57 | 10 | 32 |
| 21. Non-man, immig, London | 16 | 1 | – | 47 | 30 | 22 |
| 28. Own occ, Britain | 26 | 1 | 1 | 48 | 24 | 27 |
| 2. Rural, Britain | 29 | 1 | 3 | 52 | 12 | 32 |
| 11. Cross-section of towns, UK | 14 | 1 | 2 | 43 | 24 | 26 |
| 29. Own occ, old, S Eng | 10 | – | 2 | 45 | 22 | 27 |
| 6. Young,cross-class, Eng&Wales | 14 | 9 | 1 | 39 | 35 | 25 |
| 7. Cross-class, Eng & Wales | 24 | 7 | 1 | 42 | 33 | 24 |
| Total | 348 | 22 | 18 | 49.7 | 20.0 | 27.5 |
| **Predominantly Labour clusters (10)** | | | | | | |
| 3. Council ten, elderly, Scot | 2 | 26 | – | 21 | 48 | 21 |
| 4. Coun ten,man'l,unemp,imm,London | – | 12 | 1 | 21 | 52 | 24 |
| 26. Manual,coun ten,unemp,old,NEng | 1 | 11 | – | 30 | 47 | 22 |
| 30. Manual,unemploy,immig,London | 2 | 19 | – | 31 | 47 | 19 |
| 14. Manual, Britain | 3 | 31 | 1 | 28 | 48 | 22 |
| 16. Manual,unemp,coun ten, Eng&Scot | 1 | 15 | 1 | 23 | 50 | 20 |
| 27. Manual, coun ten, unemp, N Eng | 2 | 26 | 2 | 31 | 43 | 22 |
| 15. North of England | 4 | 18 | 1 | 32 | 40 | 22 |
| 20. Immig, manual, Eng & Wales | 14 | 15 | 1 | 38 | 39 | 22 |
| 22. Manual, own occ, old, N Eng | 9 | 11 | 2 | 32 | 38 | 18 |
| Total | 38 | 184 | 9 | 29.2 | 44.8 | 21.1 |
| **Other clusters (2)** | | | | | | |
| 1. Rural, council ten, Scot | 4 | 3 | 5 | 27 | 16 | 19 |
| 24. Rural, Scot | 7 | – | 12 | 28 | 9 | 27 |
| Total | 11 | 3 | 17 | 27.7 | 12.1 | 23.7 |

Great Britain, 11 are held by margins of less than 10 per cent. The Welsh effect is shown by the fact that while the Labour lead in this cluster averages six per cent overall, in the four Welsh seats it is always more than 28 per cent.

The Conservatives win 14 of the 25 seats in cluster 6, but the party is not hegemonic in votes, taking 39 per cent against 35 per cent for Labour. In terms of socio-economic status the cluster tends to approximate the average for Britain as a whole. It is distinctive in being low on immigrants, on agriculture, and disproportionately youthful. Eight of the nine seats won by Labour in this cluster are in Wales or the North of England. Only one of the 24 in the cluster is in the South of England. Eleven of the constituencies are held by margins of less than 10 per cent.

While every MP enters the House of Commons by winning a seat that is formally competitive, in practice the clustering of social groups inclined to the Conservative or Labour parties removes most of the competitive element from constituency contests. A Conservative fighting a seat in a middle-class constituency in the South of England where owner-occupation is high and unemployment relatively low can be virtually certain of election. Even when Labour does as badly as in 1983 a Labour candidate fighting a working-class constituency in an area of high unemployment and lots of council houses can be virtually sure of election. Of 397 Conservative MPs, 88 per cent represent constituencies where the Conservatives enjoy a hegemony of representation. Of the 209 Labour MPs, 88 per cent represent constituencies subject to Labour hegemony. In the political geography of Britain, voters supporting one party are so clustered that the competition between the parties for control of government is not reflected in constituency contests for parliamentary representation.

# XI
# Turbulence
# In Party Competition

Nobody desires turbulence for its own sake; confusion and commotion in place of what had been a predictable pattern of events is profoundly unsettling. Like it or not, the 1983 election outcome has turned the seeming regularities of electoral competition into a turbulent competition for votes, and an even more turbulent competition for seats in the House of Commons. The outcome of the 1983 election was perverse: for every one per cent of the vote that the Conservatives *lost* by comparison with 1979, the party *won* an additional 38 seats in the House of Commons. In such circumstances, politicians can no longer close their eyes to awkward facts and hope to muddle through. In the midst of a storm, the alternatives are to keep afloat, to steer toward a safe haven, or to be swept away by the deluge.

The 1983 election marked the collapse of the two-party system modelled by Sir Ivor Jennings (1961: 32), in which control of Parliament changed hands with the regularity of a pendulum swinging from the top of Westminster's Big Ben. Instead of two parties dividing the vote almost evenly on a 50-50 basis, none of the parties came near winning half the vote, and the failure of the second-place party, Labour, to win as much as a third of the vote, meant that third-force parties together took more votes than the nominal second-place party. Three major patterns of competition for seats now exist in the United Kingdom, and there are more than a dozen variations on this theme.

If Britain is said to have a two-party system, it is not the same mixture as before. In terms of votes, it is now a system with one whole party, the Conservatives, and two half parties, Labour and the Alliance. Social Democrats might argue that the Alliance itself is a coalition of two groups, each of which polls one-quarter of the votes of a normal party. Only in the sense of parties grouped into government and opposition can Britain be said to be a two-party system: the Conservatives vs Labour and the Alliance.

There is nothing sacred about competition between two parties or in the regular alternation of parties in office. It is the exception rather than the rule in the party systems of Western nations. In first-past-the-post electoral systems five different parties on average win seats in Parliament; in the 1983 British general election, five parties won seats in Britain, and five more parties won seats in Northern Ireland. In proportional representation systems, nine parties on average normally win seats in Parliament (Rose, 1983: Tables 5-6). The hegemony of a single party in government is normal in most Western nations. Among 21 Western nations Britain is unique in the even rotation of parties in and out of office; in countries such as Italy and Sweden, a dominant party can be in office for a generation (Punnett, 1981).

The British party system is dynamic, not static. Since 1885 at least four different systems of party competition have prevailed in the United Kingdom (Rose, 1980: Table 6):

(1) 1885-1918: A multi-party system in which Conservatives and Liberal Unionists opposed Liberals, Labour and Irish Nationalists.

(2) 1918-1945: A period of single-party Conservative rule alternating with coalition governments and occasional minority Labour governments.

(3) 1945-1974: Two-party competition between Conservatives and Labour.

(4) 1974--: A mixed system, in which three-party competition for the popular vote has co-existed with single-party government at Westminster.

Since 1974 the failure of any victorious party to win as large a share of the vote as the losing party normally received from 1945 to 1970 means that the two-party system as conventionally described is no longer the status quo, but the status quo *ante* . The combination of disparate attributes--a three-party division of the popular vote and a two-party division of seats in the House of Commons-- emphasizes the instability of the present mixed system.

The Conservative Party would be very happy to see the 1983 election become the basis of a new equilibrium of party competition. An election result that stabilized on the basis of the Conservatives 14.8 per cent ahead of their nearest competitor allows ample leeway for loss of votes on a scale that has been normal in the post-war era, yet would still leave the Conservatives with a majority in Parliament. However, in a turbulent political environment normal movements in votes cannot be taken for granted.

The Alliance has the greatest wish to increase turbulence, for their efforts to break the mould of British politics did not succeed fully in 1983. The election outcome did mark a significant departure from elections in the past half-century--but to the advantage of the Conservatives rather than the Alliance. The Alliance needs to win hundreds of seats in Parliament and establish a new electoral system giving it seats in proportion to votes before it can claim to have reached its goal. With only 23 seats in Parliament, the Alliance needs increased turbulence before it can hope to do this.

The Labour Party has been ambivalent in its attitude toward the 1983 election outcome. The initial shock reaction was to deny that it had happened, and there remain Labour Party activists who wish to close their eyes to the steady decline in the party's vote from 48.0 per cent in 1966 to almost half that in 1983. The election of Neil Kinnock as party leader and Roy Hattersley as deputy leader reflects a Labour desire to reverse this trend. Their first target is to win back the lost Labour voters. But this task is doubly difficult when some former Labour voters have defected to the Alliance, and others to the Conservatives; it requires a fight on two fronts. Moreover, so great is the Labour deficit in votes that to win sufficient support to become the government Labour needs more than a marginal increase in votes; it needs to secure the collapse of the Alliance or Conservative Party, or both.

Multi-dimensional party competition is intrinsically more difficult to understand than competition along a single dimension of Conservatives vs. Labour. Since voters in Continental European countries cope with such complexities all the time, there is no good reason why the British electorate cannot learn to live with complexity. Nor is there any alternative but to do so, for the parties will *not* start even at the next election; they will start from the position at which they were left on 9 June 1983. Hence, anyone who wishes to understand the next election will first need to understand the last result.

This chapter examines the 1983 election in terms of its implications for party control of government. The scale of the Conservative majority in the 1983 Parliament means that changes in votes within normal limits will now not alter control of government. For government to change hands, there must be another upheaval. The first section records the reasons why the swing concept used to analyse changes in votes in most post-war elections is no longer applicable. The second section examines multi-party competition at the constituency level. The constituency, not the region or nation, is now more than ever the territorial unit of central importance. The effect of different forms of multi-party competition is to produce multi-dimensional psephology; seats can change hands (or remain unchanged) with votes shifting very different ways. For a change of government to occur there must be discontinuity, a break with what has gone before. A third successive Conservative victory would also mark a discontinuity from the two-party system, creating Conservative hegemony in office, if not in the electorate.

The language of re-instating, re-aligning or de-aligning elections is inadequate to describe what is happening in Britain in the 1980s. Such shifts assume that the names of the parties remain constant, even if their share of the votes varies in a more or less steady fashion. What is at stake in Britain in the 1980s is *which* parties survive to contest elections in the 1990s, and *whether* the parties survive under their present names. When the names of parties change (as in the creation of a Liberal Party-Social Democratic Party Alliance) or the number competing effectively changes (as in the introduction of multi-dimensional party competition in 1983) then the difference from the 1970s is best described as a discontinuity; it is not a change in degree but a change in kind.

## The Collapse of Swing

Since 1945 British general elections have been analysed and predictions made about their outcome on the basis of the concept of swing, a simple summary measure that averages the per cent rise in the vote for one party and the fall in the vote for another (Butler, 1947: 277ff). For example, a two per cent rise in the Conservative vote (e.g. from 56 to 58 per cent) and a two per cent fall in the Labour vote (e.g. from 44 to 42 per cent) produces a swing of two per cent to the Conservatives. Notwithstanding various complications and criticisms (cf. Rasmussen, 1965; Butler, 1965), the concept proved useful for examining the results of elections in conditions characterizing British party competition for a quarter-century or more. The 1983 election marked the collapse of swing, for the conditions necessary for its use no longer exist.

Swing is calculated by comparing the result in one general election with the previous result. However, the wholesale redistribution of parliamentary constituencies following the 1979 general election meant that the boundaries on which 1983 constituency contests were fought were radically altered from the previous election. Only ten per cent of the 1979 constituencies had their boundaries left unchanged. The median 1983 constituency had one-third of its electorate added or subtracted by redistribution. A joint BBC/ITN team created notional results for the "ghost" House of Commons, that is, figures showing what each party would have secured in a new constituency if it had been fought on the 1983 boundaries in 1979. The principal source of data for these estimates were local government election results (BBC/ITN, 1983: 15ff). Although correct in terms of vote totals nationwide, the estimates inevitably have a degree of error in particular constituencies, thus constituting a less than completely accurate base for calculating vote changes in 1983.

Because swing measures the net change in the vote of two contending parties, a small estimating error in a notional 1979 result will have a disproportionate effect upon the swing figures. A one per cent estimating error can be one-quarter of a swing of four per cent. Estimating errors appear to have particularly affected the measure of the Conservative change in the vote. In the 66 constituencies completely free from estimating error because no boundary alteration occurred in 1983, the average change in the Conservative vote was

0.7, and the standard deviation 2.3 per cent, indicating a much greater pattern of dispersion than in an era of two-party competition (cf. Butler, 1965: 456). In constituencies affected by redistribution the standard deviation was almost half again as great, 3.5 per cent. The Labour vote also has estimating errors, for the average percent change in Labour's share of the vote in constituencies completely unaffected by redistribution was 4.0 per cent, whereas it was 4.8 per cent in constituencies affected by redistribution. A notable portion of the apparent difference between constituencies in calculations of 1983 constituency swings may reflect estimating errors in the 1979 constituency base.

While redistribution will not be a problem in the next general election, fundamental obstacles to the use of swing remain, because electoral competition today involves three-party competition nationwide. Between 1979 and 1983 the pattern of party competition was disrupted. Whereas 82 per cent of all constituencies in 1979 had witnessed a fight between Conservatives and Labour for first or second, in 1983 the proportion of seats in which these two parties came first and second fell to 43 per cent (Table XI.1). Whereas about one-eighth of the seats in the House of Commons could be said to change hands in 1983, the pattern of party competition changed in two-fifths of all constituencies. The shift in votes was three times as likely to produce a change of place between the second and third-place parties as a switch between the first and second-place parties. However, the movement of votes between the second and third parties and between the first and third parties is ignored by measures of swing, even though it can be large and have a major effect upon the election outcome.

Party competition in the United Kingdom today is now multi- dimensional (see Table IX.4); the same two parties do not finish first and second in every constituency. At the next election, in the 283 constituencies where the Alliance and the Conservatives finished first and second we will particularly want to

Table XI.1   CHANGING PATTERNS OF PARTY COMPETITION, 1979-83

|  | 1979 | Pattern 1983 Same | Different |
|---|---|---|---|
| Conservative & Labour | 523 | 281 | 242 |
| Conservative & Liberal/Alliance | 86 | 86 | 0 |
| Other patterns | 41 | 22 | 19 |
| Total | 650 | 389 | 261 |

know changes in votes between these two parties. By contrast, in the 285 seats in which the Conservatives and Labour finished first and second we will specially want to know about changes in votes between the two traditional contenders for government. There are also 82 seats in which the pattern of party competition is different again. Neither a Conservative vs. Labour or Conservative vs. Alliance swing is sufficient to capture the dynamics of electoral competition at present, for each only applies to a minority of parliamentary constituencies.

The very symmetry of swing is its undoing; it is designed for a system of two-party competition in which one party's gain in votes must equal another's loss. When only two parties contest a constituency, then if one party's share of the vote rises by five per cent, the other party's must necessarily fall by five per cent. When the Liberals complicated constituency contests in the 1950s and 1960s, "intervening" or "withdrawing" from constituencies, as long as the Liberals finished third the impact of the Liberals fighting or not fighting a seat could be discounted by calculating changes in the combined share of the vote of the two front-running parties (see Steed, 1965: 337ff). But when Alliance candidates finish second more often than Labour, it is unreasonable to calculate a Labour-Conservative swing, for it is between parties, normally finishing first and third.

While it is possible to sustain the concept of swing by having two sets of swing figures, one for the constituencies in which the Conservatives and the Alliance were first and second in 1983, and the other where the Conservatives and Labour finished first and second, such a tactic is mistaken. In a turbulent environment there is good reason to anticipate that the pattern of party competition will itself shift from election to election. A swing calculated between Conservatives and the Alliance on the basis of 1983 results would not be appropriate in a constituency in which Labour then came second (or even first) at the next general election. Such a calculation is fundamentally flawed because it rests upon the belief that the change in votes between any pair of parties must be symmetrical, and that the same parties must be first and second in a constituency in successive elections. However, this is not now the case.

The 1983 election witnessed a great break with symmetry, for in the majority of constituency contests the votes of the parties finishing first and second changed in the same direction (Table XI.2). The conventional pattern of change expected when a governing party wins dozens of seats, a rise in the Conservative vote and a fall in the Labour vote, occurred in only 71 constituencies. The vote of the party winning the most seats in Parliament, the Conservatives, fell in two-thirds of constituency contests. The Alliance, which did worst in terms of parliamentary seats, did best in terms of changes in the vote; there was a substantial rise in the Alliance vote in the majority of constituencies. In most of the constituencies where the vote of one party rose and the other fell, this was because of a rise in the Alliance vote and a fall in the Conservative vote.

Table XI.2   ASYMMETRIES IN THE UPS AND DOWNS OF PARTY VOTES

| | Seats | | Mean % change in vote, 1979–1983 | | |
|---|---|---|---|---|---|
| | N | | Con | Lab | Alliance |
| **Vote of both front-running parties down (212 seats)** | | | | | |
| Con down, Labour down | 209 | 33.0 | -3.4 | -7.9 | 12.1 |
| Other patterns | 3 | 0.5 | | (n.a.) | |
| **Vote of both front-running parties up (125 seats)** | | | | | |
| Con up, Alliance up | 120 | 19.7 | 1.7 | -10.2 | 9.3 |
| Other patterns of competition | 5 | 0.8 | | (n.a.) | |
| **Vote of one front-running party up, other down (296 seats)** | | | | | |
| Con down, Alliance up | 159 | 25.1 | -2.7 | -10.1 | 13.4 |
| Con up, Labour down | 71 | 11.2 | 1.8 | -11.2 | 10.7 |
| Labour down, Alliance up | 50 | 7.9 | -3.8 | -9.9 | 16.9 |
| Other patterns of competition | 16 | 2.5 | | (n.a.) | |

(Northern Ireland constituencies excluded)

___

In three-way constituency contests, changes in votes are necessarily asymmetrical: two parties must gain votes and one party lose, or vice versa. The analysis of the ups and downs of each party's vote demonstrates this. Moreover, even where the vote of both contenders went up, it rose very unequally; on average the Alliance vote went up 9.3 per cent as against a Conservative rise of 1.7 per cent. Where the votes of the two major parties went down, they did not go down equally. Whereas the Conservative vote dropped an average of 3.4 per cent in the constituencies where it fell along with Labour, the average Labour loss was more than double, 7.9 per cent. In these seats, the increased Alliance vote of 12.1 per cent could be described as a conventional swing of 2.2 per cent to the Conservatives! Where the votes of the two front-running parties moved in opposite directions, as is assumed in swing, there remained big differences between the parties. Where the Alliance vote went up 13.4 per cent on average, the Conservative vote went down 2.7 per cent.

When the assumptions of swing no longer meet the realities of multi-dimensional competition, then it is no longer 'a useful tool in forecasting', as

David Butler (1965: 457) could once fairly describe it. There is thus good reason
to discard it. In fact, this has been done in both ITN and BBC forecasts and
analyses of election results since 1974 (cf. Brown and Payne, 1975; Payne and
Brown, 1981).

The collapse of swing is literal; only by taking swing apart, that is,
disaggregating it into its component parts, can we begin to understand the
multi-dimensional nature of electoral competition today. Instead of adding
together changes in the share of the vote of the parties, these figures should be
kept separate. We can thus observe the ups and downs of each party's vote,
independently of assumptions about the vote of either of its competitors. While
the sum total of the ups and downs in votes must cancel out, in three-party
competition the process is necessarily asymmetrical; one party's gain will be
offset by the losses of two parties or the gain of two by the loss of the other party.
When examining electoral turbulence it is necessary to examine the ups and
downs of each party before considering their multi-dimensional implications.

## Multi-Party Constituency Competition

The turbulence generated by the 1983 election result requires a return to
fundamentals. For most of the post-war era, constituency contests have been
fought between two and only two parties. The attempt of the Liberals to fight
Britainwide in 1950 ended in disaster; 319 of the 475 Liberal candidates lost
their deposits. From 1945 to 1970 an average of 2.6 candidates contested a
constituency; the number fell as low as 2.2 candidates in 1951, when 495
constituencies saw straight fights without any Liberal or independent entering
the lists (Rose, 1980: Table 1). In the 1950s and 1960s, the Liberals usually
fought a quarter to one-half of parliamentary seats, almost invariably finishing
third (Craig 1981: 165).

When competition is confined to two and only two candidates, then one
candidate necessarily must win half the vote, if only by default of his opponent.
This has been the norm since 1885 (Craig, 1981: 161). In the years before the
First World War more than 95 per cent of contested seats were won with more
than half the vote. In the inter-war period, the emergence of three-party
competition involving Conservatives, Liberals and Labour decreased the
number of seats won with half the vote; the inter-war average was 76 per cent.
The range was from 46 per cent of seats won with half the vote in the atypical
1929 contest to 94 per cent in 1931. From 1945 to 1970, the proportion of seats
won by a candidate with at least half the vote was as high as 94 per cent in 1951
and 1955, in the wake of the collapse of a Liberal attempt to revive. Nearly four-
fifths (79 per cent) of all seats were won by a candidate receiving more than half
the vote.

An era of two-party competition at the constituency level ended in February, 1974, when the nationwide Liberal revival deprived MPs of being able to claim as much as half the vote in 64 per cent of constituencies. In October, 1974, this was true in 60 per cent of all constituencies. The decline in Liberal fortunes in 1979 meant that the proportion of constituencies won on a minority vote fell to 32 per cent, a higher figure than at almost every election between 1885 and 1964. In June, 1983, the surge in Alliance support meant that MPs were returned with less than half the popular vote in 51 per cent of all constituencies. Only the collapse of the Labour vote kept this figure from being higher than in 1974 (Table XI.3). In the four elections since February, 1974, 52 per cent of all MPs have been elected without a majority of the vote in their constituency. Three-party competition is now the rule.

In the 1983 general election, 335 of the 650 seats were won by a candidate polling less than half the vote (Table XI.3). Whereas the Conservatives won 59 per cent of their seats with a majority of the votes, Labour won only 33 per cent of its seats with a majority, and the Alliance 35 per cent of its small number of seats. While only two seats were won with less than one-third of the vote, signifiying a four-way contest (Renfrew West & Inverclyde and Carmarthen), 68 seats were won with less than 40 per cent of the vote, and an additional 126 seats with between 40 and 45 per cent of the constituency vote. Of the seats won with a minority of the vote, 245 were in England, 51 in Scotland, 26 in Wales, and 13 in Northern Ireland. Whereas more than half of English constituencies were won with a majority of the vote, elsewhere in the United Kingdom this was true of only one-third of seats.

Three-way competition for votes does not necessarily mean a close contest. In fact, it can have the opposite effect, increasing the number of safe seats. For

Table XI.3 THE SHARE OF THE CONSTITUENCY VOTE FOR THE WINNING PARTY

| Vote for Winner | Seats | | | | Cumulative total | |
|---|---|---|---|---|---|---|
| | Con | Lab | All. | Oth. | N | % |
| 50% plus | 233 | 68 | 8 | 6 | 315 | 48.5 |
| 45 to 49.9% | 75 | 57 | 4 | 5 | 141 | 70.1 |
| 40 to 44.9% | 60 | 56 | 6 | 4 | 126 | 89.5 |
| 35 to 39.9% | 26 | 26 | 5 | 5 | 62 | 99.1 |
| 30 to 34.9% | 3 | 2 | 0 | 1 | 6 | 100.0 |

example, if the Conservatives regularly polled 46 per cent of the vote in a constituency, the party's candidate would be defeated in a straight fight. The Conservatives would win the seat by a two per cent margin if a Liberal intervened and took 10 per cent from the previous winner's 54 per cent of the vote. The Conservatives would hold the seat by an 18 per cent margin if the Alliance candidate took second place, with 28 per cent of the vote, as against 26 per cent for Labour, and 46 per cent Conservative.

A constituency is necessarily marginal between three parties if the winning party gets no more than 40 per cent of the vote. If that happens, then in a three-way race, one or both of its opponents is sure to take at least 30 per cent of the vote. Only 68 constituencies fall into the category of three-way marginal seats, whereas 267 seats are won with at least 40 per cent of the vote but less than half. Such seats can only be marginal if the third place party does very badly. For example, in a constituency where the Conservatives won 45 per cent of the vote, the third-place also ran would need to fall below 10 per cent of the vote in order for the Conservative to lose the seat. In a seat in which each of the candidates polled the same as the party's nationwide share of the vote, the Conservative would romp home with a 15 per cent lead over Labour, and a 17 per cent lead over the Alliance Candidate.

The epigram to describe the landslide victory of Mrs. Thatcher's party in 1983 is: *Divided she conquers* . If the Conservatives had only elected MPs where their candidate won half or more of the vote, the Conservatives would be in opposition with 233 seats. Thanks to divisions among their opponents, the Conservatives won an additional 164 seats with less than half the vote.

The governing party today is vulnerable to attack on at least four different fronts. First of all, the Conservatives could lose a seat by a conventional swing of their vote to Labour, or to the Alliance, the alternative Opposition. Given that Labour more often finishes third than second to the Conservatives, this is less of a threat than a second possibility, namely, that the Conservatives lose votes to whichever party is in second place in the constituency. This would not reflect a rise in support for one opposition party so much as a rejection of the government of the day. Thirdly, the Conservatives could lose a seat held on a minority vote if support for the third-place party collapsed, with voters switching to the second-place party in order to avoid wasting their vote locally. A fourth way in which the Conservatives could lose a seat would be by a big surge in support for the third- place party--whether by taking votes from the second-place contender or from the winner or both--sufficient to make the party furthest behind in 1983 the winner at the next general election.

If there are many ways in which the Conservatives could lose seats at the next election, it follows that there are also many ways in which the government could gain or hold seats. A slight rise in the Conservative vote could add to the government's already large majority. The Conservatives would hold a seat if changes were confined to a recirculation of votes between the second and third place parties; their opponents would then find it difficult to win the seat unless it was already very marginal. Whereas a second place party that takes five per cent of the vote from the incumbent could overturn a majority of up to 10 per cent, a second place party that took five per cent of the vote from the third place candidate would not win if the Conservative majority was more than five per cent. If the circulation of votes involved the third-place candidate winning votes from the second place candidate, this would actually widen the incumbent's lead.

A Conservative MP could actually see his share of the vote drop at the next general election--as it did for most Conservative MPs in 1983--yet still be re-elected. For example, the loss of three per cent of the vote to the second place party and three per cent to the third place party would re-elect all Conservatives whose previous margin of victory was greater than nine per cent. If the front-runner's loss of six per cent went solely to the third-place party, the seat would remain secure as long as it was not very marginal.

One simple fact stands out from the welter of hypothetical possibilities canvassed in the above paragraphs, namely, that when three-party competition is the rule, we not only need to know how many votes a candidate wins or loses in a given constituency, but also which competitors suffer or benefit.

## Multi-Dimensional Competition for Government

Every election casts its shadow ahead; a distinctive feature of the 1983 election is that the shadow is bifurcated. One portion lies along the dimension of party competition between Conservatives and Labour, which has characterized British electoral politics for half a century. But the other is along a different dimension, with the Alliance the principal competitor with the Conservatives. In order to understand how changes in votes at the next general election *might* deprive the Conservatives of their majority and return a Labour or Alliance government, we must explore each dimension and then their collective implications. Exploring logical possibilities says nothing about the probability of any particular outcome, but even in a turbulent environment some logical possibilities are empirically more probable than others.

So great is the Conservative lead over the Labour opposition, 188 seats, that three different possible outcomes of the next election must be considered:

(1) *The inertia outcome* is the re-election of a Conservative government with an overall majority of seats.

(2) *A hung Parliament* in which the Conservatives lose their absolute majority without any other party securing a majority instead. In a Parliament without a majority party, the distribution of seats could take many forms.

(3) The return of *a Labour (or an Alliance) government* with an absolute majority of seats.

Conventionally, a marginal seat at a British general election is defined as a seat in which the winning party's lead over the second place party is less than 10.0 per cent. A marginal seat would therefore change hands with a conventional swing of 5.0 per cent. At ten of the eleven general elections since 1950 the swing of votes between the two parties Britainwide has been less than this, averaging 2.7 per cent. The exception was the 5.2 per cent swing to the Conservatives in 1979. A seat held by a margin of more than 10 per cent would conventionally be regarded as safe, and a seat held by a margin of more than 15 or 20 per cent would be very safe in normal times.

The 1983 election outcome forces a redefinition of the concept of a marginal seat. A Conservative loss of 5.0 per cent to the party that had been second would still leave the Conservatives by far the largest party in the House of Commons. The 77 seats the Conservatives would lose by an even movement of votes on this scale would be distributed 53 to Labour, 21 to the Alliance, and 3 to Nationalists. The net effect would be a House of Commons with 320 Conservative MPs, Labour a poor second in seats with 262 MPs, and the Alliance third with 44 seats. The Conservatives would be only six seats short of an absolute majority; the balance of power would rest in the hands of 17 Ulster MPs or seven Nationalists.

In order to see under what circumstances the Labour Party could win a majority at the next general election, or at least win more seats than the Conservatives, it is necessary to redefine marginal seats to include all the seats needed to give the Labour Party a House of Commons majority. In the present House of Commons Labour is 117 seats short of a parliamentary majority. To win this many seats from the Conservatives (allowing for Labour taking from the Alliance the five seats where it now finishes second), the Labour Party would need to sweep every seat in which the Conservative lead over Labour is 25.0 per cent or less. If the Alliance were to become the largest party in Parliament, it would have to take seats where it trails by an even greater margin.

Defining a marginal seat as a seat held by a margin of up to 25.0 per cent emphasizes the scale of the Conservative victory at the 1983 general election. To assert that seats held by such a margin are invincible would be to ignore examples of the government of the day losing even safer seats at by-elections. For example, the Conservatives lost Crosby, held by a margin of 31.6 per cent in the 1979 general election, to Shirley Williams as an SDP candidate in a 1981 by-election. But the seat was won again by the Conservatives in 1983. Even in a turbulent electoral environment, no politician would claim that it was easy to win seats where the MP's lead was 15, 20 or 25 per cent.

The territorial distribution of marginal seats is inevitably concentrated in England, given that English seats constitute more than four-fifths of the House of Commons. Since the crucial marginal seats today are Conservative-held, their location tends to follow the distribution of Conservative seats in the country. Of the seats in which the Conservatives are less than 25.0 per cent ahead of Labour, 22 are in the South of England, 22 in London, 28 in the Midlands, 29 in the North of England, 5 in Scotland and 7 in Wales. In the 132 seats in which the Conservatives lead the Alliance by a margin of less than 25.0 per cent, more than half, 69, are in the South of England.

When the government of the day holds a commanding lead in Parliament, the only way in which it can be unseated is by a tide that is Britainwide. If the Conservatives lost every seat they now hold in Scotland and Wales by a majority of less than 25 per cent over Labour, the party would still have 385 seats, a very comfortable majority in the House of Commons. Even if the Conservatives additionally lost every one of the 29 seats held in the North of England by a 25.0 per cent margin over Labour, the government would still have a comfortable parliamentary majority with 356 seats; Labour would still trail it by nearly one hundred seats. The only way in which the Labour opposition can gain control of the next House of Commons is by winning more than 70 Conservative-held seats in London, the Midlands and the South of England. A Labour strategy of mobilizing support in its territorial bastions distant from London might increase Labour's vote, but it would doom Labour to opposition in the next Parliament. Of the seats that Labour needs to win a majority in the next Parliament, 39 per cent are in the South of England or London, and 64 per cent are between the English Channel and the Mersey.

The clusters of seats where Labour must make gains if it is to have a chance of forming the government after the next general election emphasize the scale of advance required by Labour to break out of the position it had walled itself into as of 9 June 1983. If Labour simply pursued a policy of building on strength, seeking to win every seat currently held by the Conservatives in the eight clusters where it has virtually complete hegemony in representation, it would gain only 15 seats. But if the Conservatives did the same in their areas of hegemonic strength, Labour would concurrently lose seats as well (Table X.5). If Labour could also win all the seats that the Conservatives hold in two clusters where Labour now has a slight edge--clusters 20 and 22, which tend to be well above average in terms of their proportion of manual workers--then the Conservatives would be without a single seat in any of the ten predominantly Labour clusters. But Labour would only have 247 seats in Parliament, 112 less than the Conservatives.

In order for Labour to defeat the Conservatives, it must win seats in predominantly Conservative clusters. The Conservatives are most vulnerable in clusters 6, and 7, both of which are nearly average in terms of occupational class, and tend to be widely dispersed throughout England and Wales. If Labour won the 12 constituencies in cluster 6 where it is now second to the Conservatives, and the 19 in cluster 7 where it is second to the Conservatives, it would be making a substantial inroad in clusters that are two-thirds to three-quarters Conservative in parliamentary representation. But Labour's gain of 31 seats would still leave the Conservatives an absolute majority in the House of Commons with 328 seats.

In order to pull ahead of the Conservatives at the next general election, Labour must gain dozens of seats in constituency clusters that are currently overwhelmingly Conservative in Parliament. Except for cluster 21, a London group very high in immigrants but also disproportionately middle-class (e.g. Hampstead & Highgate or Streatham), the Alliance finishes second in most seats in these clusters. Adding a dozen seats in cluster 21 from the Conservatives (as against one that Labour currently holds) would deprive the Conservatives of their absolute majority, but still leave the government with 316 seats, as against 290 for Labour. To pull ahead of the Conservatives, Labour would need to win seats in social clusters where it currently has only one MP (e.g. clusters 8, middle-class, immigrant, London; cluster 11, a cross-section of United Kingdom towns; and cluster 28, owner-occupier Britain) and also win a number of seats in clusters where it is currently without a single MP (e.g. cluster 5, full employment, owner-occupier South of England; cluster 18, immigrant, elderly, South of England; and cluster 19 elderly, owner-occupier South of England).

The conventional way which an opposition is expected to win control of government is by a swing in votes from the governing party to itself in numbers sufficient to win all the marginal seats needed to gain a majority. The magnitude of Labour's difficulty is shown by the fact that to be sure of a majority in the next Parliament, the Labour Party would have to reduce the Conservative vote by 12.5 per cent in each constituency, and add every one of these votes to the Labour column.

If the Conservatives failed to win the next general election solely because of a switch of votes from the Conservatives to Labour, the following are the possibilities:

(1) The Conservatives would lose their absolute majority in the House of Commons if at least 5.7 per cent of their vote transferred to Labour. The 72nd Conservative seat in order to fall would be Nottingham South West, which the party won with 45.9 per cent of the vote, against 32.6 per cent for Labour and 20.6 per cent for the Alliance. The loss of every Conservative seat held with a majority of up to 11.8 per cent over Labour or of 5.8 per cent over other parties would leave the Conservatives with 325 seats, one less than a majority, but still

very comfortably ahead of Labour's 268 seats, the Alliance with 33, and Nationalists and Ulster MPs with 24 seats.

(2) Labour would become the largest party in the House of Commons if it could win 8.8 per cent of the vote taken by the Conservatives at the last election. The Conservatives would then lose every seat held by a 17.5 per cent margin over Labour or an 8.7 per cent lead over other parties. The 104th Conservative seat to fall would be Dover, which the Conservatives took in 1983 with 48.3 per cent of the vote, against 30.8 per cent for Labour and 20.1 per cent for the Alliance. The net result would be a Commons with 294 Labour MPs, 293 Conservatives, 38 Alliance, and 25 Nationalist and Ulster MPs.

(3) In order to win an absolute majority in the next House of Commons, Labour would need an even nationwide gain of 12.5 per cent of the total vote from the Conservatives. The Conservatives would then lose every seat held with a 25.0 per cent lead over Labour or a 12.5 per cent lead over other parties. This would give Labour 328 seats in the Commons, a commanding lead over the Conservatives with 251, the Alliance with 47 and Nationalists and Ulster MPs with 24. With poetic justice, the seat that Labour needs to achieve an absolute majority of 326 is Finchley, currently held by Mrs. Margaret Thatcher.

None of the above outcomes would mark a return to the status quo ante; each would signify a discontinuity in electoral competition. Each outcome would maintain three-party competition for the popular vote, and the disjunction between seats and votes in the House of Commons. The first possibility would leave the Conservatives without a majority but the dominant party in the House of Commons, and Labour with fewer seats in Parliament than at every election but one since 1935. The second alternative would create a hung Parliament in which the government would depend upon Alliance votes. The third alternative would produce single-party government but not a single-party opposition, for the Conservative share of the popular vote would be little more than that of the Alliance, and its parliamentary representation would be lower than in every election bar one since 1906.

In fact, a conventional swing-of-the-pendulum model of party competition grossly oversimplifies the movement of voters. Even in an era of conventional Conservative-Labour competition, Butler and Stokes calculate that in 1964 only 2.1 per cent of the electorate switched from the Conservatives to Labour. The election of a Labour government was much more dependent upon the circulation of votes to and from Liberals. The straight conversion of voters between the two parties is only one of a number of components of change in vote totals (Butler and Stokes, 1974:256; Sarlvik and Crewe, 1983).

A more realistic way in which to hypothesize the Conservatives losing the next election is to assume an even movement of votes away from the governing party to whichever group Labour, Alliance or Nationalist,is second in a given constituency. Such a trend would not benefit all parties evenly, but the Conservatives would lose all around.

(1) The Conservatives would lose their absolute majority in Parliament if the party lost 4.8 per cent of their vote to the party now second in each constituency. The loss of every Conservative seat held with a majority of 9.6 per cent or less would produce a House of Commons in which the Conservatives were still first with 325 seats, as against 260 for Labour, 40 for the Alliance, and 25 for Nationalist and Ulster MPs. Not only would the Conservatives have a larger lead in seats over Labour than in 1979, but also the Conservatives would enjoy a lead in votes, with about 38 per cent, as against 30 per cent for Labour and about 28 per cent for the Alliance.

(2) The Conservatives would lose their place as the largest party in the House of Commons by losing 7.3 per cent of their vote to the party finishing second in each constituency. A regular movement of votes of this type would produce a House of Commons in which Labour held 283 seats, the Conservatives 281, the Alliance 60 seats, and Nationalists and Ulster MPs 27. Labour might claim Downing Street, but it would be doubly vulnerable, for the Alliance would hold the balance of power in the Commons, and the Conservtives would have a larger share of the popular vote (35 per cent) than Labour, which would be virtually tied with the Alliance, each having less than one-third of the vote.

(3) In order to win an absolute majority in the next House of Commons, Labour would need to win every Conservative seat held by a majority of 25.0 per cent or less. But Labour taking 326 seats on the basis of a nationwide trend to second-place parties would produce a very different parliamentary position than a switch only to Labour, because second-place Alliance candidates would augment their vote by 12.5 per cent as well as Conservative MPs losing 12.5 per cent of their support. It would result in a House of Commons in which the Alliance was second with 162 seats, the Conservatives third with 135 seats, and Nationalist and Ulster MPs had 27 seats. A government loss of votes sufficiently large and even to produce a Labour government with a parliamentary majority could result in an extremely unconventional House of Commons.

A Conservative loss of dominance in Parliament would not mean a Conservative collapse in popular vote. In the second alternative above, an even loss by the Conservatives of 7.3 per cent of the vote to the party finishing second in the constituency would still leave the Conservatives with the largest share of the popular vote, and the only party with more than one-third of the vote. Even the third alternative, pushing the Conservatives down to third place in Parliament, would leave the Conservatives with a larger share of the popular vote than Labour or the Alliance won in the 1983 election. The absolute victor in the Commons, Labour, would have only one-third of the popular vote. In multi-dimensional party competition, this would give Labour a far greater lead over the Conservatives than Labour claimed in 1945 with nearly half the popular vote.

The previous set of hypothetical examples assumed one party, the Conservatives, would lose votes to both Labour and the Alliance. But this is not the only multi-dimensional shift in votes that could affect control of government.

Labour's chance of being the largest party or enjoying a majority in the next House of Commons would be aided if it could win some votes--but not too many--from the Alliance as well as from the Conservatives. To have a realistic chance of forming the next government of Britain, Labour must win a large proportion of its increase from the Conservatives, for only in that way can it gain sufficient seats to deprive the government of its majority *and* simultaneously make Labour the largest party in Parliament.

Every vote that Labour can win from the Alliance is only worth half as much as a vote won from the Conservatives. A vote won from the Alliance increases Labour's strength but does not diminish the Conservative lead in the constituencies that Labour needs to control the next House of Commons. Whereas a direct switch of 5.7 per cent of the votes from Conservatives to Labour would be sufficient to deprive the Conservatives of their parliamentary majority by giving Labour every seat the Conservatives held by a margin of 11.4 per cent, a 5.7 per cent boost in the Labour vote from the Alliance would only give Labour 247 MPs, as against 366 Conservative MPs, and 17 for the Alliance.

A Labour strategy based upon reviving its fortunes simply by winning back from the Alliance voters driven away by Labour's "own goals" behaviour from 1979 to 1983 would still leave the Conservatives in office. If Labour took 9.3 per cent of the vote from the Alliance, sufficient to return Labour to its 1979 share of the vote and leave the Alliance better off than the Liberals were in that election, Labour would get a limited parliamentary benefit. It would win 51 seats now held by the Conservatives by a margin of less than 9.3 per cent, and five seats held by the Alliance with leads of less than 18.6 per cent over Labour. But the Conservatives would remain comfortably in power with 354 seats, including eight gains from the Alliance.

To be the largest single party in the next House of Commons, Labour would need to take about five per cent of the Conservative vote as well as 9.3 per cent of the Alliance vote. To win sufficient seats to form the next government with an absolute majority, Labour would need to take at least 8.0 per cent of the Conservative vote as well as 9.3 per cent of the Alliance vote.

But the more votes that the Alliance loses to Labour, the greater the probability that it will also lose some votes to the Conservatives as well. In 1983 the Alliance took support from both major parties. If it loses support in this Parliament, there is no reason to believe that the losses would be solely in one direction. For example, if the Alliance vote went down 9.3 per cent at the next election and the votes lost were divided evenly among both major parties, then neither would gain a seat from the other and the Conservative lead over Labour would lengthen because of its gains from the Alliance.

If Labour benefited disproportionately from a drop in the Alliance vote, its advantage would be diminished by the extent of Alliance votes transferred to the Conservatives. For example if the Alliance vote returned to the Liberal level at the 1979 general election, by shedding 9.3 per cent to Labour and 2.3 per cent to the Conservatives, then Labour, instead of winning 54 seats thanks to the Alliance decline would gain 42 seats that the Conservatives now hold with a lead of 7.0 per cent or less. If the Alliance votes returned to the two older parties in accord with the 1983 second preferences of Alliance voters (see Rose, 1984: Epilogue Table 2), then Labour's net advantage would be slight, a one per cent narrowing of the existing Conservative lead for every five per cent decline in the Alliance share of the vote.

Perversely, the Conservatives could even benefit by losing votes to the Alliance--provided that this was in lieu of losing votes to Labour. If the Conservative vote dropped by 8.6 per cent at the next general election, this would only make Labour the largest party in the Commons if it took all of that vote. But the Conservatives would remain the largest party if any portion of that loss went instead to the Alliance. For example, if the Conservative loss were divided 4.3 per cent to each party in each constituency, each party would end up with about one-third of the popular vote. The net result would be a Commons in which the Conservatives were still the majority party with 343 MPs, Labour an extremely weak second with 248 MPs, and the Alliance third with 35 MPs.

To hypothesize the conditions under which the Conservatives might lose control of government is not to forecast a Conservative defeat. The size of the Conservative lead over Labour in popular votes is greater than that enjoyed by any governing party since 1935. The government's majority in terms of seats in the Commons is the greatest since the 1945 Labour government. Labour is in the worst position of any parliamentary opposition since the 1930s. The magnitude of Labour's task is greater ground for Conservative confidence than its own 1983 vote, which fell from 1979 notwithstanding the favourable circumstances in which the election was held.

In a turbulent electoral environment there is no reason to regard the Conservatives' present position as stable. It is necessary to consider ways in which the governing party could increase its parliamentary strength or, notwithstanding a loss in votes, retain its absolute majority in Parliament.

Almost any increase in the Conservative vote would give it more than 400 seats in the next House of Commons, barring the creation of a Labour-Alliance electoral coalition. A 1.5 per cent rise in the Conservative vote, returning it to the level of electoral support won in 1979, would give the Conservatives 417 seats in the Commons. Its parliamentary strength would be far greater than in 1979 because of the advent of three-party competition. An even 4.0 per cent rise, marking a return to the level of the Conservative vote in 1970, would give the Conservatives 437 seats.

The Conservatives could win additional seats in Parliament if there were an Alliance advance in popular support at the expense of the Labour vote. A five per cent increase in the Alliance vote at the expense of Labour would give the Alliance an additional nine seats, five at the expense of Labour, and nine at the Conservatives' expense. But it would also give the Conservatives 25 seats from Labour, thanks to the decline in the vote of a party with far more seats vulnerable to the Conservatives than to the Alliance.

The Conservatives could easily retain an absolute majority in the House of Commons, sufficient to keep the party in office into the 1990s, while losing votes. For example, if the Conservative vote fell to 37.2 per cent, the vote won by Labour when it took office without a majority after the February, 1974 election, the Conservatives would retain a comfortable absolute majority, even if all the votes were lost to Labour.

Even in the face of the loss of an absolute majority in the Commons, the Conservatives could still remain in office with a lead of upwards of 60 seats over Labour. While a positive coalition agreement with Ulster Unionists or Nationalists would not be easy to reach, the 1974-79 Labour government demonstrated that tacit or ad hoc understandings could be arrived at with all kinds of opponents. The number and variety of opposition parties needed to bring down the government could secure in office indefinitely a minority government with a substantial lead over the official opposition in the Commons.

There are such a variety of ways in which the next general election could produce an outcome leaving the Conservatives in office that it is better to think in terms of the Conservative strategies for "not losing" the election, for the Conservatives do not have to work to win in the same way that Labour or the Alliance does.

The objectives of the Alliance are different from those of the two established parties. The first aim of the Alliance partners is to survive to fight an election four years distant. The Liberals have demonstrated the stamina to continue fighting and losing elections for more than half a century. The Social Democratic Party has yet to show how well it can last out a Parliament. The second concern of the Alliance is whether it survives as an electoral pact. The difficulties of David Steel and David Owen with their parties in the months after the 1983 election are a reminder that this is not a certainty.

The Alliance emphasis upon the electoral system awarding seats in proportion to votes gives it a particular interest in seeing its share of the popular vote increase independently of its parliamentary representation. The gain of a handful of seats in Parliament is no great advantage to a third-place party, but winning more votes than Labour would strengthen the Alliance attack upon the existing first-past-the-post electoral system, and thus upon two-party politics. The even division of Alliance's vote nationwide, however, means that the party cannot easily convert a one per cent gain in votes into a one per cent gain in seats. For this to happen the Alliance needs to see its vote approach 40 per cent.

If the Alliance could win one-third of the vote at the next general election, it would gain 51 additional seats if its votes were taken from the party currently finishing first in a constituency. This would leave the Conservatives with an absolute majority in the House of Commons and Alliance third with 74 seats. But in votes the Alliance would be only five per cent behind the front-running Conservatives, and ten per cent ahead of Labour, a poor third.

The Alliance could come first in popular votes but still remain a bad third in seats in the House of Commons. If there were a transfer of 8.6 per cent of the Conservative vote to the Alliance because of government disaffection, with no movement of votes involving Labour and Conservatives, the Alliance would be first in popular votes, but have only 79 MPs. The Conservatives would remain the largest party in the Commons with 292 MPs, against 254 for Labour.

In order to exercise a great deal of political leverage in the next Parliament, the Alliance does not need to come first, or even second in seats. As long as Conservative and Labour seats were so divided that neither party approached having an absolute majority of MPs, then the Alliance would hold the balance of power in Parliament. This outcome could result from many kinds of movements in votes between the parties. Even on the most optimistic Labour scenario, that it gained all its additional votes from the Conservatives, then any Labour gain from the Conservatives of more than 5.5 per cent of the vote and less than 13.0 per cent would leave the Alliance holding the balance of power in the next Parliament.

The unusual division of the vote in 1983 makes it necessary to outline a number of alternative scenarios as *possible* outcomes of the next election. In the event, only one outcome will occur. Whatever it is, it is likely to involve turbulence on a scale unknown in British party politics since the 1920s.

# The Psephology of Discontinuities

Conventionally it is assumed that the result of an election--that is, the number of seats won by each party--will automatically determine which party controls government. But this is true only if one party wins an absolute majority of seats, which is by no means inevitable. Seven of 26 elections since 1885 have resulted in no party having an overall majority. Governments based upon a single party with a majority in Paliament have held office for less than half of the twentieth century in Britain (Butler, 1978: 112). Moreover, coalitions can form and reform during the life of a Parliament, as well as after each general election.

The 1983 election result can only be understood in terms of the psephology of discontinuities; whatever the outcome of the next British general election, it will produce a marked discontinuity from the past. If the result were simply a repeat of 1983 (or if the Conservative vote rose), this would mark a final rupture with the traditional two-party system, and the introduction of a predominant party system with one dominant party and two half parties. If a normal movement of votes occurs away from the government, this too will mark a discontinuity, for it would be insufficient to remove the Conservatives from office, nor would it necessarily mark a return to two-party competition.

The Conservatives can be turned out of office, but only by a shift in votes that represents a discontinuity with the past four elections. A Labour victory achieved at the expense of both the Alliance and Conservatives would not be a return to 1974, for it would mean the breaking of the mould-breakers, the Alliance. A Labour victory achieved in conjunction with a surge of Alliance support would represent the breaking of the Conservative Party, a defeat on a scale greater than 1945. A Parliament with no overall majority and a much larger Alliance of Liberals and Social Democrats than heretofore would test all parties to survive the turbulent politics of coalition and competition that would follow.

Multi-dimensional competition for seats at Westminster has created a fundamental discontinuity with past models of two-party competition. The British party system since 1945 has been described as competition between two parties; this is necessarily along one dimension, usually labelled the left-right dimension. It implies that voters closer to the left would vote Labour and to the right Conservative. (Figure XI.1a). While some voters do not consciously articulate left-right views, most voters can place themselves along this dimension if asked, and their views on economic issues tend to be in accord with the left-right dimension (cf. Table XI.4).

The rise of the Alliance has challenged the shape of party competition, because the Alliance leaders explicitly reject the class- ridden dimension of left-right politics. The Alliance places itself on a different dimension, which its leaders stress is equidistant from both the Conservative and Labour parties.

Figure XI.1   ALTERNATIVE MODELS OF PARTY COMPETITION

a)   One-dimensional competition for votes by two parties

Left                                                                                    Right

―――――――――――――――――――――――――――――――――――――

    Labour                                              Conservative

b)   Two-dimensional competition for votes by three parties

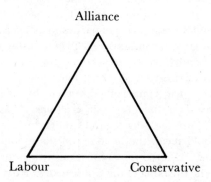

Alliance

Labour              Conservative

c)   One-dimensional competition for votes by three parties

Left                                                                                    Right

―――――――――――――――――――――――――――――――――――――

    Labour                        Alliance                    Conservative

This creates the possibility of two-dimensional competition. Locating the
Alliance at its self-defined position, equidistant from Labour and Conservatives
and also apart from class politics, changes the system's shape; it becomes
triangular competition (Figure XI.1b). At its height in the autumn of 1981 the
Alliance gained votes along both the Labour-Alliance and the Conservative-
Alliance dimensions. The revival of the Conservative Party in 1982 meant that
there was a movement back of waverers along one dimension, but the Alliance
sustained the commitment of ex-Labour voters. In this Parliament, the Alliance
can once again seek to win supporters along the Conservative to Alliance
dimension, and fight to hold off a challenge from Labour along the other axis,

Table XI.4   VOTERS AND PARTIES ON THE LEFT-RIGHT SCALE

Q.  In political matters people talk of the left and the right. How
would you place the views of (yourself/the parties) on this scale?

| | Self | Con | Placement of Lab | Lib | SDP |
|---|---|---|---|---|---|
| | % | % | % | % | % |
| Far Left | 1 | 3 | 24 | 2 | 2 |
| Substantially Left | 3 | 1 | 26 | 2 | 4 |
| Moderately left | 9 | 1 | 16 | 7 | 8 |
| Total left | (13) | (5) | (66) | (11) | (14) |
| | | | | | |
| Slightly left | 9 | 2 | 8 | 14 | 17 |
| Middle of the road | 11 | 2 | 1 | 14 | 11 |
| Slightly right | 13 | 5 | 2 | 19 | 13 |
| Total centre | (33) | (9) | (11) | (47) | (41) |
| | | | | | |
| Moderately right | 27 | 21 | 3 | 11 | 9 |
| Substantially right | 7 | 29 | 3 | 2 | 1 |
| Far right | 4 | 19 | 1 | 1 | 1 |
| Total right | (38) | (69) | (7) | (14) | (11) |
| | | | | | |
| Don't know | 16 | 17 | 18 | 29 | 33 |

Source: Calculated from Gallup Poll survey 22-27 June 1983 N = 957.

---

just as Labour needs to win back votes on both the Alliance and the
Conservative dimensions.

The triangular model is helpful in understanding the dynamics of
constituency politics, and multi-dimensional competition for control of the
House of Commons. Each of the parties is today seeking to win votes along two
not one dimensions, and to avoid losing votes along both dimensions.

However, there is another way of viewing the entrance of the Alliance into
the competition for votes, namely, to see it as a centre party, more or less
equidistant from both Labour and Conservatives *but competing along the same
dimension* (Figure XI.1c). This is consistent with many of the speeches of the
Alliance leaders, which do not promise new policies but rather a different mix of
policies, e.g. closer to Labour in supporting the welfare state, and closer to the
Conservatives in wanting to limit trade union power and opposing unilateral

nuclear disarmament. In an electorate in which turnout is already high, the Alliance cannot gain much by mobilizing additional electors. It must appeal for support from those previously accustomed to voting for parties located along the left-right dimension, but at a different point from the Alliance.

Positioning the Alliance as a half-way house between the Labour and Conservative parties is consistent with the past appeal of the Liberal Party (cf. Alt et al., 1977; Lemieux, 1977). It is also consistent with the second preferences of today's electorate. When all voters were asked just before the 1983 general election whether or not they had a second choice party, the Alliance was the favoured alternative, being named by 64 per cent of Conservative voters, and 57 per cent of Labour voters. The second choice of Alliance voters was also divided, with 43 per cent inclining to Labour, and 28 per cent to the Conservatives (Rose, 1984: Epilogue Table 2).

Studies of the issue preferences of voters emphasize that the Alliance is a coalition of supporters endorsing policies favoured by the Conservative Party, the Labour Party, or both. Alliance voters are not committed to a range of policies rejected by supporters of other parties. Among a range of 20 issues, Alliance voters agree with most Labour voters on 16 issues, and with most Conservative voters on 16 issues. A majority of Alliance voters differ from supporters of both major parties on only one of 20 issues, favouring more aid for poor nations in Africa and Asia (Gallup Poll, *Daily Telegraph*, 28 October 1983).

The great majority of voters perceive the three parties as aligned along a single left-right dimension, but at very different points on that dimension. In a 1983 post-election survey, the Gallup Poll found that 69 per cent of voters placed the Conservatives on the right, at positions ranging from the moderate to far right. Similarly, 66 per cent placed the Labour Party on the left. By comparison, 47 per cent placed the Liberal Party either in the middle of the road or only slightly to the left or right, and 41 per cent placed the Social Democratic Party in the same centre position (Table XI.4).

Collectively, 84 per cent of the electorate can readily place themselves along the left-right scale. The Conservative victory at the 1983 election is reflected in the placement of voters: 38 per cent chose one of the three right-wing positions, 33 per cent the three centre positions, and 13 per cent the three positions on the left.

When attention is focused upon the number of seats that must be shifted in order for control of government to change, then the Labour Party appears better placed than the Alliance to oust the Conservative government. Whereas Labour would have to overcome majorities of up to 25.0 per cent to win control of government, the Alliance would have to overcome majorities of almost 40 per cent to win a majority of seats in Parliament.

But when elections are examined in terms of the distance that voters must move, then the picture changes radically. As a half-way house party, the

Alliance is half the distance of Labour from the Conservatives. Therefore, a defecting Conservative voter would find it less of a distance to move to the Alliance than to Labour. This is confirmed by the fact that more than six times as many Conservatives are prepared to see the Alliance as their second-choice party rather than Labour. Equally, Labour voters find it easier to move to the Alliance than to travel double the distance to the Conservatives.

In a turbulent political environment, judgements of the electorate are subject to frequent change. Yet the basic logic of three-party competition along a single left-right dimension is clear. It is that the Conservatives are more likely to lose votes to the Alliance than to the Labour Party, and that Labour is more likely to win back (or to lose) votes to the Alliance than to the Conservatives. If both the Conservatives and Labour lost votes simultaneously, as happened in autumn, 1981, then the Alliance could make its much advertised breakthrough.

The logic of distance works in reverse as well. The Alliance is vulnerable to the loss of votes to both the Conservative and Labour parties, and its supporters are labile. For most of the Alliance's 1983 supporters a shift would not be a defection but a return to the party that they originally supported. The vulnerability of the Alliance to a loss of support on both sides was demonstrated in the final year of the last Parliament.

The central position of the Alliance is both its greatest potential strength and its biggest handicap. It is a strength because it enables the Alliance to win votes from both of the two established parties. But it is a handicap insofar as the median Labour voter is not at the centre, but sees himself or herself as moderately left, and the median Conservative voter takes a position that is moderately right. This is far enough from the middle-of-the-road to be different from the Alliance. For the Alliance to move slightly left to win more Labour votes would jeopardize its existing appeal to the Conservatives. To move slightly to the right could jeopardize its appeal to Labour supporters.

In effect, each of the parties can check the greatest ambitions of the others in a series of moves capable of producing electoral stalemate. The Alliance could inhibit a major swing of votes from the Conservatives to Labour, a necessity if Labour is to win a majority in the next Parliament. If defecting Conservatives flock to the Alliance instead of Labour, this could cost the government its parliamentary majority and create a House of Commons in which the Labour Party might have the most seats. But Labour would depend upon the Alliance on votes of confidence. The inability of the Conservatives to increase their vote in 1983 illustrates how the Alliance can block a Conservative gain of support when defecting Labour voters can stop at the Alliance half-way house.

The Conservative and Labour parties can separately or together check the ambitions of the Alliance for growth, and cut into the party's centrist vote. The Conservatives could attack by moving their profile from substantially on the right to a moderate point appealing to voters who see themselves as slightly right of centre. The Kinnock-led Labour Party has two alternatives: it can try to convert more voters to thinking of themselves as substantially to the left, or Labour can move to a sufficiently moderate left position to appeal to voters who are only slightly left. If both parties shifted toward the centre, they would not lose any significant amount of far left and far right supporters, who have no alternative party with a chance of winning seats in Parliament. Shifts to the centre could pick up support from the slightly left and slightly right wings of the Alliance. Paradoxically, if both parties successfully followed this tactic, neither would benefit compared to the other. The collective outcome would simply reduce the Alliance to a low level of support like that won by the Liberals in previous decades, when both the Conservative and Labour parties were led by centrists such as Harold Macmillan, Harold Wilson, Edward Heath and James Callaghan.

By definition, a turbulent electoral environment is not deterministic. The influence of issues is variable, not constant. The ability of the Conservatives to win a landslide victory with a postwar record level of unemployment is a reminder that assumptions about voting behaviour held at one point of time can alter under the pressure of events. The influence of social structure upon voting, while substantial, is not sufficiently strong to be deterministic at the margin, where elections are won and lost. The fluctuations in the vote from 1966 to the present are far greater--and sometimes, in opposite directions from-- changes in social structure.

Turbulence offers both promise and threat to party leaders. It offers the promise of big shifts to the advantage of any party that can take positions and adopt a style of campaigning that is most attuned to the electorate at the moment. In a turbulent environment, voters are far readier to move than in the "trench-warfare" elections between the big battalions of the Labour and Conservative parties in the 1950s. But the greater the success for one party, the greater the setback that others must suffer. In three-party competition the penalty can be more than the loss of a single election. A losing party may fall victim to the psephology of discontinuity, and become the party that makes the break by dropping out of a three-party system built for two.

# Appendix A
# Constituency Data

The following pages give detailed census and electoral data for each of the 650 parliamentary constituencies in the United Kingdom Parliament elected in 1983, this constitutes the raw material for much of the statistical analysis reported in the chapters of this book.

*Regional boundaries*

The constituencies are listed by nation, and within each nation, they are listed alphabetically within region. The national categories are self-explanatory. The regional boundaries for England are adapted by amalgamating standard regions as defined by the Central Statistical Office. Greater London is the local authority area by that name. Southern England equals the South East minus Greater London; the South West; and East Anglia. The Midlands equals the East Midlands and the West Midlands, and the North of England embraces the North West, Yorkshire & Humberside, and the North.

In Scottish and Welsh constituencies, local authority boundaries have been used as the basis to define regions by a process of aggregation providing a reasonable number of cases in each. In Scotland the categories used consist of the Central Industrial Belt (the whole of Strathclyde Region, except for Argyll and Bute); Lothian and Borders (Lothian Region, Dumfries and Galloway, and the Borders); and the North of Scotland (the Highlands and Islands region plus Angus East, Perth & Kinross, Tayside North and Argyll & Bute).

Wales is divided into Y Fro Gymraeg (Caernarvo n, Carmarthen, Ceredigion & Pembroke, Conwy, Meirionydd Nant Con and Ynys Mon); Welsh Wales (Aberavon, Blaenau Gwent, Caerphilly, Cynon Valley, Gower, Islwyn, Llanelli, Merthyr Tydfil & Rhymney, Neath, Ogmore, Pontypridd, Rhondda, Swansea, Swansea West, and Torfaen); and British Wales (Alyn & Deeside, Brecon & Radnor, Bridgend, the four Cardiff constituencies, Clwyd

North West, Clywd South West, Delyn, Monmouth, Montgomery, Newport East, Newport West, Pembroke, Vale of Glamorgan, and Wrexham).

Within Northern Ireland, constituencies are divided into those East of the River Bann, which bifurcates the Province (Antrim East, Antrim North, Antrim South, the four Belfast constituencies, Down North, Down South, Lagan Valley, Newry & Armagh, and Strangford), and those West of the River Bann (Fermanagh & South Tyrone, Foyle, Londonderry East, Mid Ulster, and Upper Bann).

*Census characteristics*

The census data reported here is from the 1981 census of the United Kingdom. The census data for Great Britain was obtained from a magnetic tape created by the Office of Population Censuses and Surveys, and made available by the Social Science Research Council Data Archive at the University of Essex. For Northern Ireland, some 1981 census data were either not available by parliamentary constituency or not available in the census. In the former instance, estimates were made from census data broken down by district council, and in the latter, estimates were made from 1971 census data. The census measures reported in the table are defined as follows:

Non-manual:% of economically active persons in socio-economic gro ups 1, 2, 3, 4, 5.1, 5.2, 6 and 7 (except in Northern Ireland, where only groups 1, 2, 3 and 4 are used).
Owner-occupier:% of households owner occupied.
Council tenants:% of households council tenants.
Unemployed:% of economically active population unemployed.
New Commonwealth:% of total population born in New Commonwealth.
Agriculture:% of total employees working in agriculture, forestr y and fisheries.
Elderly:% of total population aged 65 to 74.
Distance from London or regional capital:Road miles from London ( or in Wales, Cardiff; in Scotland, Edinburgh; in Northern Ireland, Belfast) as calculated by the Automobile Association.
Cluster:Group member assigned on the basis of the clus ter analysis. reported in Chapter X.

*Electoral Data*

The election results were provided by F.W.S. Craig and cross-checked against the pre-publication text of *Britain Votes 3* (Chichester: Parliamentary Research Services, 1984)

PA Number:Press Association number, assigned to constituencies on the basis of a single United Kingdom alphabetical ordering.

Party competition:the parties finishing first and second.

Margin:% lead of first place party over party finishing second.

Con vote: % Conservative share of total constituency vote.

Con Res: The difference residual between the actual consensus vot e, and what would be predicted by a regression analysis of the constituency's social structure as reported in Table IX.1. A plus sign indicates that the actual vote was higher than predicted, and a minus sign that the actual vote was lower.

Lab vote:% Labour share of total constituency vote.

Lab Res:The residual of the Labour vote, calculated similarly to the Conservative vote.

All vote:% vote for Liberal and Social Democratic Party candidat es running as an Alliance.

Turnout:Valid votes cast as a percentage of the registered electo rate on polling day.

# ENGLAND

| Non Man % | Own Occ % | Coun Ten % | Unem % | Born NCom % | Agric % | Aged % | Dist Lond m. | Clus | PA No | Constituency Name | Party | Marg % | Con Vote % | Con Res % | Lab Vote % | Lab Res % | All Res % | Turn Out % |
|---|---|---|---|---|---|---|---|---|---|---|---|---|---|---|---|---|---|---|
| | | | | | | | | | | SOUTH OF ENGLAND | | | | | | | | |
| 55.2 | 61.8 | 20.4 | 5.3 | 2.3 | 0.6 | 5.7 | 36 | 9 | 4 | Aldershot | Con All | 21.7 | 55.4 | 4.3 | 10.8 | -11.7 | 33.8 | 72.7 |
| 57.7 | 71.3 | 14.6 | 9.1 | 1.2 | 4.7 | 15.1 | 58 | 10 | 14 | Arundel | Con All | 30.1 | 59.6 | 5.2 | 8.2 | -4.9 | 29.5 | 69.7 |
| 34.9 | 58.4 | 33.0 | 8.7 | 0.4 | 0.8 | 8.6 | 128 | 14 | 15 | Ashfield | Lab Con | 11.8 | 30.7 | -8.8 | 42.5 | 8.8 | 26.8 | 73.7 |
| 50.9 | 59.3 | 29.7 | 8.8 | 1.4 | 6.3 | 9.2 | 54 | 17 | 16 | Ashford | Con All | 29.0 | 56.8 | 8.9 | 12.9 | -6.0 | 27.8 | 73.2 |
| 56.1 | 61.6 | 26.3 | 5.9 | 2.3 | 1.2 | 7.0 | 40 | 9 | 18 | Aylesbury | Con All | 28.7 | 58.1 | 8.4 | 12.2 | -10.8 | 29.4 | 71.5 |
| 48.4 | 54.6 | 27.9 | 7.0 | 1.3 | 3.9 | 7.5 | 72 | 17 | 20 | Banbury | Con All | 26.5 | 53.4 | 6.7 | 19.0 | -4.0 | 26.9 | 75.2 |
| 49.2 | 35.1 | 62.1 | 12.6 | 1.4 | 0.4 | 5.8 | 24 | 3 | 27 | Basildon | Con Lab | 3.0 | 38.7 | 11.4 | 35.6 | -11.6 | 25.7 | 69.0 |
| 57.8 | 53.2 | 36.9 | 6.4 | 1.9 | 1.6 | 6.3 | 47 | 13 | 28 | Basingstoke | Con All | 22.5 | 51.3 | 8.6 | 19.3 | -10.4 | 28.8 | 76.8 |
| 63.1 | 57.9 | 25.0 | 9.0 | 1.9 | 0.4 | 11.3 | 106 | 11 | 30 | Bath | Con All | 11.1 | 47.1 | 1.3 | 15.2 | -12.6 | 36.0 | 74.4 |
| 69.1 | 69.4 | 18.6 | 5.5 | 1.4 | 1.6 | 7.9 | 25 | 23 | 33 | Beaconsfield | Con All | 38.2 | 63.8 | 7.5 | 10.7 | -5.1 | 25.6 | 72.4 |
| 52.9 | 60.9 | 24.6 | 5.8 | 1.5 | 4.4 | 7.6 | 45 | 17 | 35 | Bedfordshire Mid | Con All | 29.9 | 56.8 | 6.1 | 16.2 | -1.8 | 26.9 | 76.9 |
| 57.4 | 64.3 | 20.3 | 9.0 | 5.6 | 2.1 | 7.6 | 128 | 5 | 36 | Bedfordshire N | Con All | 25.8 | 52.0 | 0.7 | 21.1 | 0.5 | 25.8 | 75.2 |
| 56.1 | 65.0 | 24.9 | 7.5 | 1.6 | 1.4 | 6.2 | 34 | 9 | 37 | Bedfordshire SW | Con All | 27.3 | 55.1 | 5.4 | 17.2 | -5.6 | 27.8 | 75.6 |
| 65.3 | 51.8 | 35.2 | 5.6 | 1.7 | 1.0 | 6.6 | 33 | 13 | 42 | Berkshire E | Con All | 26.9 | 56.8 | 11.3 | 13.3 | -14.3 | 29.9 | 73.3 |
| 58.7 | 73.1 | 12.7 | 7.7 | 1.3 | 7.5 | 17.7 | 57 | 10 | 46 | Bexhill & Battle | Con All | 43.8 | 67.3 | 8.6 | 8.0 | 2.5 | 23.5 | 72.9 |
| 61.6 | 75.6 | 19.3 | 6.9 | 1.0 | 0.6 | 5.7 | 24 | 9 | 48 | Billericay | Con All | 26.5 | 53.7 | 0.1 | 19.1 | -0.5 | 27.2 | 73.8 |
| 58.0 | 65.6 | 7.4 | 12.7 | 1.2 | 0.5 | 14.8 | 104 | 18 | 76 | Bournemouth E | Con All | 24.2 | 53.4 | 1.3 | 8.5 | -13.0 | 29.2 | 66.6 |
| 54.3 | 63.1 | 19.7 | 11.0 | 0.9 | 0.6 | 12.7 | 104 | 18 | 77 | Bournemouth W | Con All | 26.6 | 56.9 | 10.5 | 12.5 | -14.4 | 30.3 | 69.2 |
| 56.6 | 55.3 | 34.5 | 6.9 | 1.2 | 3.1 | 7.9 | 43 | 12 | 82 | Braintree | Con All | 24.0 | 52.6 | 6.9 | 18.8 | -5.6 | 28.6 | 76.2 |
| 69.0 | 67.9 | 21.1 | 5.9 | 1.2 | 2.3 | 8.0 | 22 | 12 | 88 | Brentford & Ongar | Con All | 28.1 | 58.4 | 4.3 | 11.4 | -5.4 | 30.3 | 76.6 |
| 42.9 | 59.9 | 26.6 | 9.9 | 0.6 | 6.4 | 11.3 | 142 | 10 | 90 | Bridgwater | Con All | 22.3 | 52.3 | 5.3 | 17.7 | -1.2 | 30.0 | 74.8 |
| 54.7 | 51.6 | 30.1 | 13.3 | 1.7 | 0.3 | 11.9 | 53 | 18 | 93 | Brighton Kemptown | Con Lab | 21.5 | 51.1 | 11.5 | 29.6 | -4.4 | 18.6 | 71.5 |
| 66.6 | 61.4 | 11.3 | 10.8 | 2.6 | 0.2 | 12.7 | 53 | 18 | 94 | Brighton Pavilion | Con All | 26.9 | 51.5 | 0.2 | 23.9 | 1.4 | 24.6 | 69.3 |
| 49.9 | 61.5 | 28.7 | 10.7 | 2.9 | 0.2 | 10.2 | 53 | 22 | 95 | Bristol E | Con Lab | 3.7 | 40.5 | -1.2 | 36.9 | 4.7 | 23.6 | 73.8 |
| 54.6 | 50.8 | 43.9 | 10.0 | 1.3 | 0.2 | 9.7 | 116 | 14 | 96 | Bristol NW | Con Lab | 11.3 | 43.9 | 8.4 | 32.6 | -6.0 | 23.6 | 76.9 |
| 43.5 | 47.2 | 45.1 | 14.7 | 1.0 | 0.9 | 8.7 | 116 | 14 | 97 | Bristol S | Lab Con | 8.9 | 35.1 | 3.5 | 44.0 | 2.2 | 19.5 | 68.8 |
| 73.5 | 56.6 | 9.3 | 13.5 | 4.2 | 0.1 | 9.7 | 116 | 21 | 98 | Bristol W | Con All | 19.7 | 49.1 | -5.8 | 19.5 | -0.1 | 29.4 | 70.7 |
| 59.2 | 68.8 | 23.9 | 6.0 | 1.2 | 2.5 | 7.0 | 19 | 9 | 100 | Broxbourne | Con All | 35.0 | 58.8 | 6.8 | 16.4 | -2.9 | 23.8 | 74.0 |
| 56.5 | 59.7 | 27.2 | 6.9 | 1.4 | 5.7 | 7.5 | 57 | 17 | 102 | Buckingham | Con All | 28.9 | 56.9 | 4.8 | 15.0 | 0.1 | 28.1 | 77.1 |
| 45.7 | 51.3 | 27.9 | 6.8 | 1.1 | 5.9 | 8.7 | 75 | 17 | 107 | Bury St Edmunds | Con All | 30.6 | 59.0 | 11.8 | 12.6 | -6.3 | 28.4 | 72.3 |
| 63.4 | 45.0 | 34.3 | 7.9 | 2.6 | 0.3 | 10.0 | 54 | 20 | 112 | Cambridge | Con All | 11.8 | 41.5 | 0.4 | 28.2 | -5.0 | 29.7 | 75.2 |
| 40.2 | 61.5 | 25.5 | 11.0 | 0.5 | 13.2 | 9.8 | 70 | 2 | 113 | Cambridgeshire NE | All Con | 9.7 | 40.8 | -10.2 | 8.7 | -1.3 | 50.5 | 76.3 |

| | | | | | | | | | | | | | | | | | |
|---|---|---|---|---|---|---|---|---|---|---|---|---|---|---|---|---|---|
| 53.8 | 58.8 | 24.4 | 5.6 | 1.0 | 9.0 | 70 | 17 | 114 | Cambridgeshire SE | Con All | 27.7 | 57.6 | 4.5 | 12.6 | 0.6 | 29.8 | 74.2 |
| 61.2 | 60.6 | 25.9 | 6.0 | 1.3 | 7.7 | 57 | 12 | 115 | Cambridgeshire SW | Con All | 24.0 | 56.2 | 4.1 | 11.6 | -5.3 | 32.2 | 75.9 |
| 59.2 | 64.0 | 20.8 | 8.9 | 1.5 | 11.2 | 56 | 10 | 117 | Canterbury | Con All | 30.6 | 56.5 | 4.8 | 15.4 | -0.3 | 25.8 | 70.0 |
| 55.8 | 84.3 | 10.3 | 7.8 | 0.8 | 7.8 | 30 | 28 | 126 | Castle Point | Con All | 33.8 | 58.5 | 2.6 | 16.7 | -0.5 | 24.8 | 71.3 |
| 66.8 | 65.3 | 25.2 | 4.9 | 1.5 | 7.3 | 32 | 9 | 129 | Chelmsford | Con All | 0.6 | 47.6 | -3.5 | 5.1 | -16.2 | 47.0 | 79.4 |
| 62.0 | 64.3 | 21.1 | 8.1 | 1.9 | 9.9 | 98 | 11 | 131 | Cheltenham | Con All | 9.6 | 50.6 | 1.7 | 7.6 | -16.9 | 41.0 | 75.9 |
| 68.5 | 65.7 | 17.7 | 5.8 | 1.7 | 9.4 | 21 | 25 | 132 | Chertsey & Walton | Con All | 30.9 | 58.3 | 4.8 | 13.6 | -5.7 | 27.5 | 72.5 |
| 69.1 | 73.6 | 16.3 | 4.8 | 1.2 | 7.7 | 28 | 23 | 133 | Chesham & Amersham | Con All | 29.9 | 61.0 | 3.0 | 7.8 | -5.9 | 31.2 | 75.9 |
| 59.2 | 59.7 | 21.9 | 7.7 | 1.4 | 12.5 | 63 | 10 | 136 | Chichester | Con All | 36.1 | 63.7 | 10.7 | 7.2 | -3.0 | 27.6 | 72.1 |
| 64.0 | 78.4 | 10.3 | 9.0 | 0.9 | 16.8 | 99 | 19 | 141 | Christchurch | Con All | 41.7 | 67.1 | 11.7 | 7.6 | -8.4 | 25.3 | 72.2 |
| 54.5 | 56.7 | 22.7 | 6.8 | 1.8 | 10.5 | 90 | 2 | 142 | Cirencester & Tewkes | Con All | 23.1 | 57.2 | 5.1 | 8.7 | -2.6 | 34.1 | 74.9 |
| 59.7 | 70.4 | 18.0 | 7.9 | 4.2 | 9.0 | 54 | 12 | 149 | Colchester N | Con All | 26.6 | 53.0 | -1.5 | 18.4 | 4.2 | 26.3 | 73.1 |
| 54.0 | 67.6 | 19.6 | 7.6 | 1.4 | 8.7 | 54 | 12 | 150 | Colchester S & Maldon | Con All | 20.8 | 53.6 | 0.8 | 13.6 | -2.8 | 32.8 | 73.3 |
| 46.5 | 62.2 | 20.1 | 13.6 | 0.8 | 11.5 | 220 | 2 | 156 | Cornwall N | Con All | 9.4 | 52.4 | -1.0 | 3.9 | -4.6 | 43.0 | 80.4 |
| 46.8 | 67.0 | 19.1 | 10.7 | 0.9 | 10.5 | 241 | 10 | 157 | Cornwall SE | Con All | 16.3 | 55.3 | 1.7 | 4.9 | -5.8 | 39.0 | 78.6 |
| 59.9 | 44.5 | 47.5 | 6.3 | 2.9 | 6.1 | 31 | 13 | 162 | Crawley | Con Lab | 21.9 | 48.1 | 9.8 | 26.2 | -8.8 | 25.7 | 76.4 |
| 61.7 | 64.1 | 25.2 | 7.0 | 2.3 | 7.9 | 17 | 9 | 175 | Dartford | Con Lab | 24.8 | 51.6 | 2.8 | 26.8 | 3.2 | 20.5 | 76.4 |
| 50.5 | 57.2 | 23.9 | 6.8 | 1.3 | 8.2 | 89 | 17 | 185 | Devizes | Con All | 25.1 | 53.9 | 4.3 | 16.8 | -0.4 | 28.9 | 74.9 |
| 45.5 | 66.1 | 17.4 | 9.4 | 0.8 | 11.5 | 195 | 2 | 186 | Devon N | Con All | 17.1 | 58.0 | -1.0 | 5.7 | 0.3 | 37.9 | 80.1 |
| 42.7 | 67.3 | 15.7 | 9.4 | 0.9 | 11.5 | 199 | 2 | 187 | Devon W & Torridge | Con All | 23.0 | 58.0 | 1.1 | 6.6 | 2.9 | 35.0 | 76.0 |
| 53.5 | 65.4 | 17.4 | 6.7 | 1.2 | 11.4 | 104 | 2 | 192 | Dorset N | Con All | 22.0 | 58.1 | 2.7 | 5.2 | -2.4 | 36.1 | 76.6 |
| 51.1 | 61.3 | 20.5 | 9.4 | 1.1 | 11.2 | 132 | 29 | 193 | Dorset S | Con All | 30.1 | 57.1 | 8.5 | 15.6 | -5.8 | 27.0 | 72.7 |
| 53.5 | 57.1 | 23.3 | 7.4 | 1.1 | 13.5 | 120 | 2 | 194 | Dorset W | Con All | 30.8 | 59.7 | 6.7 | 11.4 | 3.8 | 28.9 | 74.2 |
| 49.0 | 58.6 | 25.5 | 9.1 | 1.1 | 10.4 | 72 | 29 | 195 | Dover | Con Lab | 17.5 | 48.3 | 4.0 | 30.8 | -4.8 | 20.1 | 77.6 |
| 63.9 | 68.6 | 15.1 | 8.3 | 1.4 | 17.1 | 64 | 19 | 214 | Eastbourne | Con All | 25.3 | 59.1 | 9.4 | 7.1 | -16.0 | 33.8 | 73.0 |
| 58.9 | 70.3 | 21.2 | 6.6 | 1.3 | 7.5 | 71 | 9 | 216 | Eastleigh | Con All | 20.5 | 51.0 | 0.7 | 18.5 | -4.4 | 30.5 | 77.0 |
| 65.6 | 63.1 | 27.6 | 6.7 | 1.2 | 9.9 | 18 | 25 | 233 | Epping Forest | Con All | 31.7 | 56.5 | 7.1 | 17.1 | -5.7 | 24.8 | 72.8 |
| 76.8 | 75.2 | 15.7 | 4.5 | 2.5 | 11.2 | 15 | 25 | 234 | Epsom & Ewell | Con All | 33.8 | 60.4 | 3.5 | 12.9 | -3.2 | 26.6 | 72.0 |
| 76.4 | 74.0 | 13.9 | 4.8 | 2.1 | 9.9 | 15 | 25 | 237 | Esher | Con All | 35.2 | 63.3 | 2.9 | 7.2 | -4.7 | 28.0 | 73.1 |
| 59.2 | 59.9 | 24.2 | 8.9 | 1.2 | 10.0 | 170 | 11 | 238 | Exeter | Con All | 17.2 | 46.5 | 0.5 | 22.8 | -4.4 | 29.3 | 78.0 |
| 52.6 | 69.4 | 18.0 | 18.2 | 0.9 | 11.6 | 267 | 29 | 241 | Falmouth & Camborne | Con All | 22.4 | 50.0 | 1.0 | 21.2 | 0.9 | 27.6 | 75.0 |
| 59.3 | 75.0 | 15.0 | 6.7 | 1.6 | 8.0 | 72 | 9 | 242 | Fareham | Con All | 30.8 | 61.8 | 6.5 | 7.2 | -8.5 | 31.0 | 73.7 |
| 49.8 | 64.8 | 24.7 | 10.5 | 1.0 | 8.6 | 48 | 17 | 243 | Faversham | Con All | 26.0 | 53.1 | 4.7 | 19.8 | -1.0 | 27.1 | 73.5 |
| 55.3 | 65.3 | 15.4 | 10.9 | 1.4 | 12.5 | 70 | 19 | 249 | Folkestone & Hythe | Con All | 24.4 | 56.9 | 6.6 | 9.8 | -9.6 | 32.6 | 70.6 |
| 56.3 | 75.2 | 14.6 | 8.8 | 3.0 | 7.3 | 35 | 5 | 257 | Gillingham | Con All | 21.3 | 51.7 | -1.5 | 17.8 | -1.9 | 30.5 | 73.6 |
| 55.4 | 68.8 | 21.0 | 10.1 | 2.9 | 8.2 | 105 | 5 | 270 | Gloucester | Con Lab | 22.3 | 48.5 | 1.3 | 26.2 | -0.1 | 24.0 | 75.6 |
| 49.2 | 65.9 | 22.5 | 9.0 | 0.7 | 9.0 | 117 | 17 | 271 | Gloucestershire W | Con All | 16.3 | 45.8 | -4.9 | 24.7 | 8.2 | 29.5 | 79.6 |

| Non Man % | Own Occ % | Coun Ten % | Unem % | Born NCom % | Agric % | Aged % | Dist Lond m. | Clus | PA No | Constituency Name | Party | Marg % | Con Vote % | Con Res % | Lab Vote % | Lab Res % | All Vote % | Turn Out % |
|---|---|---|---|---|---|---|---|---|---|---|---|---|---|---|---|---|---|---|
| 44.9 | 63.0 | 21.1 | 8.2 | 2.3 | 0.4 | 7.8 | 77 | 5 | 273 | Gosport | Con All | 31.1 | 60.6 | 13.7 | 9.3 | -17.5 | 29.5 | 71.6 |
| 56.0 | 62.7 | 27.4 | 10.2 | 4.1 | 1.3 | 7.5 | 24 | 5 | 276 | Gravesham | Con Lab | 15.3 | 47.0 | 0.0 | 31.7 | 5.9 | 19.6 | 77.6 |
| 50.5 | 61.6 | 27.3 | 14.5 | 0.8 | 2.9 | 11.2 | 126 | 29 | 278 | Great Yarmouth | Con Lab | 25.2 | 50.4 | 6.7 | 25.2 | -1.3 | 24.3 | 70.8 |
| 66.7 | 61.7 | 23.4 | 4.9 | 1.9 | 1.8 | 9.4 | 29 | 25 | 281 | Guildford | Con All | 21.7 | 55.1 | 3.1 | 10.7 | -8.9 | 33.4 | 72.5 |
| 59.5 | 67.4 | 15.8 | 5.8 | 1.9 | 3.6 | 7.8 | 54 | 17 | 289 | Hampshire E | Con All | 31.1 | 62.8 | 6.6 | 5.5 | -7.8 | 31.7 | 74.2 |
| 50.3 | 51.1 | 26.9 | 5.9 | 1.5 | 5.8 | 7.7 | 47 | 17 | 290 | Hampshire NW | Con All | 24.8 | 57.3 | 7.8 | 10.1 | -6.9 | 32.5 | 74.4 |
| 54.1 | 31.1 | 65.6 | 9.6 | 1.8 | 1.1 | 5.6 | 25 | 3 | 293 | Harlow | Con Lab | 6.9 | 41.1 | 12.2 | 34.2 | -10.4 | 24.2 | 76.5 |
| 57.1 | 78.3 | 10.8 | 11.5 | 0.7 | 2.9 | 17.1 | 72 | 19 | 298 | Harwich | Con All | 24.7 | 54.1 | 0.1 | 16.4 | 0.7 | 29.5 | 70.2 |
| 58.1 | 59.8 | 17.8 | 12.1 | 1.4 | 1.7 | 13.4 | 63 | 18 | 299 | Hastings & Rye | Con All | 22.8 | 53.3 | 5.9 | 15.2 | -9.6 | 30.5 | 68.9 |
| 57.3 | 57.1 | 36.5 | 11.1 | 1.6 | 0.6 | 7.4 | 65 | 6 | 300 | Havant | Con All | 22.7 | 55.3 | 13.3 | 12.0 | -19.4 | 32.6 | 72.1 |
| 62.2 | 65.6 | 17.1 | 6.2 | 1.4 | 4.0 | 8.0 | 36 | 12 | 306 | Henley | Con All | 30.4 | 59.7 | 3.9 | 9.5 | -3.7 | 29.3 | 72.9 |
| 66.0 | 63.1 | 25.5 | 5.1 | 1.1 | 2.2 | 7.3 | 31 | 9 | 308 | Hertford & Stortford | Con All | 24.9 | 56.0 | 3.6 | 12.0 | -6.8 | 31.0 | 75.6 |
| 60.0 | 51.9 | 35.1 | 8.2 | 3.4 | 2.2 | 8.6 | 35 | 12 | 309 | Hertfordshire N | Con All | 16.6 | 49.0 | 4.4 | 18.6 | -8.0 | 32.4 | 79.2 |
| 65.8 | 63.6 | 26.5 | 5.8 | 1.7 | 0.9 | 9.4 | 23 | 25 | 310 | Hertfordshire SW | Con All | 21.6 | 53.6 | 2.8 | 13.9 | -8.0 | 32.0 | 75.8 |
| 60.4 | 48.1 | 44.4 | 7.6 | 1.6 | 1.0 | 6.9 | 25 | 13 | 311 | Hertfordshire W | Con All | 15.7 | 46.7 | 6.4 | 22.3 | -10.7 | 31.0 | 79.5 |
| 67.6 | 59.7 | 31.0 | 5.8 | 2.2 | 0.6 | 8.8 | 14 | 25 | 312 | Hertsmere | Con All | 27.6 | 53.2 | 4.9 | 19.2 | -5.8 | 25.6 | 73.7 |
| 52.5 | 71.2 | 16.0 | 8.4 | 1.1 | 6.4 | 16.3 | 153 | 10 | 318 | Honiton | Con All | 27.4 | 60.6 | 6.3 | 6.3 | -5.9 | 33.1 | 74.5 |
| 60.9 | 65.5 | 20.8 | 5.2 | 1.4 | 5.9 | 9.7 | 38 | 17 | 321 | Horsham | Con All | 36.3 | 63.2 | 8.2 | 8.3 | -3.3 | 26.9 | 74.5 |
| 64.0 | 57.8 | 13.1 | 10.4 | 2.0 | 0.3 | 14.7 | 53 | 18 | 323 | Hove | Con All | 36.4 | 60.5 | 10.2 | 13.8 | -9.6 | 24.1 | 65.8 |
| 50.0 | 63.1 | 20.6 | 7.0 | 1.4 | 4.5 | 7.0 | 62 | 17 | 328 | Huntingdon | Con All | 37.0 | 62.4 | 9.7 | 11.5 | -4.2 | 25.3 | 71.6 |
| 50.1 | 56.3 | 29.0 | 9.2 | 2.2 | 0.5 | 9.7 | 72 | 7 | 333 | Ipswich | Lab Con | 2.1 | 41.6 | 0.2 | 43.7 | 11.5 | 14.2 | 75.4 |
| 53.3 | 71.4 | 13.6 | 12.0 | 0.9 | 3.3 | 13.5 | 77 | 19 | 334 | Isle of Wight | All Con | 4.6 | 46.3 | -5.6 | 2.4 | -15.3 | 51.0 | 80.0 |
| 57.8 | 68.3 | 20.9 | 9.4 | 2.1 | 1.3 | 7.2 | 33 | 9 | 341 | Kent Mid | Con All | 26.4 | 53.5 | 2.5 | 18.8 | -2.7 | 27.1 | 71.4 |
| 49.4 | 68.5 | 25.4 | 7.5 | 0.7 | 0.2 | 10.1 | 112 | 7 | 346 | Kingswood | Con Lab | 3.2 | 40.4 | -4.8 | 37.1 | 8.7 | 22.5 | 77.5 |
| 63.4 | 69.9 | 16.1 | 6.8 | 1.3 | 3.0 | 13.4 | 51 | 19 | 366 | Lewes | Con All | 27.8 | 58.4 | 5.1 | 8.5 | -7.6 | 30.7 | 74.3 |
| 51.8 | 67.8 | 25.6 | 8.9 | 4.3 | 0.8 | 6.2 | 32 | 5 | 386 | Luton N | Con Lab | 22.2 | 48.3 | 0.7 | 26.2 | 0.5 | 25.5 | 77.4 |
| 48.2 | 65.9 | 18.5 | 12.3 | 7.1 | 0.2 | 8.4 | 32 | 20 | 387 | Luton S | Con Lab | 8.6 | 41.9 | -5.2 | 33.3 | 6.0 | 24.9 | 75.8 |
| 60.7 | 63.0 | 25.0 | 7.2 | 1.3 | 4.4 | 8.5 | 36 | 17 | 389 | Maidstone | Con All | 13.9 | 50.9 | -0.3 | 12.1 | -4.9 | 37.0 | 73.8 |
| 50.2 | 62.0 | 24.6 | 11.4 | 2.8 | 1.4 | 7.6 | 30 | 5 | 397 | Medway | Con Lab | 18.8 | 48.9 | 3.1 | 30.1 | 3.4 | 21.0 | 72.6 |
| 54.6 | 48.1 | 46.3 | 10.9 | 2.7 | 1.3 | 5.7 | 52 | 13 | 403 | Milton Keynes | Con All | 19.6 | 48.0 | 9.5 | 22.2 | -12.3 | 28.4 | 74.0 |
| 71.4 | 65.4 | 18.5 | 4.4 | 1.3 | 2.5 | 10.6 | 24 | 25 | 405 | Mole Valley | Con All | 30.2 | 60.8 | 5.4 | 8.5 | -6.4 | 30.7 | 75.0 |
| 60.0 | 59.4 | 23.7 | 5.9 | 1.2 | 3.4 | 8.0 | 56 | 12 | 416 | Newbury | Con All | 24.3 | 59.3 | 7.8 | 5.6 | -11.8 | 35.0 | 75.2 |
| 59.9 | 71.6 | 13.8 | 9.0 | 1.3 | 5.6 | 14.6 | 84 | 10 | 421 | New Forest | Con All | 40.6 | 66.3 | 10.5 | 7.9 | -2.9 | 25.8 | 73.5 |
| 51.0 | 68.6 | 16.5 | 7.7 | 1.0 | 9.2 | 10.2 | 106 | 2 | 428 | Norfolk Mid | Con All | 29.9 | 55.9 | -1.3 | 17.2 | 12.5 | 26.0 | 75.3 |

| No. | Constituency | A | B | C | D | E | F | G | H | I | Type | (1) | (2) | (3) | (4) | (5) | (6) | (7) |
|---|---|---|---|---|---|---|---|---|---|---|---|---|---|---|---|---|---|---|
| 429 | Norfolk N | 44.4 | 59.3 | 21.8 | 9.4 | 0.8 | 11.7 | 14.0 | 133 | 2 | Con All | 27.2 | 54.0 | 1.9 | 19.2 | 10.6 | 26.8 | 74.6 |
| 430 | Norfolk NW | 46.8 | 59.8 | 25.6 | 12.9 | 0.8 | 9.2 | 10.7 | 98 | 2 | Con All | 5.9 | 43.5 | -5.1 | 18.9 | 5.5 | 37.6 | 77.6 |
| 431 | Norfolk S | 54.5 | 67.9 | 19.6 | 6.6 | 0.7 | 8.8 | 10.5 | 94 | 2 | Con All | 21.4 | 54.2 | -2.2 | 13.0 | 6.9 | 32.8 | 77.2 |
| 432 | Norfolk SW | 38.1 | 59.7 | 24.4 | 10.0 | 0.9 | 12.2 | 10.4 | 82 | 2 | Con All | 29.0 | 55.7 | 4.9 | 17.6 | 7.4 | 26.7 | 73.1 |
| 436 | Northavon | 58.7 | 73.2 | 16.8 | 5.9 | 0.8 | 3.3 | 6.4 | 109 | 9 | Con Lab | 22.6 | 53.7 | -2.4 | 14.4 | 0.7 | 31.1 | 78.0 |
| 437 | Norwich N | 52.0 | 58.4 | 32.3 | 8.1 | 0.8 | 0.4 | 9.6 | 111 | 7 | Con Lab | 12.3 | 44.7 | 3.2 | 32.4 | 0.2 | 22.6 | 76.2 |
| 438 | Norwich S | 54.4 | 37.2 | 47.3 | 11.6 | 1.2 | 0.3 | 10.4 | 111 | 26 | Con Lab | 3.5 | 38.8 | 6.8 | 35.3 | -6.7 | 24.4 | 76.4 |
| 450 | Oxford E | 56.1 | 54.3 | 30.9 | 10.8 | 3.3 | 0.5 | 9.8 | 57 | 20 | Con All | 2.7 | 40.0 | -1.2 | 37.3 | 4.4 | 22.7 | 73.9 |
| 451 | Oxford W & Abingdon | 66.0 | 58.5 | 17.6 | 8.6 | 2.5 | 0.7 | 8.8 | 58 | 8 | Con Lab | 14.3 | 47.7 | -3.6 | 16.9 | -5.2 | 33.3 | 74.0 |
| 459 | Peterborough | 46.6 | 47.7 | 41.4 | 13.4 | 3.2 | 0.5 | 7.8 | 81 | 27 | All Con | 18.0 | 47.1 | 13.0 | 29.1 | -10.9 | 22.7 | 73.3 |
| 460 | Plymouth Devonport | 39.9 | 40.6 | 46.1 | 13.5 | 1.4 | 0.2 | 7.6 | 211 | 27 | Con All | 10.5 | 33.8 | 2.0 | 20.9 | -21.9 | 44.3 | 76.1 |
| 461 | Plymouth Drake | 50.8 | 52.9 | 19.2 | 14.9 | 1.8 | 0.2 | 11.9 | 211 | 18 | Con All | 22.0 | 50.6 | 6.3 | 20.3 | -9.7 | 28.6 | 74.3 |
| 462 | Plymouth Sutton | 55.5 | 71.1 | 14.1 | 8.7 | 1.7 | 0.7 | 8.5 | 211 | 28 | Con All | 25.6 | 55.1 | 3.6 | 14.3 | -7.4 | 29.6 | 76.4 |
| 465 | Poole | 58.2 | 70.9 | 16.5 | 9.2 | 1.2 | 0.4 | 12.3 | 106 | 19 | Con All | 27.7 | 58.3 | 9.1 | 10.7 | -13.2 | 30.6 | 73.6 |
| 466 | Portsmouth N | 50.9 | 62.0 | 26.4 | 9.1 | 1.8 | 0.2 | 9.0 | 71 | 7 | Con All | 31.7 | 55.3 | 10.6 | 21.1 | -8.0 | 23.6 | 72.9 |
| 467 | Portsmouth S | 49.5 | 56.1 | 21.5 | 11.8 | 2.6 | 0.3 | 11.7 | 71 | 18 | Con All | 24.6 | 50.0 | 5.8 | 22.6 | -7.3 | 25.4 | 67.3 |
| 472 | Reading E | 59.0 | 60.9 | 20.3 | 8.2 | 3.8 | 0.9 | 8.3 | 39 | 5 | Con All | 24.2 | 51.6 | 1.4 | 19.4 | -3.8 | 27.4 | 70.4 |
| 473 | Reading W | 61.0 | 66.1 | 19.3 | 6.9 | 3.2 | 0.5 | 7.2 | 39 | 5 | Con All | 23.8 | 52.1 | 1.4 | 19.3 | -3.8 | 28.3 | 72.5 |
| 475 | Reigate | 69.5 | 66.3 | 19.5 | 5.6 | 1.9 | 1.0 | 9.7 | 22 | 25 | Con All | 32.2 | 59.0 | 6.3 | 12.1 | -7.8 | 26.9 | 72.1 |
| 482 | Rochford | 63.0 | 82.1 | 9.7 | 5.9 | 0.9 | 2.2 | 7.7 | 42 | 9 | Con All | 25.7 | 57.8 | -1.2 | 10.0 | -1.7 | 32.1 | 73.5 |
| 484 | Romsey & Waterside | 57.2 | 70.1 | 17.7 | 6.6 | 1.0 | 1.8 | 7.7 | 76 | 9 | Con All | 25.5 | 56.6 | 4.3 | 12.3 | -7.0 | 31.1 | 75.8 |
| 495 | Saffron Walden | 57.8 | 62.5 | 22.4 | 5.7 | 0.9 | 6.6 | 8.9 | 440 | 17 | Con All | 28.6 | 57.8 | 3.2 | 11.4 | 0.5 | 29.3 | 76.9 |
| 496 | St Albans | 72.5 | 68.6 | 19.4 | 5.6 | 2.6 | 0.6 | 7.9 | 21 | 23 | Con All | 15.0 | 52.1 | -3.4 | 10.9 | -6.7 | 37.0 | 78.2 |
| 499 | St Ives | 44.8 | 63.6 | 18.7 | 14.9 | 0.8 | 10.1 | 11.8 | 279 | 10 | Con All | 16.6 | 51.4 | -2.0 | 11.2 | 1.8 | 34.8 | 73.8 |
| 501 | Salisbury | 51.3 | 51.3 | 25.0 | 7.2 | 1.7 | 4.8 | 9.3 | 84 | 17 | Con All | 13.3 | 53.5 | 6.1 | 5.8 | -14.9 | 40.2 | 72.8 |
| 505 | Sevenoaks | 64.7 | 62.4 | 22.9 | 6.2 | 1.3 | 2.9 | 8.6 | 25 | 12 | Con All | 29.9 | 58.4 | 6.5 | 12.2 | -6.2 | 28.6 | 73.7 |
| 514 | Shoreham | 60.1 | 76.3 | 16.3 | 6.5 | 1.1 | 3.2 | 14.7 | 58 | 19 | Con All | 30.7 | 61.6 | 7.4 | 7.4 | -7.9 | 31.0 | 73.7 |
| 518 | Slough | 49.5 | 56.9 | 33.3 | 9.7 | 10.1 | 0.3 | 7.7 | 23 | 20 | Con Lab | 6.0 | 42.9 | -0.8 | 36.9 | 4.9 | 18.5 | 71.5 |
| 520 | Somerton & Frome | 44.6 | 62.4 | 21.9 | 7.6 | 3.7 | 10.8 | 9.7 | 106 | 2 | Con All | 18.6 | 54.4 | 4.1 | 9.8 | 4.1 | 35.8 | 76.7 |
| 521 | Southampton Itchen | 52.9 | 55.7 | 26.7 | 12.1 | 2.1 | 0.2 | 9.6 | 77 | 20 | Con All | 10.0 | 41.5 | -0.3 | 27.1 | -5.4 | 31.5 | 73.2 |
| 522 | Southampton Test | 53.8 | 53.2 | 32.0 | 10.6 | 1.6 | 0.2 | 9.0 | 77 | 20 | Con Lab | 17.1 | 45.2 | 5.0 | 28.1 | -6.0 | 26.7 | 73.1 |
| 523 | Southend E | 59.3 | 60.2 | 17.2 | 12.0 | 1.3 | 0.2 | 12.1 | 43 | 18 | Con All | 27.4 | 55.8 | 8.9 | 15.9 | -10.9 | 28.4 | 67.6 |
| 524 | Southend W | 65.1 | 75.2 | 10.8 | 9.1 | 1.0 | 0.4 | 12.6 | 43 | 19 | Con All | 16.6 | 54.5 | 0.3 | 7.6 | -11.2 | 37.9 | 71.7 |
| 525 | South Hams | 54.9 | 66.7 | 18.0 | 11.3 | 2.0 | 7.6 | 13.3 | 212 | 10 | Con All | 22.3 | 57.2 | 3.4 | 6.9 | -4.3 | 35.0 | 74.9 |
| 530 | Spelthorne | 67.5 | 69.4 | 15.6 | 5.5 | 1.9 | 0.3 | 7.9 | 18 | 23 | Con All | 26.3 | 57.2 | -1.4 | 15.5 | -4.3 | 26.0 | 71.0 |
| 538 | Stevenage | 60.8 | 39.0 | 55.7 | 9.8 | 2.0 | 1.2 | 6.3 | 32 | 13 | Con All | 3.3 | 39.4 | 5.0 | 24.0 | -14.8 | 36.1 | 77.9 |
| 551 | Stroud | 55.0 | 64.6 | 23.8 | 7.7 | 0.8 | 4.0 | 10.0 | 102 | 29 | Con All | 19.5 | 51.3 | 1.1 | 16.8 | -1.8 | 31.9 | 77.7 |

| Non Man % | Own Occ % | Coun Ten % | Unem % | Born NCom % | Agric % | Aged % | Dist Lond m. | Clus | PA Constituency No | Name | Party | Marg | Con Vote % | Con Res % | Lab Vote % | Lab Res % | All Vote % | Turn Out % |
|---|---|---|---|---|---|---|---|---|---|---|---|---|---|---|---|---|---|---|
| 46.2 | 63.2 | 23.2 | 6.8 | 1.0 | 9.1 | 9.5 | 90 | 2 | 552 | Suffolk Central | Con All | 26.2 | 53.5 | 0.2 | 19.2 | 10.4 | 27.3 | 74.4 |
| 52.3 | 60.9 | 18.6 | 7.2 | 0.9 | 7.0 | 11.2 | 97 | 10 | 553 | Suffolk Coastal | Con All | 29.1 | 58.2 | 5.0 | 12.6 | 0.9 | 29.1 | 75.0 |
| 49.4 | 58.4 | 28.4 | 7.1 | 0.9 | 5.3 | 9.1 | 64 | 17 | 554 | Suffolk S | Con All | 19.4 | 50.6 | 2.7 | 18.1 | -1.2 | 31.3 | 76.3 |
| 69.0 | 69.2 | 18.2 | 5.2 | 1.7 | 2.1 | 9.3 | 18 | 25 | 558 | Surrey E | Con All | 35.6 | 62.9 | 6.8 | 9.8 | -5.1 | 27.3 | 74.1 |
| 66.9 | 68.6 | 17.9 | 5.1 | 2.0 | 1.2 | 6.8 | 30 | 9 | 559 | Surrey NW | Con All | 38.2 | 64.1 | 8.9 | 9.9 | -7.4 | 25.9 | 70.2 |
| 65.5 | 65.5 | 21.1 | 5.2 | 1.9 | 2.9 | 10.3 | 33 | 25 | 560 | Surrey SW | Con All | 27.6 | 59.7 | 6.2 | 8.1 | -9.0 | 32.1 | 74.5 |
| 70.9 | 74.5 | 13.0 | 4.7 | 1.6 | 2.1 | 9.1 | 30 | 12 | 561 | Sussex Mid | Con All | 29.1 | 61.4 | 3.9 | 6.0 | -7.6 | 32.3 | 74.7 |
| 49.0 | 58.1 | 35.2 | 13.0 | 2.3 | 0.2 | 7.5 | 79 | 7 | 566 | Swindon | Con Lab | 2.4 | 39.2 | -0.2 | 36.7 | 1.9 | 24.1 | 74.1 |
| 55.1 | 58.7 | 27.7 | 7.5 | 1.2 | 6.3 | 10.7 | 145 | 10 | 568 | Taunton | Con All | 23.6 | 52.9 | 4.1 | 17.9 | -0.1 | 29.2 | 75.5 |
| 53.7 | 67.4 | 17.2 | 10.0 | 0.9 | 4.2 | 13.5 | 180 | 19 | 570 | Teignbridge | Con All | 15.7 | 54.0 | 2.7 | 7.2 | -10.3 | 38.3 | 77.5 |
| 59.4 | 69.6 | 14.6 | 13.1 | 1.0 | 1.9 | 15.1 | 71 | 19 | 571 | Thanet N | Con All | 31.7 | 58.4 | 8.2 | 14.1 | -7.1 | 26.7 | 68.8 |
| 51.6 | 68.5 | 17.7 | 12.0 | 0.9 | 4.3 | 13.1 | 76 | 10 | 572 | Thanet S | Con All | 32.4 | 56.5 | 6.1 | 19.4 | 1.7 | 24.1 | 70.0 |
| 48.8 | 42.8 | 50.9 | 13.4 | 1.5 | 11.9 | 7.8 | 19 | 27 | 573 | Thurrock | Lab Con | 3.8 | 35.4 | 3.9 | 39.2 | -3.2 | 21.7 | 67.7 |
| 50.0 | 59.3 | 22.2 | 8.2 | 0.9 | 2.4 | 11.0 | 167 | 2 | 574 | Tiverton | Con All | 15.9 | 54.8 | 0.3 | 6.4 | 0.2 | 38.8 | 77.5 |
| 59.6 | 64.9 | 22.6 | 7.3 | 1.1 | 0.9 | 7.5 | 32 | 9 | 575 | Tonbridge & Malling | Con All | 24.9 | 56.1 | 5.1 | 12.7 | -7.2 | 31.2 | 74.7 |
| 59.6 | 72.5 | 9.6 | 14.9 | 0.8 | 6.0 | 14.4 | 198 | 18 | 577 | Torbay | Con All | 13.4 | 52.6 | 1.0 | 7.2 | -14.2 | 39.2 | 72.6 |
| 53.5 | 68.2 | 17.3 | 10.6 | 0.8 | 6.0 | 11.6 | 256 | 10 | 580 | Truro | All Con | 19.2 | 38.1 | -14.4 | 4.5 | -9.8 | 57.3 | 79.6 |
| 63.8 | 59.7 | 20.3 | 6.4 | 1.6 | 4.8 | 9.7 | 37 | 17 | 581 | Tunbridge Wells | Con All | 28.2 | 58.3 | 5.8 | 11.3 | -4.3 | 30.1 | 72.7 |
| 60.6 | 71.6 | 20.6 | 6.1 | 0.7 | 1.7 | 8.1 | 112 | 9 | 599 | Wansdyke | Con All | 23.3 | 50.6 | -1.7 | 21.7 | 2.3 | 27.4 | 79.0 |
| 57.0 | 58.9 | 23.5 | 6.9 | 1.2 | 4.4 | 7.7 | 61 | 17 | 601 | Wantage | Con All | 20.6 | 52.9 | 2.1 | 14.5 | -3.1 | 32.3 | 76.9 |
| 61.6 | 64.0 | 23.7 | 6.2 | 2.8 | 0.4 | 8.6 | 17 | 5 | 608 | Watford | Con All | 21.9 | 48.0 | -1.6 | 26.0 | 1.9 | 26.0 | 76.1 |
| 45.5 | 67.6 | 18.6 | 10.3 | 0.6 | 4.8 | 11.8 | 116 | 29 | 609 | Waveney | Con Lab | 24.4 | 51.8 | 3.4 | 27.4 | 7.2 | 20.8 | 75.3 |
| 62.0 | 72.6 | 13.0 | 5.7 | 1.4 | 6.0 | 11.0 | 40 | 10 | 610 | Wealden | Con All | 34.6 | 52.6 | 5.6 | 6.2 | -1.5 | 29.6 | 71.8 |
| 51.2 | 66.5 | 20.4 | 7.6 | 0.8 | 6.1 | 11.0 | 122 | 10 | 612 | Wells | Con All | 13.6 | 52.6 | -0.2 | 7.8 | -5.5 | 39.0 | 77.6 |
| 63.2 | 40.1 | 52.0 | 6.2 | 1.7 | 0.4 | 8.2 | 25 | 13 | 613 | Welwyn Hatfield | Con All | 21.2 | 47.7 | 11.4 | 25.8 | -11.8 | 26.5 | 79.4 |
| 49.7 | 65.5 | 22.2 | 7.4 | 1.4 | 4.8 | 9.6 | 96 | 17 | 617 | Westbury | Con All | 14.0 | 51.4 | 0.3 | 10.0 | -6.8 | 37.4 | 75.5 |
| 57.4 | 66.6 | 19.7 | 9.8 | 1.2 | 3.6 | 11.7 | 136 | 19 | 621 | Weston-super-Mare | Con All | 18.2 | 53.6 | 2.2 | 11.1 | -7.0 | 35.4 | 73.0 |
| 50.9 | 59.5 | 24.1 | 6.9 | 1.6 | 5.5 | 8.7 | 84 | 17 | 623 | Wiltshire N | Con All | 12.4 | 53.0 | 3.0 | 5.0 | -12.2 | 40.6 | 76.6 |
| 61.3 | 58.3 | 24.0 | 5.4 | 1.7 | 5.4 | 9.2 | 65 | 17 | 625 | Winchester | Con All | 23.5 | 57.6 | 6.1 | 8.1 | -8.2 | 34.0 | 76.2 |
| 65.8 | 65.6 | 18.1 | 5.5 | 2.4 | 1.1 | 56.2 | 23 | 5 | 626 | Windsor & Maidenhead | Con All | 32.9 | 58.2 | 6.0 | 11.5 | -8.5 | 25.3 | 70.3 |
| 51.1 | 60.3 | 19.9 | 6.4 | 1.3 | 3.9 | 7.9 | 68 | 17 | 629 | Witney | Con All | 24.5 | 55.4 | 4.5 | 13.8 | -4.5 | 30.8 | 74.7 |
| 65.6 | 68.7 | 18.1 | 5.2 | 2.0 | 1.1 | 7.7 | 26 | 23 | 630 | Woking | Con All | 28.9 | 58.3 | 3.7 | 11.7 | -6.5 | 29.4 | 71.7 |
| 73.0 | 81.9 | 10.0 | 4.2 | 1.7 | 1.0 | 5.7 | 33 | 23 | 631 | Wokingham | Con All | 28.8 | 60.4 | -1.6 | 8.0 | -2.6 | 31.6 | 76.0 |
| 65.0 | 73.8 | 16.7 | 6.3 | 0.7 | 3.3 | 8.3 | 129 | 12 | 635 | Woodspring | Con All | 27.3 | 57.6 | 1.0 | 11.8 | -1.4 | 30.3 | 77.8 |

| | | | | | | | | | | | | | | | | | | |
|---|---|---|---|---|---|---|---|---|---|---|---|---|---|---|---|---|---|---|
| 642 | Worthing | 66.9 | 76.3 | 9.4 | 7.4 | 1.4 | 1.6 | 15.4 | 58 | 19 | Con All | 28.3 | 60.9 | 4.9 | 5.9 | -10.1 | 32.6 | 71.2 |
| 645 | Wycombe | 57.5 | 62.7 | 26.7 | 6.5 | 3.5 | 0.8 | 7.0 | 31 | 5 | Con All | 26.3 | 54.2 | 4.7 | 17.2 | -6.7 | 27.9 | 71.7 |
| 646 | Wyre | 55.5 | 80.6 | 11.8 | 10.0 | 0.4 | 3.4 | 13.0 | 234 | 19 | Con All | 31.5 | 56.4 | 2.5 | 18.6 | 2.5 | 25.0 | 71.4 |
| 648 | Yeovil | 49.1 | 60.3 | 28.7 | 6.7 | 0.9 | 4.7 | 10.7 | 126 | 29 | All Con | 6.5 | 44.0 | -3.1 | -5.6 | -15.6 | 50.5 | 79.8 |
| | (Mean) | 56.7 | 62.8 | 23.3 | 8.4 | 1.7 | 3.2 | 10.0 | 79.2 | | | 22.6 | 53.2 | 3.6 | 16.3 | -4.3 | 29.9 | 74.2 |
| | (StdDev) | 7.7 | 8.9 | 9.7 | 2.7 | 1.1 | 3.2 | 4.3 | 62.0 | | | 9.0 | 6.9 | 4.6 | 9.1 | 6.3 | 6.2 | 2.9 |

## LONDON

| | | | | | | | | | | | | | | | | | | |
|---|---|---|---|---|---|---|---|---|---|---|---|---|---|---|---|---|---|---|
| 22 | Barking | 46.7 | 23.6 | 73.1 | 11.9 | 2.5 | 0.0 | 10.3 | 0 | 16 | Lab Con | 11.8 | 30.4 | 10.7 | 42.1 | -12.9 | 25.6 | 65.4 |
| 32 | Battersea | 62.7 | 28.8 | 39.2 | 14.5 | 12.6 | 0.1 | 9.0 | 0 | 30 | Lab Con | 7.5 | 36.4 | 0.7 | 43.8 | 4.2 | 17.5 | 66.6 |
| 34 | Beckenham | 73.5 | 62.8 | 15.3 | 7.7 | 4.1 | 0.1 | 9.4 | 0 | 8 | Con All | 30.8 | 57.4 | 3.3 | 15.5 | -4.4 | 26.6 | 70.0 |
| 44 | Bethnal Gr & Stephney | 42.8 | 3.6 | 78.9 | 18.1 | 17.3 | 0.0 | 10.1 | 0 | 4 | Lab All | 20.7 | 14.1 | -5.4 | 51.2 | -5.0 | 30.5 | 55.6 |
| 47 | Bexleyheath | 63.3 | 81.5 | 11.8 | 5.6 | 2.3 | 0.1 | 9.2 | 0 | 28 | Con All | 23.2 | 53.1 | -2.6 | 17.1 | -0.8 | 29.8 | 74.5 |
| 78 | Bow & Poplar | 44.2 | 5.6 | 84.4 | 18.7 | 9.3 | 0.0 | 8.5 | 0 | 4 | Lab All | 18.3 | 16.0 | -2.0 | 49.6 | -7.7 | 31.3 | 55.4 |
| 84 | Brent E | 59.4 | 41.1 | 22.5 | 14.0 | 19.1 | 0.2 | 8.7 | 0 | 30 | Lab Lab | 12.4 | 34.6 | -8.8 | 47.0 | -15.3 | 16.9 | 63.6 |
| 85 | Brent N | 68.8 | 72.5 | 15.6 | 7.9 | 15.6 | 0.0 | 9.7 | 0 | 8 | Con Lab | 33.2 | 56.3 | -2.1 | 23.1 | 7.1 | 20.6 | 70.4 |
| 86 | Brent S | 49.9 | 49.4 | 28.1 | 14.8 | 29.1 | 0.1 | 7.3 | 0 | 30 | Lab Con | 26.4 | 26.9 | -14.8 | 53.3 | 19.6 | 18.9 | 63.6 |
| 87 | Brentford & Isleworth | 66.7 | 53.6 | 24.9 | 8.4 | 9.3 | 0.0 | 9.6 | 0 | 21 | Con Lab | 18.2 | 47.4 | -1.8 | 29.3 | 3.9 | 22.1 | 74.7 |
| 125 | Carshalton & Walling | 65.5 | 58.6 | 30.7 | 6.4 | 2.4 | 0.3 | 9.4 | 0 | 11 | Con All | 21.7 | 51.3 | 5.3 | 17.5 | -10.2 | 29.6 | 72.0 |
| 130 | Chelsea | 79.7 | 34.5 | 10.3 | 12.2 | 6.4 | 0.1 | 8.8 | 0 | 21 | Con All | 39.8 | 63.2 | 13.5 | 12.8 | -12.3 | 23.5 | 56.1 |
| 137 | Chingford | 63.3 | 69.4 | 19.7 | 7.3 | 2.6 | 0.1 | 11.4 | 0 | 11 | Con All | 30.3 | 55.1 | 4.9 | 17.7 | -5.6 | 24.8 | 72.7 |
| 138 | Chipping Barnet | 71.6 | 72.5 | 15.8 | 5.7 | 5.5 | 0.3 | 10.1 | 0 | 25 | Con All | 30.0 | 56.1 | -0.6 | 16.0 | -0.9 | 26.1 | 70.7 |
| 139 | Chislehurst | 69.0 | 63.0 | 26.5 | 7.0 | 2.0 | 0.2 | 10.3 | 0 | 25 | Con All | 30.4 | 55.7 | 6.0 | 18.4 | -5.4 | 25.3 | 72.7 |
| 143 | London & Westminister | 75.9 | 21.0 | 24.5 | 10.6 | 6.8 | 0.1 | 10.2 | 0 | 21 | Con All | 38.1 | 59.1 | 17.6 | 17.1 | -16.4 | 21.0 | 51.8 |
| 165 | Croydon Central | 66.0 | 50.9 | 35.2 | 8.6 | 4.6 | 0.3 | 7.1 | 0 | 5 | Con Lab | 30.5 | 53.8 | 9.5 | 23.3 | -6.7 | 22.9 | 68.6 |
| 166 | Croydon NE | 65.9 | 63.3 | 15.7 | 7.6 | 8.2 | 0.1 | 9.4 | 0 | 8 | Con All | 27.4 | 52.5 | -0.6 | 22.4 | 1.2 | 25.1 | 67.5 |
| 167 | Croydon NW | 60.5 | 63.6 | 16.6 | 8.9 | 14.5 | 0.1 | 8.6 | 0 | 8 | Con All | 10.4 | 42.3 | -9.2 | 24.2 | 1.1 | 31.9 | 67.6 |
| 168 | Croydon S | 79.1 | 80.0 | 9.0 | 4.7 | 3.0 | 0.2 | 8.2 | 0 | 23 | Con All | 38.1 | 65.1 | 3.0 | 7.8 | -3.4 | 27.1 | 71.0 |
| 173 | Dagenham | 46.3 | 38.1 | 58.5 | 11.1 | 1.8 | 0.0 | 10.3 | 0 | 16 | Lab Con | 7.5 | 31.8 | 5.1 | 39.3 | -8.7 | 27.0 | 63.4 |
| 200 | Dulwich | 66.3 | 38.0 | 36.7 | 11.4 | 10.2 | 0.1 | 10.1 | 0 | 21 | Con Lab | 4.9 | 40.5 | 1.0 | 35.7 | 0.3 | 22.0 | 67.2 |
| 210 | Ealing Acton | 68.4 | 48.3 | 16.2 | 10.5 | 9.1 | 0.1 | 9.9 | 0 | 21 | Con Lab | 22.5 | 49.2 | -1.4 | 26.7 | 2.6 | 23.6 | 72.2 |
| 211 | Ealing N | 62.0 | 58.9 | 29.9 | 8.4 | 8.8 | 0.1 | 9.1 | 0 | 8 | Con All | 12.3 | 45.1 | -0.9 | 32.8 | 4.3 | 21.5 | 74.8 |
| 212 | Ealing Southall | 52.2 | 64.7 | 16.5 | 11.9 | 27.6 | 0.1 | 7.3 | 0 | 30 | Lab Con | 21.8 | 30.5 | -18.8 | 52.3 | 26.6 | 15.8 | 71.4 |
| 227 | Edmonton | 52.7 | 61.7 | 28.8 | 9.1 | 10.3 | 0.1 | 9.7 | 0 | 20 | Con Lab | 2.7 | 42.5 | -2.4 | 39.8 | 10.5 | 16.9 | 68.9 |
| 230 | Eltham | 63.6 | 46.2 | 43.8 | 9.4 | 2.7 | 0.1 | 9.5 | 0 | 11 | Con Lab | 18.6 | 47.9 | 10.2 | 29.3 | -7.3 | 22.1 | 74.1 |
| 231 | Enfield N | 55.7 | 61.6 | 27.9 | 7.6 | 4.5 | 0.6 | 9.4 | 0 | 11 | Con Lab | 23.8 | 51.7 | 6.5 | 27.9 | -0.4 | 19.2 | 72.4 |

| PA No | Constituency Name | Clus | Dist Lond (m.) | Aged % | Agric % | Born NCom % | Unem % | Coun Ten % | Own Occ % | Non Man % | Party | Marg % | Con Vote % | Con Res % | Lab Vote % | Lab Res % | All Vote % | Turn Out % |
|---|---|---|---|---|---|---|---|---|---|---|---|---|---|---|---|---|---|---|
| 232 | Enfield Southgate | 8 | 0 | 10.5 | 0.2 | 11.4 | 6.4 | 10.3 | 75.7 | 74.7 | Con All | 34.7 | 58.1 | -2.1 | 17.9 | 4.2 | 23.4 | 69.6 |
| 236 | Erith & Crayford | 7 | 0 | 8.4 | 0.0 | 3.9 | 8.9 | 35.7 | 57.1 | 56.6 | Con All | 2.2 | 37.1 | -4.4 | 27.3 | -5.5 | 34.9 | 73.5 |
| 244 | Feltham & Heston | 20 | 0 | 8.0 | 0.1 | 12.5 | 8.3 | 34.7 | 52.7 | 55.2 | Con Lab | 3.9 | 43.4 | 1.5 | 39.4 | 6.6 | 15.9 | 69.8 |
| 248 | Finchley | 21 | 0 | 10.4 | 0.2 | 11.8 | 7.7 | 14.6 | 61.7 | 70.1 | Con Lab | 24.2 | 51.1 | -4.8 | 26.8 | 8.3 | 20.6 | 69.0 |
| 251 | Fulham | 21 | 0 | 10.3 | 0.1 | 7.2 | 12.8 | 23.7 | 33.6 | 65.2 | Con Lab | 12.1 | 46.2 | 3.2 | 34.0 | 2.0 | 18.2 | 76.1 |
| 280 | Greenwich | 20 | 0 | 9.8 | 0.1 | 4.9 | 12.1 | 48.5 | 30.6 | 63.6 | Lab Con | 3.5 | 34.8 | 3.1 | 38.2 | -4.8 | 25.1 | 67.7 |
| 282 | Hackney N & Stoke New | 30 | 0 | 9.1 | 0.0 | 18.3 | 19.3 | 46.9 | 22.3 | 54.9 | Lab Con | 23.4 | 28.6 | -0.8 | 52.0 | 5.9 | 15.7 | 54.7 |
| 283 | Hackney S & Shore | 4 | 0 | 8.6 | 0.1 | 13.8 | 18.7 | 67.8 | 10.9 | 46.8 | Lab Con | 20.3 | 23.2 | 3.2 | 43.5 | -12.3 | 18.3 | 53.9 |
| 288 | Hammersmith | 30 | 0 | 9.4 | 0.0 | 11.4 | 14.9 | 32.5 | 26.2 | 61.9 | Lab Con | 5.9 | 35.5 | -0.5 | 41.5 | 2.2 | 15.0 | 71.3 |
| 291 | Hampstead & Highgate | 21 | 0 | 9.9 | 0.1 | 7.3 | 13.1 | 25.2 | 32.3 | 77.7 | Con Lab | 7.6 | 41.2 | -4.9 | 33.7 | 4.9 | 24.8 | 66.9 |
| 295 | Harrow E | 8 | 0 | 9.5 | 0.2 | 9.4 | 5.9 | 12.7 | 73.5 | 66.9 | Con All | 21.9 | 49.8 | -7.7 | 22.3 | 5.7 | 27.9 | 72.5 |
| 296 | Harrow W | 8 | 0 | 8.1 | 0.1 | 12.0 | 6.9 | 13.2 | 76.0 | 73.6 | Con All | 20.8 | 53.0 | -6.2 | 14.8 | 0.3 | 32.2 | 72.3 |
| 301 | Hayes & Harlington | 5 | 0 | 9.5 | 0.2 | 7.0 | 7.7 | 30.8 | 57.0 | 52.8 | Con Lab | 10.4 | 40.3 | -3.1 | 29.9 | -1.0 | 29.0 | 70.9 |
| 304 | Hendon N | 8 | 0 | 9.5 | 0.3 | 7.8 | 8.6 | 31.0 | 54.5 | 66.6 | Con All | 24.2 | 49.8 | 2.7 | 23.7 | -3.3 | 25.6 | 67.9 |
| 305 | Hendon S | 21 | 0 | 10.6 | 0.1 | 10.6 | 8.4 | 15.2 | 59.1 | 74.3 | Con All | 18.3 | 48.6 | -8.3 | 21.1 | 3.7 | 30.3 | 65.3 |
| 316 | Holborn & St Pancras | 30 | 0 | 10.0 | 0.1 | 8.8 | 15.1 | 54.1 | 14.5 | 62.5 | Lab Con | 16.8 | 30.7 | 3.5 | 47.5 | -0.8 | 21.4 | 60.2 |
| 319 | Hornchurch | 18 | 0 | 7.4 | 0.1 | 1.8 | 7.0 | 16.5 | 76.1 | 58.2 | Con Lab | 20.2 | 42.7 | -4.7 | 26.8 | 4.9 | 24.7 | 73.7 |
| 320 | Hornsey & Wood Green | 21 | 0 | 8.5 | 0.1 | 14.0 | 11.5 | 20.7 | 45.7 | 70.1 | Con Lab | 7.4 | 42.4 | -6.4 | 35.0 | 9.1 | 20.9 | 71.2 |
| 330 | Ilford N | 11 | 0 | 10.7 | 0.2 | 4.9 | 7.7 | 20.5 | 71.5 | 65.3 | Con Lab | 26.1 | 51.3 | 0.1 | 25.2 | 2.7 | 23.4 | 71.3 |
| 331 | Ilford S | 8 | 0 | 8.3 | 0.3 | 11.8 | 9.5 | 10.8 | 72.8 | 63.2 | Con Lab | 11.1 | 45.4 | -11.2 | 34.3 | 16.7 | 19.5 | 70.6 |
| 335 | Islington N | 30 | 0 | 8.6 | 0.1 | 13.7 | 17.1 | 47.4 | 21.6 | 58.9 | Lab Con | 15.2 | 25.3 | -4.8 | 40.4 | -5.1 | 22.4 | 61.6 |
| 336 | Islington S & Fins | 4 | 0 | 9.6 | 0.1 | 7.8 | 14.5 | 64.0 | 12.1 | 55.1 | Lab All | 1.0 | 26.7 | 3.8 | 36.3 | -16.4 | 35.3 | 62.0 |
| 340 | Kensington | 21 | 0 | 7.8 | 0.1 | 7.9 | 14.9 | 17.8 | 28.8 | 74.5 | Con Lab | 16.4 | 46.0 | 2.1 | 29.5 | -1.7 | 22.1 | 62.3 |
| 345 | Kingston upon Thames | 8 | 0 | 10.4 | 0.2 | 4.0 | 6.4 | 16.9 | 67.4 | 70.9 | Con All | 21.7 | 54.1 | -0.4 | 12.2 | -7.1 | 32.4 | 71.9 |
| 367 | Lewisham Deptford | 30 | 0 | 8.3 | 0.0 | 13.4 | 15.7 | 49.0 | 28.8 | 52.7 | Lab Con | 16.8 | 31.5 | 0.7 | 48.3 | 3.6 | 18.8 | 61.2 |
| 368 | Lewisham E | 20 | 0 | 10.7 | 0.1 | 5.7 | 11.3 | 45.8 | 38.5 | 61.4 | Con Lab | 4.5 | 40.4 | 5.9 | 35.9 | -4.1 | 22.0 | 69.5 |
| 369 | Lewisham W | 20 | 0 | 9.9 | 0.2 | 6.9 | 10.3 | 36.4 | 43.5 | 61.8 | Con Lab | 5.7 | 44.0 | 4.4 | 38.4 | 3.6 | 16.8 | 70.3 |
| 370 | Leyton | 30 | 0 | 9.5 | 0.0 | 13.3 | 12.5 | 24.8 | 49.6 | 52.0 | Lab Con | 11.9 | 31.6 | -11.0 | 43.5 | 11.2 | 24.9 | 65.7 |
| 404 | Mitcham & Morden | 11 | 0 | 10.3 | 0.2 | 7.1 | 8.0 | 33.7 | 55.5 | 56.0 | Con Lab | 13.9 | 42.7 | 0.4 | 28.8 | -3.1 | 27.4 | 73.1 |
| 422 | Newham NE | 30 | 0 | 8.8 | 0.0 | 18.7 | 12.4 | 33.9 | 57.5 | 50.3 | Lab Con | 21.9 | 27.8 | -16.1 | 49.7 | 18.6 | 20.5 | 62.1 |
| 423 | Newham NW | 30 | 0 | 8.0 | 0.0 | 18.8 | 15.9 | 36.0 | 39.0 | 48.8 | Lab Con | 24.7 | 21.9 | -13.6 | 46.6 | 6.7 | 18.6 | 56.1 |
| 424 | Newham S | 4 | 0 | 8.9 | 0.0 | 6.8 | 17.8 | 59.2 | 25.4 | 43.4 | Lab All | 27.1 | 23.0 | 1.8 | 50.2 | -3.7 | 23.1 | 53.6 |
| 439 | Norwood | 30 | 0 | 8.8 | 0.2 | 13.6 | 15.9 | 39.7 | 29.0 | 60.6 | Lab Con | 7.9 | 36.7 | 2.0 | 44.6 | 4.1 | 17.4 | 65.6 |
| 445 | Old Bexley & Sidcup | 23 | 0 | 8.6 | 0.4 | 1.9 | 5.3 | 8.8 | 80.7 | 71.7 | Con All | 34.1 | 60.2 | 1.7 | 13.7 | -0.9 | 26.1 | 74.1 |

| No. | Constituency | Party | a | b | c | d | e | f | g | h | i | j | k | l | m | n | o | p |
|---|---|---|---|---|---|---|---|---|---|---|---|---|---|---|---|---|---|---|
| 449 | Orpington | Con All | 76.8 | 77.1 | 16.9 | 5.5 | 1.7 | 0.4 | 8.2 | 0 | 23 | 22.7 | 57.3 | 0.6 | 7.7 | -8.9 | 34.5 | 76.0 |
| 454 | Peckham | Lab Con | 49.7 | 8.0 | 76.0 | 18.1 | 12.1 | 0.0 | 8.8 | 0 | 4 | 27.4 | 24.2 | 4.9 | 51.6 | -4.8 | 21.7 | 54.5 |
| 470 | Putney | Con Lab | 68.4 | 34.6 | 44.4 | 10.6 | 5.4 | 0.1 | 10.3 | 0 | 21 | 10.7 | 46.5 | 8.8 | 35.9 | -1.1 | 16.3 | 73.6 |
| 471 | Ravensbourne | Con All | 75.6 | 76.3 | 10.8 | 4.9 | 1.8 | 0.4 | 8.9 | 0 | 23 | 36.0 | 63.0 | 3.9 | 9.4 | -4.6 | 27.0 | 73.2 |
| 479 | Richmond & Barnes | Con All | 77.3 | 55.2 | 15.4 | 7.8 | 3.4 | 0.2 | 11.0 | 0 | 8 | 0.2 | 46.5 | -7.8 | 7.1 | -12.5 | 46.4 | 79.6 |
| 483 | Romford | Con All | 62.2 | 73.4 | 18.4 | 7.4 | 1.6 | 0.1 | 8.1 | 0 | 28 | 27.2 | 53.4 | 1.6 | 19.3 | -2.7 | 26.2 | 72.9 |
| 491 | Ruislip Northwood | Con All | 69.0 | 71.9 | 15.8 | 5.0 | 3.0 | 0.3 | 10.6 | 0 | 25 | 31.6 | 59.6 | 4.5 | 12.4 | -5.9 | 28.0 | 72.9 |
| 529 | Southwark & Bermonds | AllLab | 45.5 | 2.4 | 80.2 | 15.7 | 6.5 | 0.0 | 10.9 | 0 | 4 | 15.0 | 13.0 | -4.1 | 34.9 | -23.2 | 49.9 | 61.7 |
| 549 | Streatham | Con All | 67.3 | 38.3 | 29.8 | 13.0 | 12.6 | 0.1 | 9.5 | 0 | 21 | 15.0 | 46.5 | 3.9 | 31.5 | -0.9 | 21.2 | 65.4 |
| 557 | Surbiton | Con All | 69.2 | 70.5 | 11.2 | 5.5 | 3.4 | 0.1 | 10.2 | 0 | 8 | 26.1 | 54.5 | -2.2 | 15.5 | -1.7 | 28.4 | 71.3 |
| 562 | Sutton & Cheam | Con All | 73.8 | 78.1 | 8.8 | 4.5 | 2.8 | 0.2 | 9.9 | 0 | 25 | 21.9 | 57.1 | -2.1 | 7.6 | -6.6 | 35.2 | 74.3 |
| 576 | Tooting | Lab Con | 63.6 | 43.0 | 22.8 | 12.1 | 15.2 | 0.2 | 9.4 | 0 | 21 | 5.8 | 37.0 | -8.1 | 42.7 | 13.0 | 18.1 | 67.5 |
| 579 | Tottenham | Lab Con | 49.4 | 41.1 | 37.2 | 15.0 | 22.7 | 0.1 | 8.1 | 0 | 30 | 21.8 | 30.2 | -6.1 | 52.0 | -10.1 | 16.2 | 63.4 |
| 583 | Twickenham | Con All | 71.8 | 68.9 | 13.9 | 5.8 | 3.2 | 0.2 | 10.6 | 273 | 25 | 9.6 | 50.4 | -5.5 | 7.5 | -10.1 | 40.8 | 77.8 |
| 587 | Upminster | Con All | 62.6 | 67.4 | 27.2 | 7.3 | 1.1 | 0.5 | 8.3 | 0 | 28 | 26.8 | 52.5 | 4.3 | 20.5 | -4.6 | 25.8 | 72.1 |
| 589 | Uxbridge | Con All | 59.0 | 55.4 | 33.2 | 7.2 | 3.1 | 0.3 | 8.6 | 0 | 11 | 28.8 | 53.6 | 9.9 | 21.6 | -8.5 | 24.8 | 72.3 |
| 591 | Vauxhall | Lab Con | 56.3 | 13.7 | 58.5 | 18.5 | 14.6 | 0.1 | 7.9 | 0 | 30 | 19.8 | 26.7 | 2.9 | 46.5 | -5.6 | 21.6 | 72.3 |
| 597 | Walthamstow | Lab Con | 51.3 | 45.1 | 31.0 | 11.9 | 8.1 | 0.1 | 10.3 | 0 | 20 | 3.9 | 35.9 | -3.0 | 39.8 | 4.3 | 23.9 | 68.8 |
| 600 | Wanstead & Woodford | Con All | 74.8 | 74.6 | 14.1 | 6.4 | 3.4 | 0.1 | 10.3 | 0 | 25 | 36.4 | 60.3 | 3.0 | 13.5 | -2.8 | 21.6 | 68.4 |
| 619 | Westminster N | Con Lab | 69.0 | 19.7 | 34.9 | 14.8 | 10.4 | 0.1 | 10.4 | 0 | 21 | 3.9 | 43.2 | 7.7 | 39.4 | -0.3 | 23.9 | 64.2 |
| 624 | Wimbledon | Con All | 72.7 | 67.6 | 10.6 | 6.6 | 6.3 | 0.1 | 10.5 | 0 | 8 | 24.9 | 52.1 | -5.3 | 19.0 | 2.3 | 15.7 | 72.4 |
| 636 | Woolwich | All Lab | 51.3 | 38.4 | 48.7 | 12.5 | 6.9 | 0.0 | 8.1 | 0 | 20 | 7.1 | 25.1 | -6.2 | 33.4 | -10.1 | 27.2 | 68.0 |
| | (Mean) | | 62.6 | 49.0 | 30.8 | 10.5 | 8.7 | 0.1 | 9.3 | 3.3 | | 18.7 | 43.1 | -0.5 | 30.4 | -0.5 | 24.7 | 67.9 |
| | (StdDev) | | 9.6 | 21.5 | 18.7 | 4.1 | 5.9 | 0.1 | 1.0 | 29.8 | | 10.2 | 12.5 | 6.5 | 13.3 | 8.5 | 6.7 | 6.2 |
| | **CENTRAL ENGLAND** | | | | | | | | | | | | | | | | | |
| 5 | Aldridge Brownhills | Con Lab | 52.5 | 61.8 | 32.4 | 10.7 | 0.5 | 0.4 | 7.2 | 118 | 6 | 25.8 | 50.7 | 6.9 | 24.9 | -5.0 | 24.4 | 78.3 |
| 8 | Amber Valley | Con Lab | 39.8 | 67.7 | 23.4 | 8.0 | 0.3 | 1.0 | 9.9 | 128 | 7 | 6.4 | 41.7 | -3.5 | 35.3 | 7.7 | 21.3 | 77.2 |
| 29 | Bassetlaw | Lab Con | 42.6 | 49.5 | 34.0 | 10.8 | 0.6 | 3.3 | 8.2 | 147 | 15 | 7.9 | 37.7 | -2.7 | 45.6 | 15.9 | 16.7 | 74.2 |
| 50 | B'mingham Edgbaston | Con All | 66.2 | 51.9 | 30.1 | 13.5 | 4.1 | 0.0 | 11.1 | 110 | 18 | 31.3 | 53.7 | 9.9 | 21.0 | -9.6 | 22.4 | 66.2 |
| 51 | B'mingham Erdington | Lab Con | 44.2 | 48.3 | 38.5 | 19.7 | 3.4 | 0.1 | 9.5 | 110 | 20 | 0.6 | 39.2 | 5.4 | 39.8 | -1.2 | 21.1 | 67.0 |
| 52 | B'mingham Hall Green | Con Lab | 53.7 | 59.0 | 34.7 | 12.8 | 2.1 | 0.1 | 10.3 | 110 | 22 | 21.8 | 49.1 | 9.8 | 27.3 | -7.5 | 23.6 | 70.6 |
| 53 | B'mingham Hodge Hill | Lab Con | 38.6 | 43.3 | 50.4 | 19.5 | 2.3 | 0.2 | 9.8 | 110 | 26 | 12.3 | 35.3 | 8.9 | 47.6 | -0.6 | 15.8 | 67.6 |
| 54 | B'mingham Ladywood | Lab Con | 43.6 | 48.8 | 31.4 | 25.3 | 21.3 | 0.1 | 7.3 | 110 | 30 | 23.9 | 27.1 | -9.7 | 51.0 | 12.4 | 20.5 | 62.6 |
| 55 | B'mingham Northfield | Lab Con | 49.9 | 43.5 | 48.2 | 15.0 | 1.8 | 0.1 | 8.9 | 110 | 14 | 5.2 | 42.7 | 12.7 | 37.5 | -6.9 | 19.0 | 71.2 |
| 56 | B'mingham Perry Bar | Lab Con | 42.9 | 59.3 | 29.8 | 19.5 | 7.7 | 0.2 | 10.8 | 110 | 20 | 14.4 | 38.2 | 0.0 | 52.6 | 16.3 | 9.3 | 69.2 |
| 57 | B'mingham Selly Oak | Con Lab | 55.7 | 55.4 | 24.7 | 13.6 | 3.7 | 0.1 | 8.9 | 110 | 20 | 10.5 | 44.9 | 1.5 | 34.4 | 3.4 | 20.7 | 71.5 |

| Non Man % | Own Occ % | Coun Ten % | Unem % | Born NCom % | Agric % | Aged % | Dist Lond m. | Clus | PA No | Constituency Name | Party | Marg % | Con Vote % | Con Res % | Lab Vote % | Lab Res % | All Vote % | Turn Out % |
|---|---|---|---|---|---|---|---|---|---|---|---|---|---|---|---|---|---|---|
| 32.0 | 38.0 | 47.7 | 29.2 | 11.4 | 0.1 | 7.3 | 110 | 4 | 58 | B'mingham Sm Heath | Lab Con | 43.5 | 20.3 | -3.5 | 63.8 | 12.0 | 16.0 | 60.4 |
| 39.0 | 42.3 | 37.4 | 26.1 | 13.5 | 0.3 | 7.3 | 110 | 30 | 59 | B'mingham Sparkbrook | Lab Con | 32.0 | 27.9 | -3.7 | 59.9 | 16.1 | 10.4 | 61.5 |
| 47.2 | 59.0 | 32.3 | 16.1 | 2.1 | 0.1 | 10.7 | 110 | 22 | 60 | B'mingham Yardley | Con Lab | 6.8 | 43.2 | 5.5 | 36.4 | -0.1 | 19.5 | 72.2 |
| 55.9 | 78.1 | 14.5 | 5.9 | 1.3 | 2.2 | 7.4 | 95 | 9 | 62 | Blaby | Con All | 30.7 | 58.7 | 3.0 | 12.3 | -3.3 | 28.0 | 77.4 |
| 35.5 | 49.6 | 38.5 | 9.4 | 0.2 | 2.4 | 9.3 | 147 | 14 | 69 | Bolsover | Lab Con | 29.4 | 26.9 | -9.5 | 56.3 | 21.2 | 16.8 | 72.7 |
| 45.6 | 74.2 | 18.0 | 7.5 | 0.6 | 1.9 | 8.3 | 109 | 28 | 75 | Bosworth | Con All | 30.3 | 55.4 | 4.3 | 19.5 | -0.9 | 25.1 | 78.2 |
| 59.3 | 66.0 | 25.4 | 9.2 | 0.8 | 2.2 | 7.9 | 113 | 9 | 99 | Bromsgrove | Con All | 34.6 | 56.2 | 7.1 | 20.7 | -1.7 | 21.6 | 75.1 |
| 55.5 | 69.8 | 18.4 | 7.3 | 1.0 | 0.5 | 8.9 | 119 | 28 | 101 | Broxtowe | Con All | 28.3 | 53.5 | 3.5 | 21.3 | -1.9 | 25.2 | 76.5 |
| 46.5 | 65.5 | 22.7 | 10.2 | 0.9 | 2.9 | 8.5 | 120 | 7 | 104 | Burton | Con Lab | 21.4 | 51.1 | 3.8 | 29.8 | 6.6 | 19.1 | 75.9 |
| 47.4 | 61.4 | 31.8 | 11.1 | 0.4 | 0.4 | 6.7 | 125 | 6 | 116 | Cannock & Burntwood | Con Lab | 4.0 | 40.9 | -1.3 | 36.9 | 5.5 | 22.1 | 77.4 |
| 45.6 | 49.6 | 40.7 | 10.5 | 0.6 | 0.6 | 9.6 | 149 | 14 | 135 | Chesterfield | Lab Con | 15.6 | 32.4 | -3.7 | 48.0 | 10.5 | 19.5 | 72.6 |
| 42.6 | 41.4 | 51.2 | 19.3 | 0.7 | 2.6 | 7.9 | 82 | 15 | 155 | Corby | Con Lab | 6.5 | 42.6 | 11.5 | 36.1 | -4.4 | 20.3 | 77.5 |
| 42.7 | 61.7 | 26.3 | 20.0 | 8.3 | 0.2 | 7.7 | 92 | 20 | 158 | Coventry NE | Lab Con | 18.9 | 28.9 | -10.9 | 47.8 | 13.1 | 22.1 | 69.2 |
| 48.5 | 70.3 | 19.0 | 16.9 | 4.2 | 0.5 | 10.3 | 92 | 20 | 159 | Coventry NW | Lab Con | 7.8 | 36.5 | -8.2 | 44.3 | 15.3 | 19.2 | 74.7 |
| 50.8 | 59.2 | 28.7 | 19.9 | 6.3 | 0.1 | 8.7 | 92 | 20 | 160 | Coventry SE | Lab Con | 7.2 | 33.9 | -4.8 | 41.1 | 5.2 | 25.0 | 70.9 |
| 60.2 | 73.5 | 17.4 | 13.9 | 1.4 | 0.2 | 8.6 | 92 | 28 | 161 | Coventry SW | Con Lab | 13.1 | 45.0 | -5.2 | 31.9 | 8.3 | 22.6 | 75.9 |
| 51.3 | 60.8 | 28.1 | 6.1 | 0.8 | 6.0 | 7.5 | 65 | 17 | 176 | Daventry | Con All | 26.6 | 53.3 | 2.6 | 19.9 | 3.7 | 26.8 | 76.8 |
| 50.3 | 55.7 | 35.0 | 9.5 | 1.0 | 0.3 | 9.2 | 125 | 7 | 180 | Derby N | Con Lab | 6.9 | 43.7 | 4.5 | 36.8 | 2.3 | 19.4 | 72.5 |
| 46.8 | 57.6 | 27.8 | 13.6 | 7.4 | 0.1 | 9.4 | 125 | 20 | 181 | Derby S | Lab Con | 0.9 | 38.4 | -2.5 | 39.3 | 5.7 | 21.6 | 67.4 |
| 51.8 | 56.5 | 34.7 | 8.8 | 0.3 | 1.8 | 8.0 | 153 | 6 | 182 | Derbyshire NE | Lab Con | 3.9 | 36.9 | -6.0 | 40.8 | 11.5 | 22.2 | 75.7 |
| 48.7 | 67.0 | 22.9 | 6.2 | 0.8 | 3.1 | 8.2 | 115 | 12 | 183 | Derbyshire S | Con Lab | 14.6 | 43.8 | -5.7 | 29.2 | 8.6 | 27.0 | 78.5 |
| 49.1 | 65.6 | 18.1 | 5.7 | 0.4 | 5.5 | 10.1 | 143 | 17 | 184 | Derbyshire W | Con All | 28.8 | 55.9 | 3.5 | 17.1 | 2.0 | 27.0 | 77.4 |
| 40.0 | 45.5 | 50.0 | 15.9 | 3.0 | 0.0 | 9.0 | 119 | 27 | 198 | Dudley E | Lab Con | 10.9 | 34.9 | 5.0 | 45.8 | 1.3 | 19.3 | 71.3 |
| 49.6 | 63.6 | 32.0 | 10.7 | 0.6 | 0.1 | 7.0 | 122 | 6 | 199 | Dudley W | Con Lab | 14.8 | 46.2 | 3.1 | 31.4 | 0.5 | 22.4 | 75.9 |
| 42.9 | 64.7 | 24.3 | 10.0 | 0.8 | 0.3 | 9.0 | 125 | 7 | 235 | Erewash | Con Lab | 20.4 | 45.3 | 1.6 | 24.9 | -4.9 | 22.2 | 75.7 |
| 46.4 | 61.4 | 20.5 | 9.3 | 0.8 | 11.0 | 8.7 | 148 | 28 | 253 | Gainsborough & Horn | Con All | 10.1 | 50.9 | -3.4 | 7.7 | 1.1 | 40.8 | 75.0 |
| 55.8 | 72.4 | 18.3 | 7.1 | 1.4 | 0.3 | 8.4 | 127 | 2 | 256 | Gedling | Con All | 29.2 | 54.1 | 3.6 | 20.6 | -2.4 | 25.0 | 75.4 |
| 43.3 | 57.7 | 25.7 | 8.8 | 1.3 | 7.6 | 8.8 | 110 | 17 | 275 | Grantham | Con All | 34.3 | 57.5 | 7.6 | 19.4 | 4.7 | 23.2 | 73.5 |
| 56.0 | 66.6 | 26.5 | 9.9 | 0.9 | 0.3 | 8.7 | 122 | 28 | 284 | Halesowen & Stour | Con All | 22.8 | 48.4 | 1.7 | 25.0 | -1.9 | 25.6 | 76.4 |
| 58.8 | 76.9 | 13.6 | 6.3 | 1.8 | 2.4 | 7.7 | 84 | 9 | 292 | Harborough | Con All | 33.7 | 60.1 | 3.4 | 11.5 | -2.7 | 26.4 | 75.9 |
| 48.8 | 57.0 | 27.2 | 9.3 | 0.7 | 7.5 | 9.5 | 133 | 17 | 307 | Hereford | Con All | 4.7 | 48.1 | -0.2 | 7.6 | -9.3 | 43.4 | 75.8 |
| 50.4 | 64.3 | 22.0 | 8.6 | 0.4 | 2.2 | 9.2 | 159 | 7 | 315 | High Peak | Con All | 18.8 | 48.4 | -1.0 | 26.0 | 1.9 | 27.6 | 78.5 |
| 42.6 | 59.0 | 29.1 | 10.3 | 0.5 | 18.8 | 10.6 | 118 | 24 | 317 | Holland with Boston | Con All | 26.0 | 55.3 | 6.5 | 15.4 | 3.2 | 29.3 | 71.0 |
| 52.0 | 68.2 | 23.0 | 10.3 | 1.5 | 2.5 | 9.4 | 75 | 29 | 342 | Kettering | Con All | 17.9 | 48.4 | -0.8 | 21.1 | -0.2 | 30.5 | 76.4 |

| | | | | | | | | | No. | Constituency | | | | | | | | |
|---|---|---|---|---|---|---|---|---|---|---|---|---|---|---|---|---|---|---|
| 40.1 | 54.6 | 33.7 | 14.4 | 18.9 | 0.3 | 9.5 | 98 | 30 | 360 | Leicestershire E | Con Lab | 1.9 | 38.9 | -0.2 | 37.0 | 1.5 | 21.1 | 73.2 |
| 44.4 | 52.0 | 30.1 | 17.2 | 17.3 | 0.2 | 8.4 | 98 | 30 | 361 | Leicestershire S | Con Lab | 0.0 | 40.3 | -1.2 | 40.3 | 6.6 | 17.7 | 72.3 |
| 39.0 | 43.4 | 44.1 | 15.8 | 8.9 | 0.2 | 8.7 | 98 | 20 | 362 | Leicestershire W | Lab Con | 3.7 | 41.1 | 9.1 | 44.8 | 2.0 | 12.8 | 68.8 |
| 43.5 | 62.6 | 22.3 | 6.9 | 0.5 | 1.7 | 8.5 | 110 | 7 | 363 | Leicestershire NW | Con Lab | 12.0 | 44.6 | -3.1 | 32.6 | 8.5 | 21.7 | 81.1 |
| 44.6 | 57.2 | 17.9 | 8.4 | 0.6 | 15.5 | 10.6 | 138 | 2 | 365 | Leominster | Con All | 19.1 | 57.0 | 0.9 | 3.8 | -0.8 | 37.9 | 77.5 |
| 49.3 | 64.4 | 32.3 | 13.2 | 1.2 | 0.7 | 9.0 | 132 | 7 | 371 | Lincoln | Con Lab | 18.9 | 46.4 | 6.1 | 27.5 | -5.5 | 25.1 | 74.6 |
| 43.4 | 69.6 | 16.2 | 12.7 | 0.6 | 13.2 | 12.0 | 148 | 2 | 372 | Lindsey E | Con All | 14.7 | 53.2 | -1.5 | 8.3 | 2.3 | 38.5 | 77.7 |
| 52.4 | 58.0 | 20.5 | 7.0 | 4.2 | 1.0 | 8.8 | 109 | 5 | 384 | Loughborough | Con Lab | 29.5 | 52.9 | 2.5 | 23.4 | 1.0 | 22.2 | 74.6 |
| 47.2 | 57.0 | 21.1 | 9.3 | 0.7 | 12.5 | 9.5 | 143 | 2 | 385 | Ludlow | Con All | 23.9 | 55.7 | 1.8 | 12.6 | 5.5 | 31.7 | 70.7 |
| 41.6 | 57.0 | 33.5 | 9.7 | 0.7 | 0.5 | 8.7 | 134 | 7 | 396 | Mansfield | Lab Con | 4.9 | 35.6 | -4.2 | 40.5 | 6.7 | 23.9 | 71.6 |
| 59.7 | 55.1 | 38.5 | 13.6 | 1.2 | 1.1 | 5.9 | 82 | 13 | 399 | Meriden | Con Lab | 28.3 | 53.7 | 12.6 | 25.4 | -6.7 | 20.1 | 70.1 |
| 47.6 | 58.3 | 29.1 | 9.2 | 0.7 | 5.1 | 8.9 | 125 | 17 | 415 | Newark | Con Lab | 29.2 | 53.8 | 7.0 | 24.6 | 3.7 | 20.6 | 76.4 |
| 46.8 | 58.3 | 33.6 | 10.3 | 0.6 | 0.5 | 10.1 | 148 | 7 | 417 | Newcastle U Lyme | Lab Con | 5.5 | 36.4 | -3.7 | 42.0 | 8.6 | 21.6 | 77.3 |
| 52.1 | 60.0 | 33.9 | 10.3 | 2.9 | 0.5 | 8.1 | 65 | 7 | 434 | Northampton N | Con Lab | 20.0 | 47.0 | 4.9 | 27.0 | -4.8 | 26.1 | 72.0 |
| 54.6 | 62.9 | 27.1 | 8.5 | 2.5 | 1.4 | 8.8 | 65 | 7 | 435 | Northampton S | Con All | 30.2 | 53.6 | 6.8 | 23.0 | -2.6 | 23.4 | 72.6 |
| 44.0 | 41.7 | 37.0 | 18.6 | 4.6 | 0.1 | 10.0 | 122 | 20 | 440 | Nottingham E | Con Lab | 3.4 | 40.4 | 8.1 | 37.1 | -5.3 | 19.2 | 63.6 |
| 37.0 | 29.1 | 66.2 | 15.2 | 1.8 | 0.1 | 9.8 | 122 | 16 | 441 | Nottingham N | Con Lab | 0.8 | 39.4 | 19.6 | 38.7 | -16.1 | 19.4 | 66.1 |
| 48.5 | 42.4 | 44.9 | 13.1 | 4.1 | 0.2 | 8.9 | 122 | 14 | 442 | Nottingham S | Con Lab | 11.8 | 45.9 | 12.9 | 34.1 | -7.4 | 20.0 | 70.2 |
| 46.7 | 65.8 | 25.8 | 12.1 | 1.7 | 1.2 | 7.8 | 97 | 6 | 443 | Nuneaton | Con Lab | 9.9 | 40.5 | -4.6 | 30.6 | 3.0 | 27.9 | 77.2 |
| 59.8 | 69.7 | 19.5 | 8.5 | 2.7 | 1.8 | 8.6 | 82 | 28 | 490 | Rugby & Kenilworth | Con All | 24.5 | 50.9 | -1.0 | 22.7 | 2.7 | 26.4 | 78.1 |
| 61.9 | 70.8 | 15.5 | 6.5 | 1.2 | 2.8 | 8.3 | 112 | 12 | 492 | Rushcliffe | Con All | 37.4 | 61.5 | 5.0 | 13.5 | -0.2 | 24.1 | 76.9 |
| 47.8 | 65.9 | 17.9 | 6.8 | 1.3 | 4.8 | 7.9 | 105 | 17 | 493 | Rutland & Melton | Con All | 33.3 | 60.3 | 7.1 | 11.6 | -2.9 | 27.0 | 73.3 |
| 44.6 | 58.9 | 23.8 | 7.5 | 0.4 | 2.9 | 7.3 | 132 | 6 | 512 | Sherwood | Con Lab | 1.2 | 41.0 | -5.2 | 39.7 | 15.6 | 19.3 | 76.3 |
| 58.4 | 62.5 | 23.7 | 8.6 | 0.8 | 5.9 | 9.2 | 171 | 17 | 515 | Shrewsbury & Atcham | Con All | 17.5 | 49.5 | -1.3 | 18.4 | 6.1 | 31.6 | 74.0 |
| 46.2 | 58.2 | 24.8 | 9.3 | 0.7 | 10.9 | 9.4 | 171 | 2 | 516 | Shropshire N | Con All | 21.9 | 53.4 | 1.2 | 14.7 | 6.1 | 32.0 | 72.7 |
| 68.1 | 78.9 | 13.4 | 7.3 | 0.9 | 0.4 | 8.8 | 104 | 23 | 519 | Solihull | Con All | 33.1 | 60.8 | 4.4 | 11.6 | -5.3 | 27.7 | 71.4 |
| 57.5 | 65.1 | 22.4 | 8.1 | 1.5 | 4.4 | 8.1 | 134 | 17 | 531 | Stafford | Con All | 26.4 | 51.2 | -0.6 | 23.7 | 6.9 | 24.7 | 76.5 |
| 53.1 | 64.0 | 25.7 | 9.7 | 0.6 | 2.0 | 6.8 | 117 | 6 | 532 | Staffordshire Mid | Con All | 26.6 | 52.1 | 4.6 | 22.4 | -1.8 | 25.5 | 77.5 |
| 49.1 | 77.5 | 13.7 | 8.3 | 0.3 | 4.5 | 8.4 | 153 | 12 | 533 | Staffordshire Moor | Con Lab | 29.6 | 53.7 | -1.0 | 24.1 | 10.1 | 22.1 | 77.2 |
| 58.9 | 67.5 | 22.1 | 9.4 | 0.5 | 3.2 | 6.5 | 120 | 9 | 534 | Staffordshire S | Con All | 35.7 | 59.2 | 7.3 | 17.3 | -0.8 | 23.5 | 75.8 |
| 50.0 | 58.1 | 33.5 | 12.1 | 0.7 | 2.1 | 5.8 | 111 | 6 | 535 | Staffordshire SE | Con Lab | 22.5 | 50.7 | 6.9 | 28.2 | 0.4 | 21.1 | 76.5 |
| 47.2 | 60.7 | 26.0 | 8.1 | 0.9 | 10.8 | 9.2 | 89 | 2 | 537 | Stamford & Spalding | Con All | 24.0 | 56.5 | 3.8 | 10.9 | 2.6 | 32.6 | 74.4 |
| 35.7 | 52.9 | 35.0 | 15.3 | 1.2 | 0.1 | 9.7 | 147 | 14 | 543 | Stoke on Trent Centr | Lab Con | 18.7 | 29.4 | -6.1 | 48.1 | 9.3 | 21.4 | 65.9 |
| 34.9 | 60.2 | 35.0 | 13.6 | 0.5 | 0.2 | 9.3 | 147 | 14 | 544 | Stoke on Trent N | Lab Con | 15.4 | 30.9 | -7.2 | 46.3 | 10.5 | 22.8 | 71.0 |
| 36.6 | 58.1 | 34.0 | 12.5 | 0.6 | 0.2 | 8.9 | 147 | 14 | 545 | Stoke on Trent S | Lab Con | 14.5 | 33.6 | -4.8 | 48.0 | 12.4 | 18.4 | 69.6 |
| 55.1 | 59.4 | 23.8 | 6.9 | 0.7 | 5.7 | 9.3 | 91 | 17 | 547 | Stratford On Avon | Con All | 32.1 | 60.9 | 9.6 | 10.3 | -5.1 | 28.8 | 72.9 |
| 72.8 | 78.8 | 12.1 | 7.7 | 1.2 | 0.4 | 7.9 | 26 | 23 | 563 | Sutton Coalfield | Con All | 39.1 | 65.4 | 7.3 | 8.4 | -6.8 | 26.3 | 71.8 |

| PA No | Constituency Name | Non Man % | Own Occ % | Coun Ten % | Unem % | Born NCom % | Agric % | Aged % | Dist Lond m. | Clus | Party | Marg % | Con Vote % | Con Res % | Lab Vote % | Lab Res % | All Vote % | Turn Out % |
|---|---|---|---|---|---|---|---|---|---|---|---|---|---|---|---|---|---|---|
| 595 | Walsall N | 36.9 | 35.3 | 59.5 | 18.3 | 1.9 | 0.1 | 7.4 | 118 | 27 | Lab Con | 5.8 | 36.7 | 12.6 | 42.5 | -8.1 | 20.7 | 71.0 |
| 596 | Walsall S | 46.6 | 50.9 | 38.7 | 16.8 | 6.8 | 0.1 | 9.0 | 118 | 20 | Lab Con | 1.4 | 42.1 | 6.6 | 43.5 | 4.5 | 13.2 | 74.3 |
| 602 | Warley E | 41.6 | 48.3 | 42.2 | 18.8 | 10.4 | 0.0 | 9.9 | 116 | 20 | Lab Con | 8.6 | 37.0 | 4.9 | 45.6 | 2.9 | 16.9 | 68.9 |
| 603 | Warley W | 37.2 | 43.9 | 49.3 | 15.2 | 3.1 | 0.1 | 9.9 | 119 | 14 | Lab Con | 13.6 | 33.5 | 4.7 | 47.1 | 1.5 | 19.3 | 67.8 |
| 606 | Warwick & Leamington | 58.0 | 61.7 | 23.7 | 9.4 | 4.0 | 1.5 | 8.3 | 91 | 5 | Con All | 25.0 | 50.8 | 3.1 | 22.0 | -2.7 | 25.9 | 73.6 |
| 607 | Warwickshire N | 45.6 | 62.0 | 26.8 | 12.1 | 0.9 | 2.3 | 7.2 | 100 | 6 | Con Lab | 4.8 | 41.9 | -2.4 | 37.1 | 9.9 | 20.9 | 78.0 |
| 611 | Wellingborough | 45.8 | 62.7 | 30.0 | 9.9 | 3.5 | 1.0 | 8.7 | 68 | 7 | Con Lab | 22.9 | 48.9 | 3.8 | 26.0 | -1.9 | 24.7 | 77.8 |
| 615 | West Bromwich E | 45.6 | 48.3 | 46.6 | 16.5 | 4.5 | 0.0 | 8.1 | 115 | 27 | Lab Con | 0.7 | 37.4 | 4.5 | 38.1 | -3.6 | 24.5 | 70.2 |
| 616 | West Bromwich W | 35.9 | 32.2 | 62.1 | 19.9 | 4.3 | 0.0 | 9.6 | 115 | 16 | Lab Con | 17.8 | 32.9 | 11.2 | 50.7 | -2.5 | 16.4 | 63.8 |
| 632 | Wolverhampton NE | 40.4 | 37.9 | 57.0 | 19.2 | 5.4 | 0.1 | 7.7 | 123 | 27 | Lab Con | 0.5 | 39.6 | 13.9 | 40.1 | -9.1 | 19.0 | 70.3 |
| 633 | Wolverhampton SE | 35.5 | 34.4 | 60.2 | 21.6 | 9.4 | 0.0 | 8.5 | 123 | 4 | Lab Con | 12.9 | 31.9 | 9.1 | 44.7 | -7.7 | 23.4 | 69.1 |
| 634 | Wolverhampton SW | 60.3 | 59.6 | 27.2 | 15.4 | 9.2 | 0.3 | 9.5 | 123 | 8 | Con Lab | 23.1 | 50.6 | 5.3 | 27.5 | -1.4 | 21.5 | 72.4 |
| 637 | Worcester | 53.6 | 64.0 | 23.8 | 11.0 | 1.0 | 1.6 | 8.8 | 113 | 7 | Con All | 22.0 | 49.4 | 3.0 | 22.7 | -3.0 | 27.4 | 74.1 |
| 638 | Worcestershire Mid | 51.8 | 51.7 | 41.0 | 11.5 | 1.0 | 2.8 | 6.4 | 108 | 13 | Con Lab | 25.7 | 50.9 | 10.4 | 25.2 | -5.5 | 23.2 | 74.6 |
| 639 | Worcestershire S | 55.5 | 60.1 | 25.6 | 8.5 | 0.8 | 6.3 | 10.1 | 97 | 17 | Con All | 21.1 | 55.8 | 5.9 | 7.8 | -8.6 | 36.4 | 73.6 |
| 643 | Wrekin | 42.4 | 40.8 | 54.1 | 18.0 | 1.7 | 1.0 | 7.0 | 141 | 27 | Con Lab | 2.3 | 39.0 | 10.3 | 36.7 | -8.2 | 24.4 | 75.5 |
| 647 | Wyre Forest | 54.1 | 67.2 | 24.8 | 12.2 | 0.8 | 2.0 | 8.4 | 125 | 28 | Con All | 15.9 | 48.4 | 0.8 | 19.2 | -4.7 | 32.4 | 75.1 |
| | (Mean) | 48.2 | 58.1 | 30.8 | 12.2 | 2.9 | 2.3 | 8.7 | 115.4 | | | 17.8 | 45.5 | 2.6 | 30.4 | 1.6 | 23.5 | 73.2 |
| | (StdDev) | 7.8 | 10.8 | 11.8 | 4.9 | 4.0 | 3.6 | 1.1 | 24.0 | | | 21.0 | 9.4 | 5.9 | 13.4 | 7.1 | 5.7 | 4.1 |

## NORTH OF ENGLAND

| PA No | Constituency Name | Non Man % | Own Occ % | Coun Ten % | Unem % | Born NCom % | Agric % | Aged % | Dist Lond m. | Clus | Party | Marg % | Con Vote % | Con Res % | Lab Vote % | Lab Res % | All Vote % | Turn Out % |
|---|---|---|---|---|---|---|---|---|---|---|---|---|---|---|---|---|---|---|
| 6 | Altrincham Sale | 69.6 | 72.6 | 15.8 | 8.0 | 0.9 | 1.0 | 9.3 | 178 | 25 | Con All | 22.6 | 52.5 | -2.5 | 15.9 | -1.7 | 29.9 | 73.0 |
| 17 | Ashton-under-Lyne | 42.8 | 60.1 | 29.9 | 13.6 | 3.4 | 0.5 | 10.0 | 184 | 22 | Lab Con | 18.2 | 31.5 | -8.3 | 49.7 | 15.9 | 17.8 | 71.6 |
| 23 | Barnsley Central | 39.6 | 47.2 | 44.8 | 13.0 | 0.5 | 0.1 | 8.4 | 172 | 27 | Lab Con | 38.8 | 21.0 | -10.3 | 59.8 | 16.7 | 19.2 | 66.3 |
| 24 | Barnsley E | 35.1 | 42.6 | 43.6 | 14.2 | 0.2 | 0.8 | 8.5 | 172 | 14 | Lab All | 47.9 | 16.1 | -14.8 | 65.9 | 23.3 | 18.0 | 66.5 |
| 25 | Barnsley W & Penist | 43.8 | 50.2 | 40.8 | 10.8 | 0.2 | 1.8 | 9.4 | 172 | 15 | Lab Con | 23.3 | 27.5 | -9.4 | 50.8 | 15.6 | 21.7 | 73.2 |
| 26 | Barrow & Furness | 44.4 | 71.1 | 19.8 | 10.8 | 0.5 | 0.9 | 9.4 | 270 | 7 | Con Lab | 9.0 | 43.6 | -2.8 | 34.7 | 8.1 | 21.7 | 75.2 |
| 31 | Batley & Spen | 48.9 | 63.8 | 26.1 | 12.4 | 2.5 | 0.5 | 8.3 | 190 | 7 | Con Lab | 1.6 | 39.6 | -4.2 | 38.0 | 8.3 | 21.6 | 73.4 |
| 43 | Berwick upon Tweed | 45.4 | 37.3 | 36.2 | 9.8 | 0.4 | 13.6 | 11.1 | 336 | 24 | All Con | 19.7 | 33.0 | -9.4 | 14.3 | -4.4 | 52.7 | 77.8 |
| 45 | Beverley | 66.9 | 72.3 | 17.6 | 7.1 | 0.7 | 2.7 | 9.5 | 201 | 12 | Con All | 25.0 | 56.3 | 1.8 | 12.5 | -3.5 | 31.3 | 73.2 |
| 49 | Birkenhead | 50.3 | 50.3 | 29.9 | 22.5 | 0.7 | 0.3 | 9.1 | 196 | 14 | Lab Con | 20.7 | 28.9 | -6.6 | 49.6 | 8.8 | 21.6 | 69.7 |
| 61 | Bishop Auckland | 42.5 | 44.6 | 44.0 | 14.5 | 0.4 | 3.8 | 8.3 | 251 | 15 | Lab Con | 8.6 | 35.9 | 1.6 | 44.5 | 8.8 | 19.6 | 72.2 |
| 63 | Blackburn | 44.3 | 61.2 | 31.5 | 17.2 | 5.7 | 0.6 | 9.3 | 209 | 22 | Lab Con | 5.4 | 39.4 | 0.1 | 44.7 | 10.3 | 14.4 | 74.6 |

| | | | | | | | | | | No. | Constituency | | | | | | | | |
|---|---|---|---|---|---|---|---|---|---|---|---|---|---|---|---|---|---|---|---|
| 56.0 | 70.5 | 16.5 | 15.4 | 0.6 | 0.4 | 14.1 | 228 | 18 | 64 | Blackpool N | Con All | 25.2 | 51.1 | 3.2 | 21.7 | -3.9 | 25.9 | 70.0 |
| 51.8 | 76.4 | 9.6 | 15.1 | 0.5 | 0.4 | 12.4 | 228 | 18 | 65 | Blackpool S | Con Lab | 25.8 | 50.6 | -0.2 | 24.8 | 2.4 | 24.0 | 69.8 |
| 51.5 | 53.1 | 39.6 | 12.3 | 0.3 | 0.6 | 9.0 | 273 | 15 | 67 | Blaydon | Lab Con | 15.1 | 29.3 | -8.4 | 44.4 | 8.7 | 26.3 | 73.2 |
| 54.4 | 49.3 | 39.2 | 11.8 | 0.4 | 0.4 | 7.4 | 289 | 6 | 68 | Blyth Valley | Lab All | 7.7 | 27.8 | -8.7 | 39.5 | 2.0 | 31.8 | 72.8 |
| 41.2 | 62.8 | 31.5 | 13.8 | 2.7 | 0.4 | 8.6 | 195 | 7 | 70 | Bolton NE | Con Lab | 5.4 | 43.2 | 1.1 | 37.8 | 6.4 | 18.3 | 77.1 |
| 59.2 | 61.7 | 31.2 | 16.2 | 5.9 | 0.3 | 8.8 | 195 | 20 | 71 | Bolton SE | Lab Con | 17.6 | 30.7 | -7.8 | 48.3 | 12.7 | 20.4 | 73.6 |
| 45.9 | 73.2 | 18.0 | 10.1 | 1.6 | 0.6 | 9.3 | 195 | 28 | 72 | Bolton W | Con Lab | 13.6 | 45.1 | -5.1 | 31.5 | 8.6 | 23.4 | 78.1 |
| 48.9 | 64.8 | 22.1 | 9.5 | 0.4 | 11.4 | 8.8 | 179 | 2 | 73 | Boothferry | Con All | 32.9 | 57.7 | 3.2 | 17.5 | 11.1 | 24.8 | 73.1 |
| 45.2 | 40.4 | 40.7 | 23.1 | 0.3 | 0.1 | 8.8 | 201 | 14 | 74 | Bootle | Lab Con | 29.4 | 23.6 | -4.3 | 53.0 | 6.3 | 23.4 | 68.3 |
| 48.1 | 62.1 | 25.2 | 16.9 | 4.3 | 0.1 | 8.3 | 195 | 20 | 79 | Bradford N | Lab Con | 3.4 | 34.3 | -6.4 | 30.9 | -2.7 | 25.5 | 70.8 |
| 47.4 | 64.8 | 26.4 | 13.9 | 1.8 | 0.2 | 8.3 | 195 | 8 | 80 | Bradford S | Lab Con | 0.2 | 37.3 | -4.6 | 37.5 | 5.5 | 24.6 | 71.0 |
| 50.8 | 61.2 | 24.1 | 18.6 | 5.7 | 0.5 | 7.7 | 195 | 20 | 81 | Bradford W | Lab Con | 6.8 | 32.9 | -8.7 | 39.7 | 7.0 | 27.1 | 68.9 |
| 46.6 | 68.4 | 17.7 | 10.3 | 0.4 | 10.6 | 11.2 | 221 | 2 | 91 | Bridlington | Con All | 30.7 | 57.8 | 1.2 | 13.6 | 9.6 | 27.1 | 70.6 |
| 44.1 | 69.9 | 19.4 | 11.3 | 0.5 | 4.7 | 8.1 | 160 | 17 | 92 | Brigg & Cleethorpes | Con All | 21.4 | 50.7 | 0.9 | 20.0 | 1.2 | 29.3 | 73.6 |
| 55.5 | 69.6 | 22.5 | 14.0 | 1.1 | 0.4 | 9.7 | 205 | 22 | 103 | Burnley | Lab Con | 1.6 | 38.2 | -5.0 | 39.8 | 9.6 | 22.0 | 76.3 |
| 57.0 | 74.5 | 19.3 | 10.7 | 0.8 | 0.5 | 8.4 | 192 | 28 | 105 | Bury N | Con Lab | 5.3 | 45.5 | -4.3 | 40.2 | 16.8 | 14.4 | 79.6 |
| 49.8 | 67.7 | 24.2 | 10.2 | 0.7 | 0.3 | 10.0 | 192 | 11 | 106 | Bury S | Con Lab | 7.5 | 44.0 | -2.4 | 36.5 | 9.4 | 19.5 | 76.1 |
| 48.3 | 69.0 | 20.5 | 10.8 | 0.5 | 1.6 | 9.9 | 200 | 29 | 111 | Calder Valley | Con All | 14.3 | 43.7 | -3.6 | 27.0 | 2.3 | 29.4 | 78.5 |
| 77.5 | 49.1 | 43.5 | 11.3 | 0.5 | 0.4 | 9.5 | 298 | 14 | 122 | Carlisle | Lab Con | 0.2 | 37.3 | 2.7 | 37.5 | -1.6 | 25.1 | 76.4 |
| 61.3 | 83.1 | 10.6 | 5.7 | 1.2 | 0.7 | 7.5 | 184 | 23 | 128 | Cheadle | Con All | 18.4 | 55.7 | -6.0 | 7.0 | -4.1 | 37.3 | 76.8 |
| 53.2 | 61.2 | 26.1 | 12.5 | 0.9 | 1.5 | 9.7 | 182 | 7 | 134 | Chester City | Con Lab | 18.9 | 47.1 | 1.4 | 28.2 | 1.6 | 24.7 | 74.5 |
| 49.3 | 75.9 | 16.4 | 8.6 | 0.5 | 1.5 | 8.1 | 203 | 28 | 140 | Chorley | Con Lab | 17.8 | 48.3 | -3.7 | 30.5 | 10.6 | 20.3 | 79.2 |
| 55.4 | 74.2 | 16.0 | 10.3 | 1.7 | 1.1 | 9.4 | 196 | 28 | 151 | Colne Valley | All Con | 5.9 | 33.9 | -16.5 | 25.8 | 3.6 | 39.8 | 76.2 |
| 42.1 | 73.2 | 19.8 | 9.1 | 0.5 | 3.4 | 8.0 | 150 | 12 | 152 | Congleton | Con All | 17.2 | 48.7 | -4.4 | 19.9 | 3.2 | 31.4 | 76.9 |
| 46.2 | 45.0 | 36.1 | 11.7 | 0.4 | 3.8 | 8.3 | 302 | 15 | 154 | Copeland | Lab Con | 4.3 | 39.9 | 3.0 | 44.2 | 10.9 | 15.9 | 78.2 |
| 72.1 | 62.7 | 26.9 | 8.9 | 0.7 | 4.1 | 9.4 | 161 | 17 | 163 | Crewe & Nantwich | Lab Con | 0.5 | 40.6 | -5.6 | 41.1 | 18.4 | 18.3 | 74.7 |
| 52.6 | 81.4 | 9.4 | 9.3 | 0.6 | 0.5 | 7.8 | 203 | 23 | 164 | Crosby | Con All | 5.2 | 47.2 | -10.3 | 10.2 | -5.3 | 42.0 | 77.9 |
| 63.9 | 64.2 | 25.0 | 12.9 | 1.1 | 0.4 | 9.5 | 242 | 7 | 174 | Darlington | Con Lab | 6.8 | 44.6 | 1.5 | 37.8 | 7.2 | 17.4 | 77.1 |
| 45.0 | 65.1 | 24.2 | 10.1 | 1.0 | 0.3 | 8.1 | 184 | 5 | 177 | Davyhulme | Con All | 18.8 | 46.0 | -1.7 | 26.9 | 0.7 | 27.2 | 73.9 |
| 50.4 | 57.8 | 33.0 | 13.1 | 0.7 | 0.1 | 9.9 | 184 | 22 | 179 | Denton & Reddish | Lab Con | 10.3 | 34.0 | -4.0 | 44.3 | 8.3 | 21.7 | 72.8 |
| 49.2 | 60.1 | 30.7 | 10.8 | 1.7 | 2.0 | 8.8 | 185 | 7 | 188 | Dewsbury | Con Lab | 4.0 | 39.4 | -4.1 | 35.3 | 7.0 | 25.3 | 74.0 |
| 37.3 | 52.6 | 36.0 | 15.0 | 1.4 | 0.3 | 8.8 | 162 | 14 | 189 | DoncasterCentral | Lab Con | 5.0 | 37.1 | 0.3 | 42.0 | 4.8 | 20.9 | 70.8 |
| 45.8 | 49.6 | 38.5 | 15.6 | 0.4 | 1.9 | 7.7 | 162 | 4 | 190 | Doncaster N | Lab Con | 25.2 | 27.6 | -7.4 | 52.8 | 15.7 | 19.7 | 69.9 |
| 56.2 | 56.3 | 34.5 | 12.6 | 0.5 | 1.9 | 7.8 | 157 | 6 | 191 | Don Valley | Lab Con | 12.7 | 32.4 | -8.3 | 45.1 | 14.0 | 22.5 | 69.9 |
| 52.3 | 47.3 | 42.6 | 10.4 | 0.6 | 1.6 | 8.3 | 260 | 15 | 207 | Durham City | Lab All | 4.0 | 31.0 | -6.3 | 36.5 | 1.3 | 32.5 | 74.4 |
| 48.9 | 50.3 | 43.8 | 16.7 | 0.3 | 0.8 | 8.7 | 266 | 15 | 208 | Durham N | Lab All | 25.9 | 24.0 | -10.6 | 51.0 | 12.2 | 25.0 | 72.7 |
| | 50.5 | 38.5 | 22.0 | 0.3 | 3.2 | 10.5 | 272 | 15 | 209 | Durham NW | Lab Con | 14.8 | 29.8 | -5.8 | 44.6 | 9.8 | 25.6 | 70.7 |

| Non Man % | Own Occ % | Coun Ten % | Unem % | Born NCom % | Agric % | Aged % | Dist Lond m. | Clus | PA No | Constituency Name | Party | Marg | % | Con Vote % | Con Res % | Lab Vote % | Lab Res % | All Vote % | Turn Out % |
|---|---|---|---|---|---|---|---|---|---|---|---|---|---|---|---|---|---|---|---|
| 36.9 | 30.2 | 56.0 | 13.9 | 0.2 | 0.9 | 8.7 | 272 | 16 | 213 | Easington | Lab | All | 33.3 | 16.5 | -7.3 | 58.4 | 8.5 | 25.1 | 67.5 |
| 48.3 | 48.5 | 40.3 | 13.7 | 0.8 | 0.1 | 10.6 | 196 | 26 | 219 | Eccles | Lab | Con | 12.7 | 33.2 | -0.2 | 45.9 | 5.1 | 19.9 | 70.1 |
| 56.7 | 63.5 | 25.3 | 10.5 | 0.6 | 5.0 | 7.7 | 162 | 17 | 220 | Eddisbury | Con | All | 27.9 | 53.5 | 2.7 | 21.0 | 4.1 | 25.5 | 74.3 |
| 50.5 | 59.2 | 34.0 | 13.7 | 0.5 | 1.6 | 6.9 | 188 | 6 | 228 | Ellesmere P & Neston | Con | Lab | 13.4 | 45.9 | 5.0 | 32.6 | 1.0 | 21.5 | 75.8 |
| 57.0 | 61.3 | 31.7 | 7.5 | 0.5 | 1.6 | 7.7 | 190 | 6 | 229 | Elmet | Con | Lab | 15.5 | 47.3 | 1.1 | 31.8 | 5.9 | 20.9 | 75.4 |
| 64.6 | 72.0 | 11.8 | 7.1 | 0.7 | 3.6 | 12.2 | 226 | 19 | 252 | Fylde | Con | All | 38.6 | 62.9 | 6.4 | 10.9 | -1.8 | 24.3 | 71.2 |
| 46.8 | 30.6 | 53.4 | 17.3 | 0.4 | 0.2 | 9.2 | 273 | 27 | 255 | Gateshead E | Lab | Con | 21.7 | 26.6 | 1.7 | 48.3 | -1.3 | 25.1 | 69.6 |
| 45.8 | 58.9 | 33.8 | 18.6 | 1.2 | 1.7 | 8.0 | 160 | 6 | 258 | Glanford & Scunth | Con | Lab | 1.2 | 38.5 | -0.9 | 37.3 | 4.5 | 24.3 | 73.5 |
| 40.7 | 64.2 | 26.5 | 14.3 | 0.8 | 1.3 | 9.0 | 164 | 14 | 277 | Great Grimsby | Lab | Con | 1.4 | 34.9 | -5.3 | 36.3 | 3.4 | 28.8 | 73.8 |
| 45.6 | 66.9 | 23.4 | 12.5 | 1.0 | 0.3 | 9.7 | 193 | 22 | 285 | Halifax | Lab | Con | 3.4 | 40.9 | -1.6 | 37.4 | 6.1 | 21.7 | 75.1 |
| 45.1 | 48.4 | 44.8 | 15.4 | 0.4 | 0.4 | 7.6 | 197 | 27 | 286 | Halton | Lab | Con | 12.8 | 33.6 | 1.9 | 46.4 | 4.0 | 20.0 | 73.3 |
| 66.9 | 71.1 | 12.1 | 6.8 | 1.0 | 2.7 | 10.3 | 204 | 19 | 294 | Harrogate | Con | All | 31.6 | 60.2 | -4.7 | 10.2 | -4.4 | 28.6 | 69.0 |
| 43.1 | 50.6 | 40.0 | 20.7 | 0.4 | 1.2 | 7.9 | 254 | 27 | 297 | Hartlepool | Lab | Con | 6.4 | 39.1 | 6.2 | 45.5 | 5.1 | 15.3 | 69.8 |
| 63.0 | 72.3 | 18.8 | 8.4 | 0.5 | 0.6 | 8.9 | 177 | 28 | 302 | Hazel Grove | Con | All | 4.1 | 46.1 | -6.2 | 12.0 | -8.8 | 41.9 | 77.2 |
| 38.6 | 46.5 | 41.2 | 11.6 | 0.3 | 1.3 | 8.1 | 171 | 14 | 303 | Hemsworth | Lab | All | 38.1 | 19.6 | -13.7 | 59.3 | 19.6 | 21.2 | 68.6 |
| 58.9 | 56.5 | 23.7 | 6.5 | 0.5 | 10.8 | 10.0 | 282 | 2 | 313 | Hexham | Con | All | 20.0 | 51.5 | -3.3 | 17.0 | 10.9 | 31.5 | 76.4 |
| 46.3 | 50.5 | 43.6 | 15.0 | 0.5 | 0.6 | 8.1 | 190 | 14 | 314 | Heywood & Middleton | Lab | Con | 9.5 | 33.8 | 0.5 | 43.3 | 2.8 | 22.1 | 69.9 |
| 48.6 | 35.6 | 58.9 | 14.6 | 0.3 | 0.4 | 6.7 | 265 | 3 | 322 | Houghton & Washington | Lab | All | 27.3 | 23.9 | -2.9 | 51.7 | 4.2 | 24.4 | 66.9 |
| 46.7 | 57.5 | 32.1 | 15.8 | 5.5 | 0.5 | 9.7 | 186 | 20 | 324 | Huddersfield | Lab | Con | 8.2 | 33.2 | -5.8 | 41.4 | 6.4 | 24.8 | 71.1 |
| 43.6 | 33.9 | 56.1 | 17.8 | 0.4 | 0.5 | 8.4 | 205 | 27 | 325 | Hull E | Lab | Con | 21.3 | 28.6 | 4.6 | 49.9 | -0.2 | 21.5 | 67.6 |
| 49.0 | 38.9 | 48.3 | 17.8 | 0.8 | 1.0 | 8.2 | 204 | 27 | 326 | Hull N | Lab | Con | 12.0 | 30.5 | 0.9 | 42.5 | -1.6 | 26.6 | 67.5 |
| 41.0 | 41.6 | 35.7 | 20.1 | 0.8 | 1.2 | 10.9 | 205 | 26 | 327 | Hull W | Lab | Con | 10.0 | 31.9 | 1.1 | 41.9 | -0.7 | 26.1 | 63.5 |
| 44.2 | 77.8 | 15.7 | 11.6 | 0.4 | 0.6 | 9.8 | 205 | 22 | 329 | Hyndburn | Con | Lab | 0.0 | 42.2 | -5.8 | 42.2 | 17.3 | 14.6 | 77.4 |
| 48.9 | 28.2 | 65.3 | 19.8 | 0.3 | 0.4 | 8.1 | 277 | 3 | 338 | Jarrow | Lab | Con | 30.5 | 24.8 | 3.0 | 55.3 | 2.7 | 20.0 | 71.4 |
| 50.8 | 74.7 | 15.2 | 10.8 | 1.1 | 1.3 | 9.7 | 205 | 28 | 339 | Keighley | Con | Lab | 5.5 | 37.0 | -7.5 | 31.4 | 14.7 | 19.8 | 78.9 |
| 41.2 | 22.6 | 72.8 | 31.7 | 0.3 | 0.4 | 5.8 | 202 | 3 | 348 | Knowsley N | Lab | Con | 44.5 | 20.1 | 3.1 | 64.5 | 6.7 | 14.8 | 69.5 |
| 49.1 | 38.5 | 55.6 | 23.2 | 0.4 | 0.4 | 7.1 | 202 | 27 | 349 | Knowsley S | Lab | Con | 24.6 | 29.2 | 4.7 | 53.8 | 3.8 | 17.1 | 70.3 |
| 52.3 | 57.9 | 34.5 | 14.4 | 0.6 | 5.2 | 7.5 | 203 | 17 | 351 | Lancashire W | Con | Lab | 12.5 | 46.3 | 1.1 | 33.8 | 11.2 | 20.0 | 74.4 |
| 52.7 | 67.4 | 17.9 | 11.7 | 1.1 | 6.1 | 10.2 | 233 | 10 | 352 | Lancaster | Con | Lab | 25.4 | 50.3 | -0.5 | 24.9 | 8.8 | 24.4 | 74.7 |
| 52.6 | 62.5 | 29.2 | 16.2 | 0.5 | 1.1 | 6.5 | 251 | 6 | 353 | Langbaurgh | Con | Lab | 10.4 | 41.7 | -1.2 | 31.4 | 1.5 | 26.9 | 75.0 |
| 39.1 | 32.9 | 48.8 | 19.9 | 2.9 | 0.1 | 10.9 | 190 | 26 | 354 | Leeds Central | Lab | Con | 21.1 | 23.6 | -1.3 | 47.9 | -1.9 | 26.9 | 61.7 |
| 49.3 | 44.2 | 47.1 | 17.9 | 2.9 | 0.3 | 9.6 | 190 | 26 | 355 | Leeds E | Lab | Con | 14.5 | 29.3 | -1.0 | 43.8 | -0.3 | 25.8 | 66.3 |
| 69.7 | 64.6 | 21.3 | 11.3 | 5.2 | 0.7 | 9.8 | 190 | 25 | 356 | Leeds NE | Con | All | 19.5 | 47.6 | -3.5 | 23.8 | 1.6 | 28.1 | 70.7 |

| 1 | 2 | 3 | 4 | 5 | 6 | 7 | | | | | | | | | | | | |
|---|---|---|---|---|---|---|---|---|---|---|---|---|---|---|---|---|---|---|
| 68.4 | 60.5 | 22.5 | 9.6 | 2.5 | 0.7 | 9.6 | 190 | 8 | 357 | Leeds NW | Con All | 17.6 | 46.6 | -3.5 | 22.2 | -1.1 | 29.0 | 71.3 |
| 45.2 | 44.1 | 47.0 | 12.4 | 0.7 | 0.7 | 9.3 | 190 | 14 | 358 | Leeds S & Morley | Lab Con | 14.2 | 31.8 | -0.4 | 45.9 | 4.5 | 22.3 | 67.9 |
| 45.9 | 47.4 | 42.4 | 13.5 | 1.2 | 0.3 | 9.9 | 190 | 14 | 359 | Leeds W | All Lab | 4.4 | 26.8 | -6.0 | 34.0 | -7.1 | 38.4 | 69.0 |
| 41.7 | 60.9 | 32.3 | 13.5 | 0.3 | 0.5 | 9.0 | 194 | 14 | 364 | Leigh | Lab Con | 25.1 | 26.8 | -11.0 | 51.9 | 16.1 | 21.3 | 72.2 |
| 54.5 | 68.4 | 23.2 | 9.5 | 0.7 | 0.7 | 8.5 | 184 | 28 | 374 | Littleborough & Sadd | Con All | 11.8 | 42.8 | -4.8 | 25.3 | -0.0 | 31.0 | 74.8 |
| 54.5 | 52.4 | 21.9 | 19.1 | 0.7 | 0.1 | 10.8 | 197 | 22 | 375 | L'pool Broadgreen | Lab Con | 8.3 | 32.6 | -6.2 | 40.9 | 5.5 | 11.2 | 72.1 |
| 52.8 | 38.6 | 54.4 | 22.1 | 0.6 | 0.2 | 9.0 | 197 | 27 | 376 | L'pool Garston | Lab Con | 8.7 | 37.9 | 11.3 | 46.6 | -1.3 | 15.5 | 71.6 |
| 59.2 | 58.2 | 15.1 | 17.4 | 1.4 | 0.2 | 10.4 | 197 | 11 | 377 | L'pool Mossley Hill | All Con | 9.1 | 31.8 | -12.7 | 26.8 | -2.6 | 40.9 | 73.4 |
| 40.5 | 19.5 | 53.0 | 36.5 | 2.9 | 0.3 | 9.3 | 197 | 4 | 378 | L'pool Riverside | Lab Con | 45.2 | 19.8 | 2.0 | 65.0 | 7.8 | 14.0 | 62.4 |
| 45.6 | 45.6 | 29.3 | 21.6 | 0.5 | 0.1 | 10.2 | 197 | 26 | 379 | L'pool Walton | Lab Con | 27.6 | 25.1 | -5.5 | 52.7 | 9.1 | 21.4 | 69.6 |
| 46.8 | 28.3 | 66.8 | 26.6 | 0.4 | 0.1 | 8.5 | 197 | 16 | 380 | L'pool W Derby | Lab Con | 27.0 | 27.5 | 10.6 | 54.5 | -3.4 | 18.0 | 69.5 |
| 64.1 | 70.0 | 20.0 | 7.4 | 0.7 | 2.4 | 8.6 | 166 | 12 | 388 | Macclesfield | Con All | 37.7 | 59.4 | 6.3 | 18.1 | 18.5 | 21.6 | 75.0 |
| 47.9 | 66.1 | 28.5 | 12.4 | 0.4 | 0.6 | 6.9 | 184 | 6 | 390 | Makerfield | Lab Con | 21.3 | 27.9 | -14.8 | 49.3 | 18.5 | 22.8 | 73.7 |
| 50.4 | 44.0 | 43.0 | 16.7 | 1.0 | 0.1 | 11.6 | 184 | 26 | 391 | M'chester Blackley | Lab Con | 15.4 | 32.6 | 2.2 | 48.1 | 4.2 | 19.3 | 69.7 |
| 36.6 | 19.4 | 68.6 | 28.3 | 5.4 | 0.1 | 9.3 | 184 | 4 | 392 | M'chester Central | Lab Con | 44.1 | 21.2 | 3.4 | 65.3 | 7.7 | 11.8 | 60.6 |
| 46.8 | 47.5 | 27.6 | 20.1 | 4.5 | 0.1 | 9.3 | 184 | 30 | 393 | M'chester Gorton | Lab Con | 22.7 | 28.5 | -9.3 | 51.2 | 14.2 | 19.0 | 67.9 |
| 65.0 | 46.0 | 29.2 | 14.5 | 2.9 | 0.2 | 10.1 | 184 | 21 | 394 | M'chester Withington | Con Lab | 5.1 | 39.2 | -3.5 | 34.2 | 2.2 | 26.2 | 72.3 |
| 46.7 | 20.5 | 75.8 | 18.6 | 0.9 | 0.4 | 10.5 | 184 | 16 | 395 | M'chester Wythenshawe | Lab Con | 25.2 | 29.4 | 13.1 | 54.6 | -3.7 | 15.9 | 69.6 |
| 44.4 | 49.0 | 40.4 | 27.0 | 1.3 | 0.1 | 7.8 | 247 | 27 | 401 | Middlesborough | Lab Con | 23.1 | 31.6 | -1.9 | 50.7 | 5.4 | 21.2 | 66.5 |
| 56.5 | 77.4 | 7.4 | 11.7 | 0.5 | 2.9 | 13.9 | 237 | 19 | 411 | Morecambe & Lunesdal | Con All | 31.4 | 56.6 | 1.5 | 17.7 | 2.6 | 25.2 | 72.9 |
| 64.0 | 44.1 | 34.3 | 14.5 | 2.2 | 0.3 | 10.3 | 273 | 11 | 418 | N'castle U Tyne Cen | Con Lab | 5.0 | 40.8 | 1.4 | 35.8 | 1.0 | 22.3 | 71.0 |
| 48.7 | 33.2 | 51.3 | 17.4 | 0.9 | 0.1 | 12.2 | 273 | 26 | 419 | N'castle U Tyne E | Lab Con | 17.7 | 27.8 | 2.1 | 45.5 | -3.3 | 26.7 | 71.0 |
| 57.5 | 45.7 | 46.5 | 12.9 | 0.6 | 0.7 | 8.2 | 273 | 15 | 420 | N'castle U Tyne N | Lab Con | 5.1 | 32.5 | -2.0 | 37.6 | -1.7 | 29.9 | 72.8 |
| 49.3 | 58.5 | 32.8 | 7.5 | 0.5 | 1.1 | 8.8 | 183 | 7 | 433 | Normanton | Lab Con | 9.7 | 33.9 | -8.5 | 43.6 | 13.2 | 22.6 | 70.4 |
| 40.7 | 55.9 | 37.0 | 14.9 | 3.0 | 0.3 | 9.5 | 184 | 22 | 446 | Oldham Cen & Royton | Lab Con | 7.4 | 34.0 | -0.9 | 41.4 | 2.4 | 24.5 | 66.9 |
| 43.4 | 63.3 | 29.0 | 12.4 | 1.6 | 0.0 | 9.4 | 184 | 22 | 447 | Oldham W | Lab Con | 7.9 | 36.2 | -3.8 | 44.1 | 10.0 | 19.3 | 69.8 |
| 41.4 | 75.5 | 17.1 | 11.8 | 0.6 | 1.4 | 10.3 | 209 | 22 | 456 | Pendle | Con Lab | 11.9 | 44.2 | -2.7 | 32.3 | 7.0 | 23.5 | 79.7 |
| 46.1 | 58.2 | 17.6 | 7.9 | 0.3 | 15.7 | 9.9 | 281 | 2 | 457 | Penrith & Border | Con All | 31.0 | 58.8 | 3.9 | 13.3 | 7.4 | 27.9 | 73.1 |
| 36.7 | 43.8 | 47.3 | 12.1 | 0.4 | 1.0 | 8.3 | 177 | 27 | 463 | Pontefract & Castlef | Lab Con | 31.3 | 25.8 | -5.3 | 57.1 | 15.0 | 17.0 | 67.4 |
| 42.1 | 54.3 | 35.0 | 19.4 | 6.0 | 0.4 | 10.1 | 211 | 20 | 468 | Preston | Lab Con | 14.9 | 31.8 | -3.3 | 46.7 | 7.6 | 21.5 | 71.9 |
| 59.8 | 70.1 | 23.1 | 7.5 | 0.7 | 0.6 | 8.8 | 190 | 28 | 469 | Pudsey | Con All | 9.9 | 45.7 | -3.2 | 17.8 | -6.4 | 35.8 | 75.8 |
| 46.6 | 53.2 | 41.6 | 21.0 | 0.5 | 0.3 | 7.8 | 252 | 27 | 474 | Redcar | Lab Con | 6.9 | 33.7 | 1.3 | 40.6 | -1.2 | 25.7 | 71.3 |
| 61.3 | 79.7 | 9.2 | 5.3 | 0.8 | 5.6 | 9.4 | 214 | 12 | 478 | Ribble Valley | Con All | 40.4 | 63.4 | 3.3 | 13.5 | 6.4 | 23.1 | 76.8 |
| 46.0 | 56.9 | 21.2 | 7.6 | 0.9 | 11.8 | 8.9 | 234 | 2 | 480 | Richmond Yorks | Con All | 35.0 | 62.6 | 7.8 | 9.7 | 3.6 | 27.7 | 68.7 |
| 49.8 | 56.4 | 35.8 | 17.0 | 2.3 | 0.3 | 8.7 | 190 | 7 | 481 | Rochdale | All Lab | 16.0 | 22.4 | -15.4 | 30.1 | -6.0 | 46.1 | 70.8 |
| 45.6 | 68.8 | 24.1 | 11.7 | 0.7 | 0.8 | 9.2 | 203 | 22 | 486 | Rossendale & Darwen | Con Lab | 15.2 | 47.0 | 1.8 | 31.8 | 4.0 | 21.2 | 77.8 |

| Non Man % | Own Occ % | Coun Ten % | Unem % | Born NCom % | Agric % | Aged % | Dist Lond m. | Clus | PA No | Constituency Name | Party Marg | Con Vote % | Con Res % | Lab Vote % | Lab Res % | All Vote % | Turn Out % |
|---|---|---|---|---|---|---|---|---|---|---|---|---|---|---|---|---|---|
| 47.1 | 40.7 | 51.8 | 16.2 | 0.5 | 0.3 | 8.9 | 163 | 27 | 487 | Rotherham | Lab Con | 28.6 | 25.7 | -3.7 | 54.3 | 9.5 | 20.0 | 67.0 |
| 48.0 | 55.2 | 33.7 | 10.9 | 0.3 | 1.1 | 6.8 | 163 | 6 | 488 | Rother Valley | Lab Con | 18.4 | 28.1 | -12.4 | 46.5 | 14.1 | 25.4 | 71.9 |
| 48.6 | 65.8 | 15.8 | 6.4 | 0.7 | 10.7 | 10.6 | 230 | 2 | 494 | Ryedale | Con All | 28.7 | 59.2 | 1.9 | 10.3 | 6.9 | 30.5 | 71.8 |
| 49.3 | 55.8 | 36.9 | 13.6 | 0.3 | 1.0 | 7.9 | 191 | 15 | 497 | St Helens N | Lab Con | 17.5 | 30.4 | -8.6 | 47.9 | 13.8 | 21.8 | 74.5 |
| 46.7 | 60.0 | 29.0 | 15.4 | 0.5 | 0.4 | 8.3 | 191 | 7 | 498 | St Helens S | Lab Con | 19.8 | 27.1 | -12.4 | 46.9 | 12.7 | 22.4 | 70.6 |
| 43.4 | 30.2 | 53.8 | 22.1 | 1.0 | 0.1 | 10.1 | 184 | 26 | 500 | Salford E | Lab Con | 24.0 | 29.7 | 7.1 | 53.7 | 1.5 | 15.5 | 62.3 |
| 50.9 | 64.1 | 20.6 | 12.8 | 0.7 | 5.8 | 12.1 | 231 | 10 | 502 | Scarborough | Con All | 27.0 | 54.3 | 5.1 | 18.5 | 0.3 | 27.2 | 71.3 |
| 45.2 | 45.9 | 45.9 | 13.5 | 0.3 | 2.9 | 9.3 | 252 | 15 | 503 | Sedgefield | Lab Con | 18.4 | 29.2 | -4.0 | 47.6 | 9.9 | 22.6 | 72.9 |
| 49.5 | 68.0 | 19.8 | 6.5 | 0.6 | 6.3 | 8.5 | 182 | 17 | 504 | Selby | Con All | 33.9 | 56.7 | 2.0 | 20.5 | 9.6 | 22.8 | 72.1 |
| 45.0 | 43.4 | 49.0 | 11.5 | 0.7 | 0.1 | 10.0 | 159 | 14 | 506 | S'field Attercliff | Lab Con | 25.9 | 25.6 | -5.0 | 51.5 | 7.8 | 22.9 | 69.7 |
| 38.7 | 25.2 | 68.8 | 16.2 | 0.8 | 0.1 | 11.2 | 159 | 16 | 507 | S'field Brightside | Lab All | 34.5 | 17.9 | 0.9 | 58.0 | 0.2 | 23.4 | 65.5 |
| 38.5 | 24.1 | 61.8 | 21.4 | 3.4 | 0.1 | 10.7 | 159 | 4 | 508 | S'field Central | Lab All | 40.8 | 19.2 | 0.9 | 60.2 | 3.5 | 19.4 | 61.6 |
| 75.3 | 72.7 | 10.3 | 7.9 | 1.6 | 0.4 | 9.9 | 159 | 25 | 509 | S'field Hallam | Con All | 22.2 | 50.6 | -7.9 | 19.7 | 4.9 | 28.4 | 72.8 |
| 48.6 | 40.4 | 52.2 | 11.9 | 0.7 | 0.1 | 11.7 | 159 | 26 | 510 | S'field Heeley | Lab Con | 15.9 | 29.9 | 1.3 | 45.8 | 0.1 | 24.3 | 70.5 |
| 51.1 | 60.3 | 29.1 | 8.9 | 0.4 | 1.0 | 9.4 | 159 | 7 | 511 | S'field Hillsborough | Lab All | 2.8 | 28.3 | -14.7 | 37.2 | 7.5 | 34.5 | 75.4 |
| 63.0 | 70.3 | 21.7 | 9.2 | 0.7 | 0.6 | 9.5 | 201 | 28 | 513 | Shipley | Con All | 22.0 | 49.7 | -0.4 | 21.6 | -1.4 | 27.7 | 77.0 |
| 48.1 | 65.3 | 15.3 | 6.2 | 0.7 | 11.4 | 10.6 | 214 | 2 | 517 | Skipton & Ripon | Con All | 28.9 | 60.6 | 2.4 | 7.8 | 5.3 | 31.6 | 74.9 |
| 68.4 | 74.2 | 6.7 | 11.5 | 0.7 | 1.0 | 11.9 | 210 | 19 | 526 | Southport | Con All | 9.9 | 50.4 | -4.3 | 8.3 | -9.5 | 40.5 | 72.5 |
| 55.9 | 76.7 | 18.2 | 8.6 | 0.6 | 1.8 | 7.7 | 211 | 28 | 527 | South Ribble | Con Lab | 22.5 | 49.1 | -2.9 | 26.6 | 6.9 | 24.3 | 77.7 |
| 45.0 | 34.8 | 47.3 | 18.8 | 0.6 | 0.1 | 9.8 | 276 | 27 | 528 | South Shields | Lab Con | 15.6 | 30.9 | 3.9 | 46.5 | -1.0 | 22.7 | 66.2 |
| 46.4 | 53.9 | 39.9 | 13.7 | 1.3 | 0.4 | 8.8 | 184 | 14 | 536 | Stalybridge & Hyde | Lab Con | 9.1 | 36.4 | 0.4 | 45.5 | 7.7 | 17.4 | 70.5 |
| 59.1 | 70.1 | 15.0 | 11.1 | 1.0 | 0.1 | 9.2 | 184 | 28 | 540 | Stockport | Con Lab | 13.2 | 42.1 | -8.2 | 29.0 | 5.4 | 27.6 | 74.6 |
| 47.1 | 49.3 | 44.0 | 19.9 | 0.6 | 0.3 | 7.1 | 243 | 27 | 541 | Stockton N | Lab Con | 3.8 | 33.3 | 1.1 | 37.1 | -4.9 | 29.6 | 70.3 |
| 56.7 | 70.8 | 21.3 | 14.8 | 0.8 | 0.7 | 6.8 | 243 | 6 | 542 | Stockton S | All Con | 0.2 | 36.6 | -11.2 | 26.3 | 0.7 | 36.7 | 72.1 |
| 52.1 | 52.1 | 25.2 | 18.1 | 7.8 | 0.2 | 8.7 | 184 | 30 | 550 | Stretford | Lab Con | 10.8 | 34.1 | -6.9 | 44.9 | 10.9 | 20.3 | 70.0 |
| 44.8 | 38.7 | 52.5 | 23.2 | 0.4 | 0.2 | 8.9 | 269 | 27 | 555 | Sunderland N | Lab Con | 13.8 | 32.5 | 6.8 | 46.3 | -2.4 | 21.2 | 66.5 |
| 52.1 | 39.8 | 50.9 | 19.9 | 0.8 | 0.2 | 8.3 | 269 | 27 | 556 | Sunderland S | Lab Con | 11.1 | 34.6 | 5.5 | 45.7 | 0.4 | 19.7 | 66.6 |
| 62.2 | 64.1 | 26.1 | 8.2 | 0.6 | 3.5 | 9.2 | 166 | 12 | 567 | Tatton | Con All | 27.3 | 54.6 | 3.6 | 18.2 | -0.3 | 27.2 | 74.3 |
| 43.7 | 25.9 | 53.6 | 24.3 | 1.1 | 0.1 | 9.6 | 273 | 16 | 584 | Tyne Bridge | Lab Con | 31.3 | 25.2 | 5.1 | 56.5 | 1.6 | 18.3 | 61.5 |
| 60.0 | 55.1 | 29.8 | 13.6 | 0.6 | 0.5 | 9.8 | 281 | 7 | 585 | Tynemouth | Con Lab | 17.3 | 48.6 | 6.9 | 31.3 | -0.6 | 20.1 | 74.6 |
| 52.3 | 50.5 | 42.0 | 9.1 | 0.6 | 0.9 | 8.3 | 181 | 15 | 592 | Wakefield | Lab Con | 0.8 | 39.6 | 1.7 | 40.4 | 5.1 | 19.3 | 69.3 |
| 55.0 | 62.7 | 20.5 | 16.4 | 0.6 | 0.1 | 10.2 | 199 | 22 | 593 | Wallasey | Con Lab | 13.5 | 46.0 | 3.4 | 32.5 | 1.0 | 21.6 | 72.6 |
| 50.3 | 35.2 | 52.8 | 14.6 | 0.4 | 0.3 | 8.9 | 273 | 27 | 594 | Wallsend | Lab Con | 23.1 | 26.0 | -1.4 | 49.1 | 2.2 | 24.9 | 71.1 |

| Non Man % | Own Occ % | Coun Ten % | Unem % | Born NCom % | Agric % | Aged % | Dist Card m. | Clus | PA No | Name | Par | Con Mar Vote | Con Res Vote | Lab Mar Vote | Lab Res Vote | All Vote | All Res Vote | PC Vote | Turn Out |
|---|---|---|---|---|---|---|---|---|---|---|---|---|---|---|---|---|---|---|---|
| 46.0 | 42.7 | 40.9 | 10.4 | 0.4 | 0.9 | 10.0 | 289 | 14 | 598 | Wansbeck | Lab All | 17.0 | 22.9 | -10.5 | 47.0 | 7.3 | 30.1 | | 72.9 |
| 50.5 | 53.2 | 38.2 | 12.8 | 0.5 | 0.9 | 8.7 | 183 | 15 | 604 | Warrington N | Lab Con | 10.4 | 30.8 | -6.2 | 41.2 | 4.9 | 27.5 | | 72.6 |
| 55.2 | 62.5 | 30.2 | 11.5 | 0.6 | 0.9 | 7.1 | 183 | 6 | 605 | Warrington S | Con Lab | 11.9 | 41.9 | -2.7 | 30.0 | 1.5 | 27.3 | | 74.5 |
| 42.0 | 41.7 | 48.9 | 14.2 | 0.2 | 0.4 | 8.2 | 167 | 27 | 614 | Wentworth | Lab Con | 36.9 | 22.2 | -8.0 | 59.1 | 15.3 | 18.7 | | 69.7 |
| 52.6 | 62.3 | 18.9 | 6.5 | 0.5 | 8.5 | 12.3 | 247 | 10 | 620 | Westmorland & Lonsdale | Con All | 34.2 | 61.3 | 8.0 | 9.9 | -1.1 | 27.2 | | 72.3 |
| 43.7 | 55.3 | 37.3 | 13.7 | 0.4 | 0.5 | 9.4 | 196 | 14 | 622 | Wigan | Lab All | 31.6 | 22.5 | -13.2 | 54.5 | 16.7 | 22.9 | | 75.6 |
| 63.0 | 72.2 | 14.2 | 9.9 | 0.6 | 1.0 | 9.4 | 192 | 28 | 627 | Wirral S | Con All | 30.0 | 53.7 | 1.5 | 22.6 | 2.2 | 23.7 | | 75.8 |
| 65.8 | 70.6 | 21.1 | 12.3 | 0.6 | 0.8 | 9.8 | 201 | 28 | 628 | Wirral W | Con All | 33.5 | 55.9 | 5.9 | 21.8 | -1.1 | 22.4 | | 79.6 |
| 43.1 | 52.2 | 28.2 | 14.1 | 0.3 | 3.3 | 9.4 | 303 | 15 | 640 | Workington | Lab Con | 16.0 | 36.1 | -4.4 | 52.0 | 21.9 | 11.9 | | 74.7 |
| 52.8 | 54.0 | 42.0 | 12.7 | 0.5 | 0.6 | 8.4 | 190 | 15 | 641 | Worsley | Lab Con | 7.7 | 32.6 | -4.4 | 40.3 | 4.0 | 27.1 | | 74.7 |
| 52.2 | 58.3 | 29.8 | 9.5 | 0.9 | 0.3 | 10.8 | 196 | 22 | 650 | York | Con Lab | 6.2 | 41.3 | 1.1 | 35.1 | 1.6 | 23.0 | | 75.1 |
| 50.4 | 55.4 | 33.0 | 13.9 | 1.1 | 1.6 | 9.2 | 208.0 | | | (Mean) | | 17.6 | 37.8 | -2.2 | 37.4 | 5.1 | 24.2 | | 72.0 |
| 8.2 | 14.4 | 14.6 | 5.2 | 1.3 | 2.8 | 1.3 | 38.4 | | | (StdDev) | | 11.3 | 11.4 | 5.8 | 14.3 | 6.7 | 6.7 | | 3.9 |

# WALES

| Non Man % | Own Occ % | Coun Ten % | Unem % | Born NCom % | Agric % | Aged % | Dist Card m. | Clus | PA No | Constituency Name | Par | Con Mar Vote | Con Res Vote | Lab Mar Vote | Lab Res Vote | All Vote | All Res Vote | PC Vote | Turn Out |
|---|---|---|---|---|---|---|---|---|---|---|---|---|---|---|---|---|---|---|---|
| | | | | | | | | | | **BRITISH WALES** | | | | | | | | | |
| 49.5 | 66.9 | 24.9 | 16.0 | 0.6 | 2.3 | 8.0 | 143 | 6 | 7 | Alyn & Deeside | Lab Con | 3.1 | 37.2 | -7.6 | 40.3 | 13.5 | 21.6 | 0.9 | 78.1 |
| 44.8 | 57.7 | 24.5 | 9.5 | 0.5 | 17.2 | 11.1 | 42 | 2 | 83 | Brecon & Radnor | Con Lab | 23.2 | 48.2 | -3.8 | 25.0 | 16.2 | 24.4 | 1.7 | 80.1 |
| 57.8 | 66.3 | 25.7 | 14.0 | 0.7 | 0.7 | 9.2 | 26 | 28 | 89 | Bridgend | Con Lab | 3.2 | 38.4 | -7.0 | 35.2 | 7.4 | 23.2 | 3.2 | 77.0 |
| 66.3 | 65.4 | 11.4 | 13.5 | 2.8 | 0.3 | 7.7 | 0 | 8 | 118 | Cardiff Central | Con All | 8.9 | 41.4 | -11.2 | 24.2 | 2.7 | 32.6 | 1.8 | 72.1 |
| 67.8 | 74.5 | 17.5 | 8.8 | 1.0 | 0.3 | 11.1 | 0 | 25 | 119 | Cardiff N | Con All | 16.6 | 47.1 | -5.4 | 20.0 | -0.6 | 30.5 | 2.4 | 77.3 |
| 52.4 | 54.4 | 33.9 | 17.7 | 1.6 | 0.5 | 9.4 | 0 | 7 | 120 | Cardiff S & Penarth | Lab Con | 5.4 | 35.9 | -2.0 | 41.3 | 5.4 | 20.9 | 1.6 | 71.0 |
| 56.6 | 52.8 | 33.1 | 15.7 | 2.2 | 0.3 | 9.0 | 0 | 20 | 121 | Cardiff W | Con Lab | 4.4 | 38.0 | -1.9 | 33.6 | -0.7 | 25.5 | 2.1 | 69.6 |
| 55.7 | 68.5 | 16.8 | 15.1 | 0.6 | 2.7 | 13.9 | 169 | 19 | 145 | Clwyd NW | Con All | 21.9 | | 1.5 | 16.3 | -5.2 | 29.1 | 3.7 | 73.1 |
| 47.9 | 62.8 | 34.8 | 12.5 | 0.3 | 10.4 | 10.4 | 158 | 24 | 146 | Clwyd SW | Con All | 3.6 | 33.8 | -11.7 | 27.4 | 9.8 | 30.2 | 8.5 | 77.3 |
| 52.4 | 71.1 | 22.0 | 17.3 | 0.4 | 3.2 | 10.4 | 146 | 29 | 178 | Delyn | Con Lab | 12.2 | 41.6 | -5.1 | 29.4 | 5.8 | 25.8 | 3.2 | 77.8 |
| 57.5 | 61.4 | 27.5 | 10.5 | 0.7 | 8.1 | 9.3 | 36 | 17 | 408 | Monmouth | All Con | 21.1 | 49.2 | -1.5 | 21.7 | 7.0 | 28.0 | 1.1 | 78.8 |
| 39.5 | 52.1 | 30.1 | 8.9 | 0.3 | 21.2 | 9.9 | 93 | 24 | 409 | Montgomery | Lab Con | 6.5 | 33.1 | -8.5 | 39.6 | 8.4 | 25.6 | 1.7 | 76.6 |
| 49.2 | 62.9 | 29.6 | 16.8 | 0.8 | 1.3 | 7.9 | 12 | 6 | 425 | Newport E | Con Lab | 1.4 | 38.0 | -3.2 | 36.6 | 4.3 | 24.2 | 1.7 | 77.5 |
| 59.7 | 58.1 | 33.3 | 15.1 | 1.1 | 0.7 | 8.5 | 12 | 7 | 426 | Newport W | Con Lab | 17.6 | 46.9 | -0.9 | 29.2 | 12.5 | 20.7 | 2.0 | 78.1 |
| 47.8 | 55.7 | 30.8 | 13.1 | 0.7 | 9.0 | 8.7 | 97 | 17 | 455 | Pembroke | Con Lab | 22.3 | 48.0 | -1.7 | 25.8 | 4.3 | 23.9 | 2.3 | 74.2 |
| 58.4 | 63.3 | 23.0 | 11.7 | 0.8 | 2.5 | 7.6 | 10 | 9 | 590 | Vale of Glamorgan | Con Lab | | | | | | | | |
| 50.2 | 50.4 | 41.2 | 15.9 | 0.6 | 3.2 | 8.7 | 140 | 15 | 644 | Wrexham | Lab Con | 0.9 | 33.4 | -4.6 | 34.3 | 1.7 | 29.7 | 2.6 | 77.5 |
| 53.7 | 60.8 | 27.0 | 13.6 | 0.9 | 4.9 | 9.4 | 63.8 | | | (Mean) | | 10.3 | 41.3 | -4.8 | 28.7 | 5.2 | 27.0 | 2.7 | 76.2 |
| 7.3 | 7.3 | 7.5 | 2.9 | 0.7 | 6.3 | 1.6 | 65.2 | | | (StdDev) | | 8.3 | 6.0 | 3.7 | 9.0 | 5.9 | 5.5 | 1.9 | 3.0 |

| Non Man % | Own Occ % | Coun Ten % | Unem % | Born NCom % | Agric % | Aged % | Dist Card m. | Clus | PA No | Constituency Name | Par | Par Mar % | Con Vote % | Con Res Vote % | Lab Vote % | Lab Res Vote % | All Vote % | PCTurn Out % |
|---|---|---|---|---|---|---|---|---|---|---|---|---|---|---|---|---|---|---|
| | | | | | | | | | | **WELSH WALES** | | | | | | | | |
| 40.2 | 53.5 | 42.5 | 21.5 | 0.3 | 0.5 | 9.6 | 30 | 14 | 1 | Aberavon | Lab All | 38.4 | 16.3 | -13.6 | 58.8 | 14.9 | 20.3 | 4.6 73.6 |
| 38.9 | 55.5 | 40.1 | 22.0 | 0.2 | 0.2 | 9.9 | 30 | 14 | 66 | Blaenau Gwent | Lab All | 54.9 | 11.2 | -19.5 | 70.0 | 26.6 | 15.1 | 3.8 76.9 |
| 48.7 | 58.6 | 32.6 | 16.9 | 0.4 | 0.7 | 7.2 | 10 | 6 | 109 | Caerphilly | Lab All | 24.4 | 19.7 | -18.9 | 45.6 | 10.7 | 21.2 | 13.6 74.5 |
| 41.0 | 65.7 | 25.9 | 17.0 | 0.3 | 0.7 | 9.7 | 50 | 22 | 172 | Cynon Valley | Lab All | 35.4 | 14.2 | -26.0 | 56.0 | 22.9 | 20.6 | 9.3 73.4 |
| 57.7 | 71.9 | 20.7 | 11.3 | 0.3 | 1.4 | 10.5 | 46 | 28 | 274 | Gower | Lab Con | 2.7 | 35.4 | -14.3 | 38.1 | 15.5 | 23.4 | 3.2 78.7 |
| 40.8 | 53.1 | 38.1 | 15.5 | 0.3 | 0.7 | 8.6 | 20 | 14 | 337 | Islwyn | Lab All | 36.8 | 14.1 | -20.8 | 59.3 | 20.7 | 22.5 | 4.0 77.7 |
| 43.3 | 60.8 | 32.9 | 17.1 | 0.3 | 2.0 | 11.1 | 61 | 22 | 382 | Llanelli | Lab Con | 28.3 | 19.9 | -18.9 | 48.2 | 15.1 | 18.9 | 12.2 75.4 |
| 38.5 | 52.8 | 39.8 | 20.6 | 0.3 | 0.4 | 9.4 | 27 | 14 | 400 | Merthyr Tydfil & Rhy | Lab All | 52.7 | 12.6 | -18.4 | 67.3 | 24.5 | 14.7 | 4.8 72.5 |
| 44.5 | 60.3 | 30.1 | 15.4 | 0.3 | 0.6 | 10.5 | 37 | 22 | 414 | Neath | Lab All | 32.2 | 17.4 | -21.8 | 53.6 | 19.5 | 21.4 | 7.2 76.5 |
| 38.4 | 64.9 | 33.2 | 16.2 | 0.3 | 1.1 | 8.4 | 12 | 14 | 444 | Ogmore | Lab All | 44.0 | 14.7 | -22.4 | 59.2 | 23.2 | 15.3 | 7.9 76.9 |
| 54.0 | 64.9 | 29.0 | 13.3 | 0.6 | 0.5 | 7.3 | 12 | 6 | 464 | Pontypridd | Lab All | 19.7 | 22.9 | -20.4 | 45.6 | 15.3 | 25.8 | 4.7 72.7 |
| 37.8 | 76.1 | 17.5 | 22.5 | 0.3 | 0.2 | 10.4 | 30 | 22 | 477 | Rhondda | Lab All | 44.8 | 8.3 | -33.4 | 61.7 | 29.9 | 16.9 | 10.2 76.2 |
| 44.8 | 58.1 | 36.0 | 17.0 | 0.3 | 0.2 | 8.1 | 40 | 14 | 564 | Swansea E | Lab All | 33.0 | 19.7 | -16.1 | 54.4 | 16.0 | 21.4 | 3.7 71.5 |
| 58.1 | 57.4 | 28.8 | 16.0 | 1.3 | 0.1 | 10.7 | 40 | 11 | 565 | Swansea W | Lab Con | 5.5 | 36.6 | -4.9 | 42.1 | 9.6 | 18.8 | 1.9 73.5 |
| 47.1 | 39.5 | 55.8 | 16.9 | 0.4 | 0.7 | 8.1 | 22 | 27 | 578 | Torfaen | Lab All | 19.0 | 22.3 | -3.7 | 47.3 | -0.6 | 28.3 | 2.0 74.4 |
| 44.9 | 59.4 | 33.5 | 17.3 | 0.4 | 0.7 | 9.3 | 31.1 | | | (Mean) | | 31.5 | 19.0 | -18.2 | 53.8 | 17.6 | 20.3 | 6.2 75.1 |
| 6.9 | 8.7 | 9.3 | 3.2 | 0.3 | 0.5 | 1.3 | 14.8 | | | (StdDev) | | 15.3 | 8.0 | 7.4 | 9.2 | 7.6 | 3.9 | 3.7 2.1 |
| | | | | | | | | | | **Y FRO GYMRAEG** | | | | | | | | |
| 49.3 | 62.8 | 23.2 | 16.2 | 0.3 | 8.6 | 11.3 | 164 | 10 | 108 | Caernarfon | PC Con | 31.7 | 21.1 | -28.7 | 19.4 | 4.8 | 6.8 | 52.7 78.6 |
| 43.9 | 65.0 | 22.1 | 10.8 | 0.3 | 17.0 | 11.1 | 65 | 2 | 123 | Carmarthen | Lab Con | 2.2 | 29.4 | -24.7 | 31.6 | 24.9 | 11.0 | 27.0 82.1 |
| 48.3 | 64.6 | 18.3 | 10.9 | 0.7 | 17.0 | 11.4 | 106 | 2 | 127 | Ceredigion & Pembrok | All Con | 12.0 | 29.8 | -27.0 | 14.5 | 10.6 | 41.8 | 12.9 77.8 |
| 58.2 | 60.3 | 25.2 | 13.3 | 0.7 | 2.9 | 12.8 | 173 | 29 | 153 | Conwy | Con All | 10.8 | 41.7 | -2.7 | 17.1 | -9.4 | 30.8 | 10.4 76.4 |
| 42.9 | 66.6 | 23.9 | 13.6 | 0.3 | 12.0 | 11.9 | 145 | 2 | 398 | Meirionnydd Nant Con | PC Con | 10.7 | 28.5 | -22.2 | 15.1 | 4.5 | 17.2 | 39.2 81.3 |
| 49.0 | 59.0 | 27.6 | 15.6 | 0.6 | 6.7 | 9.3 | 173 | 17 | 649 | Ynys Mon | Con PC | 4.2 | 37.5 | -8.8 | 16.9 | -3.7 | 12.3 | 33.3 79.6 |
| 48.6 | 62.0 | 23.4 | 13.4 | 0.5 | 10.7 | 11.3 | 137.7 | | | (Mean) | | 11.9 | 31.3 | -19.0 | 19.1 | 5.3 | 20.0 | 29.3 79.3 |
| 5.4 | 2.4 | 3.1 | 2.2 | 0.2 | 5.7 | 1.2 | 43.7 | | | (StdDev) | | 10.4 | 7.3 | 10.7 | 6.3 | 11.9 | 13.5 | 16.1 3.2 |

# SCOTLAND

Constituency Name: CENTRAL INDUSTRIAL BELT

| Non Man % | Own Occ % | Coun Ten % | Unem % | Born NCom % | Agric % | Aged % | Dist Edin m. | Clus | PA No | Constituency Name | Par | Mar Vote % | Con Vote % | Con Res % | Lab Vote % | Lab Res % | All Vote % | SNP Vote % | Turn Out % |
|---|---|---|---|---|---|---|---|---|---|---|---|---|---|---|---|---|---|---|---|
| 62.3 | 50.6 | 43.8 | 13.1 | 0.6 | 1.5 | 10.4 | 72 | 15 | 19 | Ayr | Con Lab | 16.0 | 42.8 | 4.0 | 26.8 | -6.7 | 25.6 | 4.9 | 76.7 |
| 39.4 | 21.7 | 69.0 | 17.0 | 0.3 | 7.1 | 8.6 | 93 | 1 | 124 | Carrick Cumm & Doon | Lab Con | 27.4 | 24.1 | -0.2 | 51.5 | 10.0 | 17.9 | 6.5 | 74.3 |
| 44.2 | 27.4 | 67.4 | 13.8 | 0.4 | 1.5 | 7.6 | 28 | 3 | 144 | Clackmannan | Lab SNP | 26.8 | 18.0 | -5.8 | 45.8 | -3.5 | 17.2 | 19.0 | 75.6 |
| 57.2 | 26.3 | 69.4 | 17.2 | 0.4 | 0.1 | 8.4 | 50 | 3 | 147 | Clydebank & Milngavie | Lab All | 20.0 | 20.3 | -2.6 | 44.8 | -6.9 | 24.8 | 9.2 | 75.9 |
| 51.0 | 36.2 | 56.3 | 14.8 | 0.4 | 4.4 | 7.9 | 42 | 1 | 148 | Clydesdale | Lab Con | 10.6 | 28.2 | -4.4 | 38.8 | 2.5 | 21.5 | 11.4 | 76.5 |
| 55.9 | 27.8 | 70.6 | 13.7 | 0.5 | 0.8 | 5.1 | 35 | 3 | 169 | Cumbernauld & Kilsyth | Lab All | 29.4 | 13.6 | -10.8 | 49.2 | -0.6 | 19.8 | 17.4 | 76.5 |
| 51.6 | 45.2 | 47.7 | 18.3 | 0.4 | 3.0 | 9.8 | 74 | 15 | 170 | Cunninghame N | Con Lab | 4.1 | 38.7 | 4.2 | 34.6 | -1.7 | 18.1 | 8.6 | 75.7 |
| 44.2 | 20.7 | 76.2 | 21.1 | 0.3 | 0.9 | 6.7 | 70 | 3 | 171 | Cunninghame S | Lab Con | 32.9 | 21.2 | 4.0 | 54.1 | -2.8 | 17.8 | 6.9 | 73.6 |
| 52.1 | 35.0 | 54.3 | 16.4 | 0.7 | 1.2 | 7.8 | 58 | 27 | 201 | Dumbarton | Lab Con | 4.9 | 31.8 | 2.1 | 36.7 | -7.0 | 22.8 | 8.7 | 75.1 |
| 49.8 | 24.1 | 64.0 | 20.4 | 1.0 | 0.4 | 9.0 | 55 | 16 | 203 | Dundee E | SNP Lab | 10.8 | 15.5 | -5.6 | 33.0 | -20.3 | 7.7 | 43.8 | 73.7 |
| 52.6 | 21.9 | 66.6 | 17.2 | 0.9 | 0.1 | 10.1 | 55 | 16 | 204 | Dundee W | Lab Con | 21.7 | 21.7 | 1.9 | 43.5 | -11.3 | 17.1 | 17.1 | 74.4 |
| 37.6 | 19.2 | 74.0 | 12.4 | 0.6 | 1.3 | 8.5 | 16 | 3 | 205 | Dunfermline E | Lab Con | 31.5 | 18.8 | -0.8 | 51.5 | -2.3 | 20.1 | 7.2 | 72.0 |
| 52.5 | 38.2 | 52.9 | 10.0 | 0.7 | 0.9 | 7.7 | 16 | 27 | 206 | Dunfermline W | Lab Con | 6.9 | 29.2 | -3.0 | 36.0 | -5.0 | 26.2 | 7.8 | 73.5 |
| 57.3 | 30.2 | 67.1 | 13.2 | 0.4 | 1.4 | 5.7 | 41 | 3 | 215 | East Kilbride | Lab All | 9.2 | 24.3 | -3.4 | 37.1 | -8.7 | 27.9 | 10.1 | 77.0 |
| 74.5 | 70.7 | 26.1 | 8.3 | 0.5 | 0.9 | 7.6 | 48 | 23 | 218 | Eastwood | Con All | 19.0 | 46.6 | -6.9 | 20.1 | 0.7 | 27.6 | 5.8 | 76.2 |
| 46.3 | 25.7 | 70.0 | 14.3 | 0.4 | 0.6 | 8.0 | 26 | 3 | 239 | Falkirk E | Lab Con | 26.7 | 21.0 | -0.3 | 47.7 | -5.4 | 18.5 | 11.9 | 72.3 |
| 50.1 | 24.0 | 71.3 | 15.2 | 0.4 | 0.7 | 8.9 | 26 | 3 | 240 | Falkirk W | Lab Con | 24.5 | 21.0 | 0.3 | 45.6 | -7.8 | 20.4 | 13.0 | 74.0 |
| 41.7 | 24.0 | 70.0 | 14.8 | 0.6 | 1.2 | 7.5 | 31 | 3 | 246 | Fife Central | Lab All | 19.8 | 22.5 | 1.6 | 43.1 | -9.6 | 23.4 | 6.6 | 72.5 |
| 54.7 | 48.7 | 33.8 | 8.9 | 1.0 | 8.2 | 11.5 | 49 | 2 | 247 | Fife NE | Con All | 5.9 | 46.1 | -0.1 | 6.5 | -11.2 | 40.2 | 6.6 | 73.7 |
| 62.0 | 43.6 | 45.2 | 14.3 | 0.5 | 0.1 | 10.9 | 44 | 14 | 259 | Glasgow Cathcart | Lab Con | 10.9 | 30.5 | -3.8 | 41.4 | 1.5 | 22.5 | 5.6 | 75.8 |
| 46.3 | 27.6 | 51.5 | 24.4 | 1.5 | 0.1 | 12.2 | 44 | 26 | 260 | Glasgow Central | Lab Con | 34.1 | 19.0 | -3.6 | 53.0 | 0.8 | 16.7 | 10.3 | 62.8 |
| 47.2 | 7.9 | 87.3 | 24.3 | 0.3 | 0.0 | 10.8 | 44 | 16 | 261 | Glasgow Garscadden | Lab Con | 38.6 | 15.4 | -0.1 | 56.2 | -3.2 | 17.6 | 10.2 | 69.1 |
| 48.4 | 23.2 | 64.2 | 20.9 | 0.3 | 0.2 | 12.3 | 44 | 16 | 262 | Glasgow Govan | Lab All | 35.2 | 19.4 | 1.6 | 55.0 | -1.7 | 19.7 | 6.0 | 71.6 |
| 69.3 | 48.6 | 21.9 | 13.9 | 2.8 | 0.1 | 10.8 | 44 | 8 | 263 | Glasgow Hillhead | All Lab | 2.8 | 23.6 | -22.0 | 33.3 | 4.5 | 36.2 | 5.4 | 72.0 |
| 46.9 | 16.6 | 68.6 | 24.8 | 2.5 | 0.1 | 9.7 | 44 | 4 | 264 | Glasgow Maryhill | Lab All | 33.0 | 14.8 | -2.7 | 55.2 | -2.6 | 22.2 | 7.1 | 65.5 |
| 50.5 | 27.1 | 64.6 | 22.4 | 1.1 | 0.1 | 7.6 | 44 | 3 | 265 | Glasgow Pollok | Lab Con | 31.8 | 20.5 | -1.1 | 52.3 | -1.0 | 17.4 | 9.9 | 68.2 |
| 36.6 | 2.6 | 93.3 | 33.7 | 0.1 | 0.1 | 6.5 | 44 | 3 | 266 | Glasgow Provan | Lab All | 49.5 | 10.8 | -5.7 | 64.4 | 5.8 | 15.0 | 8.8 | 65.2 |
| 50.8 | 27.5 | 67.4 | 20.0 | 0.2 | 0.1 | 8.7 | 44 | 3 | 267 | Glasgow Rutherglen | Lab All | 20.5 | 18.0 | -3.1 | 48.3 | -5.4 | 27.8 | 5.5 | 75.2 |
| 46.1 | 26.3 | 65.3 | 24.3 | 0.2 | 0.2 | 10.4 | 44 | 16 | 268 | Glasgow Shettleston | Lab Con | 35.0 | 19.1 | 0.9 | 54.2 | -2.1 | 18.5 | 7.9 | 68.3 |
| 40.3 | 17.8 | 71.0 | 26.1 | 0.3 | 0.0 | 9.7 | 44 | 16 | 269 | Glasgow Springburn | Lab All | 50.7 | 13.1 | -2.7 | 64.7 | 5.7 | 14.1 | 8.1 | 65.1 |
| 41.3 | 18.0 | 74.8 | 21.2 | 0.3 | 0.3 | 8.5 | 66 | 3 | 279 | Greenock & P Glasgow | Lab All | 10.5 | 9.8 | -6.7 | 46.8 | -11.5 | 36.3 | 6.8 | 74.2 |
| 52.8 | 28.4 | 67.5 | 21.0 | 0.3 | 0.6 | 6.9 | 37 | 3 | 287 | Hamilton | Lab All | 32.3 | 19.2 | -4.3 | 52.4 | 1.6 | 20.1 | 8.2 | 75.7 |
| 46.1 | 29.9 | 65.6 | 15.3 | 0.3 | 3.0 | 8.7 | 60 | 3 | 343 | Kilmarnock & Loudoun | Lab Con | 19.0 | 24.7 | -0.8 | 43.6 | -2.2 | 22.7 | 9.0 | 75.6 |

| Non Man % | Own Occ % | Coun Ten % | Unem % | Born NCom % | Agric % | Aged % | Dist Edin m. | Clus | PA No | Constituency Name | Party Marg | Marg Vote % | Con Vote % | Con Res % | Lab Vote % | Lab Res % | Lab All Res Vote % | SNP Vote % | Turn Out % |
|---|---|---|---|---|---|---|---|---|---|---|---|---|---|---|---|---|---|---|---|
| 50.7 | 30.8 | 62.8 | 12.9 | 0.5 | 0.9 | 10.1 | 25 | 15 | 347 | Kirkcaldy | Lab Con | 14.0 | 26.3 | 0.8 | 40.3 | -7.6 | 24.3 | 9.0 | 71.9 |
| 47.3 | 18.0 | 79.0 | 21.7 | 0.2 | 0.9 | 6.6 | 34 | 3 | 406 | Monklands E | Lab Con | 27.4 | 23.9 | 6.8 | 51.2 | -6.0 | 16.0 | 8.9 | 73.1 |
| 54.2 | 27.3 | 69.0 | 18.9 | 0.2 | 0.8 | 7.3 | 36 | 3 | 407 | Monklands W | Lab Con | 32.2 | 22.0 | -0.0 | 54.2 | 2.1 | 17.3 | 6.5 | 75.7 |
| 43.1 | 14.9 | 81.6 | 22.0 | 0.3 | 0.6 | 7.4 | 35 | 3 | 412 | Motherwell N | Lab Con | 42.2 | 15.5 | -1.2 | 57.8 | -0.1 | 14.1 | 12.6 | 75.0 |
| 46.3 | 17.4 | 79.8 | 20.6 | 0.2 | 0.2 | 8.7 | 35 | 3 | 413 | Motherwell S | Lab Con | 32.5 | 20.0 | 3.8 | 52.4 | -6.2 | 17.8 | 9.8 | 72.9 |
| 51.5 | 31.5 | 60.0 | 17.3 | 0.5 | 0.2 | 9.5 | 51 | 16 | 452 | Paisley N | Lab All | 21.9 | 21.4 | -2.2 | 45.6 | -5.3 | 23.7 | 8.0 | 68.6 |
| 54.7 | 23.8 | 72.3 | 15.4 | 0.3 | 0.3 | 7.9 | 51 | 3 | 453 | Paisley S | Lab All | 17.3 | 20.7 | 0.7 | 41.4 | -13.3 | 24.1 | 13.0 | 72.5 |
| 60.7 | 45.1 | 47.6 | 10.2 | 0.6 | 1.4 | 6.8 | 66 | 13 | 476 | Renfrew W & Invercly | Lab All | 3.2 | 32.7 | -5.6 | 29.0 | -5.5 | 29.5 | 8.7 | 78.1 |
| 62.3 | 43.3 | 44.3 | 10.9 | 0.8 | 4.1 | 8.8 | 37 | 15 | 539 | Stirling | Con Lab | 12.0 | 40.0 | -0.2 | 27.9 | -1.0 | 23.9 | 8.2 | 75.7 |
| 73.0 | 66.9 | 28.9 | 7.3 | 1.1 | 0.4 | 6.1 | 46 | 9 | 548 | Stra'kelvin & Bearsd | Con Lab | 7.7 | 36.4 | -14.4 | 25.6 | 2.9 | 28.7 | 9.2 | 79.4 |
| 51.2 | 29.8 | 62.4 | 17.3 | 0.6 | 1.2 | 8.6 | 45.3 | | | (Mean) | | 22.4 | 23.8 | -2.1 | 44.0 | -3.4 | 23.0 | 10.1 | 73.2 |
| 8.6 | 13.8 | 15.7 | 5.5 | 0.5 | 1.8 | 1.7 | 15.5 | | | (StdDev) | | 12.5 | 9.0 | 5.1 | 11.9 | 5.7 | 6.3 | 6.2 | 3.7 |

## LOTHIAN AND BORDERS

| Non Man % | Own Occ % | Coun Ten % | Unem % | Born NCom % | Agric % | Aged % | Dist Edin m. | Clus | PA No | Constituency Name | Party Marg | Marg Vote % | Con Vote % | Con Res % | Lab Vote % | Lab Res % | Lab All Res Vote % | SNP Vote % | Turn Out % |
|---|---|---|---|---|---|---|---|---|---|---|---|---|---|---|---|---|---|---|---|
| 45.5 | 42.1 | 43.1 | 11.1 | 0.4 | 9.3 | 9.4 | 73 | 24 | 202 | Dumfries | Con All | 20.7 | 44.5 | 3.4 | 20.8 | -0.7 | 23.9 | 10.8 | 73.0 |
| 52.9 | 30.4 | 59.1 | 10.0 | 0.5 | 5.9 | 9.7 | 24 | 1 | 217 | East Lothian | Lab Con | 13.1 | 30.8 | -1.4 | 43.9 | 8.9 | 20.9 | 4.4 | 76.2 |
| 73.3 | 62.5 | 8.8 | 11.0 | 2.1 | 0.4 | 11.9 | 0 | 18 | 221 | Edinburgh Central | Con Lab | 6.9 | 38.0 | -13.9 | 31.1 | 9.4 | 25.6 | 4.9 | 64.9 |
| 57.6 | 47.7 | 43.5 | 13.8 | 0.7 | 0.3 | 10.6 | 0 | 14 | 222 | Edinburgh E | Lab Con | 16.3 | 28.6 | -4.7 | 44.9 | 4.2 | 21.0 | 5.5 | 70.4 |
| 54.3 | 46.1 | 38.2 | 14.0 | 0.9 | 0.1 | 10.8 | 0 | 14 | 223 | Edinburgh Leith | Lab All | 12.2 | 26.3 | -7.6 | 39.7 | -0.7 | 27.5 | 6.5 | 67.3 |
| 65.4 | 51.5 | 38.8 | 8.2 | 1.2 | 0.5 | 7.7 | 0 | 13 | 224 | Edinburgh Pentlands | Con All | 9.9 | 39.2 | -2.1 | 23.9 | -8.6 | 29.3 | 6.1 | 73.4 |
| 70.6 | 53.4 | 33.8 | 10.4 | 1.6 | 0.7 | 10.4 | 0 | 11 | 225 | Edinburgh S | Con All | 8.2 | 36.8 | -6.3 | 28.6 | -1.9 | 28.6 | 5.0 | 71.7 |
| 69.0 | 58.4 | 31.1 | 6.1 | 0.9 | 0.6 | 10.3 | 0 | 28 | 226 | Edinburgh W | Con All | 1.1 | 38.2 | -7.1 | 20.1 | -7.9 | 37.1 | 4.6 | 75.7 |
| 42.4 | 40.2 | 40.4 | 12.4 | 0.4 | 20.1 | 10.3 | 86 | ○24 | 254 | Galloway & U Niths | Con SNP | 13.9 | 44.7 | -3.5 | 11.4 | -8.7 | 13.1 | 30.8 | 75.8 |
| 46.9 | 23.8 | 71.3 | 14.1 | 0.4 | 1.5 | 6.9 | 18 | 3 | 373 | Linlithgow | Lab Con | 26.0 | 19.1 | -2.6 | 45.1 | -6.5 | 17.0 | 18.4 | 75.2 |
| 49.1 | 22.6 | 72.1 | 13.7 | 0.7 | 1.8 | 5.4 | 15 | 3 | 381 | Livingston | Lab All | 11.9 | 23.9 | 0.9 | 37.3 | -12.3 | 25.4 | 13.3 | 71.7 |
| 53.0 | 27.5 | 60.9 | 8.4 | 0.5 | 2.0 | 7.1 | 7 | 3 | 402 | Midlothian | Lab All | 13.6 | 21.9 | -6.8 | 42.7 | -0.7 | 29.2 | 6.2 | 75.0 |
| 40.7 | 32.7 | 48.1 | 8.4 | 0.4 | 15.4 | 11.2 | 51 | 24 | 489 | Roxburgh & Berwicks | All Con | 10.7 | 39.6 | 2.0 | 7.4 | -16.4 | 50.3 | 2.7 | 75.8 |
| 49.3 | 40.6 | 42.8 | 7.8 | 0.5 | 9.1 | 11.2 | 46 | 24 | 582 | Tweeddale Ettrick | All Con | 29.6 | 28.9 | -13.3 | 7.6 | -11.8 | 58.5 | 5.0 | 77.8 |
| 55.0 | 41.4 | 45.1 | 10.7 | 0.8 | 4.8 | 9.5 | 22.9 | | | (Mean) | | 13.9 | 32.9 | -4.0 | 28.9 | -3.8 | 29.1 | 8.9 | 73.1 |
| 10.7 | 12.7 | 16.7 | 2.7 | 0.5 | 6.4 | 1.9 | 29.5 | | | (StdDev) | | 7.5 | 8.3 | 5.6 | 13.9 | 7.8 | 12.3 | 7.6 | 3.7 |

## NORTH OF SCOTLAND

| No | Constituency | Prof Man % | Own Occ % | Coun Ten % | Unem % | Cath % | Agric % | Aged % | Dist Belf | Clus |
|---|---|---|---|---|---|---|---|---|---|---|
| 2 | Aberdeen N | 46.9 | 15.3 | 79.1 | 9.4 | 0.9 | 0.7 | 9.3 | 119 | 16 |
| 3 | Aberdeen S | 64.8 | 52.7 | 28.5 | 7.2 | 1.5 | 1.0 | 10.8 | 119 | 11 |
| 9 | Angus E | 52.6 | 40.7 | 43.6 | 9.9 | 0.7 | 6.9 | 9.3 | 84 | 1 |
| 13 | Argyll & Bute | 50.2 | 40.9 | 37.0 | 12.6 | 0.7 | 12.4 | 10.7 | 123 | 24 |
| 21 | Banff & Buchan | 40.0 | 41.1 | 46.8 | 9.1 | 0.3 | 15.2 | 8.5 | 162 | 24 |
| 110 | Caithness & Suther | 46.2 | 37.6 | 42.4 | 11.3 | 0.4 | 10.4 | 9.3 | 288 | 24 |
| 272 | Gordon | 54.0 | 50.4 | 32.7 | 4.5 | 0.8 | 9.5 | 6.7 | 134 | 1 |
| 332 | Inverness Nairn | 56.0 | 39.1 | 45.8 | 11.6 | 0.6 | 5.6 | 8.7 | 158 | 1 |
| 344 | Kincardine & Deeside | 58.7 | 45.3 | 38.5 | 5.9 | 1.0 | 7.5 | 8.7 | 105 | 1 |
| 410 | Moray | 40.7 | 41.2 | 39.7 | 10.2 | 0.5 | 10.0 | 8.5 | 161 | 1 |
| 448 | Orkney & Shetland | 43.7 | 50.2 | 29.0 | 6.6 | 0.8 | 14.7 | 9.1 | 378 | 24 |
| 458 | Perth & Kinross | 55.6 | 42.8 | 40.9 | 9.5 | 0.7 | 6.4 | 10.5 | 44 | 1 |
| 485 | Ross Cromarty & Skye | 48.7 | 44.9 | 36.6 | 11.5 | 0.6 | 9.6 | 8.4 | 207 | 24 |
| 569 | Tayside N | 47.8 | 40.3 | 37.3 | 10.0 | 0.6 | 12.8 | 11.1 | 69 | 24 |
| 618 | Western Isles | 38.4 | 64.3 | 23.8 | 17.1 | 0.3 | 4.9 | 10.8 | 273 | 29 |
| | (Mean) | 49.6 | 43.1 | 40.1 | 9.8 | 0.7 | 8.5 | 9.4 | 161.6 | |
| | (StdDev) | 7.4 | 10.3 | 12.6 | 3.0 | 0.3 | 4.4 | 1.2 | 90.6 | |

| Constituency | Party | | | | | | | | |
|---|---|---|---|---|---|---|---|---|---|
| Aberdeen N | Lab All | 22.3 | 18.1 | 1.4 | 47.0 | -10.7 | 24.7 | 9.3 | 65.0 |
| Aberdeen S | Con Lab | 9.1 | 38.9 | -5.2 | 29.9 | 0.6 | 26.2 | 5.0 | 68.7 |
| Angus E | Con SNP | 8.1 | 44.1 | 2.9 | 36.0 | -16.1 | 11.4 | 36.0 | 73.5 |
| Argyll & Bute | Con All | 11.1 | 38.6 | -5.8 | 9.3 | -7.6 | 27.5 | 24.6 | 72.9 |
| Banff & Buchan | Con SNP | 2.3 | 39.7 | -1.2 | 7.8 | -12.8 | 15.0 | 37.4 | 67.0 |
| Caithness & Suther | All Con | 29.4 | 22.7 | -17.5 | 14.3 | -9.0 | 52.0 | 11.0 | 75.4 |
| Gordon | All Con | 1.8 | 42.0 | -8.3 | 8.5 | -4.1 | 43.8 | 5.7 | 70.1 |
| Inverness Nairn | Con All | 16.3 | 29.8 | -7.9 | 14.4 | -15.5 | 46.1 | 9.8 | 70.5 |
| Kincardine & Deeside | Con SNP | 18.3 | 47.7 | 2.2 | 15.2 | -4.4 | 29.4 | 7.7 | 71.5 |
| Moray | Con SNP | 4.0 | 39.2 | -2.7 | 7.3 | -15.1 | 18.3 | 35.2 | 71.1 |
| Orkney & Shetland | All Con | 20.3 | 25.6 | -23.3 | 13.1 | 0.7 | 45.9 | 15.4 | 67.8 |
| Perth & Kinross | Con SNP | 15.1 | 40.2 | -1.6 | 9.9 | -14.1 | 24.7 | 25.1 | 72.3 |
| Ross Cromarty & Skye | All Con | 4.9 | 33.7 | -10.1 | 14.0 | -5.3 | 38.5 | 13.8 | 72.6 |
| Tayside N | Con SNP | 26.8 | 51.0 | 7.4 | 5.4 | -12.1 | 19.2 | 24.3 | 72.6 |
| Western Isles | SNP Lab | 24.5 | 9.6 | -33.4 | 30.1 | 3.0 | 5.8 | 54.5 | 66.5 |
| (Mean) | | 14.3 | 34.7 | -6.9 | 15.6 | -8.2 | 28.6 | 21.0 | 70.5 |
| (StdDev) | | 9.2 | 11.5 | 10.8 | 11.4 | 6.3 | 14.0 | 14.6 | 3.0 |

## NORTHERN IRELAND

WEST OF R. BANN

| PA No | Constituency Name | Prof Man % | Own Occ % | Coun Ten % | Unem % | Cath % | Agric % | Aged % | Dist Belf m. | Clus |
|---|---|---|---|---|---|---|---|---|---|---|
| 245 | Fermanagh & S Tyrone | 7.7 | 57.1 | 33.7 | 21.2 | 40.1 | 32.4 | 8.0 | 86 | 24 |
| 250 | Foyle | 9.4 | 40.2 | 52.3 | 24.7 | 54.7 | 8.1 | 6.1 | 72 | 1 |
| 383 | Londonderry E | 9.7 | 47.7 | 42.2 | 19.8 | 28.2 | 19.0 | 6.9 | 55 | 24 |
| 427 | Newry & Armagh | 8.3 | 50.4 | 42.4 | 21.2 | 46.1 | 21.5 | 7.1 | 40 | 24 |
| 586 | Ulster Mid | 7.6 | 54.3 | 36.4 | 23.3 | 42.0 | 35.5 | 7.2 | 71 | 24 |
| 588 | Upper Bann | 10.0 | 41.3 | 49.6 | 16.4 | 30.4 | 9.6 | 7.2 | 25 | 1 |
| | (Mean) | 8.8 | 48.5 | 42.8 | 21.1 | 40.2 | 21.0 | 7.1 | 58.2 | |
| | (StdDev) | 1.0 | 6.8 | 7.2 | 2.9 | 9.9 | 11.3 | 0.6 | 22.7 | |

| Constituency Name | PartyMarg | OU Vote % | DU Vote % | AP Vote % | SDL Vote % | SF Vote % | Oth Vote % | TO % |
|---|---|---|---|---|---|---|---|---|
| | PM | OU | DU | AP | SDL | SF | Oth | TO |
| Fermanagh & S Tyrone | OU SF | 12.8 | 47.6 | 0.0 | 0.0 | 16.5 | 34.8 | 1.1 | 88.7 |
| Foyle | SDL DU | 15.6 | 0.0 | 30.5 | 2.1 | 46.0 | 20.3 | 1.1 | 78.1 |
| Londonderry E | OU DU | 14.1 | 37.9 | 23.8 | 4.7 | 18.3 | 13.8 | 1.6 | 76.3 |
| Newry & Armagh | OU SDL | 3.3 | 40.0 | 0.0 | 0.0 | 36.8 | 20.9 | 2.3 | 76.1 |
| Ulster Mid | DU SF | 0.1 | 13.1 | 30.0 | 3.2 | 22.4 | 29.9 | 1.4 | 84.4 |
| Upper Bann | OU SDL | 39.0 | 56.9 | 10.4 | 0.0 | 17.8 | 9.4 | 5.5 | 72.0 |
| (Mean) | | 14.2 | 32.6 | 15.8 | 1.7 | 26.3 | 21.5 | 2.2 | 79.3 |
| (StdDev) | | 13.7 | 21.6 | 14.2 | 2.0 | 12.2 | 9.5 | 1.7 | 6.1 |

## EAST OF R. BANN

| PA No | Constituency Name | Prof Man % | Own Occ % | Coun Ten % | Unem % | Cath % | Agric % | Aged % | Dist Belf m. | Clus | Party Marg | OU Vote % | DU Vote % | AP Vote % | SDL Vote % | SF Vote % | Oth Vote % | TO % |
|---|---|---|---|---|---|---|---|---|---|---|---|---|---|---|---|---|---|---|
| 10 | Antrim E | 11.2 | 44.6 | 45.0 | 13.6 | 23.3 | 5.9 | 7.0 | 29 | 15 | OU DU | 37.4 | 36.4 | 19.9 | 2.7 | 0.0 | 1.5 | 65.1 |
| 11 | Antrim N | 13.2 | 50.3 | 43.9 | 15.1 | 10.9 | 19.9 | 7.5 | 22 | 11 | DU OU | 24.3 | 54.2 | 0.0 | 14.0 | 6.5 | 0.0 | 69.9 |
| 12 | Antrim S | 9.8 | 40.4 | 49.0 | 12.6 | 15.3 | 7.6 | 5.7 | 18 | 1 | OU DU | 45.7 | 28.2 | 11.9 | 8.7 | 4.2 | 1.4 | 65.6 |
| 38 | Belfast E | 12.2 | 58.6 | 22.3 | 11.3 | 4.6 | 0.2 | 10.6 | 0 | 22 | DU OU | 24.8 | 45.3 | 24.1 | 1.3 | 1.8 | 1.1 | 70.1 |
| 39 | Belfast N | 10.3 | 51.3 | 29.6 | 19.3 | 24.2 | 0.0 | 10.1 | 0 | 22 | OU DU | 36.2 | 19.5 | 9.1 | 14.0 | 12.9 | 5.7 | 69.4 |
| 40 | Belfast S | 11.1 | 56.0 | 18.5 | 12.2 | 16.1 | 0.2 | 11.3 | 0 | 18 | OU AP | 50.0 | 12.2 | 23.9 | 8.6 | 3.0 | 2.3 | 69.6 |
| 41 | Belfast W | 10.1 | 32.3 | 58.0 | 28.0 | 54.0 | 0.2 | 6.4 | 0 | 27 | SF SDL | 5.5 | 5.4 | 0.0 | 24.6 | 36.9 | 4.3 | 74.3 |
| 196 | Down N | 21.0 | 63.7 | 26.8 | 7.9 | 5.9 | 3.9 | 8.5 | 12 | 12 | Oth AP | 20.3 | 0.0 | 22.1 | 1.6 | 0.0 | 56.1 | 66.3 |
| 197 | Down S | 9.4 | 48.8 | 41.8 | 17.9 | 42.4 | 18.4 | 7.3 | 22 | 24 | OU SDL | 40.3 | 7.3 | 3.6 | 39.2 | 7.9 | 1.7 | 76.7 |
| 350 | Lagan Valley | 16.3 | 50.0 | 41.0 | 11.4 | 16.1 | 1.8 | 6.7 | 9 | 13 | OU DU | 59.2 | 16.8 | 11.3 | 6.4 | 4.3 | 2.0 | 67.6 |
| 546 | Strangford | 27.3 | 51.3 | 40.2 | 10.1 | 9.5 | 6.9 | 7.8 | 9 | 17 | OU DU | 48.8 | 30.0 | 15.8 | 4.4 | 0.0 | 0.0 | 65.0 |
| | (Mean) | 13.8 | 49.8 | 37.8 | 14.5 | 20.2 | 5.9 | 8.1 | 11.0 | | | 35.7 | 23.2 | 12.9 | 11.4 | 7.0 | 1.8 | 69.0 |
| | (StdDev) | 5.6 | 8.6 | 12.1 | 5.6 | 15.4 | 7.1 | 1.8 | 10.5 | | | 15.7 | 17.3 | 9.1 | 11.5 | 10.7 | 1.8 | 3.8 |

# Appendix B

The 1981 census contains approximately 5,000 separate variables for each parliamentary constituency, ranging from the occupational structure of the population to the amenities possessed by each housing unit. Previous ecological analyses have often treated this large pool of variables in a fragmented and unsystematic way. A typical approach has been to throw dozens of census variables into an ad hoc pool of potential predictors, extracting a few of them on the basis of their relationship to voting behaviour, and then attempting to make conceptual sense of the heterogeneous assortment of predictors that emerge.

This method has two major weaknesses. Firstly, it leads to highly speculative interpretations of the meaning of the results that emerge from the analysis, with the accompanying risk that however plausible the predictors may be, they can easily be misinterpreted. Secondly, as the census variables are often highly inter-correlated, it is easy to obtain unstable results, depending heavily on chance differences among the predictors, and likely to produce a spurious appearance of change in subsequent analysis (Hanushek and Jackson, 1977: 95-6)

An alternative procedure, which is used here, is to subject the matrix of census variables to factor analysis, a statistical technique which detects underlying patterns of relationships between a wide range of variables (see Kim and Mueller, 1978). Factor analysing the 1981 census variables produced four clear, unambiguous factors which represent the contextual characteristics of British parliamentary constituencies (see Table B.1). After a series of analyses in which a wide range of variables were included and then rejected, a final solution involving 16 variables was arrived at. The factor loadings for these final 16 variables are given in Table B.1. The factor loadings represent the correlation between each individual item and the four underlying factors identified in the analysis.

The first factor, labelled socio-economic status, differentiates constituencies which have high proportions of professional and managerial workers, and owner occupiers, and low proportions of unskilled and semi-skilled manual workers, the unemployed and council tenants. The second factor, immigrants, focuses on constituencies which have high proportions of households living in rented furnished accommodation, and sharing either a bathroom or toilet with another household. It reflects a high proportion of

Table B.1  FACTOR LOADINGS FOR CONSTITUENCY SOCIAL STRUCTURE
1981 CENSUS

| | Factor loadings | | | |
|---|---|---|---|---|
| | I | II | III | IV[a] |
| | (varimax rotation)[a] | | | |
| **Socio-economic status** | | | | |
| 1. % Workforce unskilled manual workers | -.89 | -.01 | -.01 | .04 |
| 2. % Workforce professional or managerial workers[b] | .87 | -.14 | .02 | -.14 |
| 3. % Workforce unemployed | -.85 | -.10 | -.05 | .14 |
| 4. % Households council tenants | -.83 | -.09 | .28 | .09 |
| 5. % Households owner occupiers | .81 | .24 | .17 | .00 |
| 6. % Workforce semi-skilled manual workers[c] | -.80 | .10 | -.08 | -.11 |
| **Immigrants** | | | | |
| 7. % Households sharing bathroom or toilet | -.09 | .91 | .20 | -.13 |
| 8. % Households renting furnished accommodation | -.15 | .87 | .20 | -.06 |
| 9. % Population born in Irish Republic | .10 | .84 | -.05 | -.11 |
| 10. % Population born in New Commonwealth | .08 | .77 | -.07 | -.16 |
| **Elderly** | | | | |
| 11. % Population age 70 to 74 | -.12 | .04 | .97 | .08 |
| 12. % Population age 65 to 69 | -.05 | .02 | .97 | .08 |
| 13. % Population retired | .03 | .16 | .94 | .04 |
| **Agriculture** | | | | |
| 14. % Workforce farm employers | -.09 | -.16 | .07 | .96 |
| 15. % Workforce agricultural workers | -.08 | -.15 | .08 | .95 |
| 16. % Workforce employed in agricultural industry | -.03 | -.12 | .06 | .95 |

[a]  Varimax rotated factor loadings from a principal components factor analysis with unities in the main diagonal. The eigenvalues of the four factors are, with variance explained in brackets: 4.65 (29%); 3.73 (23%); 3.00 (19%); 1.89 (12%). No other factor had an eigenvalue greater than one.

[b]  Registrar-General's socio-economic groups 1, 2, 3, 4 and 13.

[c]  Registrar-General's socio-economic groups 7, 10 and 15.

persons born in the Irish Republic and the New Commonwealth. Constituencies which have large numbers of the elderly make up the third factor, measured by persons aged 65 to 74, and by persons who have retired from the workforce. Finally, agriculture identifies constituencies which have high proportions of the workforce employed in different sectors of the agricultural industry.

The order in which the factors emerged from the analysis does not indicate that one is more important than the other, for example, that socio-economic status is a more important social structural measure than immigrants; on the contrary, it merely reflects the number of variables included in the final solution which loaded on each factor. The first factor, with an eigenvalue of 4.65, explained 29 percent of the variance, while the second, immigrants, had an eigenvalue of 3.73 and explained 23 percent of the variance. The remaining two factors, the elderly and agriculture, had eigenvalues of 3.00 and 1.89, and explained 19 percent and 12 percent of the variance respectively.

The use of these four multiple-item scales has four major advantages over the use of single-item indicators. Firstly, they are intuitively meaningful, whereas the general significance of many single items is often obscure or misleading. Secondly, multiple item scales reduce measurement error, since any error affecting one item is averaged out over all the items in the scale. Thirdly, they are statistically more reliable than single items, since there is less danger that an analysis will be biased by the idiosyncracies of any one item. Fourthly, the use of multiple item scales as predictors in regression analyses avoids the risks of multicollinearity (see Bohrnstedt and Carter, 1971; Kelley and McAllister, 1983)

Ideally the four scales should be unrelated to one another, as they are designed to measure different aspects of the social structure of parliamentary constituencies. The independence of each factor from the others is demonstrated in Table B.2, which gives the correlations between the scales. The results show that the scales have little association with one another; the strongest relationship is a negative correlation of -.28 between immigrants and socioeconomic status. The median correlation falls between .13 and .17 .

Table B.2   CORRELATIONS BETWEEN CONTEXTUAL SCALES

|                          | 1     | 2    | 3    | 4    |
|--------------------------|-------|------|------|------|
| 1.  Socio-economic status | –     | .02  | .13  | .17  |
| 2.  Immigrants            | -.02  | –    | .24  | -.31 |
| 3.  Elderly               | .13   | .24  | –    | .13  |
| 4.  Agriculture           | .17   | -.31 | .13  | –    |

For use in regression analysis, each factor was transformed into multiple -item scales by summing their component parts:

Socio-economic status = (% ProfMan + % ownOcc - % SkillMan - % Unemployed - % CounTen - % SemSkillMan)/Total N of items

The equations for the other three are as follows :

Immigrants = (% Share BathToilet + % FurnAcc + % Irish + % NewCom)/Total N of items

Elderly = (% Aged 70-74 + % Aged 65-69 + % Retired)/Total N of items

Agriculture = (% FarmEmp + % AgricWor + % AgricInd)/Total N of items

The resulting scales often had extreme outliers, which could have been potential sources of bias in the regression analyses. For example, the natural scale for agriculture had a minimum value of zero, a maximum value of 15.7, and a mean and standard deviation of 1.4 and 2.1, respectively. To cope with skewed distributions, constituencies which had a score greater than 2.5 standard deviations on either side of the mean were collapsed, being assigned the value of 2.5 standard deviations from the mean. This transformation affected a small number of constituencies at the lowest end of the socio-economic status scale, at the highest end of the agriculture and elderly scales, and at both ends of the immigrants scale.

As the resulting measures had no natural metric, they were transformed into 0 to 100 scales, so that a constituency with highest socio-economic status would score 100 and a constituency with the lowest socio-economic status would score 0. These linear transformations are intended to aid interpretation; they have no effect on the results of regression analyses which utilise the scales.

The means and standard deviations for the four scales used in the regression analysis

Table B.3 MEANS AND STANDARD DEVIATIONS OF SCALES BY NATION

|  | England Mean | Std Dev | Wales Mean | Std Dev | Scotland Mean | Std Dev | N.Ireland Mean | Std Dev |
|---|---|---|---|---|---|---|---|---|
| Socio-economic status | 57 | 21 | 55 | 13 | 28 | 22 | 43 | 15 |
| Immigrants | 26 | 26 | 12 | 13 | 10 | 11 | 14 | 9 |
| Elderly | 57 | 22 | 60 | 19 | 47 | 22 | 53 | 21 |
| Agriculture | 18 | 26 | 29 | 35 | 28 | 35 | 56 | 41 |

are given for each nation in Table B.3. It should be emphasised that the mean values are simply locations on the standardised 0-100 scales; for example, a score of 67 on the socio-economic status scale simply means that the constituency in question is 13 per cent above the mean constituency with a socio-economic status of 54. Since the status measure is a composite of the constituency's characteristics, namely occupational structure, unemployment level, and housing types, the score of 67 cannot be related to any one component entering the scale. The actual census values for the principal elements in the four scales are given for each constituency in Appendix A.

# References

ALLEN, D. Elliston (1968), *British Tastes*, (London: Hutchinson).

ALT, J., CREWE, I. and SARLVIK, Bo (1977), 'Angels in Plastic: the Liberal Surge in 1974', *Political Studies* 25: 343-368.

BALSOM, Denis, MADGWICK, Peter and VAN MECHELEN, Denis (1982), *The Political Consequences of Welsh Identity* (Glasgow: University of Strathclyde Studies in Public Policy No. 97).

BARNETT, Joel (1982), *Inside the Treasury* (London: Deutsch).

BBC-ITN (1983), *The BBC-ITN Guide to the New Parliamentary Constituencies* (Chichester: Parliamentary Research Services).

BERGLUND, Sten and LINDSTROM, Ulf (1978), *The Scandinavian Party System(s)* (Lund: Studentlitteratur).

BINDER, B.J.A. (1982), 'Relations between Central and Local Government since 1975: are the Associations Failing?', *Local Government Studies* 8:35-44

BIRCH, Anthony (1959), *Small-Town Politics* (London: Oxford University Press).

BLUMLER, Jay G. *et al.* (1971), 'Attitudes to the Monarch: their Structure and Development during a Ceremonial Occasion', *Political Studies* 19: 149-171.

BOGDANOR, Vernon (1981), *The People and the Party System* (Cambridge: Cambridge University Press).

BOHRNSTEDT, G.W. and CARTER, T.M. (1971), 'Robustness in Regression Analysis', in H.L. Costner, ed., *Sociological Methodology*, (San Francisco: Jossey-Bass), 118-146.

BOSANQUET, Nick (1983), *After the New Right* (London: Heinemann).

BRAND, J.A. (1978), *The National Movement in Scotland* (London: Routledge and Kegan Paul).

BRAND, J.A., McLEAN, D. and MILLER, William L. (1983), 'The Birth and Death of a Three-Party System: Scotland in the Seventies', *British Journal of Political Science* 13: 463-488.

BROWN, Philip J. and PAYNE, Clive (1975), 'Election Night Forecasting', *Journal of the Royal Statistical Society*, Series A, 138: 463-498.

BULPITT, Jim (1967), *Party Politics in English Local Government* (London: Longman).

BULPITT, Jim (1982), 'Conservatism, Unionism and the Problem of Territorial Management', in Peter Madgwick and Richard Rose, eds., *The Territorial Dimension in United Kingdom Politics* (London: Macmillan).

BULPITT, Jim (1983), *Territory and Power in the United Kingdom* (Manchester: Manchester University Press).

BUTLER, David E. (1947), 'The Relation of Seats to Votes', in R.B. McCallum and A. Readman, *The British General Election of 1945* (London: Oxford University Press), 277-295.

BUTLER, David E. (1951), 'An Examination of the Results', in H.G. Nicholas *The British General Election of 1950* (London: Macmillan), 306-333.

BUTLER, David E. (1965), 'A Comment on Professor Rasmussen's Article', *Parliamentary Affairs* 18: 455-457.

BUTLER, David E., ed., (1978), *Coalitions in British Politics* (London : Macmillan).

BUTLER, David E. (1983), *Governing without a Majority* (London: Collins).

BUTLER, David E. and KAVANAGH, Dennis (1980), *The British General Election of 19 79*(London: Macmillan).

BUTLER, David E. and KAVANAGH, Dennis (1984), *The British General Election of 1983* (London: Macmillan).

BUTLER, David E. and STOKES, Donald (1974), *Political Change in Britain* (London: Macmillan, 2nd edition).

BUTT PHILIP, Alan (1975), *The Welsh Question: Nation alism in Welsh Politics 1945-1970* (Cardiff: University of Wales Press).

CAIN, Bruce E., FEREJOHN, John A. and FIORINA, M.P. (1979), 'The House is not a Home: MPs and their Constituencies', *Legislative Studies Quarterly* 4: 501-523.

CAIRNCROSS, Alexander (1976), 'The Market and the State', in Thomas Wilson and Andrew Skinner, eds., *The Market and the State: Essays in Honour of Adam Smith* (London: Oxford University Press).

CAMPBELL, Angus,CONVERSE, Philip, MILLER, Warren and STOKES, Donald (1960) *The American Voter* (New York: John Wiley).

CMND 6453 (1976), *Local Government Finance* (London: HMSO).

CMND 6813 (1977), *Local Government Finance* (London: HMSO).

CMND 8085 (1980), *Government Observations on the First Report of the Committee on Welsh Affairs* (London: HMSO).

CMND 8449 (1981), *Alternatives to Domestic Rates*(London: HMSO).

CMND 8798 (1983), *Third Periodical Report of the Boundary Commission for Wales* (London: HMSO).

CONGDON, Tim (1978), *Monetarism: An Essay in Definition* (London: Centre for Policy Studies).

CONSERVATIVE CENTRAL OFFICE (1976), *The Right Approach* (London: Conservative Central Office).

CORNFORD, James, ed., (1975), *The Failure of the State* (London: Croom Helm).

CRAIG, F.W.S. (1981), *British Electoral Facts 1832-1980* (Chichester: Parliamentary Research Services).

CREWE, Ivor (1983) 'Dealignment and Realignment in the British Party System', (Chicago: American Political Science Association annual meeting).

CRITCHLEY, Julian (1973),'Strains and Stresses in the Conservative Party', *Political Quarterly* 44:401-410.

CROMPTON, Paul (1982), 'The Lothian Affair: A Battle of Principles?', in D. McCrone, ed., *The Scottish Government Yearbook 1983, 33-48*

CSE (1980), *The Alternative Economic Strategy* (London: Conference of Socialist Economists London Working Group).

CURTICE, John and STEED, Michael (1982), 'Electoral Choice and the Production of Government', *British Journal of Political Science* 12: 249-298.

DAVISON, W. Phillips and GORDENKER, Leon, eds., (1980), *Resolving Nationality Conflicts* (New York: Praeger Publishers).

DEWAR, Donald (1980), 'The Select Committee on Scottish Affairs', in H.M. and N.L. Drucker, eds., *The Scottish Government Yearbook 1981*(Edinburgh: Paul Harris), 9-25.

DRUCKER, H.M. (1982), 'The Curious Incident: Scottish Party Competition since 1979', in D. McCrone, ed., *The Scottish Government Yearbook 1983*, 16-32.

ELLIOTT, Sydney and WILFORD, R.A. (1983), *The 1982 Northern Ireland Assembly Election* (Glasgow: University of Strathclyde Studies in Public Policy No. 119).

EMERSON, Rupert (1960), *From Empire to Nation* (Boston: Beacon Press).

ESMAN, Milton, ed., (1977), *Ethnic Conflict in the Western World* (Ithaca, NY: Cornell University Press).

EVERITT, Brian (1974), *Cluster Analysis* (London: Heinemann).

FITTON, Martin (1973), 'Neighbourhood and Voting: a Sociometric Examination', *British Journal of Political Science* 3: 445- 472.

FOULKES, David, JONES, J. Barry and WILFORD, R.A., eds., (1983), *The Welsh Veto: the Wales Act 1978 and the Referendum* (Cardiff: University of Wales Press).

FRANKLIN, Mark N. and MUGHAN, Anthony (1978), 'The Decline of Class Voting in Britain', *American Political Science Review* 72: 523-34.

FRIEDMAN, Milton (1963), *Capitalism and Freedom* (Chicago: University of Chicago Press).

GOODHART, C.A.E. and BHANSALI, R.J. (1970), 'Political Economy', *Political Studies* 18: 43-106.

GREENWOOD, Royston (1982), 'The Politics of Central-Local Relations in England and Wales Since 1975',*West European Politics* 5: 253-269.

GREGORY, Roy (1980), 'Executive Power and Constituency Representation in United Kingdom Politics',*Political Studies* 28: 63-83.

GYFORD, John and JAMES, Mari (1983), *National Parties and Local Politics*(London: Allen and Unwin).

HANHAM, H.J. (1959), *Elections and Party Management*(London: Longman).

HANUSHEK, E.A. and JACKSON, J.E. (1977), *Statistical Methods for Social Scientists* (New York: Academic Press).

H.C. 731 (1980), *The Role of the Welsh Office and Associated Bodies in Developing Employment Opportunities in Wales* (London:HMSO).

HEALD, David (1983), *Public Expenditure* (Oxford: Martin Robertson).

HECHTER, Michael (1975), *Internal Colonialism: the Celtic Fringe in British National Development, 1885-1966* (London: Routledge and Kegan Paul).

HESELTINE, Michael (1983), *Reviving the Inner Cities* (London: Conservative Political Centre).

HIRSCH, Fred (1977), *Social Limits to Growth*(London: Routledge and Kegan Paul).

HOGWOOD, Brian W. and KEATING, Michael, eds., (1982), *Regional Government in England* (Oxford: Clarendon Press).

HOLLAND, Stuart (1975), *The Socialist Challenge*(London: Quartet) .

HOOD, Christopher and WRIGHT, Maurice, eds., (1981), *Big Government in Hard Times*(Oxford: Martin Robertson).

JACKSON, P.M. (1982), 'The Impact of Economic Theories on Local Government Finance', *Local Government Studies* 8:21-34.

JENNINGS, Sir Ivor (1961), *The British Constitution*(Cambridge: Cambridge University Press 4th edition).

JONES, G.W. and STEWART, John (1983), 'The Treasury and Local Government', *Political Quarterly* 54: 5-15.

JONES, J.Barry and KEATING, Michael (1982), 'The British Labour Party: Centralisation and Devolution' in Peter Madgwick and Richard Rose, eds. *The Territorial Dimension in United Kingdom Politics* (London: Macmillan).

JOSEPH, Sir Keith (1975), *Reversing the Trend*(London: Barry Rose) .

KEATING, Michael and BLEIMAN, David (1979), *Labour and Scottish Nationalism* (London: Macmillan).

KELLAS, James G. (1973), *The Scottish Political System* Cambridge: Cambridge University Press).

KELLAS, James G. and MADGWICK, Peter (1982), 'Territorial Ministries: the Scottish and Welsh Offices', in Peter Madgwick and Richard Rose, eds, *The Territorial Dimension in United Kingdom Politics* (London: Macmillan).

KELLEY,Jonathan and McALLISTER,Ian (1983), 'The Methodology of Aggregate Analysis: Errors in Traditional Methods and Suggestions for Improvement' *Quality and Quantity* 17:461-474.

KELLEY, Jonathan, McALLISTER, Ian and MUGHAN, Anthony (1983), 'The Decline of Class Revisited' (Canberra: Australian National University Working Papers in Sociology).

KIM, J.O. and MUELLER, Charles W. (1978), *Factor Analysis: Statistical Methods and Practical Issues* (Beverly Hills and London: Sage University Papers No. 07-014).

KREJCI, Jaroslav and VELIMSKY, Vitezslav (1981), *Ethnic and Political Nations in Europe* (New York: St. Martin's Press).

LABOUR PARTY (1983), *The New Hope for Britain: Labour's Manifesto 1983* (London: Labour Party).

LABOUR PARTY SCOTTISH COUNCIL (1981), *Interim Policy Statement on Devolution* (Glasgow: Labour Party).

LABOUR PARTY SCOTTISH COUNCIL (1983), *The New Hope for Scotland: Labour's Manifesto* (Glasgow: Labour Party).

LAIDLER, David (1981), 'Monetarism: An Interpretation and An Assessment', *The Economic Journal* 91: 1-28.

LEE, J.M. (1963), *Social Leaders and Public Persons* (Oxford: Clarendon Press).

LEMIEUX, Peter H. (1977), 'Political Issues and Liberal Support in the February, 1974 British General Election', *Political Studies* 25: 323-342.

LERUEZ, Jacques (1983), *L'Ecosse: une nation sans état* (Lille: Presses Universitaires de Lille).

McALLISTER, Ian (1982), 'United Kingdom Nationalist Parties: One Nationalism or Three?', in Peter Madgwick and Richard Rose, eds, *The Territorial Dimension in United Kingdom Politics* (London: Macmillan).

McALLISTER, Ian and ROSE, Richard (1984), *A Cluster Analysis of United Kingdom Parliamentary Constituencies* (Glasgow: University of Strathclyde Studies in Public Policy).

McALLISTER, Ian, PARRY, Richard and ROSE, Richard (1979), *United Kingdom Rankings: the Territorial Dimension in Social Indicators* (Glasgow: University of Strathclyde Studies in Public Policy No. 44).

McCRONE, D., ed., (1982), *The Scottish Government Yearbook 1983* (Edinburgh: Unit for the Study of Government in Scotland).

McDONALD, J.F. (1982), 'Members of Parliament: a Regional Perspective?', in Brian Hogwood and Michael Keating, eds, *Regional Government in England* (Oxford: Clarendon Press).

MADGWICK, Peter and ROSE, Richard, eds., (1982), *The Territorial Dimension in United Kingdom Politics* (London: Macmillan).

MAUDE, Angus, ed., (1977), *The Right Approach to the Economy* (London: Conservative Central Office).

MEADOWS, W.J. (1981), 'Local Government', in P.M. Jackson, ed., *Government Policy Initiatives 1979-80* (London: RIPA).

252

MIDWINTER, A., KEATING, M. and TAYLOR, P. (1983), 'Excessive and Unreasonable: the Politics of the Scottish Hit List', *Political Studies* 31: 394-417.

MILLER, William L. (1978), 'Social Class and Party Choice in England', *British Journal of Political Science* 8: 285-312.

MILLER, William L. (1979), 'Class, Region and Strata at the British Election of 1979', *Parliamentary Affairs* 32: 376-382.

MILLER, William L. (1981), *The End of British Politics?* (Oxford: Clarendon Press).

MILLER, William L. (1982), 'Variations in Electoral Behaviour in the United Kingdom' in Peter Madgwick and Richard Rose, eds, *The Territorial Dimension in United Kingdom Politics* (London: Macmillan)

MORI (1983), *British Public Opinion: General Election 1983* (London: Market & Opinion Research International).

MOSER, C.A. and SCOTT, Wolf (1961), *British Towns* (Edinburgh: Oliver and Boyd).

NAIRN, Tom (1982), *The Break Up of Britain* (London: Verso).

NAUGHTIE, James (1982), 'The Year at Westminster', in D. McCrone, ed., *The Scottish Government Yearbook 1983*, 5-15.

NEWTON, K. (1981), 'The Local Financial Crisis in Britain: a New Crisis which is neither Local nor Financial', in L.J. Sharpe, ed., *The Local Fiscal Crisis in Europe* (London: Sage Publications), 195-228.

OPCS (1983), *Census 1981: Parliamentary Constituency Monitors, 1983 Boundaries* (London: Office of Population Censuses and Surveys).

ORRIDGE, Andrew (1981), 'Uneven Development and Nationalism', *Political Studies* 29: 1-15, 181-190.

PAGE, Edward C. (1978), 'Michael Hechter's Internal Colonialism Thesis: Some Theoretical and Methodological Problems', *European Journal of Political Research* 6: 295-317.

PAGE, Edward (1982), *Laws and Orders in Central-Local Government Relations* (Glasgow: University of Strathclyde Studies in Public Policy No. 102).

PARRY, Richard (1981), 'Territory and Public Employment: a General Model and British Evidence', *Journal of Public Policy* 1: 221-250.

PAYNE, Clive and BROWN, Philip J. (1981), 'Forecasting the British Election to the European Parliament', *British Journal of Political Science* 11: 235-245.

PELLING, Henry (1967), *Social Geography of British Elections, 1885-1910* (London: Macmillan).

PRESCOTT, J.L. (1981), *Alternative Regional Strategy* (London: Parliamentary Spokesman's Working Group).

PULZER, Peter (1967), *Political Representation and Elections in Britain* (London: Allen and Unwin).

PUNNETT, R.M. (1981), 'Must Governments Lose? British Inter-Party Competition in Comparative Perspective', *Parliamentary Affairs* 34: 392-408.

RASMUSSEN, Jorgen (1965), 'The Disutility of the Swing Concept in British Psephology', *Parliamentary Affairs* 18: 442-454.

RIFKIND, Malcolm (1981), 'Reflections of a Scottish Office Minister', in H.M. and N.H. Drucker, eds., *The Scottish Government Yearbook 1982* (Edinburgh: Paul Harris), 57-68.

ROKKAN, Stein and URWIN, Derek W. (1983), *Economy, Territory, Identity: Politics of West European Peripheries* (London and Beverly Hills: Sage Publications).

ROSE, Richard (1968), 'Class and Party Divisions: Britain as a Test Case', *Sociology* 2:129-162 .

ROSE, Richard (1970), *The United Kingdom as a Multi-National State* (Glasgow: University of Strathclyde Survey Research Centre Paper No. 6).

ROSE, Richard (1971), *Governing without Consensus: An Irish Perspective* (London: Faber and Faber).

ROSE, Richard (1974), 'Britain: Simple Abstractions and Complex Realities', in Richard Rose, ed., *Electoral Behavior* (New York: Free Press), 481-541.

ROSE, Richard (1974a), 'Comparability in Electoral Studies', in Richard Rose, ed., *Electoral Behavior*(New York: Free Press), 3-25.

ROSE, Richard (1974b), *The Problem of Party Government* (London: Macmillan).

ROSE, Richard (1976), *Northern Ireland: A Time of Choice* (London Macmillan).

ROSE, Richard (1980), *Class Does Not Equal Party: the Decline of a Model of British Voting* (Glasgow: University of Strathclyde Studies in Public Policy No. 74).

ROSE, Richard (1982), *Understanding the United Kingdom: the Territorial Dimension in Government* (London: Longman).

ROSE, Richard (1982a), 'From Simple Determinism to Interactive Models of Voting: Britain as an Example', *Comparative Political Studies* 15: 145-169.

ROSE, Richard (1982b), 'Is the United Kingdom a State? Northern Ireland as a Test Case', in Peter Madgwick and Richard Rose, eds, *The Territorial Dimension in United Kingdom Politics* (London: Macmillan), 100-136.

ROSE, Richard (1983), 'Elections and Electoral Systems: Choices and Alternatives', in Vernon Bogdanor and David E. Butler, eds., *Democracy and Elections* (Cambridge: Cambridge University Press), 20-45.

ROSE, Richard (1984), *Do Parties Make a Difference?* (London: Macmillan expanded 2nd edition).

ROSE, Richard (1984a), 'The Value of National Pride', (Glasgow: University of Strathclyde, CSPP typescript).

ROSE, Richard and KAVANAGH, Dennis (1976), 'The Monarchy in Contemporary Political Culture',*Comparative Politics* 8: 548-576.

ROSE, Richard and McALLISTER, Ian (1982), *United Kingdom Facts* (London: Macmillan).

ROSE, Richard McALLISTER, Ian and MAIR, Peter (1978), *Is There a Concurring Majority in Northern Ireland?* (Glasgow: University of Strathclyde Studies in Public Policy No. 22).

ROSE, Richard and MOSSAWIR, Harve (1967), 'Voting and Elections: a Functional Analysis', *Political Studies* 15: 173-201.

ROSE, Richard and URWIN, Derek W. (1969), 'Social Cohesion, Political Parties and Strains in Regimes', *Comparative Political Studies* 2: 7-67.

ROSE, Richard and URWIN, Derek W. (1975), *Regional Differentiation and Political Unity in Western Nations* (London and Beverly Hills: Sage Contemporary Political Sociology Series No. 06-007).

RUSSEL, Trevor (1978), *The Tory Party: Its Policies, Divisions and Future* (Harmondsworth: Penguin).

SARLVIK, Bo and CREWE, Ivor (1983), *Decade of Dealignment* (Cambridge: Cambridge University Press).

SBRAGIA, Alberta (1983), *Capital Markets and Central-Local Politics in Britain: The Double Game* (Glasgow: University of Strathclyde Studies in in Public Policy No. 109).

SCHAEFER, Roberta and SCHAEFER, David (1983), 'The Political Philosophy of J.M. Keynes', *The Public Interest*.

SKIDELSKY, Robert, ed., (1977), *The End of the Keynesian Era* (London: Macmillan).

SMITH, John (1981), 'Portrait of a Devolutionist', *The Bulletin of Scottish Politics* 1: 44-55.

STEED, Michael (1965), 'The Results Analysed', in David E. Butler and Anthony King, *The British General Election of 1964*(London: Macmillan), 337-359.

THOMSON, Andrew (1982), 'Local Government as an Employer', in Richard Rose and Edward Page, eds., *Fiscal Stress in Cities* (Cambridge: Cambridge University Press), 107-136.

TOBIN, James (1981), 'The Monetarist Counter-Revolution Today: An Appraisal', *The Economic Journal* 91: 29-42.

VAN MECHELEN, Denis P. (1982), *The Growth of Third Party Support in Britain* (London: PhD thesis, London School of Economics).

WALD, Kenneth (1983), *Crosses on the Ballot: Patterns of British Voter Alignment since 1885* (Princeton: Princeton University Press).

WAPSHOT, Nicholas and BROCK, George (1983), *Thatcher*(London: Futura).

WEATHERFORD, M. Stephen (1980), 'Comment on Franklin and Mughan', *American Political Science Review* 74: 460-462.

WEBBER, Richard (1978), *Parliamentary Constituencies: a Socio-economic Classification* (London: Office of Population Censuses and Surveys Occasional Paper No. 13).

WEBBER, Richard A. and CRAIG, John (1978), *Socio-economic Classification of Local Authority Areas* (London: Office of Population Censuses and Surveys Studies on Medical and Population Subjects No. 35).

WOOD, David (1978), '1978 is now or never for Mrs. T', *The Times*, 9 January 1978.

WORMS, J.P. (1980), 'Le Decentralisation: Une Strategie Socialiste de Changement Sociale', *Recherche Sociale* 75.

WRIGHT, Maurice (1982), 'Pressures in Whitehall', in Richard Rose and Edward Page, eds., *Fiscal Stress in Cities*(Cambridge: Cambridge University Press), 17-43.

# Index